Surely few men in the history of the world have had a more extraordinary life journey than Sir Walter Ralegh. Elizabethan to his finger tips, master of the pen and the sword, he lived and fought like Drake, although he had the mind of a Marlowe, with whom, indeed, he collaborated. It is not enough to say that every detail of his life appears in these pages. The author has gone to enormous pains to get at every shred of evidence, and yet to write about it with perspective and with fire. Sir Walter's life necessarily makes easy reading because everything he did was dramatic and because the times were the quintessence of drama. Queen Elizabeth, the Spanish Armada, Mary Queen of Scots, revolt in Ireland, plots in London—almost any name or event that you mention has in it something of the excitement of sudden death. So to say that Mr. Thompson's book is exciting is to give it no especial praise. But to say that it is beautifully written, that the man and the events are seen in proportion, and that besides all this it has around it the feel and texture of daily life—that is to say the book is unusual.

SIR WALTER RALEGH

PAINTER UNKNOWN

FORMERLY ATTRIBUTED TO ZUCCARIO

Sir Walter
RALEGH

Last of the Elizabethans

By Edward Thompson

New Haven · Yale University Press
1936

That rare and renowned knight, whose fame
shall contend in longevity with the island itself.

JAMES HOWELL to Carew Ralegh, 1645.

Preface

IT is difficult to believe in Sir Walter Ralegh. There is and always has been something legendary, something fantastic and not quite credible about him."[1] The image his name calls up in the general mind is that of a splendid ruffler. We think quickly of his spreading a cloak in the mire in front of his Queen.

To a smaller, but considerable, public, that of historical students, he is the supremely unsuccessful man. It is hard to reconcile his achievements and reputation, or to explain such a whirl of contradictions in one person. There have been greater Englishmen; but none so variously capable, so endowed (and almost cursed) with a "restless vitality."[2] He "could carry on half a dozen enterprises abreast";[3] was historian, poet, philosopher, writer on naval affairs, courtier, statesman, soldier, admiral, privateer, shipbuilder, patriot, chemist, colonizer, empire-planner, Member of Parliament, administrator, patron of authors and scientists and unpopular thinkers, intriguer, martyr. "So may we say to the memory of this worthy Knight, Repose your self in this our Catalogue under what Topick you please. . . . His worth unlocks our closest Cabinets, and provides both room and welcome to entertain him."[4] Yet in every capacity his effort was flawed and disappointing: "his history was never finished, and his poetry is lost" (except for pieces whose ascription to him is rarely free from uncertainty). His work was all "tainted by a curious impermanence," and had "something sketchy and amateurish about it." He took up an activity, and it "sparkled at his touch; but let him abandon it, and at once the fire was out."[5]

Living in an age which was ready to try all things, he tried more than any other man, as impersonally bent on knowledge as Marlowe's Faustus planned to be. A versatile and unpausing improvisation made up the "groundwork" of his life, and his incalculable quality kept men continually surprised. "No family muniment room can be ex-

1. Agnes M. C. Lathom, *The Poems of Sir Walter Ralegh*, p. 1.
2. William Stebbing, *Sir Walter Ralegh*, pp. ix, 265.
3. Edward Edwards, *The Life of Sir Walter Ralegh*, p. xxx.
4. Thomas Fuller, *The History of the Worthies of England* (1662), p. 261.
5. Lathom, p. 2.

plored without traces of him. Successive reports of the Historical Manuscripts Commission testify to the vigilance with which his doings were noted."[6]

He held contemporary attention to a unique degree. Nor has his reputation ever sunk into the calm that allows of dispassionate examination. A wind of controversy blows about it, as about the names of Cromwell and Warren Hastings; and at times has blown with peculiar shrillness. "Historians, with whom Ralegh has never been a favourite,"[7] have judged his actions by international standards of a day which did not dawn until long afterwards. Those standards were of dubious acceptance when Nelson bombarded Copenhagen; were ignored when Andrew Jackson raided far into Florida and hanged and shot British subjects living under the sovereignty of Spain; were set aside by the British press when Dr. Jameson invaded the Transvaal and delighted that love of direct action which exists in every nation. When Ralegh employed his privateering fleets, or sailed to Guiana, these standards simply did not exist.

Biographers (unlike historians) are convinced that his reward from his own generation was iniquitous. A new *Life of Ralegh* appears every few years, and in two centuries half a dozen of these have been good ones. My own debt is greatest to the earliest important *Life,* by William Oldys; to Edwards' rich full study (which prints Ralegh's letters) on the contemporary background; to Stebbing's more concentrated study, admirable in wisdom and style; to Hume's, which so extended our knowledge of Gondomar's part in Ralegh's ruin, by its transcripts from Spanish documents; to Mr. Milton Waldman's *Ralegh;* and to Mr. Harlow's *Ralegh's Last Voyage.* Mr. Harlow seems to me to have stopped short of finding the nature of Kemys's offense and Ralegh's real plan. But his book has made obsolete every previous study of Ralegh's last expedition. Since its appearance, a new *Life,* that took his conclusions into account, has been needed.

The *pax Victoriana* has vanished. My own generation, from the insecurity and changes and variety of our experience, seems to me closer in sympathy to the Elizabethans than any intervening generation has been, so that a career which has always seemed like a preposterous

6. Stebbing, *Ralegh,* p. 85.
7. *Ibid.* Sir Charles Firth is almost the only exception to this statement.

fairy-tale now takes on semblance of humanity. I have tried to relate that career to the age of which it was such a startlingly vivid epitome and illumination. My main reason for writing this book is that for nearly forty years Ralegh has been a major interest of mine, and at last I found I wanted to write about him.

Footnotes are out of fashion, and readers have become intolerant of documented studies. But I have stuck to personal preference, hoping to find some who agree with me in liking to know a quotation's source without having to turn up an appendix. Those who find footnotes teasing can ignore them. It is quite easy to do this.

Except very occasionally, and for special reason, when quoting I have modernized spelling, as is the practice with all Elizabethan literature that has passed into general currency. But the original text's capital letters have been left undisturbed, for, although these are largely haphazard, they sometimes correspond to an emphasis in the writer's mind. I have kept also my authorities' spelling of proper names, instead of making Ralegh's "Honduraes" into "Honduras," and his "Campeach" into "Campeachy," and so on.

E. T.

Boars Hill, Oxford.

Contents

		PAGE
PREFACE		V
I.	THE ENGLAND OF RALEGH'S CHILDHOOD	1
II.	STUDENT AND SOLDIER	7
III.	IRELAND	14
IV.	THE RISING COURTIER AND ADMINISTRATOR	27
V.	PRIVATEER, EXPLORER, COLONIZER	37
VI.	VIRGINIA	46
VII.	THE ARMADA	58
VIII.	NEW RIVALRIES	64
IX.	POET; AND FRIEND OF POETS	69
X.	MARRIAGE; AND DISGRACE	84
XI.	GUIANA	100
XII.	SEA EXPLOITS. THE TAKING OF CADIZ	119
XIII.	THE ISLANDS VOYAGE	131
XIV.	THE DEATH OF ESSEX	144
XV.	ELIZABETH'S LAST YEARS	164
XVI.	JAMES, BY THE GRACE OF GOD, KING	185
XVII.	TRIAL AND CONDEMNATION	195
XVIII.	THE KING'S MERCY	220
XIX.	FIRST YEARS IN THE TOWER	230
XX.	SHERBORNE; AND *The History of the World*	246
XXI.	RELEASE	263
XXII.	AN ADMIRAL AT LAST	284
XXIII.	THE FIGHT AT SAN THOMÉ	311
XXIV.	THE RETURN	331
XXV.	THE LORDS OF THE COUNCIL	354
XXVI.	THE SCAFFOLD	369
XXVII.	AFTERWARDS	384
APPENDIX A.	THE SPELLING OF RALEGH'S NAME	394
APPENDIX B.	THE "POOR DAUGHTER" LETTER	395
BIBLIOGRAPHY		398
INDEX		408

Illustrations

Sir Walter Ralegh (by Zuccario) . . . . *Frontispiece*

Map Illustrating Action in Cadiz Harbor 122

Sir Walter Ralegh and his Elder Son (by Giesharz) . . . 214

Count Gondomar (by Velasquez; engraved, R. Cooper) . . 272

Ralegh after Release from the Tower 284

Map Illustrating Ralegh's Voyages to Guiana 312

Thanks are due to the Trustees of the National Portrait Gallery, for the frontispiece portrait of Ralegh; to Sir Stephen Lennard and Mr. W. Packe, who allow me to reproduce the portrait of Ralegh and his son which is preserved at Wickham Court; to the Trustees of the British Museum, for permission to reproduce the portrait of Count Gondomar; to the Walpole Society and their honorary secretary, Mr. J. W. Goodison, and to the Oxford University Press, for use of their plate of the portrait of Ralegh after Release. I have not reproduced either of the two extant portraits of Lady Ralegh; I am not satisfied of their authenticity. The woodcut of Sir Walter Ralegh as an old man is from the contemporary broadsheet, *Newes of Sir Walter Rauleigh from the River of Caliana* (1618). No map of Ralegh's Virginia is needed. It is now North Carolina; his islands lie between Cape Henry and Cape Lookout, and are shown on any good map of the United States.

SIR WALTER RALEGH

CHAPTER I

The England of Ralegh's Childhood

Sir Walter Ralegh was one that, it seems, fortune had picked out of purpose, of whom to make an example, or to use as her tennis-ball, thereby to show what she could do; for she tossed him up of nothing, and to and fro to greatness, and from thence down to little more than to that wherein she found him, a bare gentleman. SIR ROBERT NAUNTON, *Fragmenta Regalia*.

> O for my sake do you with Fortune chide,
> The guilty goddess of my harmful deeds!
> SHAKESPEARE.

THE date of Ralegh's birth is generally given as 1552; it may have been 1554. He was "a Gentleman of good Alliance in the West of England, and very well descended";[1] "at one period five knightly branches of the house flourished simultaneously in the county of Devon."[2] But his own branch became somewhat depressed after Henry VII's rapacious lawyers, Empson and Dudley, found an excuse to fine his grandfather, Wimund Ralegh. Wimund's son Walter left his manor-house at Fardell, on Dartmoor border, and moved to Hayes Barton, a farm near Budleigh Salterton.[3] Our Walter Ralegh was born here.

The Tudors encouraged a new nobility, to balance the old nobility who so readily set themselves up as king-makers and king-breakers. These quickly accepted themselves, and found enough of the old-established families left to strengthen their arrogance. Elizabeth herself never advanced anyone not of gentle blood. Nevertheless, by old and new nobility alike, Ralegh was considered an upstart and they brought him to ruin. Yet, as his contemporary Naunton noted[4]—in a judgment

1. Sir William Sanderson, *The Lives and Reigns of Mary and James*, p. 282.
2. William Stebbing, *Ralegh*, p. 1. See also Edward Edwards, *Ralegh*, i, 7.
3. *Transactions, Devonshire Association*, xxi, 312–320.
4. *Fragmenta Regalia, Sir Walter Ralegh*.

into which are compressed the pity, admiration and scorn that accompanied his career—he could not be brought lower than he began. He began as a gentleman.

The Raleghs remained distinguished enough, and individual enough, to be often in peril, of which two instances have come down from the life of Sir Walter's father. In 1549 Catholic Devonshire rose against the Protestant innovations of Edward VI's Council—to be massacred at Clyst St. Mary, an earlier Sedgmoor in the unavailing valor of the West Country peasantry and their sufferings after defeat. Mr. Walter Ralegh overtook an old woman telling her beads and rebuked her for breaking the law. She hurried to church, all flustered, and poured out a hysterical tale that the gentry intended to burn the poor folks' houses down, unless they gave up their religion. Her fellow-worshippers, "in all haste like a sort of wasps they flying out,"[5] swarmed in chase of Mr. Ralegh, who fled into another church, where they besieged him. He escaped, only to be caught by other insurgents and shut up in St. Sidwell Church, Exeter, with frequent threats that he was going to be hanged —a prospect which the rebellion's suppression swept away.

The second story shows the family Protestant amid the still greater perils of the Marian reaction. When a poor woman, Agnes Prest, afterwards burnt to death, was imprisoned in Exeter Castle:

There resorted to her the wife of Walter Ralegh—a woman of noble wit and of good and godly opinions, who coming to the prison and talking with her, she said the *Creed* to the gentlewoman. When she came to the article, "He ascended," there she stayed, and bade the gentlewoman to seek His blessed body in Heaven, not on earth; and said that God dwelleth not in temples made with hands; and that Sacrament to be nothing else but a remembrance of His blessed Passion. And yet (said she) as they now use it, it is but an idol, and far wide from any remembrance of Christ's body— which will not long continue, and so take it, good Mistress.

Mrs. Ralegh reported to her husband

that in her life she never heard any woman of such simplicity to see, to talk so godly and so earnestly; insomuch that if God were not with her she could not speak such things. I was not able to answer her—I, who can read, and she cannot.[6]

5. Holinshed, *Chronicle* (1807 reprint), iii, 94.
6. John Foxe, *Acts and Monuments*, etc. (1684), iii, 748.

Anecdotes of great men's parents are rarely of relevance. But these two show that Ralegh came from a home of exceptional independence and fearlessness. Mrs. Ralegh's immunity after her brave action is one more proof of the way the family have been underrated. At Court the Raleghs may have seemed of no importance. But within Devon they were powerful. The Marian terror's crowning disgrace was that it struck down friendless victims, and left the wealthy and high-ranking alone. Agnes Prest was burnt; Katharine Ralegh was free to visit her in prison. It is no obscure yeoman family that twice swims up into clear light of history. In later life, Ralegh was able to refer to "more than a hundred gentlemen of my kindred." Devon, as we shall have frequent occasion to observe, was like an English outpost of the Scottish clan spirit.

Walter Ralegh married thrice, and had four sons and two daughters. Sir Walter was the second of two sons by the third marriage; his elder brother of whole blood, Carew Ralegh,[7] himself became a distinguished seaman, and was knighted. Their mother's cousin, Sir George Carew, "the prettiest man and the finest seaman in England," was drowned in his ship, the *Mary Rose,* one of Henry VIII's new great vessels, when the French attempted the Isle of Wight in 1545. His nephew, Sir Peter Carew, a man without fear, hesitation or pity, had a career turbulent even for Tudor times. He opposed the Spanish marriage, and fled overseas, Walter Ralegh lending his ship for the purpose (another instance of the Ralegh courage); was arrested in Antwerp, brought back and imprisoned in the Tower—to be released by Elizabeth, and to join the Devon adventurers trying to put down rebellion in Ireland. The connection between Carews and Raleghs was close and cherished.

Katharine Ralegh brought into the family other great seafaring names also. She had been Katharine Champernoun, and her brother, Sir Arthur Champernoun, was Vice-Admiral of Devon, commanding at Plymouth. (For fifty years the Raleghs and their kinsmen managed to keep this post in their grip—a very present help to sea-prowlers in trouble.) When she married Walter Ralegh, she was Otho Gilbert's widow, and mother of John, Humphrey and Adrian Gilbert, who all won fame as navigators, explorers, colonizers.

The song which alleges that whenever Queen Elizabeth was in diffi-

7. ?1550–?1625.

culties "she used to send for a Devon man" is not far astray. At her accession (1558), "the merchant navy of England *engaged in lawful commerce* amounted to no more than 50,000 tons, and the royal navy in commission consisted only of seven cruisers, the largest 120 tons, and eight armed merchant brigs."[8] But there had been a great unofficial augmentation of this strength when Mary's marriage to Philip was followed by the three years' intensive persecution. Large sections of the West Country population took to an amphibious existence, living with one foot always ready to spring on shipboard. Many of these fliers belonged to the first families, and preserved loyal feelings by blaming the burnings on to the Queen's foreign husband. Their precarious fugitive manner of living made piracy at all times a temptation, and at many times near to a necessity. The temptation was easily and often yielded to. Mary died; and England continued in official amity with Spain, while a main business of her western seaboard was pillage of Spain.

The situation was unethical, but justifiable. Catholic Europe, regarding England as a third-rate Power lapsed into the sin of heresy, demanded that Elizabeth should "restore religion." In Spain, only her Ambassador was allowed to use the Anglican service; his household were required to attend mass. Later, even his personal exemption was withdrawn. It was impudence, heightened by insistence that Catholics in England must have the fullest freedom of public worship. Europe howled at any abbreviation as a monstrous outrage, never heard of among even the most heathenish people. Meanwhile, Devon was the region most active in mercantile and naval enterprise. Her seamen were the spearhead to which London and Bristol furnished the heavy haft of financial support; they had no choice but to let their skill and valor idly rust in harbor, or go armed while using them, for Spain was tenacious of her duty to be the hammer of heretics wherever found. His countrymen died, all through Ralegh's childhood, to please the loungers of Lima and Seville and Valladolid. On January 10, 1563, Elizabeth's chief minister, Sir William Cecil,[9] stated that in the year just ended twenty-six Englishmen had been burnt at the stake in Spain. Piracy answered bigotry; in May, 1565, Cecil listed sixty instances of downright pillage of Spain. And robbery was emphatically robbery with vio-

8. Hume, p. 6. My italics.
9. Afterwards Lord Burghley.

lence, savagery was matched with savagery, as when Thomas Cobham in 1564 replied to Spanish brutalities by sewing up a vessel's crew in their own sails, sending eighteen bodies drifting on to the Galician shores—"cruelty without example, of which but to hear was enough to break the heart."

We must shed our knowledge, then, of all that *England* has meant to patriotic love during the last two hundred years: "the Mother of Parliaments," "the modern Rome," the pioneer against the slave trade, the builder of new nations, the rebuilder of decayed old ones. A tiny half-island, disunited in religion, was passing ever deeper under the menace of foreign conquest; and (apparently) kept independence only by sufferance of France and Spain, mutually hostile. To north lay Scotland in civil dissension; westward were Wales and Cornwall speaking foreign tongues; further west still, Ireland in agony of hatred. And while to us the word *Elizabethan* calls up Shakespeare, Kit Marlowe and his strutting Tamburlaine, the Mermaid Tavern, elves and the idle glamour of *A Midsummer-Night's Dream* and Prospero's enchanted island, madrigals, morrice dances, lutes and virginals, a lovely ecstatic world beginning with Sidney, chivalry's perfect flower, and with—

> Calm Spenser, moving through his clouded heaven
> With the moon's beauty and the moon's soft pace—

the Elizabethan world of fact was one the imagination dare not confront. The mob, like the mob everywhere else, was fed with cruelty like any Roman one, with traitors flung alive on the quartering block and occasional Socinians or Anabaptists burnt (to show Philip of Spain that the English monarch was still a Defender of the Faith) "in great horror, crying and roaring." London streets abounded in beggary, in suffering, in swashbuckling. And not in England only, in every land warfare, plottings, executions, poisonings abounded, to an extent that renders moral judgments an absurdity. Tragedy ceased to be impressive, except when some outstanding figure had the luck to play it out on a public scaffold.

No one realized that *our* Europe was taking on shape and outline; for many a day yet its peoples were to be regarded as appanages to lands lying at the disposal of kings and conquerors. International arrangements were between sovereigns, not necessarily between their subjects. If you disliked Spain, the fact that your country was at peace with Spain did not mean that you must be at peace. You could get a privateering commission from Powers who *were* at war with Spain, could serve as nominally under the Prince of Condé or the Prince of Orange. This sufficiently regularized your position with your own ruler if confronted with responsibility for you. Englishmen's attitude toward the privateering into which Ralegh came, almost as if into a hereditary trade, was "very much that of an American citizen towards a bootlegger. They disapproved, but bought the goods the pirate carried in."[10] Few even disapproved. And, especially when Spain and England became engaged in veiled but deadly warfare, as irregular seconds in fighting that went on steadily in the Low Countries and Ireland, Devon seamen saw no reason why the situation should not yield them profit as well as peril. The peril, and the appalling penalties attached to failure, ennobled the breach of international morality. Their Queen dared not acknowledge them, or do other than repudiate them if caught. But she was glad that they should dog her enemy with misgivings that grew ever more frightening, until his Invincible Armada came to the clash like a man half expecting defeat. Her circumstances, unprecedentedly hard, were surmounted with success; and England passed into the modern world. Drakes, Courtenays, Champernouns, Grenvilles, Carews, Gilberts, Raleghs—these were the darts that flew from England, when she dared not let her left hand know what her right was doing.

10. William McFee, *Sir Martin Frobisher* ("Golden Hind" series), p. 16.

CHAPTER II

Student and Soldier

His approaches to the University and Inns of Court were the grounds of his improvement. But they were rather incursions than sieges or settings down, for he stayed not long in a place; and being the youngest brother, and the house diminished in patrimony, he foresaw his own destiny, that he was first to rule (through want and disability to subsist otherwise) before he could come to a repose. NAUNTON, *Fragmenta Regalia*.

RALEGH was never "educated," except by himself. Though known throughout life as "an indefatigable reader,"[1] incessantly seeking after information of every kind, his mind closed against nothing of interest, he evaded normal courses almost entirely.

Anthony à Wood says he entered Oriel College, Oxford, in 1568, as a Commoner (aged only fourteen, if he was born in 1554), and that he stayed three years, "the ornament of the juniors; and was worthily esteemed a proficient in oratory and philosophy."[2] No doubt he was. But his attendance was fitful and broken. Two incidents only survive. Aubrey relates[3] one (often cited with reprobation by biographers who have forgotten their own student days—or else imagine that Universities foster an uncomfortably high standard of honesty):

I remember that Mr. Thomas Child of Worcestershire told me that Sir Walter Ralegh borrowed a gown of him when he was at Oxford (they were both of the same College), which he never restored, nor money for it.

And Francis Bacon[4] quotes Ralegh's reply to a fellow-student who was a coward but a fine archer, and sought advice as to how to get satisfaction for an affront. He was recommended to challenge his adversary to a shooting match.

Ralegh's name appears in the Oxford Register for 1572, as still an undergraduate. But we know that in the interim he had been fighting

1. Naunton, *Fragmenta Regalia*. 2. *Athenae Oxonienses* (1721), *Ralegh*.
3. *Brief Lives*, ii, 179. 4. *Apophthegms*.

in France. His cousin Gawain Champernoun was married to Gabrielle de Montgomeri, daughter of a Huguenot leader, and Gawain's brother Henry took a hundred Devon mounted volunteers to help the Protestant cause. Their standard showed a corpse with severed head on a black ground, and the motto, *Det mihi virtus finem,* "Let valor end my life." (It turned out to be prophetic; on June 26, 1574, Count Gabriel de Montgomeri, Ralegh's connection-by-marriage, was beheaded after capitulating.) Ralegh is thought to have been one of the volunteers. But it seems likely that he had already drifted into the French wars, in the isolated manner that marked his actions; for these volunteers did not arrive until two days after the battle of Moncontour (October 3, 1569), whereas he tells us he was present at both that battle and the earlier Huguenot defeat at Jarnac (March 13). He praises Count Louis of Nassau for his skilful conduct of the retreat after Moncontour, "of which myself was an eyewitness, and was one of them that had cause to thank him for it."[5]

Ralegh's references to his experiences convey an impression of distaste hanging about the memory. He remarks once that by civil war no nation's condition was ever bettered; and is thinking especially of the inadvisability of writing about contemporary events frankly, when he says:

> Whosoever in writing a modern history shall follow Truth too near the heels, it may haply strike out his teeth.

The mind stirs with pity and amazement to think of a boy of sixteen[6] as combatant in such a war. Over the volunteers hung their knowledge of what had happened in 1562, when their Queen was openly allied with the Prince of Condé. A barge full of soldiers, sent to serve under the Earl of Warwick, had been washed ashore, and they were taken and hanged, under scrolls setting forth that this was "for having come, contrary to the wish of the Queen of England, to serve the Hugenots."[7] Ralegh's whole military life was in campaigns where neither he nor his enemies recognized any rules except kill, and kill anyhow. We may let

5. *History of the World,* Book V, chapter II, 38. See Oldys, *Life of Ralegh,* p. 24.
6. Fourteen, if he was born in 1554.
7. "*Pour avoir venus contra la volunté de la Royne d'Angleterre au service des Huguenotz.*"

his apprenticeship go at that, with this glimpse of the Huguenots catching a band of opponents in caves in Languedoc,

which we knew not how to enter by any ladder or engine, till at last, by certain bundles of lighted straw let down by an iron chain with a weighty stone in the midst, those that defended it were so smothered, that they surrendered themselves, with their plate, money, and other goods, therein hidden; or they must have died like bees that are smoaked out of their hives.[8]

Presumably he had returned from France by February, 1575, after Montgomeri's failure and execution, for in that month he was entered as a Member of the Middle Temple. But again the evidence is confused. On trial for his life, in 1603, Ralegh affirmed that he had never read a word of law. Hume is justified in saying of him (as of any other Elizabethan) that "neither on this, or any other occasion, is it safe to take his word with absolute literalness."[9] On the other hand, if he had ever used the Inns of Court as anything more than a club—a fashionable use in those days[10]—he would have been a fool to allege that he had never read a word of law, when the generation of those who *had* studied in the Middle Temple during his young manhood were still only middle-aged, and were many of them engaged in, or present at, his trial. Membership of the Temple is by no means inconsistent with legal ignorance. A further proof that he spoke truth is furnished by his own carelessness in legal matters. He lost his much-loved home at Sherborne because of this.

Probably he still fought, at any rate occasionally, on the Huguenot side, or was a nearby observer of the fighting, until 1575. He then spent at Islington two or three exceedingly obscure years, which Aubrey says were turbulent and irregular, a statement supported by other evidence, in which we may include Lady Ralegh's in 1613, when Ralegh rebuked his own son for playing humiliating tricks on Ben Jonson. She found them amusing, and reminded the father that he himself had behaved similarly at the same age.[11] And in December, 1577, Ralegh had to bail

8. *History of the World,* Book V, chap. II.

9. *Sir Walter Ralegh,* p. 18.

10. The Inns of Court "was always the place of esteem with the Queen, which she said, fitted youth for the future" (*Aulicus Coquinariae,* p. 74).

11. See Jonson's *Conversations with William Drummond of Hawthornden* (Gifford and Cunningham's *Works of Ben Jonson,* iii, 483).

out two servants of his, committed for defying the watch. Thirdly, there was his brawl with Perrot—of which more presently.

It is not only in brawls, however, that his name crops up. He had found his almost tempestuously eager interest in intellectual matters. His spirit plunged him into action, thought, intrigue simultaneously. But throughout his troubled and disastrous life the things of the mind meant most to him. Of this a proof comes in his earliest-known verses, which are complimentary to *The Steel Glass*[12] of that bright swash-buckler, George Gascoigne, like him a Member of the Inns of Court and an adventurer in the Continental wars. They have some value, and contain a couplet which is one of the few passages of his verse that are at all remembered, enshrining a somber truth his own experience was to bring home to him:

> For whoso reaps renown above the rest
> With heaps of hate shall surely be oppressed.

In later life Ralegh used as his own Gascoigne's motto, *Tam Marti quam Mercurio*—a proud confession of his double dedication to war and the sciences.

Oldys remarks[13] that the poem's opening line—

> Sweet were the sauce should please each kind of taste

—discovers "a great air of that solid axiomatical vein, which is observable in other products of Ralegh's muse." The comment brings in aptly Mr. Milton Waldman's criticism[14] that "one of the gravest defects" of Ralegh's writings "is their lack of humour." But humor runs in fashions. The Elizabethans are accepted as a humorous generation; they laughed uproariously, revelled and roistered, enjoyed life zestfully. But their humor seems no great matter, except formerly to themselves. Apart from Falstaff, little of even Shakespeare's humorous writing is alive to-day, unless we artificially make it dance again, jerking it and our own wits up to make it seem funny. Ralegh's own few jokes were practical ones, either brutal or (in one instance) dreadful; or else were verses about the gallows. We have, then, to give him up as a humorous

12. Published 1576.   13. *Life of Ralegh* (1736), p. xi.
14. *Ralegh* ("Golden Hind" series), p. 9.

writer; and may as well do it now, at the very beginning. He had, however, a biting irony, as we shall have frequent occasion to observe.

His career for some years closely followed that of his half-brother Humphrey Gilbert, a Puritan before the time of the Puritan ascendancy, devoutly terrible. Gilbert built up a reputation for being unlucky, and (unlike Ralegh) was little loved by his own men. After a horrible campaign in Ireland, for which he was knighted, in 1572 he commanded the English contingent helping the Low Countries' rebellion against Spain. Here, too, the English were hanged if captured (in that age, it can hardly have been worth while to surrender); and Gilbert, who believed in doing his reprisals in advance, hanged his own prisoners. But he did small good, and in November, 1572, decided to transfer his activities to other fields. So he returned to England, pretending (under instructions) to be in dread of the Queen's displeasure. The grave farce accomplished, he was free to approach her (March, 1574), in company with Richard Grenville and others, for leave to prosecute

an enterprise by them conceived; and with the help of God under the protection of Her Majesty's most princely name and goodness, at their own charges and adventure, to be performed, for discovery of sundry rich and unknown lands, fatally, and it seemeth by God's providence, reserved for England and for the honour of Her Majesty.[15]

In 1576, two years later, Gascoigne (author of *The Steel Glass,* already mentioned) revealed other strands of Gilbert's complicated and ambitious thinking by publishing the latter's *Discourse to Prove a Passage by the North-West to Cathaia*—the frost-set glimmer that was to draw so many brave spirits to their deaths. Gilbert, temporarily concentrating on a less visionary plan, urged on the Privy Council that "the northern part of America . . . inhabited by a savage people of a mild and tractable disposition" was "of all other unfrequented places the only most fittest and most commodious for us to meddle withal." And at last, in June, 1578, he was granted his patent to discover and annex "any remote, barbarous and heathen lands not possessed by any Christian prince or people." By then, Ralegh was definitely a principal in the project—whose very language was to reappear in his own last en-

15. R. Pearse Chope (*Devonshire Association Transactions,* 1917, pp. 217–218) rejects Gilbert's name from this project, on what seem to me unconvincing grounds.

terprise. While it was maturing he seems to have served in the Low Countries, again in characteristically detached and amateur fashion. He reëmerges into clear light when his and Gilbert's fleet was ready.

Gilbert had been living unemployed, at Limehouse, London, for five years, during which he worked out his scheme, along with a modification that would make it financially sound. This was to surprise the Newfoundland fishing fleet, whose personnel was mainly Catholic and included almost half Spain's sailors; to sell the captured vessels in the Low Countries, build warships with the proceeds, and wrest the New World from Spain.[16] The Privy Council made no reply to his "Discourse," which they may have found somewhat advanced for a Government officially at peace with its proposed victims. But they perhaps showed that they had thought about it, when they came down on an action of some of Gilbert's men. These had seized in Dartmouth harbor a Seville merchant's boat and cargo of oranges and lemons (which would be useful in a sea-journey, against scurvy). This could hardly be glossed over as patriotism, and the eldest Gilbert, Sir John, was ordered "to see the said Spaniard restored to his bark and goods, or otherwise sufficiently recompensed." The Council added that they understood his brothers, Sir Humphrey Gilbert and Walter Ralegh, had not yet sailed; he was "required friendly to advise them . . . to remain at home to answer such as have been, by their company, damaged." The Sheriffs, Vice-Admiral and Justices of Devon were commanded to hold up the expedition. We do not know the upshot, or if the Spaniard recovered his fruit. But fines were paid, by Ralegh and others, in 1579, which perhaps, as some suggest, implies that the Council had been disobeyed.

Meanwhile the fleet sailed into the winter storms of 1578. The voyage suffered from the disloyalties and desertions which beset Elizabethan enterprises, and ended prematurely. Ralegh, commanding the *Falcon,* with motto *Nec mortem peto nec finem fugio* ("I neither seek death nor flee the end") seems to have held on longest, refusing to return until tempests and want of supplies drove him also back. He fought a severe action with Spaniards, lost many men and was nearly killed

16. "How Her Majesty might annoy the King of Spain by fitting out a fleet of warships under pretence of a voyage of discovery, and so fall upon the enemy's shipping, destroy his trade in Newfoundland and the West Indies, and possess both Regions" (November 6, 1577).

himself. At Plymouth afterwards, he and some fellow-officers formally charged the Queen's kinsman Knollys, before the Mayor, with desertion.

Next year Gilbert was on the prowl again, ostensibly guarding Ireland from invasion. It happened in spite of him. But he sacked a monastery in Galicia, thereby gratifying both his piety and his patriotism. Ralegh may have been with him.

CHAPTER III

Ireland

He first exposed himself to the land service of Ireland (a militia), which then did not yield him food and raiment, for it was ever very poor; nor had he patience to stay there. NAUNTON, *Fragmenta Regalia.*

SPAIN and England for some time had been fighting out part of their first campaign in Ireland—then, as later, England's weakness, eager to welcome foreign aid. Some, especially Irish Catholic writers like Sir John Pope-Hennessy,[1] have denied that religion was at the root of hatred. But religion racked that whole generation with a fever of spite and suffering. Both England and Ireland, in different ways, were fighting for life, and Protestantism had not yet accepted toleration as safe. The English did what Catholic Powers did, they suppressed other forms of worship than their own. No Irish Catholic could doubt that, if their rule ever became effective, the Anglican religious compromise would be everywhere enforced.

The Anglican bigotry was folly (but we cannot expect men three centuries ago to have seen this), because some of the Irish were beginning to see the advantages of a settled way of existence. In Waterford, Cork, Dublin and other ports, a flourishing trade was growing up. Already the country custom whereby "every petty gentleman lives in a stone tower, where he gathers into his service all the rascals of the neighbourhood (and of these towers there is an infinite number)"[2] looked the barbarism it was. These ports would never have jeopardized their prosperity by turning to Spain, unless their people's religion had been threatened. England's case—consisting in her peril from Ireland and in a stupidity then universal—is completed if we add that there was more justification than Nationalist idealization now admits, for the belief that the Irish were savages. Their ancient civilization did not prevent incessant civil war; and England, treating them as wild beasts, kept them in the wild beast way of living.

1. In *Ralegh in Ireland.*   2. Report of a Spanish agent to Philip II, 1579.

For all this, Devon men had the main responsibility. When Elizabeth had been ten years on the throne, nearly thirty West Country gentlemen volunteered (February 12, 1569) to end the Irish wars and colonize Munster, as if it were some wild new-discovered region, clearing it of wolves and natives. Their attitude (as has often been noted) was exactly paralleled in America later. The Irish, like "Injuns," being "p'ison," wherever found,

their extinction was contemplated with as much indifference as the destruction of the Red Indians of North America by the politicians of Washington, and their titles to their lands as not more deserving of respect.[3]

Ireland was regarded by most Englishmen of that day as New England was regarded by the Colonists of the following century. It was territory to be cleared of its savage inhabitants and settled by civilised people.[4]

It was to be made into a New Devon, overflowing with cream, and tumbling with apples and pasties. The intending colonists stipulated only that they should keep fully their English nationality, not becoming "banished men" but rather being allowed "to carry England to Ireland."

We know how the big-game hunter thinks and feels and looks; we have his photograph in the illustrated papers, and his memoirs, "Sport in Many Lands," "Leaves from a Happy Life." His quarry can express themselves only by unseemly acts of outrage—slipping, wounded, into thickets and rushing out just when guns happen to be unloaded. The Irish did this, and answered savagery with savagery. Thereupon Devon, under Humphrey Gilbert as military commandant in Munster, settled down to make a job of it. Gilbert held the view, not yet obsolete, "that no conquered nation will ever yield willingly their obedience for love, but rather for fear." His methods—which were not essentially different from those of another kinsman of Ralegh, Sir Peter Carew,[5] who had gone to Munster in 1568, as a first swallow of the Devonian spring— were set down by himself, in a complacent letter to Sir Henry Sidney, Lord Deputy of Ireland and his own immediate superior:

My manner of dealing was to show them all that they had more need of Her Majesty, than she of their service; neither yet that we were afraid of

3. Froude, *Queen Elizabeth*, iv, 11.   4. McFee, *Frobisher*, p. 21.
5. See p. 3.

any number of them, our quarrel being so good. I slew all those from time to time that did belong to, feed, accompany, or maintain any outlaws or traitors; and after my first summoning of a castle or fort, if they would not presently yield it, I would not afterwards take it of their gift, but won it perforce—how many lives soever it cost; putting man, woman, and child of them to the sword.

There is no suspicion of anything shameful behind that summary. The writer, bent on extirpation, has tracked mischievous beasts to their lairs, and there "strangled the cubs and rooted out the entire broods."[6] Nor did Sir Henry Sidney, Sir Philip Sidney's father, see anything blameworthy in it. He praised Gilbert to Lord Burghley (January 4, 1570):

The highways are now made free, where no man might travel unspoiled. . . . Yet this is not the most, nor the best he hath done, for the estimation that he hath won to the name of Englishman there, before almost not known, exceedeth all the rest.

Ethics came late to the men of Ralegh's generation, and their coming was not hastened by this using of Ireland as a finishing school to the French religious wars and the semi-piracy of privateering.

There were some, however, who thought Gilbert's methods erred "by a little too much warmth and presumption." His terms of office anywhere were always brief, and in 1570 he was superseded by Sir John Perrot, who was gentler—Ralegh (as he recorded later) thought, too gentle. Perrot was a remarkable old ruffian, closely resembling Henry VIII, whose son by Mary Berkley, before she married Thomas Perrot, he was generally accepted as being. Frankly regarding Elizabeth as his sister, he habitually showed the mettle of his pedigree by a broad vigor of expression as lusty as hers or her father's. According to Ralegh, "in the great chamber of Dublin," after the Queen had followed up sharp letters with a kindly one, in which she warned him to watch for a Spanish invasion, he laughed and broke out into unquotable coarseness, adding "for fear of the Spaniards, I am again one of her white boys!" —a speech which Naunton (who married Perrot's granddaughter) censures as having—

tended to some disreputation of his sovereign and serve for instruction to

6. Froude, iv, 23.

persons in place of honour and command, to beware of the violences of nature, and especially the exorbitance of the tongue.

As President of Munster (1570–1573) Perrot was adequately (but not outstandingly) successful by Elizabethan standards, killing in fight or hanging eight hundred rebels, with a loss of only eighteen English. He was a bull-headed blundering ruler, of the sort our detractors are pleased to style typically British—strong and without any nonsense except of his own roaring kind. The Irish sent his hair white, and it was probably a relief when he left his presidency, 1573, and took over naval command, passing on to an element which must have seemed quietness itself after the unruliness of men. Gilbert served under him off the Irish coast, watching against the peril which had moved the Queen to write the letter whose friendliness so amused her brother. We may be sure that he served Perrot with the critical freedom of the Elizabethans, who had nothing of the modern code of strict subservience to superior authority. Both had been removed from Munster, and admirers compared their tenures. No subsequent governors of Munster (Ralegh insisted, eleven years later) approached the standard set by his half-brother, acting independently under Lord Ormond, the nominal President.

Perrot, who served many years in Ireland, differed from the Devon men on a point of policy, as well as in comparative mildness:

to save the Queen's purse (which herself and my Lord Treasurer Burleigh ever took for good services), he imposed on the Irish the charge of bearing their own arms, which both gave them the possession, and taught them the use, of weapons, which proved in the end a most fatal work.[7]

Here the Devon "squatters" were right; if you are going to keep down by ruthlessness and a tiny force a country in rebellion, you must not give the enemy arms or instruction in their use. It seems a certainty that it was out of the jealousies excited by rivalry that the quarrel arose between Ralegh and Sir Thomas Perrot, Sir John's son. In 1579,[8] when Perrot and Gilbert were expecting the Spanish invasion, there was an affray which landed Ralegh and Thomas Perrot in Fleet Prison for six days. It left a lasting quarrel between the former and a family as iras-

7. Naunton, *Fragmenta Regalia, Sir John Perrot.*
8. February.

cible as his own. No man ever had more quarrels on hand, at practically any moment of his career; this one was to be permanent.

Sir John Perrot's later vicissitudes are interesting enough to justify a digression to summarize them. He became Lord Deputy of Ireland, 1584. But he could never bring himself to take his sister seriously as Queen. Ralegh always held that the men of his time who lost their sovereign's favor lost it, not because of "treason" but of sheer disrespect (which she found much harder to pardon). "That which most exasperated the Queen, and gave advantages to his enemies, was (as Sir Walter Rawleigh takes into his observation) words of disdain" (those left unquoted are specially meant); Perrot was recalled in 1588, sent to the Tower, and in 1592 condemned for high treason. Even in this strait he remained his picturesquely outspoken self, and "having a carnation in his hand, he said, I care not for death the value of this flower."[9] He attributed his fall to the machinations of Sir Christopher Hatton. "God's death!" he burst out. "Will the Queen suffer her brother to be offered up a sacrifice to the envy of his frisking[10] adversary?" Elizabeth, when these words were reported to her, swore that he was a true man, and should not die. But "the haughtiness of his spirit, which accompanied him to the last . . . brake in pieces the cords of his magnanimity," and he died suddenly, still a prisoner.

Ralegh was not in the first wave of Devonian invasion. But in the summer of 1580, during the Earl of Desmond's rebellion, as their captain he took over to Ireland a hundred infantry. In August he and Sir Warham St. Leger, provost-marshal in Munster, were the commission who sentenced the Earl's brother, Sir James Fitzgerald,[11] to be hanged and quartered, at Cork. Their instructions (August 23, 1580) from the Lord Justice of Ireland, Sir William Pelham, were: "proceed to his arraignment and condemnation; which done, you shall have farther direction for his execution."[12] Butchery followed automatically (though with the pretense of legal sanction). The victim's ghost had vengeance, in the almost simultaneous killing of Ralegh's kinsman, Sir Peter Carew, by ambushed Fitzgeralds (August 25). They nearly killed

---

9. *Fragmenta Regalia.*   10. *Ibid.* See p. 27.

11. The Fitzgeralds, of course, like many of the leading rebels, were Anglo-Irish, not true Irish.

12. *Calendar of the Carew MSS.,* 1575–1588, ed. J. S. Brewer and William Bullen (1867), p. 299. See also entry of August 15, 1580, same volume, p. 294.

Peter's brother George also; but he escaped, and played an important part in Ralegh's life.

The stories which have come down illustrate, by the lurid flame which plays over Elizabethan Ireland, Ralegh's ruthlessness and valor, that of a man known widely and eagerly followed. He would dash back to rescue a wounded follower alone in a mob of enemies; he would, by a mixture of sharp practice and courage, capture a suspected chieftain in his own castle; he would hold a ford single-handed. One story, told originally (as Stebbing observes[13]) approvingly, as an example of the English way of handling rebels properly, without any sentimental nonsense, appeals to us to-day rather as showing the forlorn pluck of a nameless peasant. Ralegh, who had noticed how quickly the Irish prowled into their enemies' deserted camps, to pick up what they could find, made an ambush after he had pretended to go, and caught a man with a lot of withies. He asked what they were for, and received the defiant reply, "to hang up the English churls." They would do, said Ralegh, to hang up the Irish kern, and so used them.

Ralegh in Ireland is an unpleasant memory. If it had been civilized warfare, with some honorable courtesy in the intervals of fighting, we might be happy to see that most attractive quality of his—refusal to desert a follower. He became detested as no other contemporary was; but throughout his life, those nearest to him, and especially those under his orders, worshipped him. We can tell why, when we read of him "standing with a pistol in one hand and his iron-shod quarterstaff in the other,"[14] holding off a small army while his tiny escort passed a river safely.

The opposition was similar to that which England (led, often, by the same Anglo-Irish strain) was one day to meet in India. Writing for King James's information, in 1603, Ralegh remarks that the Irish were armed with darts only. An arrogant rush by their well-armed confident enemies easily scattered large parties. Toward the end of Elizabeth's reign, the rebels managed to get hold of decent weapons, and fought the invaders on level terms, inflicting severe defeats. Massacre became what it was to remain, a two-edged sword.

The resistance of the conquered to attempts to civilize them always

13. *Ralegh*, pp. 16–17.   14. Martin Hume, p. 26.

puzzles their conquerors. "There lieth some secret mystery in this universal rebellious disposition," a Lord Deputy[15] wailed, in 1592, of the Irish recalcitrance, perhaps not knowing that another Englishman[16] had, three years previously, put his finger on the explanation: "the real cause of the mischief was the Devil, who would not have Ireland reformed." And in September, 1580, the Devil's captain-general, the King of Spain, permitted a filibustering expedition to the island. Most of its officers were Italians, and it sailed under the Papal flag, with Philip approving. Their first prospecting party had found out Smerwick, a ruined fort in Kerry; the main body followed, and made it their headquarters.

Europe was watching, and Sir Nicholas Malby, President of Connaught, wrote to Walsingham (September 7): "It is now a quarrel of religion, and the expectation of foreign aid doth much further it." Invasion drew the troubles to a head. The invaders brought four thousand stand of arms for the rebels, and three hundred of their personnel of about a thousand went inland to find the Earl of Desmond. The new Lord Deputy, Lord Grey de Wilton, invested Smerwick with a force of only two hundred soldiers, and after two days' bombardment the garrison asked for quarter. Their messengers had to admit themselves adventurers, with no Spanish commissions, and no official support but the Pope's. That support merely made their case the blacker in the eyes of Lord Grey, a stern Puritan. Refusing terms, he "left them to their choice, to yield and submit themselves, or no." They yielded, and "the Lord of Hosts" having "delivered the enemy to us . . . then put I in certain bands"—under Ralegh and Mackworth, the captains of the day—"who fell straight to execution."[17] Only officers were reserved for ransom. Six hundred stripped bodies, "as gallant and goodly personages as ever were beheld,"[18] were laid out on the sands. "The country was thus weeded of these noxious foreigners."[19]

Spenser (present as Lord Grey's personal secretary) went out of his way[20] to defend his master from the charge that he had been cruel, and had even broken promises (or, at any rate, half-promises) of quarter. Apologists stressed, and still stress, how small was his force, and the

15. Sir William Fitzwilliams.   16. George Wise.
17. Lord Grey to the Queen, November 12, 1580.
18. Lord Grey to the Privy Council.
19. Oldys, *Life of Ralegh* (Ralegh's *Works*, Vol. i).
20. *View of the Present State of Ireland* (Globe ed. of *Works*, p. 656).

impossibility of keeping a crowd of dangerous prisoners in a land wild with revolt. Nor were the invaders men whose value we need assess highly. They were the sweepings of Italian and Spanish jails: their own first prospecting party, on its way to Smerwick, had come across a Bristol trader, whose crew they flung into the sea. But all that need be said is that the massacre was horrible, but ordinary. The prisoners were

legally pirates, who had without valid commissions stirred up the native Irish to rebellion; and English adventurers in the same legal position on the Spanish main, although they were free from the added imputation of inciting to rebellion, had been mercilessly slain.[21]

Ralegh's share in the deed was, again, under orders, but there can be little doubt that he approved of it. It is, however, an excessive economy of words to summarize it as Lingard does. "Sir Walter Raleigh" ("the gallant but unprincipled Sir Walter Raleigh")[22] "entered the fort, received their arms, and then ordered them to be massacred in cold blood."[23] A mere captain has not such power.

Of the desperation to which the native Irish were driven their oppressors bear witness, as Spenser does on every page of his illuminating pamphlet, which contains *passim* such eyewitness stories as this, of the execution of "a notable traitor," Murrogh O'Brien, at Limerick:

I saw an old woman, which was his fostermother, take up his head whilest he was quartered, and sucked up all the blood running thereout, saying, that the earth was not worthy to drink it, and therewith also steeped her face and breast, and tore her hair, crying out and shrieking out most terribly.

It is this "gentle poet," and no fierce soldier, who has left us the most heart-rending picture of the misery which alien cruelty and their own inveterate civil quarrels, working together, had brought down on the rich and beautiful province of Munster, within less than two years of ravage:

Out of every corner of the woods and glens they came creeping forth upon their hands, for their legs could not bear them. They looked like anatomies of death; they spake like ghosts crying out of their graves; they

---

21. *D.N.B., Ralegh.*   22. *History of England* (1825), lx, 225.
23. *Op. cit.*, viii, 156.

did eat of the dead carrions, happy were they if they could find them, yea, and one another soon after, insomuch as the very carcasses they spared not to scrape out of their graves. And if they found a plot of watercresses or shamrocks, there they flocked as to a feast for the time, yet not able long to continue therewithal.

Ralegh in Ireland was disgruntled. Having found a patron (or hoping to find one) in Robert Dudley, Earl of Leicester, he told him (August 25, 1581):

I have spent some time here under the Deputy, in such poor place and charge, as, were it not for that I know him to be one of yours, I would disdain it as much as to keep sheep.

"Your Honor, having no use of such poor followers, hath utterly forgotten me." He corresponded with Burghley and Walsingham, freely criticizing Lord Grey, his superior. Stebbing finds his "apology, such as it is . . . in his just sense of a masterly capacity."[24] But no apology is called for; his conduct was deplorable, disloyal—and characteristically Elizabethan. Everyone wrote behind everyone's back.

Writing to Walsingham, February 25, 1581, Ralegh contrasted the feeble slackness of later authorities in Munster with Gilbert's vigor, a decade previously:

Would God your Honor and Her Majesty, as well as my poor self, understood how pitifully the service here goeth forward. Considering that this man, having now bin Lord General of Munster now about two years, there are at this instant a thousand traitors more than there were the first day. Would God the service of Sir Humfry Gilbert might be rightly lookt into! who with the third part of the garrison now in Ireland ended a rebellion not much inferior to this, in two months!

Gilbert's reappointment would work immediate miracles,

for I never heard nor read of any man more feared than he is among the Irish nacion. And I do assuredly know that the best about the Earl of Desmond, yea! and all the unbridled traitors of these parts, would come in here and yield themselves to the Queen's mercy, were it but known that he were come among them.

24. *Ralegh*, p. 20.

In December, 1581, Ralegh's company was disbanded, and he himself sent to London with dispatches. Naunton's story that he was presently in personal conflict with Lord Grey, before the Privy Council—"where he had much the better in telling of his tale; and so much that the Queen and the Lords took no small mark of the man and his parts"—may not be accurate in detail. But it is certain that his errand brought him before Elizabeth, whose ear "he got in a trice":

she began to be taken with his elocution, and loved to hear his reasons to her demands; and the truth is, she took him for a kind of oracle, which nettled them all.[25]

Nor need we reject Fuller's story of "this Captain Ralegh coming out of Ireland to the English Court in good habit (his clothes being then a considerable part of his estate)," and spreading his cloak in "a plashy place," "whereupon the Queen trod gently over, rewarding him afterwards with many suits for his so free and seasonable tender of so fair a foot cloth."[26] Nor even Fuller's other story, of his scrawling with a diamond on glass that would meet the Queen's eyes:

Fain would I climb, yet fear I to fall;

and of Elizabeth's writing thereunder:

If thy heart fails thee, climb not at all.[27]

All testimony agrees that Ralegh's person, the decision and imperious carriage won by years of hard unlovely warfare, the quickness and flashing brightness of his speech, were remarkable. Yet the extant portraits, with perhaps one exception, do not bear out this witness. The face is somber, and close to Aubrey's description:

He had a most remarkable aspect, an exceeding high forehead, long-faced and sour eye-lidded, a kind of pig-eye.[28]

Aubrey, however, was born after Ralegh's death.

Burghley, on January 1, 1582, passed on to Lord Grey what the

25. *Fragmenta Regalia.* 26. *Worthies*, p. 262.
27. "However, he at last climbed up by the stairs of his own desert" (Fuller).
28. *Brief Lives*, ii, 186.

latter indignantly characterized as proposals "for the lessening of" Her
Majesty's "charges here in the province of Mounster . . . offering a
very plausible show of thrift and commodity, which might easily occasion Her Majesty to think that I have not so carefully as behoved
looked into . . . Her Majesty's profit." He turned them down, and
warned Burghley that this climber was specious and unsound:

I doubt not but you will soon discern a difference between the judgments
of those who, with grounded experience and approved reason, look into the
condition of things, and those who, upon no ground but seeming fancies,
and affecting credit with profit, frame "plots" upon impossibilities for
others to execute.

But some of Ralegh's criticisms begin to show that even in Ireland he
had the capacity to outstrip his fellows by independence of thought. He
urged the policy of winning over the minor chieftains, who resented
indiscriminate violence—he made distinctions between what he considered military severity and wanton cruelty, though he was willing to
take the former to appalling lengths. The smaller men (he noted)
feared that Elizabeth, weary of the endless expense, would let Desmond
make his peace, and leave him free to avenge himself on those who had
taken part against him. He objected[29] to the employment of the Earl of
Ormond to suppress his own countrymen, partly because he thought
him too lenient, but also for the valid reason that Irishmen resented
coercion by an Irishman. The Geraldines "will rather die a thousand
deaths, enter into a million of mischiefs and seek succour of all nations,
rather than they will ever be subdued by a Butler."

Ralegh did not immediately become one of those close to the Queen's
person. She wrote a letter (April, 1582)[30] signifying her interest in him,
and reappointing him in Ireland to a company whose captain had died:

our pleasure is to have our servant Walter Rawley trained some time longer
in that our realm for his better experience in Martial affairs, and for the
special care we have to do him good in respect of his kindred, that have
served us some of them (as you know) near about our Person.[31]

29. Letter to Walsingham, February 25, 1581.
30. To the Lord Deputy (Lord Grey).
31. Humphrey Gilbert had been her page.

But Elizabeth "loved a soldier, and had a propension in her nature to reward, and always to grace them."[32] This soldier she soon decided she liked too well to want him to go and "get knockt on the head, as that inconsiderate fellow Sidney was."[33] Recalled after what must have been an excessively brief term of renewed service, he was allowed to send a deputy. Grey had angrily acknowledged his reappointment, with resentment of Ralegh's indiscipline: "I like neither his carriage nor his company; and therefore, other than by direction and commandment, and what his right can require, he is not to expect at my hands." Ireland was obviously closed as a career, for the time being.

Wonder has often been expressed that a man so outstandingly gifted should have had Ralegh's poor success throughout life. But the world is not made for those who pursue their ideas with his impersonal fierceness. He was a poor judge of men, and especially of what they were thinking about him. He accepted enthusiastically, in the best clan spirit, the views of Gilbert, Grenville, Frobisher and the other Devon men in Ireland; and when he clashed with Lord Grey, he pushed past him to those who held the reins of government in London. No man can do this kind of thing without suffering casualties. And Ralegh either did not notice (or did not take seriously) that even in Elizabethan times there was beginning another school of opinion concerning Ireland, one ashamed and weary of the whole business. Elizabeth herself, when Europe interfered at Smerwick, was about to try leniency. Burghley, who "possessed the rare quality of being able to recognise the faults of his own countrymen,"[34] wrote (June 10, 1582):

The Flemings had not such cause to rebel against the oppression of the Spaniards as the Irish against the tyranny of England.

"Wise Walsingham thought it no treason to wish" Ireland "buried in

32. *Fragmenta Regalia.*

33. Her ungracious reference, a few years later, to the eclipse in Zutphen skirmish, of—

> "the perfect knight,
> The soldier, courtier, bard in one,
> Sidney, that pensive Hesper-light
> O'er Chivalry's departed sun."
> Sir William Watson.

34. Froude, *Queen Elizabeth,* iv, 237.

the sea, considering the charge it brought."[35] It was the extreme of un-wisdom to urge sterner, and ever sterner, measures on men sick of those already enforced, and enforced against their protests. Ralegh's career was one of disappointment, the more intense because his ambition was so quick and active; it was now that dislike of the young soldier—so pushing, so hardened, and so immediately successful with the Queen—took root. It "nettled them all" that a fine presence should achieve so much; his great intellectual qualities were to emerge later, and be ac-knowledged reluctantly and inadequately. When at length the dislike of men like Burghley and Walsingham had ceased to be an obstacle, Ralegh's marriage (1592) and the circumstances of it completed his failure, leaving him to struggle henceforward with the Queen's undy-ing resentment.

Luckily for Ralegh's admirers, Ireland was not to see him again, ex-cept in brief and unwarlike visits. We have reached a point at which his biographers can never suppress their satisfaction, realizing that henceforward that brutally used country need call for only perfunctory mention. Almost everyone who has written of him has been unable to resist the temptation to quote Goldwin Smith's remark:

The eagles took wing for the Spanish main, the vultures descended on Ireland.

Pope-Hennessy adds, "Ralegh seems to have united some of the char-acteristics of both"[36]—a remark true of all Elizabethan men of action.

35. Osborne's *Traditional Memoirs of the Reign of Elizabeth*, no. 22.
36. *Sir Walter Ralegh in Ireland*, p. 61.

CHAPTER IV

The Rising Courtier and Administrator

If ever man drew virtue out of necessity, it was he, therewith was he the great example of industry. . . . For it was a long time before he could brag of more than he carried at his back; and when he got on the winning side, it was his commendation, that he took pains for it, and underwent many various adventures for his after perfection, and before he came into the public note of the world . . . he came up, *per ardua, per varios casus, per tot discrimina rerum*—not pulled up by chance, or by any gentle admittance of fortune. NAUNTON, *Fragmenta Regalia*.

. . . It is reported of the Women in the Balear Islands, that, to make their Sons expert archers, they will not, when children, give them their breakfast before they had hit the mark. Such was the dealing of the Queen with this Knight, making him to earn his Honour, and by pain and peril to purchase what places of credit or profit were bestowed upon him. Indeed, it was true of him, what was said of Cato Uticensis, *That he seemed to be born to that only which he went about*—so dextrous was he in all his undertakings. FULLER, *History of the Worthies of England*.

LORD GREY'S protest fell dead. Ralegh's star had risen far above his; he "came from the mud of obscure campaigns to the most brilliant court in Europe, a plain captain, and for ten years that court held no more brilliant figure."[1] When he visited the Low Countries, in the train of the Earl of Leicester, William the Silent picked him out to take back dispatches, and through him put up his appeal to the Queen, whose vacillations were so sore a trial. "Say for me to the Queen, *Sub umbra alarum tuarum protegimur*."

Robert Dudley, Earl of Leicester, was still Elizabeth's first favorite, but had ceased to be a passion. As "second string" she had Sir Christopher Hatton, her vice-chamberlain and mouthpiece in the House of Commons. As we have seen, according to Sir John Perrot he owed his success to nothing more remarkable than a pair of skipping feet. He "came to the Court . . . by the galliard . . . a mere vegetable of the

1. Agnes Latham, *Poems of Ralegh*, p. 3.

Court that spring up at night and sink again at his noon." With her trick of nicknaming her gallants, Elizabeth called him by various pastoral titles, her "mutton," her "bell-wether," and so on. He and Sir Thomas Heneage, who had "now dropped out of the active list of lovers"[2] decided that something must be done about the newest favorite. Accordingly, on an October morning in 1582, as the Queen was mounted "to ride abroad in the great park to kill a doe," Heneage emerged from a thicket, to hand her three tokens, a book, a bucket, a jewelled bodkin. The bucket referred to Ralegh, whose nickname with Elizabeth was "water" (a play on the pronunciation of his name). The meaning of this touching little drama was that her bell-wether would kill himself unless measures were taken to remove the water. Elizabeth was delighted, and affirmed of Hatton that "there never was such another." She tried to fix the bodkin, but her horse was excited by her excitement, and she had to give back bodkin and book (containing letter) till she had managed him to a standstill. Then she and Heneage went through a little flirtation by proxy. She read her bell-wether's reproaches "with blushing cheeks, and uttered many speeches (which I refer till I see you), most of them tending to the discovery of a doubtful mind, whether she should be angry or well pleased"; but came home to the answer that,

If Princes were like gods, as they should be, they would suffer no element so to abound as to breed confusion. And *Pecora campi*[3] was so dear unto her, that she had bounded her banks so sure, as no *water* nor floods should ever overthrow them. And for better assurance unto you that you shall not fear drowning, she hath sent you a bird that, together with the rainbow, brought the good tidings that there should be no more destruction by water. . . . You should remember she was a shepherd, and then you might think how dear her sheep was unto her.

Heneage concludes, "*water* hath been more welcome than were fit for so cold a season."

Water, however, continued to be an element growing in favor. In April, 1583, Ralegh's career gained its first sound financial basis, by All Souls College, Oxford, granting him (under royal instructions) two

2. Hume, *Ralegh,* p. 36. "Lover" in the romantic sense only.
3. "Sheep of the field," Elizabeth being a shepherdess.

leases.[4] In the same year, we find him so established that Lord Burghley himself begs his intercession for his son-in-law, the Earl of Oxford, who had wounded, and been wounded by, a gentleman of the Privy Chamber. Ralegh consented, with a distaste he frankly owned (May 12, 1583). "I am content to lay the serpent before the fire, as much as in me lieth, that having recovered strength, myself may be more in danger of his poison and sting." His intercession was successful, but the favor he granted so tactlessly was accepted without gratitude. Oxford continued his enemy, and later became one of the most aggressive of the anti-Ralegh faction who excited the Earl of Essex.

It is almost sufficient to list Ralegh's appointments and public activities, to show how impressive was his rise. In 1583, he and Carew Ralegh, his elder brother of whole blood, were on a panel from which a committee was to be appointed to inquire into the state of the navy. The same year, Ralegh received a commission to clear the seas of Don Antonio's privateers. Don Antonio was leading a Nationalist revolt against Spain, which had annexed Portugal in 1580, and his ships had become a general nuisance. In 1584 there was an attempt to found a company to enter the lucrative Eastern trade, then strongly attracting English merchants. A paper, endorsed by Burghley, "29 November 1584. The charge of the navy to the Moluccas," lists the Queen as adventuring £7000 in shipping and £10,000 in capital, Leicester as adventuring £3000, John Hawkins £2500, Drake £7000, William Hawkins £1000, Hatton £1000, Ralegh £400. As the last sum shows, Ralegh was not yet a wealthy man. The expedition was to consist of a thousand mariners, a hundred gunners, and five hundred soldiers; its purpose was plainly no gentle trading, but nothing less than the occupation of the Moluccas, with which Drake had set up treaty relations in 1579. But the proposal came to nothing, for Elizabeth's long period of infirm and halting action had set in. It was Holland who went into the Moluccas.

In 1584 Ralegh was elected one of Devon's two M.P.'s, and entered on what was not the least (though the least noticed) of his astoundingly varied activities, his long steady service in Parliament. He was knighted the same year.

Elizabeth "used to pay her servants part in money, and the rest with

4. See *Egerton Papers,* p. 94.

grace."[5] To Ralegh, in May 1583, she granted the farm of wines; he was entitled to collect from every vintner one pound annually, for his license. When passions had died down, it was admitted that he used his power gently (in 1592, his accounts estimated that he made only £2000 a year by it). But no one who interferes between the Englishman and his drink, with a demand for additional payment, is going to be popular, and the patent aroused universal obloquy. In 1584 it brought him in conflict with a strong vested interest, his sub-agent Brown having granted a license in Cambridge, where the University Vice-Chancellor claimed licensing rights. The students took up the reigning publican's cause, beat up the intruder, and nearly frightened his wife to death. "By violence offered" she "was in case by sundry swoons and passions to have died."[6] The Vice-Chancellor backed up this spirited action by sending Brown's nominee to jail. Ralegh had to write three temperate letters before the University replied. The dispute was ultimately decided against him, and the Universities expressly excluded from the operation of his patent. Brown proved dishonest, and in 1588, Ralegh, in order to get rid of him, went the length of having his own license revoked and then regranted for twenty-one years, from August 9, 1588. Even so, he had to compensate Brown handsomely.

In March 1584, and in 1585, 1587, and 1589, he was granted a license to export woollen broadcloths, on payment of a rent to the Queen. Burghley thought he profiteered in these, which seems likely enough, even allowing for contemporary exaggeration of his extravagance. That extravagance must certainly have been considerable; all testimony concurs that, even in that age of boyish "showing-off," he was almost the most gorgeously dressed. The Middlesex Registers (April 26, 1583), record that "Hugh Pewe, gentleman," was tried for stealing a jewel worth £80, a hatband of pearls worth £30, and five yards of damask silk worth £3, all the property of Ralegh. Drexelius, the Flemish Jesuit, calls him[7] "the darling of the English Cleopatra" ("*Gualterus Raiolaeus, ille apud Anglicanam Cleopatram nimis gratiosus homo*"), and says that his shoes were computed to be worth more than 6600 gold pieces. In 1583, the Queen gave Ralegh the use of Durham

5. Naunton, *Fragmenta Regalia.*
6. Ralegh to the Vice-Chancellor and Senate, July 9, 1584.
7. *Trismegistus Christianus* p. 469.

House in the Strand; he kept here forty men and forty horses in attendance:

> I well remember his study, which was on a little turret that looked into and over the Thames, and had a prospect which is as pleasant as any in the world.[8]

For all this splendor, Ralegh needed money. One way of getting money was by interceding for condemned traitors. In 1586 occurred Babington's inept plot to assassinate Elizabeth, recognized as peculiarly base, its participators being young men of good family trusted with easy access to their Queen:

> upon the discovery of this dreadful Plot, and the taking up of these Rebels and bloody-minded Traitors, the City of London made extraordinary Rejoicings, by publick Bonfires, ringing of Bells, Feastings in the Streets, singing of Psalms, and such like.[9]

The night before execution (September 19, 1586) Babington still hoped that a friend who had offered Ralegh £1000 might come with word of his pardon. Ralegh cannot possibly have thought him a case deserving help, and there is not the slightest evidence that he ever hinted he might help him. However, "few men have had more conspicuously than" Ralegh "the fortune to be much written about by writers possessing extremely lax notions of the laws of evidence";[10] some of these have assumed a kind of "double-crossing" of the unhappy youth because of his hope, and because the Queen granted Ralegh most of the traitor's vast estates, situated in five counties, directing that her grant should pass the great seal without fee. Loss of life and lands was an ordinary casualty of those uncertain days; Ralegh was to experience similar pillage himself. For some of the Essex conspirators, over a dozen years later, Ralegh consented to intercede, and was well paid for saving their lives. The Queen, and everyone else, on such occasions understood perfectly what was happening. It was the State's way of paying for services, before a proper civil and military system existed—a bad way, but it was the way.

8. Aubrey, *Brief Lives,* ii, 183.
9. John Strype, *Annals of the Reformation* (1785 edition), Vol. iii, Book II, chap. V, p. 417.
10. Edwards, *Life of Ralegh,* i, 68.

In the same year as he stepped into Babington's shoes, Ralegh was granted in Munster, now being settled after having become a wilderness inhabited by wolves and foxes, a seignory of the standard size (twelve thousand acres). Another two and a half seignories were granted to him and two associates, who are assumed to have been practically "dummies." He set to work immediately to plant his sub-province with Devonshire men.

It is a mixed story, and much of it offends modern decency. Yet part of it, on the narrative's very face, proves Ralegh different from Elizabeth's other favorites. He is recognized as a naval authority, and is in high and responsible employment. "Posterity, misled by tradition, has never been sure whether his distinctive vocation were not that of a fine gentleman."[11] His contemporaries slowly learnt better, though they never learnt the whole truth. Everyone has heard the younger Cecil's confession, "I know that he can toil terribly." Bacon respected him; and respect, rendered with surly grudging, appears even in Ben Jonson's comments on him to Drummond of Hawthornden.

Ralegh's work for the West of England, though not his most famous, was some of his greatest work. In July, 1585, he became Lord Warden of the Stannaries—that is, head of the Devon and Cornwall tin-miners, a commonwealth with laws of their own, which he overhauled. The courts were held in the heart of Dartmoor, on Crockern Tor, where formerly stood a granite table and seats, hewn out for use of Warden and "stannators." Here Ralegh and his miners, a folk he understood and was understood by, sat in a desolation so high and lonely that often they were cloaked from the world, with thick mists drifting all about them. It was not the courtier with the shoes that flashed with gems, whom these wild regions saw; but the other Ralegh, who kept to his death-day his burring accent,[12] which amused Queen Elizabeth.

In September, 1585, he was appointed Lieutenant of the County of Cornwall, and presently, Vice-Admiral of the counties of Cornwall and Devon. In 1587 he became Captain of the Queen's Guard, an ornamental post which kept him near her person. He selected young men of tall fine presence, who carried in her food, guarded her from poison or

11. Stebbing, *Ralegh,* p. 27.
12. "He spoke broad Devonshire to his dying day" (Aubrey, *Brief Lives,* ii, 182).

the assassin's dagger, and went in and out with messages. He himself, a figure more splendid than them all, at all times stood within summons, and often within hearing of her conversation. The post brought in no payment (unless, as is likely, and would be ordinary by the time's standards, he took a fee for admission to the Guard). The sole emoluments were a uniform:

To our right trusty and well beloved servant Sir Walter Rawley, knight, Captain of our Guard, six yards of tawny medley, at thirteen shillings and fourpence a yard; with a fur of black budge, rated at ten pounds; sum, fourteen pounds; given to him for the office of Captain of our Guard.[13]

This was the highest favor he ever reached, and his success with Elizabeth was solely personal. He was far older than nobles who were of her Council or served as commanders. He never reached the Privy Council, and until his last most miserable voyage of all—that resulting in his execution—was never in the place of first command. And his unpopularity was intense, and grew steadily, an evil name with commons and courtiers alike. In May, 1587, he was described[14] as "the best hated man of the world, in Court, city, and country." Even men essentially base in their own employments thought they might take a chance on this dislike of Ralegh. Richard Tarleton, the player, a dissipated disreputable fellow, seeing him with the Queen pointed at him, and said, "See, the Knave commands the Queen," "for which he was corrected by a frown from Her Majesty."[15]

Ralegh's failure to win the first place as naval or military commander need not surprise us. It was not unusual to have a titled blunderer as the nominal chief, while someone like Ralegh was present to provide experience on which that chief could rely. As to exclusion from the Council, here he paid the price always paid by the man whose genuine greatness is accompanied by versatility. He was too clever; and too variously clever. It is obvious that even Elizabeth thought he lacked balance. Her nickname of "water" may not have been altogether friendly.

Personal unpopularity had much to do with his failure. He was an "upstart," and the age was peculiarly jealous of upstarts, though it is

13. Warrant, April 7, 1592.   14. By Sir Anthony Bagot.
15. *Fragmenta Regalia.*

hard to see why, the Queen herself being daughter of a country knight's child who was adjudged an adulteress and executed. The Tudors had risen recently, from no great matter. The all-powerful Earl of Leicester was grandson of a mere "squire," the Dudley who sheared Henry VII's woollier subjects for him, and was beheaded when Henry VIII looked round for ways of winning applause. However, when a man has once definitely arrived, with the plumes of title nodding above him, people quickly forget that he was lately nobody. Ralegh, of an ancient line of gentlemen, was not of the nobility; the nobility, and those who loved the nobility, scorned him accordingly as an adventurer.

There were also faults of deportment. "Damnable proud,"[16] he treated backbiting with a contempt more galling than open wrath. "If any man accuseth me to my face, I will answer him with my mouth, but my tail is good enough to return an answer to such who traduceth me behind my back."[17] Yet he suffered, conscious of a host of enemies and enviers, from an inferiority complex, which betrayed him into acts and attitudes alternately inflated and unduly humble.

When he was made Lord Warden of the Stannaries, an indignant correspondent wrote to Burghley (July 7, 1586):[18]

Her Majesty and you have placed Sir Walter Ralegh as Lord Warden of the Stannaries, but amongst so rough and mutinous a multitude, 10,000 or 13,000 of the most strong men of England, it were meet their governor were one whom the most part well accounted of, using some familiarity and biding amongst them, whereas no man is more hated than him—none more cursed daily of the poor, of whom in truth numbers are brought to extreme poverty through the gift of the cloths to him—his pride is intolerable, without regard for any, as the world knows.

But that complaint bears throughout the marks of its secondhand character. Ralegh's intense unpopularity (which surprises all who write about him) stopped short at the West Country borders. Here, except (apparently) in Exeter, he was as beloved as elsewhere he was hated. Something of this may be set down to local pride in one who was at no pains to hide his origin, but even in the Queen's presence talked as he did at home. Yet this local pride exacted a penalty at Court, where

16. Aubrey, *Brief Lives*, ii, 182.   17. Fuller, *Worthies*, p. 262.
18. *Calendar of State Papers, Domestic*, Elizabeth, Addenda, 1580–1625, p. 182.

Devon's greatest figure was "backed by the vast family circles of the Gilberts and Champernouns,"[19] and by Carews, Courtenays, Grenvilles, "Old Uncle Tom Cobley and all." Many ears disliked the grating music made when these Devon men ground each other's axes.

At least once, Ralegh went out of his way to disarm hostility.

There had been a time when Elizabeth's relations with Lord Leicester were reported daily in every chancellery of Europe. When his wife was found with broken neck at the foot of the stairs of Cumnor manor-house, where he kept her retired, her death was assumed to have been arranged to free him for supremely great alliance. But he had been too unpopular for the Queen to dare to marry him; it would have seemed like Mary's marriage with Bothwell after Darnley's "elimination."

In 1586, however, all this was a half-forgotten story, of more than a quarter of a century earlier. According to general belief, Elizabeth still kept Leicester as her lover, but had tried many others, Hatton and Ralegh among them, only to ascertain that she was not meant to be anything but a Virgin Queen. The time's indecent assumption has been set down by Ben Jonson in classic words (which the curious may look up in their context)[20] that have furnished, in the medical history of Queen Elizabeth, yet one more detail in the multifarious problem of this astonishing and obscure woman. But by 1586 her relations with Leicester had sunk into the placid course of habit, which neither pursued with any zest. Nevertheless, Leicester could be roused to jealousy; when it was reported that a Devon squire, his own protégé, had supplanted him while he was away fighting his mistress' battles in the Low Countries,[21] his satellites seem to have prevailed on his indolence, and he complained. Ralegh took the complaint up with the Queen, who made Walsingham write to Leicester (March, 1586):

Her wish was . . . to assure you, upon her honor, that the gentleman hath done good offices for you; and that, in the time of Her displeasure, he dealt as earnestly for you as any other in the world that professeth the most goodwill for your Lordship. This I write by Her Majesty's command.

At the same time, Ralegh himself, having occasion to send Leicester

19. Stebbing, p. 24.
20. *Conversations with William Drummond.*
21. They had chosen him as their Governor.

some West Country miners for whose assistance he had asked, took the opportunity to add (March 29) :

The Queen is in very good terms with you, and, thanks be to God, well pacified. You are again her "Sweet Robyn."

For Ralegh's own relations with the Queen, contemporaries assumed that they were that of lovers in the technical, physical sense. It is still commonly assumed; even Hume and Mr. Harlow, as well as Edwards, accept it. But the belief is one that cannot bear examination. Ralegh's own testimony in later days was that to be the Queen's "minion" was no great distinction, except in your selection for constant service and endurance of her moods. The belief that he was her lover in a physical sense is based entirely on the slanders of her enemies, who chose to assert that her ruling passions were sensual. There is no evidence whatever of this relationship between her and Ralegh.

CHAPTER V

Privateer, Explorer, Colonizer

She made it her constant practice to annoy the Spaniard through the conduct of those Sonnes of Neptune, Drake, Furbusher, Cavendish, Sir Walter Rawly, &c. FRANCIS OSBORNE.

THE income which provided Ralegh's splendor came (not, as was assumed, filched from the drink and clothing of the poor, but) from privateering, his main business. Up to 1584, he seems to have conducted it under cover of commissions from the Prince of Condé or the Prince of Orange. In April, 1585, that zealous leader of the Church militant, the Rev. Richard Hakluyt, chaplain of the English Embassy in Paris, wrote to Walsingham:

The rumours of Ralegh's fleet, and especially the preparation of Sir Francis Drake, so vexes the Spaniard that I wish, if Drake's voyage be stayed, the rumour of it be continued.[1]

Ralegh's name here appears subordinate to the dreaded Dragon's. To be cited as casting a menace additional to that flung by Drake's far-feared shadow is sufficient honor!

Moreover (and this gives him his outstanding place), in Ralegh's naval enterprises was a creative aim absent from Drake's. Drake was the destroyer and pillager in chief, in whom the Elizabethan naval effort reached its highest offensive and destructive point. But Ralegh, in that steadfast terrible way of his, year after year, worked to make an overseas empire. Capture of galleons and carracks merely brought in goods, many of them decorative rather than useful; and their bringing in was often demoralizing. To plant "New Englands," linked in blood and language and affection to the mother-country, providing homes for her surplus population and vigorous auxiliaries in her hour of danger —as they themselves grew in importance, providing also "a vent" for England's woollen goods, while sending back raw materials and food—

1. *Calendar of State Papers, Domestic,* Elizabeth, Addenda, 1580–1625, p. 141.

this was a dream which came to him almost alone, and stayed with him, unshaken by adversity or the triumph of enemies or death itself.

When a Devon group, Ralegh and Gilbert their leaders, first approached the Queen with a proposal

to discover and to plant Christian inhabitants in place convenient, upon those large and ample countries extended Northward from the cape of Florida, lying under very temperate climes, esteemed fertile and rich in Minerals, yet not in the actual possession of any Christian prince,

she was unenthusiastic. Her Court was beset by visionaries whose eyes held a gleam as wild as those of the Ancient Mariner himself. They testified to silver mines on the river Norumbega, to Indian chiefs in banqueting houses of crystal pillared with precious shining metals, and to the ease with which their ships could whip the Spanish ships. Gilbert, the most pertinacious of all, Elizabeth considered a pleasant person to have about Court (where he preferred to waste as little time as possible), but "a man noted for no good hap at sea." Ralegh, however, made her listen to him.

· Part of his scheme was, of course, religious; it would hardly have been Elizabethan otherwise. When John Hawkins infested African estuarial swamps with the *Jesus* and the *John the Baptist,* kidnapping negroes, he had done it in order to lift them out of their "beastly manner" of existence and give them, not merely a life of servitude to sound Christian masters, but a chance of Paradise when it finished; Hakluyt writes of his voyages as if they were missionary ones. Paradise (without preliminary kidnapping) was what Gilbert hoped to give the heathen —stirred in his "virtuous and heroical mind, preferring chiefly the honour of God, compassion of poor infidels captived by the devil tyrannising in most wonderful and dreadful manner over their bodies and souls." It was no sin that patriotic zeal worked concurrently with pity, for

advancement of his honest and well disposed countrymen, willing to accompany him in such honourable actions, relief of sundry people within this realm distressed: all these be honourable purposes, imitating the nature of the munificent God, wherewith He is well pleased, who will assist such an actor beyond expectation of man.

All this was deeply and sincerely felt. These were the years when the religious tension was growing to its fiercest. For twenty years Elizabeth had held her Puritans in check. There had been no reprisals for the Smithfield burnings, indignation had been compelled to spare even "bloody Bonner." But her Protestantism slowly grew, and grew from political roots and the need for self-preservation. In 1570 the Pope excommunicated her, an action anticipated in the Catholic rising of the north in 1569, which was put down with ferocity quite exceptional in her reign. In 1572, at last political executions began, with the Duke of Norfolk's beheading. He was followed by the Earl of Northumberland, who (like other State offenders in her time) paid the penalty of ungentlemanly behavior, rather than of treason. He had called her a bitch, and "may be truly said to have gone 'indignant to the shades.' "[2] In 1577 men began to die for religion along with treason.[3] Two years later, Cardinal Allen, one-time Fellow of Oriel, founded the English College at Rome. Its members, all Jesuits and most of them Oxford men, were trained in the atmosphere of anticipated martyrdom. The excommunication had cleared the issues, and for strict Catholics Elizabeth's deposition became a duty, though one softened by absolution from it *ad illud tempus,* "until that time" when some foreign invasion gave rebellion a chance of success. Mary in imprisonment grew ever more hopeful, the center of a vast web of excited plotting. The execution of the Babington conspirators was deliberately savage, as an answer. Unless we see in what a fever England was moving to the open clash, we cannot understand the apocalyptic exultation with which Gilbert, a man whose blood always ran hotly, went forward to his colonizing, expecting enemies both human and spiritual, and death at any moment.

The quickening of decisions directly affected the plans of Gilbert and Ralegh. As war with Spain, and with it the likelihood of civil war, plainly approached, moderate Catholics sought to save both life and conscience. In 1582 a group of them were told by Walsingham that if they would join with Gilbert, the Queen would permit them to enjoy full religious liberty in the proposed New England, while keeping their estates in the Old England. Sir Philip Sidney stood their friend, and the

2. John Bayley, *The History and Antiquities of the Tower of London,* p. 83.
3. Execution of Cuthbert Mayne at Launceston. As often happens, this first execution was the one most open to objection, even from the legal side.

proposal attracted. Gilbert delegated authority (June, 1582) to two Catholic gentlemen to explore the coast between Florida and Cape Breton, and settle there. He was to follow himself, to establish a second England modelled on the one he knew, with parishes exactly three miles square, and churches in the middle of each, served by a clergy endowed with glebe and tithes. There would be gentry, yeomanry, commonalty, with generous grants of land according to their degree; and common spaces, "with such allowance for housebote, hedgebote and ploughbote as the country may serve." By December, 1582, his scheme was ready.

Ralegh, who was to be Gilbert's Vice-Admiral, spent £2000 building the *Bark Ralegh,* of 200 tons—not to be confused with the more famous *Ark Ralegh,* also built by him, Lord Howard's flagship against the Armada. (Lord Howard testified that she was "the oddest ship in the world, and the best for all conditions.") Ralegh's shipbuilding won the puzzled admiration of contemporaries. But on posterity's attention he has so many greater claims, that this, like his parliamentary distinction, can be mentioned only, as one activity in what must have been almost the busiest and most versatile career on record.

Then Elizabeth forbade Ralegh to sail, and for long refused leave even to Gilbert. Gilbert was in despair. During the Irish rebellion, his ships had been pressed into State service and stolen, and the remainder of his resources had gone into the long effort to give shape to his dreams of a North-West Passage and a New England. He had written to Walsingham (July, 1581) that he had been forced "to sell his wife's clothes from her back," which for that heroic woman's sake we may hope was seaman's hyperbole. Beset by both brothers, at last the Queen consented as regards Gilbert; and Ralegh notified him of her relenting, in a letter charming in itself, and bringing out also the courtly grace which gave that age a glamour even for itself and has kept that glamour alive during three centuries, despite our ability now to see behind its fine façade of drama and lyric and voyaging after the rainbow:

RICHMOND, 17TH March, 1583.
BROTHER,

I have sent you a token from Her Majesty, an anchor guided by a lady, as you see; and farther, Her Highness willed me to send you word that she wished you as great good hap, and safety to your ship, as if her self were there in person: desiring you to have care of your self, as of that which she tendereth; and therefore for her sake you must provide for it accordingly.

Further, she commandeth me that you leave your picture with me. For the rest, I leave till our meeting, or to the report of this bearer, who would needs be messenger of this good news. So I commit you to the will and protection of God, Who send us such life or death as He shall please or hath appointed.

Your true brother,
W. RALEGH.

The present age has travelled far from the delight of Lamb and Swinburne in quite minor dramatists and from indiscriminate eulogy of poetry written to a convention. The worship once so loud and joyous is liable to interruption by distinguished barrackers. Rossetti's protest—

> O ruff-embastioned vast Elizabeth,
> Bush to these bushel-bellied casks of wine,
> Home-growth, 'tis true, but rank as turpentine!

—has been continued by Mr. E. M. Forster, raising his voice against a wicked and parthenolatrous generation, himself "thankful to have escaped" the days of Queen Elizabeth:

> Gone was the dear Pope, overseas, underground; gone the traditions that echoed out of the past and whispered of future unity, and in their place, closing every vista, stood a portentous figure shaped like a dinner-bell. The hard reverberations of this creature filled the air, her feet twinkled in a septuagenarian dance, she made progresses and rude metallic jokes, she exploited a temper naturally violent, she was a public virgin—and all she did she did for the honour of England.[4]

Yet the "public virgin," who to us appears so preposterously called Virgin, still abides our question, not easily dismissed; and a letter like Ralegh's shows that the application of what now seems an outmoded chivalric legend was not entirely *blague*. It is cruel to judge any age by its more conventionalized portraiture; and for posterity the vivid reality has completely disappeared from sight, behind that "portentous figure shaped like a dinner-bell." Her own subjects remembered other pictures, stirring pity and immense admiration: the girl whose child-

4. E. M. Forster, "Peeping at Elizabeth" (*Nation and Athenaeum*, August 8, 1925).

hood had been so helpless; her own mother humiliated and executed; the scaffold's shadow dark over her own obscure yet closely watched existence, when London was crowded with gibbets and Smithfield pyres were burning, before the dear Pope had been thrust overseas and underground. Out of these perils she had been plucked by a miracle of which her own discretion and courage had been part: she had held a course still full of terrors, until England had been raised to where her sons were raised above all threats. There was something to quicken the blood here; I submit there is something to quicken it still, unless we put imagination and sympathy utterly to sleep. Elizabeth and her servants were both alike innocent of ethics: ruthless often, liars always (but by degrees not so "always"). But they were at least resolute to keep out of their country the desolation of cruelty which the Continent miscalled "religion," and they were working out some kind of ideals which later on would take even ethical shape. The people could recognize courage when they saw it; and they saw it in their Queen. She scolded her servants, she was capricious, grasping, vain, insulting; she exacted service which often ended in repudiation (though never to the extent of flinging their lives to England's enemy, as her successor was to fling Ralegh's). But her regard for them was real and personal, and more honorably based than the crude psychological theories of our age allow. I am not going to speak of her servants as "her Paladins." Yet the stale phrase expresses the fact. She was Gloriana, not merely in verse but in their thoughts of her; Gloriana maddeningly hesitant often, halting and withdrawing when (as after the Armada's rout) she should have let them press home; often more dishonest than even a Queen has any right to be. But still Gloriana, the most courageous brain in Christendom. She sent Gilbert out to what she and he both knew, and he at least knew with entire cheerfulness, might prove his death, and he took with him "an anchor guided by a lady."

The rest of the enterprise lives forever, as one of the mightiest stories of even the English race. The fleet sailed, June 11, 1583, five ships that amounted altogether to the monstrous burden of 410 tons. Two days later, after a night of "great storm of thunder and wind" the *Bark Ralegh* fled back, at one stroke robbing the expedition of half its tonnage and personnel. Her commander alleged that a contagious sickness had prostrated his men, which the historian allows as perhaps true,

perhaps false, but in any case disgraceful: "Sure I am, no cost was spared
by their owner Master Ralegh in setting them forth. Therefore I leave
it unto God." Gilbert himself wanted to leave it to a lower authority,
who was likely to act promptly. "I pray you, solicit my brother Ralegh
to make them an example to all knaves."

Gilbert reached Newfoundland, and annexed it. Never losing sight
of his and Ralegh's main purpose, to persuade as many as possible to
pitch their lives in these new countries, he gave the land away generously, to himself and his followers. Then, on August 20, having sent
his sick back to England, he continued his voyage. The astonishing
band kept their spirits high:

most part of this Wednesday night, like the Swan that singeth before her
death, they in the Admiral, or Delight, continued in sounding of Trumpets,
with Drums and Fifes: also winding the Cornets, Hautboys: and in the end
of their jollity, left with the battle and ringing of doleful knells.

But their luck was over, and omens began to gather, in a tale as stark
and threatening as that Icelandic one of Burnt Njal. Some made "frivolous reports . . . of strange voices" in the night, "which scared some
from the helm." Next day the wind rose, fogs densely shut them in, and
they ran into shoal water where the *Delight* went aground, a loss of 120
tons of their trivial burden and over a hundred lives. The other ships
stood in as near as they could, while the sea's fury dashed it to pieces:
"all that day, and part of the next, we beat up and down as near unto
the wrack as was possible for us, looking out, if by good hap we might
espy any of them." Twelve only escaped, and after six terrible days and
nights reached Newfoundland.

There remained now the *Golden Hind,* 40 tons, and the *Squirrel,* 10
tons. Gilbert made the latter, the point of gravest danger, his ridiculously tiny "flagship." Cruising up and down, they grew daily more
discouraged. The coast was unknown: the sea promised yet wilder tempests. Starving and in rags, the men pointed to their mouths and their
clothes in ribbons; and Gilbert consented to return:

Reiterating these words, Be content, we have seen enough, and take no
care of expense past. I will set you forth royally the next Spring, if God send
us safe home. Therefore I pray you, let us no longer strive here, where we
fight against the elements. . . .

So upon Saturday in the afternoon the 31 of August, we changed our course and returned back for England, at which very instant, even in winding about, there passed along between us and towards the land which we now forsook a very lion to our seeming, in shape, hair and colour—not swimming after the manner of a beast by moving of his feet, but rather sliding upon the water with his whole body (excepting the legs) in sight . . . confidently shewing himself above water without hiding, notwithstanding we presented ourselves in open view and gesture to amaze him, as all creatures will be commonly at a sudden gaze and sight of men. Thus he passed along, turning his head to and fro, yawning and gaping wide, with ugly demonstration of long teeth and glaring eyes, and to bid us a farewell (coming right against the *Hind*) he sent forth a horrible voice, roaring or bellowing as doth a lion. . . . What opinion others had thereof, and chiefly the General himself, I forbear to deliver. But he took it for Bonum Omen, rejoicing that he was to war against such an enemy, if it were the Devil. . . .

They staggered on till near the Azores. Here the Atlantic broke up in tempest. Gilbert refused to leave the *Squirrel,* whose 10 tons burden was weighed down with cargo and artillery. "I will not forsake my little company going homeward, with whom I have passed so many storms and perils." And the stars, pitying so brave a spirit, granted it a going hence sublime as itself; literature holds no grander picture than this one of the passing of the "man noted for no good hap at sea":

Men which all their lifetime had occupied the Sea never saw more outrageous Seas. We had also upon our main yard an apparition of a little fire by night, which seamen do call Castor and Pollux. But we had only one, which they take an evil sign of more tempest: the same is usual in storms.

Monday, the ninth of September, in the afternoon, the Frigate was near cast away, oppressed by waves yet at that time recovered; and giving forth signs of joy, the General sitting abaft with a book in his hand, cried out to us in the *Hind* (so oft as we did approach within hearing), "We are as near to heaven by sea as by land"—reiterating the same speech, well beseeming a soldier, resolute in Jesus Christ, as I can testify he was.

The same Monday night, about twelve of the clock, or not long after, the Frigate being ahead of us in the *Golden Hind,* suddenly her lights were out, whereof as it were in a moment, we lost the sight, and withal our watch cried, the General was cast away, which was too true. For in that moment the Frigate was devoured and swallowed up of the Sea.

Nearly a fortnight later (September 22), the *Golden Hind* limped into Falmouth harbor, and her captain reported to Sir John Gilbert.

In his "true brother" Humphrey, Ralegh suffered a deep personal loss. John and Adrian Gilbert continued the quest for the North-West Passage, and he helped them, generously and steadily, but was too occupied to sail personally. In 1584, Adrian Gilbert and John Davies were granted control[5] of the Passage and any trade thereby, customs-free for sixty years. But the search had definitely passed out of the world of reality, into that of the poetry and tragedy of human endeavor.

5. *Calendar of State Papers, Domestic,* Elizabeth, Addenda, 1580–1625, p. 104.

CHAPTER VI

Virginia

We have discovered the main to be the goodliest soil under the cope of heaven, so abounding with sweet trees, that bring such sundry rich and pleasant gums, grapes of such greatness, yet wild, as France, Spain nor Italy have no greater, so many sorts of Apothecary drugs, such several kinds of flax, and one kind like silk, the same gathered of a grass, as common there as grass is here. RALPH LANE (first Governor of Virginia) to Richard Hakluyt, 1585.

RALEGH'S greatest fame with posterity comes from the foundation of Virginia, a land he never visited. He received his letters-patent, March 24, 1584; and two barks sailed, a week later (April 2). On July 13 they reached the island of Wokoken, where they landed and took possession in Elizabeth's name. On the third day the natives ventured near them. The English learnt that the country was called Wingandacoa, and its Prince Wingina, names near enough to that which they now gave it, in honor of their own Queen—Virginia. A great friendliness was established, cemented by gifts of trinkets. The ships cruised in the archipelago, and learnt something of the mainland, and then returned to England, taking two natives. They had opened up a country to all seeming like their own, endowed with temperate comforts.

Of the second Virginian expedition we get a glimpse before it sailed, in a report of the Spanish ex-Ambassador. Detected in constant plotting and dismissed from London (January, 1584), he still kept a watch on English naval activities (by espionage from Paris), and on Ralegh's in particular. He wrote to Philip II (February 25, 1585):

The Queen has knighted Ralegh, her favourite, and has given him a ship of 180 tons burden, with five pieces of ordnance on each side, and two culverins in the bows. Ralegh has also bought two Dutch flyboats of 120 tons each, to carry stores, and two other boats of 40 tons, in addition to which he is having built four pinnaces of 20 to 30 tons each. Altogether, Ralegh will fit out no fewer than 16 vessels, in which he intends to convey 400 men. The Queen has assured him that if he will refrain from going himself she will defray all the expenses.

Ralegh's fleet, he added, was sailing almost immediately for the mysterious river Norumbega.

Rumor's sixteen vessels materialized as ten, including three pinnaces; they sailed, April 9, 1585, with Grenville in Ralegh's place. Nothing could have been more mixed than Anglo-Spanish relations were now; and Grenville, who was broad-minded even for an Elizabethan, after prowling the Indies and capturing two Spanish frigates, refreshed himself in happy civilities with the Spaniards of Cuba, in "banquetting houses covered with green boughs." "In recompense of our courtesy" (their throats had not been cut) the settlers provided what was as near to a Devon stag-hunt as that barbarous age and country could provide. They—

caused a great herd of white bulls and kine to be brought together from the mountains, and appointed for every Gentleman and Captain that would ride a horse ready saddled, and then singled out three of the best of them to be hunted . . . so that the pastime grew very pleasant for the space of three hours, wherein all three of the beasts were killed, whereof one took the Sea, and there was slain with a musket.

Business followed sport: "the next day we played the Marchants in bargaining with them by way of truck and exchange." Then the visitors departed, in high good humor but pondering the enemy's friendliness, which "the wiser sort" decided was due to their own strength and grim watchfulness:

for doubtless, if they had been stronger than we, we might have looked for no better courtesy at their hands, than Master John Hawkins received at Saint John de Ulloa, or John Oxenham near the Straits of Darien, and divers others of our countrymen in other places.

In which surmise they may have been right.

News of the bull-hunt infuriated the Spanish Government. But their settlers were in hard case, cut off from their native land by swarming foes. The English were everywhere. This very summer, a ship called the *Primrose* kidnapped[1] the Governor of Biscay, in his own port of

1. In self-defense originally.

Bilbao; and Elizabeth countered Philip's embargo on English ships in Biscayan harbors by granting seventy fresh letters of marque. Spanish colonists had no choice but to keep on good terms with the privateers.

Grenville lives forever in Ralegh's and Tennyson's praise, for his last superhuman battle. But he was a poor exponent of Ralegh's aims, a man as cruel and insensate as he was brave. Because of such agents, this earlier Virginian settlement failed. In the Bahamas and South Carolina he met with trust and kindness always, and when they reached the Virginian archipelago the English "were well entertained of the Savages." But a silver cup was stolen, which the chief of a neighboring village failed to recover. So next day saw the impressive first lesson of the educative process which was to convince the savages that there was no great difference between one European nation and another, where they were concerned. "We burnt and spoiled their corn and Town, all the people being fled." Ralegh's judgment on this and succeeding brutalities can be traced in his extreme care in Guiana later, to prevent any violence.

To Grenville his deed was merely an incident. He looked for no Nemesis, but proceeded to inaugurate England's first colony, 107 settlers, under Governor Ralph Lane, on the island of Wokoken; and sailed away, leaving supplies and promising to return within nine months. On the way home the English boarded a Spanish ship of 300 tons, on an improvised raft of boxes that sank as they came alongside. A fine string of pearls was in the booty; and Sir Lewis Stukeley ("Judas Stukeley," who betrayed Ralegh to his death, and whose father was in this Virginian voyage) says Ralegh complained that the Queen seized it, "without so much as even giving him one pearl." Ralegh had the honor, not only of mainly financing the enterprise but of being held responsible by Spaniards for it. Philip's Ambassador supplied this information from a German sailor whom Grenville had forced to accompany him:

The ship which this captain says was taken by Ralegh's expedition, with so large a freight of gold, silver, pearls, cochineal, sugar, ivory and hides, was the one I advised Your Majesty of months ago, as having arrived in England, and that Ralegh himself had gone down to the port to take possession of her cargo, to prevent it from being distributed amongst the sailors.

For awhile Virginia prospered. Lane was enthusiastic, and not in official letters only. But fear and treachery undid what was well begun, and finally ruined it. The Indians watched with disquiet the indefatigable explorations of their coast: the settlers accused the Indians of plotting their extermination. It came to fighting (June 1, 1586), and the Indian chief was slain. Eight days later a letter arrived from Sir Francis Drake, who followed in person next day. Happy with loot from Cartagena and Santo Domingo, he had gone out of his way to look up fellow-Devonians. He offered provisions and ammunition, but their yearning was all for England, to which the entire settlement sailed with him (June 19):

For fear they should be left behind they left all things confusedly, as if they had been chased from thence by a mighty army: and no doubt so they were; for the hand of God came upon them for the cruelty and outrages committed by some of them against the native inhabitants of that country.

They did not gloss their case over by talk about deceitful savages. They had raised the countryside against them, and they knew it. The Elizabethans had the merit of perfect frankness about their crimes.

They were "too quick despairers," nevertheless. Their precipitate flight was hardly begun, when a vessel sent by Ralegh to relieve their necessities arrived. After hunting up and down, it had to return with stores intact. Grenville himself reappeared, a fortnight later, with three ships. Puzzled to find no trace of the colony he had established, he decided to try once more, and left on Roanoke fifteen men with two years' stores. Then he sailed away, to swoop dragon-like on the Azores (which far more than the Bermoothes might in these years have been termed "still-vext"):

on some of which Islands he landed, and spoiled the towns of all such things as were worth carriage, where also he took divers Spaniards. With these and many other exploits done by him in this voyage, as well outward as homeward, he returned into England.

Spaniards who lived by the sea, particularly in isolated and insular positions, must have scanned the ocean-horizons with dread. Every sail might be a pirate.

It is as true in history as in life, that one man may steal a horse, while another may not even look over a hedge. Ralegh has been reprobated more freely than any other Elizabethan, for greed no worse than that of contemporaries who have "got away with it" with posterity. The sources of his opulence were the usual ones, tapped by all who could get near them. But he stood alone in the generosity with which he squandered his money on impersonal ends. Through good and evil days alike, he spent it to make an English nation in Virginia.

Equally noteworthy was his steady and generous help of every original and fearless mind, regardless of the risks that helping such entailed. At the outset of his career, in 1580, when he must have had precious little money, he persuaded young Thomas Hariot, at the age of twenty just graduated B.A. from St. Mary's Hall, Oxford, to join him as his mathematical tutor. Hariot was the greatest astronomer and mathematician of his day (a fact Ralegh must have the credit of first perceiving): he first saw the 1607 comet,[2] afterwards known as Halley's; he noted sunspots; he gave algebra its modern form. He remained in the closest friendship with Ralegh throughout the latter's life—was his constant visitor during the long Tower imprisonment, and at times even had rooms close to his patron's cell.

Hariot was in the Virginian expedition. When most of the settlers were retracting their first glowing stories and blaming on to the country's defects the failure due to their own cowardice and uneasy sense of Nemesis couched in the surrounding swamps and forests, he published (1588) his *Brief and True Report of the new-found land of Virginia*—a lasting witness to his wide and acute intelligence. In this he made the strongest claims for what (though he did not foresee this) was to prove the chief result of these earliest Virginian enterprises, the habit of smoking, now introduced to England. Its medicinal virtues "would require a volume" to relate. "Men and women of great calling," Ralegh most of all, swiftly popularized it. Everyone has heard of his servant, appalled to see smoke issuing from his master, in the belief that he was on fire drenching him with water. A better authenticated story shows Ralegh deliberately ill-mannered in his bravado to seem singular. "In a stand at Sir Robert Poyntz' park at Acton," he "took a pipe of tobacco,

2. On September 17, from Ilfracombe. He used telescopes that magnified up to fifty times.

which made the ladies quit it till he had done."[3] Another story tells how he won a bet from Elizabeth.[4] Urging the merits of his beloved vice, he bragged that he understood tobacco so well that he could even say what its smoke weighed. The Queen, quick to pick up what seemed easy money, took him up with a wager; and Ralegh, first weighing a quantity of tobacco, smoked it and weighed the ashes. The Queen proved a sportswoman, and turned the loss of the wager off with a dry jest:

what was wanting in the prime weight of the tobacco Her Majesty did not deny to have been evaporated in smoke, and further said that many labourers in the fire she had heard of, who turned their gold into smoke, but Ralegh was the first who had turned smoke into gold.

Ralegh with his long silver pipe and gold tobacco-case became famous; and posterity remembers him smoking, almost as tenaciously as it remembers him sweeping his fine cloak in the mud before his Queen. Smoke played a part in bringing him to the scaffold, deepening King James's angry detestation of him. Maintaining to the last the picture his own choice and his fellows' expectation had made for him, he took a pipe the morning he was to die.

Another strand of the web which finally caught him was weaving now. The privateering by which he financed his Virginian attempts roused in Spain an indignation that settled in a concentration of hatred against his name. He only of the great privateers outlived his Queen and this indignation was therefore smoldering long after Drake and "Achines"[5] were merely memories. Sarmiento, James I's Ambassador, who finally procured Ralegh's execution, had an intimate knowledge of the relations of Spain and Devon during half a century, and to him "Guatteral" was always "that old pirate," the last and wickedest of a corsair brood whose holds were in the rocky westernmost counties. And in 1586 Ralegh's pinnaces, the *Serpent,* 35 tons, and the *Mary Spark,* 50 tons, patrolled the Spanish coast and the Azores, taking many prizes; and returned, bringing as part of their loot a notable prisoner,

3. Aubrey, ii, 181.   4. *Epistolae Ho-Elianae*, p. 522.
5. John Hawkins, against whose name (spelled thus) in Spanish reports Philip II repeatedly scribbled horrified recognition.

Don Pedro Sarmiento de Gamboa, Governor of Magellan. Ralegh met his captains at Plymouth and took over their seizures, treating his sailors with his invariable generosity. To their distinguished captive he was exceedingly courteous, and accepted him as a greatly desired guest.

With Sarmiento's name a shadow falls on our narrative. The later Sarmiento was nephew of this one; it was a long-standing debt that he settled with the famous admiral. There is also a tradition that the younger Sarmiento was taken by one of Ralegh's ships in 1589, and held to ransom. If this is true, Ralegh's name stood for impoverishment of the Sarmiento fortunes and humiliation twice endured.

Our business, however, is with the elder Sarmiento, in an episode which has caused perhaps needless perplexity. Both Spain and England, after drifting on to a course which apparently could not halt short of open war, repeatedly tried to draw back. Sarmiento presently told his King, through the banished Spanish Ambassador, Mendoza, in Paris, that he had been discussing affairs with Ralegh privately,

and signified to him how wise it would be for him to offer his services to Your Majesty, as the Queen's favour to him could not last long. If he would attend sincerely to Your Majesty's interests in England, apart from the direct reward he would receive Your Majesty's support when occasion arose, that might prevent him from falling.

Ralegh had promised to block the attempts of Don Antonio, the Portuguese pretender (which, as a matter of fact, he thought rather foolish ones), to launch expeditions against Spain. He further offered to sell one of his excellent heavily armed ships for 5000 crowns. He was one of six gentlemen, Mendoza told Philip (March, 1586), in a plot to assassinate Elizabeth.[6]

Sarmiento had interviews with the Queen and Burghley also, and was released without ransom, as a sort of envoy.[7] But the Huguenots arrested him while he was passing across France. Mendoza immediately let Ralegh know, and Ralegh asked Henry of Navarre, in the Queen's name, to let Sarmiento proceed. These good offices pleased Mendoza, who wrote to his master (February 18, 1587):

6. Obviously the Babington conspiracy. See p. 31.
7. *Calendar of State Papers, Spanish*, 1587–1603, p. 23.

I am assured that he is very cold about these naval preparations, and is trying secretly to dissuade the Queen from them. He is much more desirous of sending to Spain his own two ships for sale, than to use them for robbery.[8]

Philip, through Mendoza, told Ralegh that "his aid would be highly esteemed, and adequately rewarded."

In all this, though there is obscurity, there seems no cause for perplexity, if we make the effort to set ourselves back in the period. The Elizabethans stood on a quag, with underneath continual mine and countermine. If you were at all prominent you could not help living dangerously. You had your spies out, as everyone else had: you neglected no possible retreats or methods of insuring your safety if events swung against your party. Ralegh, too, was one of the many who enjoyed intrigue for its own sake. He always had his connections with foreign courts, with France now and later, even to the end of his life (this connection played a part, with a little justice,[9] in bringing him to grief ultimately)—with Denmark—occasionally with Spain. Mendoza's belief that he was in a plot to murder Elizabeth is plainly absurd. But it does not follow that he did not know that this plot was preparing. An Elizabethan courtier knew a great deal; and he knew it with a detached interest that may seem to us cold-blooded. The wild beast has quicker and more watchful senses than ours. To *feel* danger while the bush is as yet only shaking is often the only way to escape death.

As to Babington's ridiculously mismanaged plot, very many knew of it. Some of Ralegh's knowledge of it must have come from others who were also watching it, from Walsingham or the Queen. There was no disloyalty, even by contemporary standards, in seeming to listen to overtures, if you kept your Government informed. Ralegh was always ready to listen to anyone who wanted to talk to him on any subject, and the "anyone" frequently included plotters. This readiness, partly due to disinterested intellectual curiosity, helped to undo him when the Queen who understood him died, and James who hated him took her place. But in Mendoza's report we probably have the reason why Babington hoped Ralegh might save him; some of his group had blabbed

8. *Ibid.*, p. 26.   9. But only a little.

to Ralegh, who had gravely taken it in without denouncing them to their faces.

The offer to sell a ship to Spain may shock the reader who forgets the admirably impartial manner in which munition firms of our own day supply what are technically called "weapons of precision" to any country that can pay for them. But Ralegh could not have carried it out without the Queen's knowledge and sanction. She knew at least part of the Sarmiento negotiations, for she was in them. I have no doubt that she knew the whole. It is on record that the dreaded "Achines" himself over a long period drew enemy pay and kept enemy confidence (having informed Philip that he was weary of his Queen and would assist a Spanish attempt to dislodge her), while scoffingly reporting everything to Elizabeth and Walsingham. Fear that Ralegh might be fooling him soon dawned on Philip, who warned his Ambassador:

As for his sending for sale the two ships he mentions, that is out of the question, in the first place to avoid his being looked upon with suspicion in his own country, in consequence of his being well treated whilst all his countrymen are persecuted; and secondly, to guard ourselves against the coming of the ships under this pretext being a feint or trick upon us (which is far from being improbable). But you need only mention the first reason to him.

The part of the negotiations which attempted to bring Spain and England into smoother relations was made at the Queen's direct instance and was entirely genuine. When it failed, the next news of Ralegh showed him the busiest of those working against the projected Armada, in the exposed counties of the West. Sarmiento and Mendoza and Philip must then have known the anguish of the man who has been "double-crossed." To the Sarmiento count against Ralegh, destined to lengthen as the years passed, another item was written down.

The second Virginian colony of fifteen were murdered, or carried off to die in the interior later. Ralegh sent out another hundred and fifty, April 26, 1587, with a Charter, and a Governor (John White) who had been with Grenville. Following Spanish precedent closely, they began with a municipality. White and a Council of twelve formed "the Governor and Assistants of the City of Ralegh in Virginia." Forbidden to stray off on looting expeditions, after what must have been a torturingly peaceful cruise through West Indian islands the colonists reached Roanoke, which they found deserted, its fort razed, "but all the houses standing unhurt, saving that the nether rooms of them, and also of the fort, were overgrown with Melons of divers sorts, and Deer within them, feeding on those Melons." They set to work repairing. But the war of the white man and the red had begun. It was on July 23 that the Governor first walked over the ruins; on the 28th, the savages ambushed one of his Council, and,

being secretly hidden among high reeds, where oftentimes they find the Deer asleep and so kill them, espied our man wading in the water alone, almost naked, without any weapon save only a small forked stick, catching Crabs therewithal, and also being strayed two miles from his company, and shot at him in the water, where they gave him sixteen wounds with their arrows: and after they had slain him with their wooden swords, they beat his head in pieces, and fled over the water to the main.

Even under this provocation Ralegh's far-sighted pacific aims so far prevailed that, when the attackers were able to prove they themselves had been wronged by the previous colony, a peace was patched up. But to follow this peace through was more than the settlers could manage. Determined to avenge their predecessors' murder on the actual offenders, they crept through pre-dawn murk on August 9, on some "miserable souls herewith amazed," of whom they shot one before finding they were friends. This was awkward. However, "finding ourselves thus disappointed of our purpose, we gathered all the corn, Pease, Pompions, and Tobacco that we found ripe, leaving the rest spoiled," and took off hostages. "The mistaking of these Savages somewhat grieved Manteo," the Indian sub-chief with whom the peace had been made. But four days later, "by the commandment of Sir Walter Ralegh" (i.e., the instructions they had brought out), he was baptized, and so put on an ethical equality with his allies.

The autumn storms were beginning, and the colonists grew frightened of starvation. Their Governor, reluctantly giving way to clamor, returned to England for stores, leaving an ill-balanced community of 89 men and 17 women. He reached home at a bad time to press plans for anything so fantastic as the founding of New Englands. Mary of Scotland's execution had brought even Philip of Spain's "leaden foot" within measurable distance of springing. All available shipping was being held against invasion, and Sir Richard Grenville was stopped from fitting out another Virginian expedition. Ralegh could hardly get permission to release two ships, with the stores and additional colonists he had promised. Their crews had little heart for such sailings then; falling in with French pirates, they used the excuse to return to England, and left the settlement to God.

It has often been said that Ralegh deserted his colonists, indifferent to their fate. The opposite is the truth. He had spent £40,000, a sum representing at least four times that amount to-day, and "it would have required a prince's purse to have followed out"[10] what he had begun. In March, 1589, he handed his patent over to a London company, and henceforward had no responsibility for Virginia. Nevertheless, after White had sailed once more, in August, 1589, and failed to find the settlers (who had moved to another island, sixty miles from Roanoke), he sent out five expeditions in thirteen years.[11] The Virginia Company did nothing, but he did much, to try to find the unfortunate men—vainly, for Powhatan (father of Pocahontas) had killed them all. On the eve of his own ruin, he sent his last expedition (1602), and wrote: "I shall yet see it" (Virginia) "an English nation." When in the Tower, he begged Queen Anne, James's consort, to obtain permission for him to join the Jamestown foundation, in 1607, and in the same year his nephew, Ralph Gilbert, sailed there on his behalf. Though debarred from direct share in that actual successful foundation, he is rightly remembered as the real founder of the great and lovely State of Virginia.

Failure was not his fault, as the man best qualified to judge, John White, the Governor of Virginia, admitted, writing not to Ralegh but to Hakluyt (February 4, 1593). The "evils and unfortunate events had not chanced, if the order set down by Sir Walter Ralegh had been observed." How did he ever find time at all, in that eve of expectation of the Spanish attack, to do anything for Virginia? The answer is, he had an unrivalled power of doing many things at once.

His interest in exploration never slept. He lavished his money on assisting, not merely those who voyaged, but those who wrote about

10. Hakluyt.   11. *Purchas his Pilgrimes,* iv, 1653.

voyagings. John Hooker calls him "rather a servant than a commander to his own fortune." His help was gratefully acknowledged in dedications by Richard Hakluyt. One detail of that help was his purchasing for £60 the manuscript of the Portuguese story of Da Gama's voyage in 1541 to the Red Sea, which he presented to the historiographer. It is only his long imprisonment that has brought down the early East India Company's record to us without his name inscribed on its pages.

CHAPTER VII

The Armada

That morrice dance upon the waters. SIR HENRY WOTTON.

Their Navy, which they termed Invincible, consisting of 240 sail of ships, not only of their own kingdom, but strengthened with the greatest Argosies, Portugal Carracks, Florentines and huge Hulks of other countries, were by thirty of Her Majesty's own ships of war, and a few of our own Marchants, by the wise, valiant, and most advantageous conduction of the Lord Charles Howard, High Admiral of England, beaten and shuffled together, even from the Lizard in Cornwall, first to Portland—where they shamefully left Don Pedro de Valdes, with his mighty ship—from Portland to Calais, where they lost Hugo de Monçado, with the Gallias of which he was Captain—and from Calais, driven with squibs from their anchors: were chased out of the sight of England, round about Scotland and Ireland, where, for the sympathy of their barbarous religion, hoping to find succour and assistance, a great part of them were crusht against the rocks, and those other that landed, being very many in number, were notwithstanding broken, slain, and taken, and so sent from village to village, coupled in halters to be shipped into England. Where Her Majesty, of her Princely and Invincible disposition disdaining to put them to death, and scorning either to retain or entertain them, they were all sent back again to their countries, to witness and recount the worthy achievements of their Invincible and dreadful Navy. Of which the number of soldiers, the fearful burthen of their ships, the commanders' names of every squadron, with all other their magasins of provisions, were put in print, as an Army and Navy unresistable and disdaining prevention. With all which so great and terrible an ostentation, they did not in all their sailing round about England so much as sink or take one ship, bark, pinnace, or cockboat of ours, or ever burnt so much as one sheepcote of this land. Whenas on the contrary Sir Francis Drake, with only 800 soldiers, not long before, landed in their Indies, and forced Santiago, Santo Domingo, Cartagena, and the Forts of Florida. RALEGH, *Report of the Truth of the Fight . . . betwixt the Revenge and an Armada. . . .* (The passage is ascribed by Strype to Sir Francis Drake.)

BY luck and opportunism, Elizabeth had held her course of precarious independence. Continental opinion did not rate England's resources highly but they were considered enough to turn the balance of power between France and Spain. Philip, therefore, however indignant at heresy and piracies, would not let France (through Mary of Scotland, who had once been Queen of France also[1]) obtain control of them. But there was, in addition, an element of chivalrous memory, usually overlooked, in his quite amazing forbearance through decades of provocation; and Elizabeth was woman enough to feel and take pleasure in it. He had known her as the helpless and infinitely more attractive younger sister of his gaunt wife; and, if he could not marry her himself, he long hoped to marry her to some dependent. Her heresy had not at first looked serious. In doctrine she had begun as hardly a Protestant at all. She had had moods when she beguiled the first Spanish Ambassador, the able and pertinacious Alvarez de Quadra, into half believing she had been led astray against her will—that, if his master would support her, she would bring England back, and offer it as a humble but serviceable pawn in the conquest of France. England had survived, because her enemies were divided, and because she had in her service the finest spies and seamen of an age when spies swarmed like nerves in the body of Europe. She had *appeared,* long after she had ceased to be, the earthen pot between two iron pipkins. She was not the earthen pot now.

In 1587, Mary's execution swept a sponge over the story of her errors and crimes, and stirred pity and indignation. Before dying she bequeathed her claims to both Scottish and English crowns away from her son James to Philip II, a generosity men still took seriously as establishing a valid claim in law. Elizabeth was left with few friends. The Scots would probably have executed Mary, twenty years previously, had she not escaped to England, but were naturally outraged when she died by another kingdom's judicial sentence. In Europe the heretic Queen who slew the martyrs and the Catholic lady who had voluntarily come into her power was regarded as a monster of cruelty and sin—a Jezebel for whose destruction God was seeking volunteers.

Pretense of any kind of peace was fairly abandoned in April, when Drake appeared in Cadiz harbor, and without loss of a boat or a man

1. 1559–1560, at the opening of Elizabeth's reign.

sank an armament assembling to sail against England. He peeped also
into Tagus mouth, where the veteran Spanish admiral, Santa Cruz,
was fretting himself into his grave. He did nothing here (beyond leaving such terror as a dragon leaves when he has shown his teeth in some
shelter of "tame villatic fowl"), but on his way back he captured a
huge East India galleon, the *San Felipe*. Even Philip's long-suffering
patience saw that the islanders were incorrigible, except by chastise-
ment. He and his advisers concluded—with what sorrow we can
imagine—

that certain it was that the Study of Novelties was inserted, as it were by
Nature, in the English. For that if any read the History of that People, he
should find Seditions, Conspiracies, Treasons and the like had fixed, as it
were, a Dwelling Place for themselves in that Island.[2]

There was nothing for it but severity.

   Severity Elizabeth's Government expected, and prepared for. In November, a special Council of War discussed measures to meet it. Ralegh
served on this Council; and he drew up a list of places particularly exposed to invasion, going as far afield in person as King's Lynn, to advise the Norfolk coastal authorities.[3] Acting under Privy Council instructions, he conferred with the magnates of Devon, and of Exeter in
particular, "for the drawing together of 2,000 foot and 200 horse." Some
thought this too heavy a burden, but Sir John Gilbert—who acted always as Ralegh's deputy in his absence—the Earl of Bath and Sir Richard Grenville, "being more zealous both in religion and Her Majesty's
service,"[4] thought otherwise. Ralegh also stirred up Cornwall. People
assured Don Antonio that "Admiral Raleich with a great fleet"[5] was
about to take him back to Portugal—a prospect which filled him with
gloom, for he knew that Ralegh had no great opinion of him, and he
feared the English were making fun of him. Then the Spanish peril
seemed to lift a little, and be no longer imminent. In early 1588, Ralegh
was in Ireland, serving as Mayor of Youghal, and seeing to his estates.
But he had to hurry back to see to fortifications and be ready for extraordinary consultations.

   2. Strype, *Annals of the Reformation*, III, II, xv, 525.
   3. See Gosse, *Ralegh*, p. 38.   4. Ralegh's letter, December 20, 1587.
   5. *Calendar of State Papers, Spanish*, 1587–1603 (January 4, 1588), p. 188.

This was in part premature. *La Felicissime Armada* was not off Scilly yet. But it sailed at last, and on the afternoon of July 20, 1588, its vast assemblage showed itself, slowly rolling off Cornwall. That night, "under a gibbous moon, little more than a half circle,"[6] threescore English ships glided out behind it. Next morning began the stormy shepherding, the Spaniards lurching onward in unsteady crescent, while their assailants raked them with fire—declining to set themselves at stupendous disadvantage by boarding and pitting their few men against those which even one galleon could carry.

Graphic pictures have been painted of Ralegh's share in the weeklong battle which followed. Hume, on the other hand, points out that "Not the slightest reference to his presence appears in any of the official correspondence,[7] and in any case he had no command and cannot have taken an active part." Neither Hume nor the more picturesque biographers seem quite in the right. It is true that Ralegh was too responsibly placed to indulge in knight-errantry by flying to the battle-front. But his duties did not necessitate his stay in Devon when the Armada had been brushed up-Channel. On July 23, his subordinates, John and Adrian Gilbert, joined the fleet. During the battle, powder was sent to the navy in "the *Roebuck,* a fine ship built by Sir Walter Ralegh."[8] (The Lord Admiral's flagship, the *Ark Ralegh,* was of his building, as we have seen.) He did all his official position allowed, in preparing the threatened West, and in lending his own shipping. Then he seems to have been kept chafing in London, but won release when news came of the enemy stranded before Gravelines; "the Queen thereupon sent Richard Drake and Ralegh with all speed to order the Admiral to attack the Armada in some way, or to engage it, if he could not burn it."[9]

They found the Admiral had his own views about boarding a fleet with far superior strength of personnel; and Ralegh, looking back on these days long afterwards, in a famous passage of his *History of the World,* noted that—

6. Froude, *Queen Elizabeth,* p. 406.

7. *Ralegh,* p. 93. The statement is an exaggeration, as the following pages show.

8. *Calendar of State Papers, Domestic,* Elizabeth, 1581–1590 (July 30), p. 517.

9. *Calendar of State Papers, Spanish,* p. 392. This statement seems to contradict that made by previous biographers, that Ralegh was enabled to go aboard Lord Howard's flagship as a volunteer, as soon as the Armada had passed the coast of Devon.

there is a great deal of difference between fighting loose or at large, and grappling. To clap ships together without consideration belongs rather to a madman than to a man of war; for by such an ignorant bravery was Peter Strozzi[10] lost at the Azores, when he fought against the Marquess of Santa Cruz. In like sort had Charles Howard, Admiral of England, been lost in the year 1588, if he had not been better advised than a great many malignant fools were that found fault with his demeanour. The Spaniards had an army aboard them, and he had none; they had more ships than he had, and of higher building and charging; so that, had he entangled himself with those great and powerful vessels, he had greatly endangered this kingdom of England. For twenty men upon the defences are equal to a hundred that board and enter; whereas then the Spaniards, contrariwise, had a hundred for twenty of ours to defend themselves withal. But our admiral knew his advantage and held it; which had he not done he had not been worthy to have held his head.

It is hard to explain the Armada's failure to attempt anything at any point of the English coast. Even when the fireships had dispersed it, and it was being driven north, past the mouth of the Thames and still farther and farther, England's peril remained great. Expectation was that the enemy would go north to Denmark, refit and rest there, and return; and Ralegh urged the Queen[11] to follow them, and complete their ruin in those northern waters. However, as we know, Spain's navy, depleting continually, rounded Scotland instead; and off Ireland sustained its heaviest losses, miseries (wrote Sir George Carew) "to be pitied in any but Spaniards."[12] The Atlantic strewed eleven hundred bodies on one shore alone. And those who escaped the sea's fury were received by their Irish friends in a manner no one had anticipated. One chieftain "killed eighty with his gallowglass axe." The English rejoiced, foreseeing "perpetual diffidence" between their enemies, "as long as this memory endureth":[13]

This people was very doubtful before the victory was known to be Her Majesty's, but when they saw the great distress and weakness that the enemy was in, they did not only put as many as they could to the sword,

10. Don Antonio's admiral.
11. *State Papers, Domestic,* 1581–1590 (August 12), p. 530.
12. *MSS. Ireland,* September 28.
13. Edward Fenton to Lord Burghley, September 19.

but are ready with all their forces to attend the deputy in any service. The ancient love between Ireland and Spain is broken.[14]

The English bore their victory modestly, as the Prince of Parma testified. The medal they struck claimed merely that God "blew with His winds and they were scattered," "ascribing to the watchful Providence of God and His viewless couriers a result that might without undue arrogance have been in part attributed to their own skill and courage."[15] As to Philip, according to Camden,[16] he bore his loss "patiently and thanked God it was no worse"; according to Strype[17] he pointed to a candle and swore a great oath to waste his kingdom till it was of that worth, seeking revenge. England and Spain remained officially at war until Elizabeth died.

14. Sir George Carew to Burghley, September 18: "that friendship being broken, they have no other stranger to trust to."
15. G. M. Trevelyan, *History of England*, p. 354.
16. *Elizabeth*, p. 418.
17. *Annals of the Reformation*, III, ii, xv, 525. The candle story was a *cliché* of the time. See footnote, p. 134.

CHAPTER VIII

New Rivalries

He still continued in some lustre of a favoured man, like billows that sink by degrees, even when the wind is down that first stirred them. *Reliquiae Wottonianae.*

THE Armada temporarily diverted notice from Elizabeth's dalliance with a new favorite. As Sidney's star set in the Zutphen skirmish (1586), that of Robert Devereux, Earl of Essex, simultaneously rose; at the age of nineteen, he was there created knight banneret, for valor. Already he began to embody in men's eyes, as he embodied it to the end, all of swift and lovely and youthful that comes to us in the word "Elizabethan"; the mantle of Sidney's chivalrous fame was his henceforward.

The Queen was soon infatuated with him, "nobody near her but my Lord of Essex; and at night, my Lord is at cards, or one game or another, with her, till the birds sing in the morning."[1] He marked down Ralegh for jealousy. No one took seriously the gambolling affection of Sir Christopher Hatton, or Elizabeth's petting of him in return, as if he were a nice clumsy dog. But Ralegh was a different matter. In the summer of 1587 the Queen snubbed Essex's sister, wife of Sir Thomas Perrot, Ralegh's old antagonist. That antagonism was still smoldering; and, though Elizabeth's dislike of Lady Perrot was of long standing and had a well-understood reason, Essex asserted that her incivility was—

only to please that knave Ralegh, for whose sake I saw she would both grieve me and my love, and disgrace me in the eye of the world. From thence she came to speak of Ralegh; and it seemed she could not well endure anything to be spoken against him; and taking hold of one word, "disdain," she said there was "no such cause why I should disdain him." This speech did trouble me so much that, as near as I could, I did describe unto her what he had been, and what he was.

1. Anthony Bagot to Edward Dyer (May, 1587).

He heightened his impertinence by speaking loudly and clearly, so that Ralegh, standing as Captain of the Guard, might hear it. When the Queen defended Ralegh, he pettishly saw in her only a resolve "to cross me," and told her,

I had no joy to be in any place, but was loth to be near about her, when I knew my affection so much thrown down, and such a wretch as Ralegh highly esteemed of her. . . . This strange alteration is by Ralegh's means; and the Queen, that hath tried all other ways, now will see whether she can, by these hard courses, drive me to be friends with Ralegh, which rather shall drive me to many other extremities.[2]

In the autumn of 1588 the rivals exchanged challenges to a duel, which the Privy Council forbade.

Then Essex's influence, after carrying all before it, underwent eclipse. In 1589 the English Government decided on reprisals for the Armada. The Portuguese patriots were accepted as useful, and an army of 16,000 soldiers and a fleet of nearly 200 ships were got together to attack Lisbon. It was now that Essex's ascendancy did Ralegh a good turn; he was at last allowed to sail on an expedition, while Essex was kept at home. But to be left outside the enterprise of vengeance after victory was more than the latter could bear. He rode disguised to Plymouth, and joined the *Swiftsure,* on which was his friend Sir Roger Williams, the military second-in-command. She justified her name by immediately sailing, and the Queen's couriers arrived too late. Elizabeth poured out her fury on Drake and Norris, the sea and land commanders, sending them word that they should bear the entire costs of the campaign, above a mere £20,000. Williams was promised execution, a threat which he either never heard, or else ignored.

The fleet wasted ten days on the peninsula's northern fringes, besieging Corunna, destroying, pillaging. Meanwhile, the *Swiftsure,* in the undisciplined Elizabethan manner, kept out at sea, and did not join until the others were about to go south once more. Drake, seconded by Ralegh, now wished to force the Tagus and sack Lisbon. But a nobleman, however young and inexperienced, carried absurdly disproportionate weight. Essex urged that they should march overland and invest the city; Don Antonio and Norris supported him. The army did this

2. Essex to Edward Dyer (Tanner MSS. [Bodleian Library, Oxford]).

accordingly—unsuccessfully, with heavy losses by sickness and desertion. For some reason, probably flattery of Essex, a legend sprang up that it was a fine exploit; Ralegh himself, two years later, generously so described it. He and Drake more usefully employed their time in sweeping enemy shipping off the seas. They burnt two hundred vessels in the Tagus estuary.

Returning, Ralegh used some of Sir Roger Williams' men to navigate one of his prizes, which that commander therefore claimed as his and their booty. But Essex, his patron, was skulking away from Court, and the claim was rejected. The Queen gave Ralegh a gold chain, an action taken as it was meant, as a snub to Essex; Williams wrote to the Privy Council, that he himself deserved a chain just as much. "He was probably unaware that only a few weeks before the Queen had peremptorily ordered Drake and Norris to give him a halter."[3]

But Essex attracted Elizabeth too strongly to remain in disgrace. There is a story that, a year or so before this, she sent for him and told him she had at last decided to marry, and to marry one of her English nobles, not any foreign prince. What was his advice? He applauded her resolution, and, wilfully blind to hint after hint, strongly recommended the Earl of Leicester. She hid her humiliation as best she could. The story's evidence, apart from whatever plausibility we may concede to it, is not of the best. But there is no doubt of her affection for him. Had it been less, their relations would never have reached their miserable ending, in his insolence later and her rage of mortification.

After the Lisbon fiasco, Sir Francis Allen wrote:[4] "My Lord of Essex hath chased Mr. Ralegh from the court and confined him in Ireland." Ralegh was aware of this interpretation, and vigorously denied it. Back in London again (December, 1589), he told Sir George Carew: "For my retreat from court, it was upon good cause, to take order for my prize."[5] This was to "Cussen George." Yet the misconception (if it were one) persisted, and his eclipse was popular. English squatters found they might presume on it; the Irish crept back into territory of which they had been dispossessed. The Lord Deputy, Sir William Fitzwilliams,

3. Hume, p. 102.
4. To Anthony Bacon, August 17 (Birch, *Memoirs of the Reign of Queen Elizabeth*, i, 56).
5. Letter, December 27. We do not know what prize this was; possibly the one over which Ralegh had had his altercation with Sir Roger Williams.

supported offenders against one he believed fallen never to rise again. He did not wish to see so brilliant a man establishing a great seignory inside his rule; magnificently rebuilding Lismore Castle; putting into practice his expert mining knowledge; exercising his restless curiosity as to plants and crops; accidentally making the Irish his debtors, by introducing the potato; draining bogs; afforesting. Ralegh, furious, told Carew:

If in Ireland they think that I am not worth respecting they shall much deceive themselves. I am in place to be believed not inferior to any man, to pleasure or displeasure the greatest, and my opinion is so received and believed as I can anger the best of them. And therefore, if the Deputy be not as ready to stead me as I have bin to defend him—be it as it may!

When Sir William Fitzwilliams shall be in England, I take myself far his better by the honourable offices I hold, as also by that nearness to Her Majesty which still I enjoy, and never more. I am willing to continue towards him all friendly offices, and I doubt not of the like from him as well towards me as my friends.

That he did not take his temporary eclipse too seriously the not-too-respectful playfulness of the letter's conclusion shows: "The Queen thinks that George Carew longs to see her; and therefore see her. Farewell, noble George, my chosen friend and kinsman, from whom nor time, nor fortune, nor adversity, shall ever sever me."

The glimpses thrown up in contemporary records show this eternally restless man troubled as well as troubling. In February, 1589, his ship the *Roebuck* plundered the *Angel Gabriel,* a Flemish, not a Spanish vessel, and therefore drawing down official notice. Such activities, and they were many, brought Ralegh into conflict with the Admiralty Courts and the Privy Council; the latter, especially, must sometimes have wished that Sir Walter Ralegh did not exist. His views of property on the high seas were the accepted West Country ones; he vigorously contested those held in London. Seeing how ready the Queen and her Councillors were to invest money in his ventures, it is not easy to show where they would have drawn the line of demarcation between piracy and patriotism. But there *was* a divergence, and the embarrassment he caused did much to keep him from ever being given official status as a responsible adviser. He was too much of a freelance, and a troublesome freelance. He fought now against orders to restore the *Angel Gabriel*, pointing out that under neutral colors Spanish goods were being carried, and Dutch and Flemings were keeping the war alive.

Such people are Spaniards in disguise, seeking the good and profit of the common enemy, with the loss and hindrance of such of Her Majesty's subjects as, to their great charge, do venture upon reprisals.

In the same year (June 25, 1589), the Perrot feud flared up again. This time Sir Thomas quarrelled with his allies also; he was accused of plots against Essex, Ralegh, and others.[6] In 1590, contemporaries, noting Ralegh's unpractical interest in madcap schemes, marked him thinking not of Virginia only, but of "Dorado"[7]—a name deeply significant in his story, and now occurring in it for the first time. In February, 1591, he and Essex are coupled as both in disgrace. A month later (March 16), John Prestall, a renegade who had been in Spanish service and was arrested in England, tells what Catholic Europe was saying, namely, that the Queen "made such knights as other countries spoke much shame of, meaning Sir Walter Ralegh and Sir Francis Drake."[8] Ralegh and Drake—the two are henceforward linked, in foreign as well as national opinion.

On May 17th Ralegh was instructed to send a pinnace from Plymouth to Lord Thomas Howard, warning him that another Spanish Armada was off Scilly; and to go west himself, taking ships and men to defend Cornwall and Devon. It proved a false alarm. While guarding against the chances of its reality, he found time to see about ransoming a captive in Barbary and to disapprove of plans for Portsmouth fortifications. Many details show his career at this period taking a downward curve; he was undoubtedly under a cloud, which might have passed (but did not, because of his marriage in 1592). But under that cloud he did not abate one jot of his unpausing energy. Ralegh's presence near the Queen, though of splendid scenic quality, wrongs him, keeping posterity still thinking only of a showy *flâneur*.

6. *Calendar of State Papers, Domestic,* 1581–1590, p. 674.
7. *Ibid.,* p. 710.
8. *Ibid.,* 1591–1594, p. 19.

CHAPTER IX

Poet; and Friend of Poets

I sat (as was my trade)
Under the foot of Mole, that mountain hoar,
Keeping my sheep amongst the cooly shade
Of the green alders by the Mulla's shore.
There a strange shepherd chanced to find me out,
Whether allurèd with my pipe's delight,
Whose pleasing sound yshrillèd far about,
Or thither led by chance, I know not right:
Whom when I askèd from what place he came
And how he hight, himself he did yclepe
The Shepherd of the Oceän by name
And said he came far from the main-sea deep.
He, sitting me beside in that same shade,
Provokèd me to play some pleasant fit;
And when he heard the musick which I made
He found himself full greatly pleased at it.
Yet, aemuling my pipe, he took in hond[1]
My pipe (before that aemulèd of many),
And played thereon (for well that skill he conned),
Himself as skilful in that art as any.
He piped, I sung; and when he sung, I piped;
By change of turns, each making other merry,
Neither envying other nor envied—
So pipèd we, until we both were weary.

SPENSER, *Colin Clout's Come Home Again.*

RETURN to Ireland, however caused and motived, brought him his greatest friendship—one of the noble friendships of literature. Edmund Spenser, Lord Grey's secretary at Smerwick, and serving in Ireland ever since, was settled at Kilcolman. Here Ralegh unexpectedly visited him. The poet's story (which we may take as reasonably close to prosaic fact) suggests that their previ-

1. Hand.

ous acquaintance had been slight. But of course he knew who this splendid apparition was, and that the pastoral charge of "the Shepherd of the Ocean" was mainly Spanish merchandise that strayed within reach of his privateering c▮▮▮ The meeting was immortalized in *Colin Clout's Come Home ▮▮▮n,* dedicated to "The Right Worthy and Noble Knight Sir Walter Ralegh, Captain of Her Majesty's Guard, Lord Warden of the Stannaries, and Lieutenant of the County of Cornwall." It tells not only what Colin sang, but what his visitor sang, under Mulla's green alders:

> His song was all a lamentable lay
> Of great unkindness and of usage hard,
> Of Cynthia, the Lady of the Sea,
> Which from her presence faultless him debarred,
> And ever and anon, with singults[2] rife,
> He crièd out, to make his undersong,
> "Ah, my love's queen and goddess of my life!
> Who shall me pity, when thou dost me wrong?"

The two went off to London—which gives excuse for a picture of the sea's terrors, and the fine new ships dancing on it, an enthusiasm we can think caught from Ralegh. In London Ralegh introduced the poet to Cynthia, who was persuaded to be generous as well as gracious, granting him a pension of £50, despite Lord Burghley's dismay at "all this for a song."

The Faerie Queen, begun with Philip Sidney's patronage, was continued with Ralegh's. Its first instalment was printed with a letter, addressed to Ralegh, explaining its plan and meaning. The best of the introductory verses are by Spenser and Ralegh, and are of a stately beauty which makes it a pleasure to transcribe them. They carry the sincerity of unselfish affection. Ralegh's won from Milton the compliment of remembrance.[3] It is conceited (in the literary sense). But its rhythmical strength is noble: its imagery clear in outline and of a mournful dignity recalling the funerary monuments of which it speaks. The concluding brag is superb hyperbole.

2. Sighs.
3. In the sonnet beginning "Methought I saw my late espousèd Saint."

Methought I saw the grave where Laura lay,
Within that Temple where the vestal flame
Was wont to burn; and, passing by that way,
To see that buried dust of living fame,
Whose tomb fair Love and fairer Virtue kept,
All suddenly I saw the Faery Queen!
At whose approach the soul of Petrarch wept.
And from thenceforth those Graces were not seen
(For they. this Queen attended), in whose stead
Oblivion laid him down on Laura's hearse.
Hereat the hardest stones were seen to bleed,
And groans of buried ghosts the heavens did pierce,
    Where Homer's spright did tremble all for grief,
    And cursed the access of that celestial thief.

In this poem, at any rate, there seems a lovely inner pulse of wit, if not of that humor whose absence from Ralegh's writings Mr. Waldman has noted. No man can without a smile call an admired friend a "celestial thief" and picture divine Homer as shaking because this friend has climbed into Poetry's heaven of heavens! The sonnet witnesses to the spontaneous delight out of which it was born.

Spenser's poem equals this in charming hyperbole. He pretends his poem is worthless, knowing very well that it is such verse as English never previously produced; and pretends, too, that Ralegh's own verses are far, far better, which he and Ralegh both knew was not so. It is an interchange of Chinese compliments, in numbers delighting in their own grace and turns of phrase and emphasis.

To thee, that art the summer's Nightingale,
    Thy sovereign Goddess's most dear delight,
Why do I send this rustick Madrigal,
    That may thy tuneful ear unseason quite?
    Thou only fit this Argument to write,
In whose high thoughts Pleasure hath built her bower
    And dainty Love learnt sweetly to endite!
My rimes I know unsavoury and sour
To taste the streams that like a golden shower
    Flow from thy fruitful head, of thy Love's praise

(Fitter, perhaps, to thunder martial stower,
  Whenso thee list thy lofty Muse to raise).
  Yet, till that thou thy Poem wilt make known,
  Let thy fair Cynthia's praises be thus rudely shown.

The hope of that concluding couplet was never fulfilled. In youth, Ralegh wrote verse better than all but a few of the Elizabethans, and with a full share of the charm that clings to even the poorest verses of the time, making posterity unduly kind to them. But in later life he moved away from poetry, and his verse, like that of his rival Essex, became occasional. His half dozen really notable pieces were wrung out of him by crises of emotion. The poem that showed fair Cynthia's praises, which was to have been his masterpiece, was never finished, and what was written was supposed to be lost, until over five hundred lines in his handwriting were found at Hatfield.

Ralegh was "temperamental," and sank into despairs. One of his best poems, *The Lie,* savagely resents the opinion that regarded him as an upstart now sinking to deserved oblivion. It dates itself as obviously written in these years when eclipse was a new experience, to which he was not yet reconciled.

Go, Soul, the body's guest,
  Upon a thankless arrant;[4]
Fear not to touch the best;
  The truth shall be thy warrant:
    Go, since I needs must die,
    And give the world the lie.

Say to the Court, it glows
  And shines like rotten wood;
Say to the Church, it shows
  What's good, and doth no good.
    If Church and Court reply,
    Then give them both the lie.

4. Errand.

Tell potentates they live
    Acting by others' action:
Not loved unless they give,
    Not strong but by a faction:
        If potentates reply,
        Give potentates the lie.

Tell men of high condition,
    That manage the Estate,
Their purpose is ambition,
    Their practice only hate:
        And if they once reply,
        Then give them all the lie. . . .

Tell zeal it wants devotion;
    Tell love it is but lust;
Tell time it is but motion;
    Tell flesh it is but dust:
        And wish them not reply,
        For thou must give the lie.

Tell age it daily wasteth;
    Tell honour how it alters;
Tell beauty how she blasteth;
    Tell favour how it falters:
        And as they shall reply,
        Give every one the lie. . . .

So when thou hast, as I
    Commanded thee, done blabbing—
Although to give the lie
    Deserves no less than stabbing—
        Stab at thee he that will!
        No stab the soul can kill!

Such plainly genuine fury made him an easy victim of the many reprisals it aroused. His attack on Church and Court inspired the retort:

> The Court hath settled sureness
>   In banishing such boldness;
> The Church retains her pureness,
>   *Though Atheists show their coldness;*
>   The Court and Church, though base,
>   Turn lies into thy face.
>
> The potentates reply,
>   Thou base, by them advancèd,
> Sinisterly soar'st high
>   And at their actions glancèd:
>   They for this thankless part
>   Turn lies into thy heart.

I have italicized a line containing a charge which followed Ralegh all his life. Those who wish to be daring without paying a price had better follow the majority, by showing valor in some field where victory has long been won. Ralegh, when two forms of doctrine and religious government, the Catholic and the Anglican, were engaged in unpitying warfare, sat loose to both. It is worth noting that we never find his name in connection with any action against Catholics as such, a fact which is negative evidence of the theological tolerance for which we have abundant positive evidence. That he held a deep faith of his own, which could pass for being substantially orthodox by Anglican standards, in the end he all but convinced contemporaries. But he achieved this only on the scaffold, and even then with reservations. When finally telling him he must die, without hope of further reprieve (October 28, 1618), the Lord Chief Justice went out of his way to express satisfaction that at any rate he was not dooming an unbeliever:

Your religion has been much questioned, but I am resolved you are a good Christian, for your *History,* which is an admirable work, doth testify as much.

Next morning men listened for his last words with unexampled eagerness. He had always been Ralegh the Atheist, a term covering all who were not strictly Nicene and Athanasian on the doctrine of the Person of Jesus Christ. What would this notoriously reckless thinker, comrade of every daring spirit of his time, say when about to pass to eternal judgment? He edified his hearers; and George Abbot, Archbishop of Canterbury, who had with misgiving sanctioned Ralegh's sacrifice to Spain, was able to salve his conscience with the reflection[5] that God had found a way of saving his soul by punishing his body. Ralegh had

questioned God's being and omnipotence, which that just Judge made good upon himself in overhumbling his estate, but last of all in bringing him to an execution by law, where he died a religious and Christian death.

Even so, some remained dissatisfied. *Was* the illustrious convict really sound on the all-important question? Aubrey notes that even his dying speech, though not "atheist" was "a-Christ."[6] It is probable that it was, as was Ralegh's own thought.

To be intellectually unusual was an immediate passport to Ralegh's kindness, and he was utterly indifferent to the likelihood of his consorting with men under suspicion bringing him under suspicion also. For example, there was John Dee, mathematician, geographer, astrologer, spiritualist, who managed to escape a succession of excellent chances of being burnt. Bishop Bonner had closely watched him as a possible wizard and a probable heretic; and, when close on fourscore years of age, he begged King James, the hammer of sorcerers, to clear him formally of the scandal of witchcraft, and was rebuffed. Elizabeth, however, had a kindness for this scientist who was liable to be "visited by a spiritual creature at midnight"; whenever she noticed him "making his obeisance" as she rode by, she would call him up to walk beside her horse, while they chatted. She would ask him to come to Court and to let her know when he was coming. This happened repeatedly; and Ralegh encouraged her friendliness, and added his own. Thus, on April 18, 1583:[7]

The Queen went from Richmond toward Greenwich, and at her going on horseback, being new up, she called for me by Mr. Rawly his putting her in mind . . . and gave me her right hand to kiss.

On July 31, Dee's *Diary* notes: "Mr. Rawlegh his letter unto me of Her

5. In a letter to Sir Thomas Roe in India.
6. *Brief Lives*, ii, 189.
7. *The Private Diary of Dr. John Dee*, ed. J. O. Halliwell (Camden Society 1842), p. 20.

Majesty's good disposition unto me."[8] On October 9, 1595,[9] Dee dined with Ralegh at Durham House.

Dee, despite his magic glasses and angelic friendships, escaped the magician's and atheist's doom. Francis Ket, Fellow of Corpus Christi College, Cambridge, did not. He was an Elizabethan Blake, as lovable and irresponsibly original in speculation and beliefs, though without the gift of divine verse and painting. He held that Christ was "not God, but a good man who suffered once for his own sins, and would suffer again for the sins of the world and be made God after his second resurrection"; he was "now personally in Judaea," with his Apostles, "gathering of his Church," and the faithful must go to Jerusalem to meet him and be fed there on Angels' food. Elizabethan Anglicanism had other food for such visionaries, and Ket was burnt alive, 1589. Some spirit of pity preserved him from the blackness of desolation, as the body died in pain. William Burton, who calls him "a devil incarnate," tells how he went to the fire clothed in sackcloth, leaping and dancing; and that in the fire itself, "above twenty times together clapping his hands he cried nothing but 'Blessed be God!' "

Ket had been Christopher Marlowe's tutor; and against the pupil a warrant for arrest on charges of atheism and blasphemy was issued in 1593. Luckily, before, it could be executed, he died in the brawl at Deptford, May 30, 1593. After his death a Commission on Atheism sat at Cerne Abbas, in Dorset. Before it Marlowe was alleged to have torn leaves from a Bible to dry tobacco on; and, "when he was like to die, being persuaded to make himself ready to God for his soul, he answered he would carry his soul up to the top of a hill, and run god, run devil, fetch it that will have it"—a recklessness of mockery we might dismiss, if it did not so ring with a laughter wilder than the solemn witnesses could have imagined. The general tenor of the charges is well supported by the shocked impression Marlowe made on contemporaries, which comes out in the deathbed lamentations of his former companion Greene. The strongest evidence, however, is in *Dr. Faustus*. There, side by side with imbecile and tiresome comic patches,[10] are flights of philosophical and imaginative beauty, and tides of rhythmical

8. *Op. cit.*, p. 21.
9. *Op. cit.*, p. 54. Stebbing, by a slip, has 1593 for 1595 (*Ralegh*, p. 104).
10. Which I, at least, cannot believe are by Marlowe.

subtlety and passion, which make Marlowe, despite his untimely death, the peer of Shakespeare and Milton, and challenge Robert Bridges' conclusion that

if one English poet might be recalled to-day from the dead to continue the work which he left unfinished on earth, it is probable that the crown of his country's desire would be set on the head of John Keats.

Some of us might vote for Christopher Marlowe. Even to-day astonishment comes with Mephistopheles' replies to his master's "frivolous demands" (which "strike a terror" to his "fainting soul"):

> Hell hath no limits, nor is circumscrib'd
> In one self place; for where we are is hell,
> And where hell is, there must we ever be:
> And to conclude, when all the world dissolves,
> All places shall be hell that are not heaven.

Remembering the crude theology over which Marlowe's contemporaries were burning and slaughtering each other, and the centuries of hardly less crude theology still to follow, our respect rises high for a dramatist who dared risk such doctrine on the stage, and risk it with the freedom and detachment apparent on every page of his play. Respect rises, too, for his audience, who could not have been intellectually so much inferior to some of our own day.

No one who has read much of the relevant literature can doubt the close connection of Marlowe and Ralegh, though only peaks of the evidence remain, thrusting above a sea of circumstantial suggestion. It is not simply that the circle of men who mattered in Elizabethan England was small, and circumscribed by London, so that, as in the Athens of Pericles, we may almost safely affirm that every great mind had at least exchanged thoughts with each important contemporary. We have definite proof. The Cerne Abbas Commission examined charges against both men.[11] One Richard Charley, himself accused of atheism, testified that "Marlowe told him that he had read the Atheist lecture"—whatever that was—"to Sir Walter Ralegh and others." The Reverend Ralph Ironside, parson of Winterbottom, gave evidence (March, 1594) of a

11. Charges were also made against Ralegh's elder brother, Carew Ralegh.

conversation at Sir George Trenchard's table, at Walveston, on a summer evening in 1593, when Ralegh questioned some of his theological reasoning, and had gone so far as to say he was dissatisfied with the Aristotelian definition of God as *"Ens Entium,"* "for neither could I learn hitherto what God is." The clergyman had stoutly withstood him, whereupon Ralegh slipped away by the expedient of asking him to say grace, "for that, quoth he, is better than this disputacion."

Most convincing of all is the natural bond between Ralegh and Marlowe in "the combination in both men of penetrating intellect with profound religious instinct." They were "both men in whom keenness of intellect was inseparable from clarity and grace of expression."[12] Miss Ellis-Fermor justly asserts:

If there was any mind in Elizabethan England that could command or impress Marlowe's, whose leadership he would have consented to follow even in part, that mind was Ralegh's. And the darker and graver personality of Ralegh is the only one of his contemporaries that outstrips Marlowe's in originality and independence of spirit.

The same admirable critic's summary of the character of *Dr. Faustus* seems to me, though she does not suggest this, to show the hell-doomed sorcerer's as close to Ralegh's as anything imagined can be to anything actual. In Ralegh, as in Faustus, we shall find[13]

alternating moods continue, with increasing violence, up to the last scene: a macabre and sombre series of contradictory passions: triumph, mirth, terror, repentance, despair and recklessness, until Faustus is beyond repentance, beyond salvation, and looks back over his last delusion with clear eyes. . . .

And Mr. V. T. Harlow indicates a theme calling for research far more strongly than the overworked and trivial questions often pursued (persecuted would be a better word) by students seeking to justify their name: "The closeness of the personal contact between the two" (Ralegh and Marlowe) "is well attested by documentary evidence, but the degree of their mental affinity has not yet been thoroughly examined."[14]

Something of that mental affinity lies on the surface of Ralegh's

12. V. M. Ellis-Fermor, *Christopher Marlowe*, pp. 163, 165.
13. *Ibid.*, p. 65. I have omitted Miss Ellis-Fermor's last words in this passage, as inapplicable to Ralegh (though finely applicable to Dr. Faustus).
14. *The Discoverie of Guiana*, pp. xxxiv–xxxv.

pleasantly realist answer to Marlowe's *Passionate Shepherd to his Love,*
a poet's answer to a poet, a friend "chaffing" a friend:

(MARLOWE)	(RALEGH)
Come, live with me and be my love	If all the world and love were young,
And we will all the pleasures prove	And truth in every shepherd's tongue,
That valleys, groves, hills and fields,	These pretty pleasures might me move
Woods or steepy mountain yields:	To live with thee, and be thy love.
And we will sit upon the rocks,	Time drives the flocks from field to fold,
Seeing the Shepherds feed their flocks	When rivers rage, and rocks grow cold,
By shallow rivers, to whose falls	And Philomel becometh dumb,
Melodious birds sing madrigals:	And Age complains of cares to come;
And I will make thee beds of roses,	And fading flowers in every field
And a thousand fragrant posies,	To winter floods their treasures yield.
A cap of flowers, and a kirtle	A honeyed tongue, a heart of gall,
Embroidered all with leaves of myrtle:	Is Fancy's spring, but Sorrow's fall.
A gown made of the finest wool,	Thy gowns, thy shoes, thy beds of roses,
Which from our pretty lambs we pull,	Thy cap, thy kirtle, and thy posies,
Fair-linèd slippers from the cold,	Soon break, soon wither, soon forgotten,
With buckles of the purest gold:	In folly ripe, in reason rotten.
A belt of straw, and ivy buds,	Thy belt of straw, and ivy buds,
With coral clasps, and amber studs;	Thy coral clasps, and amber studs,
And, if these pleasures may thee move,	All these in me no means can move,
Come, live with me, and be my love!	To come to thee and be thy love.
The Shepherd swains shall dance and sing,	But, could youth last, and love still breed,[15]
For thy delight, each May-morning!	Had joys no date, nor age no need,
If these delights thy mind may move,	Then these delights my mind might move,
Then live with me, and be my love!	To live with thee, and be thy love.

15. That is, keep continuing.

These verses were cast off in Ralegh's lighter moments, to be read in a circle of common friends. But no reader can miss their sincerity and gravity. Though they are not to be taken too seriously, they *are* to be taken seriously; and the mind which cast them off was always serious, with a deep imaginative melancholy. Every writer points out that Ralegh lived in an age greedy for power and money (as if any age were not greedy for these things). What is seldom remembered is that he was marked apart by his habit of reminding himself that all this strife in which he and his fellows were engaged was *māyā,* illusion. The world was passing away, and the fashion thereof: "the long day of mankind draweth fast towards an evening, and the world's tragedy and time are nearly at an end." Is it fanciful to find in this habit, and in the loosening of grip and effort which must have come with it, part reason of that practical failure which so puzzles those who see how amazing and varied his abilities were, and who feel that surely his contemporaries *must* have seen this too? Suddenly Ralegh would feel the effort not worth while, the prizes trivial—and in that moment another would have passed him and would have grasped what he himself had so lately been desiring.

Marlowe's famous verses were not printed till 1599, when their author had been six years dead. But obviously they had been known for years, as had been Ralegh's reply. We can connect the two men by another link. We have seen that in 1580 Ralegh engaged young Thomas Hariot as his mathematician, and that Hariot went to Virginia for him and drew up a report on that region. It is a natural surmise that Ralegh brought Marlowe and Hariot together; Marlowe's enthusiasm for Hariot was unbounded, and was expressed with characteristically reckless excitement. Marlowe asserted that "Moses was but a juggler," working his miracles before Pharaoh, "and that one Harriot can do more than he." It is to Hariot that Thomas Nash, in *Pierce Pennilesse his Supplication to the Divell* (1592), refers (with revelation of another modernist heresy, centuries before Bishop Colenso): "I hear say there be Mathematicians abroad, that will prove men before Adam." Robert Parsons, the Jesuit, also in 1592, speaks[16] of this same iniquitous Hariot, whom Marlowe so admired, *"Astronomo quodam necromantico,"* the archpreceptor of the *"schola frequens de Atheismo"* (the School for Athe-

16. *Responsio ad Elizabethae edictum.*

ism) which Ralegh notoriously held in his house—a school in which "both Moyses and our Saviour, the old and the new Testament, are jested at, and the scholars taught, among other things, to spell God backward." However childish all this seems to us, we shall misunderstand the whole period and be needlessly puzzled by Ralegh's later ruin, if we do not see how passionately and angrily interested men were. Hariot was the theologian who made a philosophy, "wherein he cast off the Old Testament, and then the New one would (consequently) have no foundation"—a subversive system which he "taught to Sir Walter Ralegh, Henry earl of Northumberland, and some others."[17] And these three—Hariot, Marlowe, Ralegh—were persistently named together, and their wicked doings discussed constantly and widely, reaching (among others) that ultra-orthodox busybody, James VI of Scotland. In 1594, however, the charges apparently collapsed, and went into general vague talk, where they worked as one more reason for hatred of Ralegh, who outraged common opinion so variously.

It was his consistent wish that opinion should be left free. When John Udal, a Puritan clergyman who criticized the Bishops,[18] was sentenced to death in 1591 for high treason (on the grounds that they were an essential part of the State, as of course they were), certain laymen who were shocked by the judgment saved him from the gallows. Of these Ralegh and Essex were the most prominent. Thomas Phelippes, of the Government's secret intelligence service, observes (March 22, 1591): "The Puritans hope well of the Earl of Essex, who makes Ralegh join him as an instrument from them to the Queen, upon any particular occasion of relieving them." It is pleasant to note them joined in such a deed. (It is pleasant, too, to remember that James of Scotland, of whom we shall not have much to say that is good, interceded, from his admiration for Udal's exceptional scholarship.) Udal received a note:

If you will write half a dozen lines to Sir Walter Ralegh concerning those doctrines [i.e., doctrines alleged against him, which had prejudiced the Queen greatly], that he may show it to Her Majesty, he hopes to obtain your life. I know it is very easy for you to answer all those things, there-

17. Aubrey, i, 287.
18. He wrote that they "cared for nothing but the maintenance of their dignities, be it the damnation of their own souls and infinite millions more."

fore do it with speed; and in your writing to Sir Walter take knowledge that he hath sent you such word.[19]

Udal did as he was advised, stressing his devotion to "Her Majesty's happy government" and begging her, not without dignity, "that the land may not be charged with my blood—to change my punishment from death to banishment." The bishops were scandalized by proposals of leniency. But Ralegh successfully championed the offender "against the same lying spirit of legal casuistry which was to destroy himself,"[20] and in June, 1592, Udal was pardoned. He remained in prison awhile longer, as too dangerous to be at large in a Christian country, though possibly safe for more heathen regions; he died while it was being debated whether he could be allowed "to carry his anti-prelatic zeal and immense learning into a chaplaincy in Guinea."

It is anticipating a little, but this seems a fitting place to draw attention to the honorable stand Ralegh made in the House of Commons (April 4, 1593), when the full tide of the Queen's anger and his own disgrace was running, against a bill proposing to put Brownists to death. He wisely evaded the stubborn rush of ignorant bigotry, and conciliated opposition by arguments not based on religion or creed. He admitted that "the Brownists are worthy to be voted out [of] a Commonwealth." This may strike us as ungenerous; but the men he was defending would have shown little tolerance, had they possessed power, to his own freedom of speculation. He meant to save their lives, nevertheless; and urged that:

The law is hard that taketh life, or sendeth into banishment, where men's intentions shall be judged by a jury, and they shall be judges what another man meant.

He was not willing to have twelve blunt common-sense men deciding what some lonely enthusiast meant, on the matters that lie most hid, and judging whether he should die for thinking differently from bishop and grocer. He had no respect for the man in the street's opinion; after

19. Cf. Thomas Birch, *Memoirs of the Reign of Queen Elizabeth,* i, 62: "Sir Walter Ralegh was made an instrument of the prolonging hitherto of Udal's life" (Anthony Bacon, March 11, 1591).
20. Stebbing, p. 55.

bitter experience of crowds he found them "like dogs, that bark at those they know not."[21]

He was also one of the few Elizabethans who, while convinced Protestants, would not have persecuted Catholics. John Cornelius, the only son of Irish parents settled in Cornwall, became a Jesuit priest, one of the mission to convert England. He was renowned for his power over demons; they fled at his command, "uttering terrible curses, and vociferating that they could by no means withstand the charity of the Father, whose very approach sometimes put them to flight."[22] One evicted devil sardonically offered him twopence to buy a halter, saying he would be hanged within the year (as, indeed, he was). When Cornelius was arrested in the West Country, Ralegh, "one of the most learned men in England, a famous mathematician, and of a subtle spirit," was moved with interest in him, as once in Dr. Dee, and

passed the whole night with him alone, that he might have certain doubts cleared up; nor would such a man rest contented with mere questions and doubts, but would go into matters more deeply. He was so pleased with the Father's conviction and reasoning and with his modest and courteous manner, that he offered to do all he could in London for his liberation, and this although the Father had greatly reproved him for his mode of life and conversation.

He saw that Cornelius was no traitor. But it was 1594, at the deepest point of his disgrace and powerlessness, and he could not save the enthusiast.

21. *History of the World,* Preface.
22. Henry Foley, S. J., *Records of the English Province of the Society of Jesus* (1878), iii, 446 ff.

CHAPTER X

Marriage; and Disgrace

When she smiled it was a pure sunshine that everyone did choose to bask in if they could. But anon came a storm, and the thunder fell in wondrous manner on all alike. SIR JOHN HARINGTON on Queen Elizabeth.

IN September, 1588, after the Armada's repulse, Ralegh and Grenville were ordered to sweep away its relics from the western coasts of Ireland. The work proved unnecessary, the seas having already accomplished it. But the two were to knit their names together once more, in an association which has moved into the immortalities of history and literature alike.

It happened in 1591. Those unhappily placed islands, the Azores, were marked out for a fresh descent (much as a tiger marks out a river-brink where he has repeatedly killed), and Ralegh received his first high naval command, as Vice-Admiral under Lord Thomas Howard. They were to wait at the Azores for Spain's silver fleet returning from America. But Elizabeth again decided he must not sail, so Grenville took his place.

With what quickening of interest Ralegh followed what happened we know from one of the most challenging and ringing pieces of prose in the language. This time the hunter was caught. Six ships of war (five royal vessels, and the *Bark Ralegh*), five cargo boats and some pinnaces, were close inshore, watering and waiting for sick men who had been sent on land to recover. An enemy armament of fifty-three ships crept up, their approach "shrouded . . . by reason of the island" but reported by an English captain, Middleton, who in the light confident manner of his countrymen coolly kept abreast for three days while he took stock of their strength. The English had "scarce time to weigh their anchors, but some of them were driven to let slip their cables and set sail." Grenville was the last, for the entirely honorable reason that he would not abandon his sick on shore. When these had been collected, he was too late to catch the wind, but still had a chance of escape.

Escape, however, did not suit with his magnificence of valor, which was of that uncomfortable kind that brings a commander fame but too often leaves those under his command in a premature grave:

Sir Richard utterly refused to turn from the enemy, alleging that he would rather choose to die than to dishonour himself, his country, and her Majesty's ship, persuading his company that he would pass through the two Squadrons in despite of them: and enforce those of Sivill to give him way.

> "Let us bang these dogs of Seville, the children of the devil,
> For I never turned my back upon Don or devil yet."

He would thrust his majestic way athwart them, and the deer would timidly give place!

After the disaster it was rumored that Ralegh had challenged Lord Thomas Howard to a duel for "deserting" his kinsman. Ralegh's account makes it plain that no shadow of blame could possibly attach to Howard. He has left on record in enough places his opinion of Grenville's kind of courage—that it is superb and splendid (of course) and all that, but nevertheless rather silly. He puts it on record here, with the gentlest of strictures on the recently dead who had died so grandly:

But the other course had been the better, and might right well have been answered in so great an impossibility of prevailing. Notwithstanding, out of the greatness of his mind, he could not be persuaded.

The *Revenge,* becalmed in a towering forest of galleons, fought for fifteen hours, repelling rush after rush of boarders, until, her decks slippery and foul with carnage, her bulk riddled and shattered from the 800 shot she had received, her commander mortally wounded, she was surrendered against Grenville's will. The Spaniards, partly from admiration, partly from terror to board again a ship possessed by such a devil incarnate as this world-renowned corsair—who would not hesitate to blow the vessel to the four winds, with himself and her captors on her—promised that there should be no galleys or Inquisition, but that quarter should be granted and the captives sent to England, where the "better sort" alone should "pay such reasonable ransom as their estate would bear." Sir Richard was then carried on board their flagship, where he lingered for three days, happy in his conquerors' unstinted admiration and awing them (according to the Dutch traveller Van Linschoten, who was then in the Azores and talked with survivors of the battle) by an appalling trick of crushing glasses till the blood ran from his mouth, and then swallowing the splinters. This seems hard to believe, and was probably part of the Spanish legend of the terrible sea-rover.

Some extravagance of gesture, however, Grenville felt was due to his situation. These Devon captains, as Ralegh himself was to show more finely than any of them, lived in an exaltation of mood which made them dramatic at all great moments, and never more dramatic than when foes were watching them die. Sir Richard's words to his captors, in their own tongue, as he passed from them and from captivity, have never been forgotten: "Here die I, Richard Grenville, with a joyful and quiet mind, having ended my life like a true soldier that has fought for his country, Queen, religion and honour."

Ralegh's pamphlet, his earliest-known publication, was written in answer to detractors who alleged that the English had shown coward-ice: first, in the fleeing of five vessels, and next, in being beaten at all. The Spaniards had published great reports of their victory, which was, as a matter of fact, their first since the disastrous sailing of the Armada. It was a poor triumph, costing a thousand casualties; and what Grenville's headstrong valor had not been able to accomplish the sea achieved, in a storm that sank fifteen war vessels and another fif-teen merchantmen, drowning ten thousand men. The pirate's soul, the Spaniards believed, had sunk straight down into Hell, and rerisen with all its devils to help him to vengeance. In that holocaust the shot-riddled *Revenge* herself went to the ocean depths, with her host of victims accompanying, in a burial which stirs Ralegh to a paean.

After his story of the actual fight, Ralegh's account flags into mere bigotry and prejudice for the most part, though often finely expressed. Even so, the prejudice had more reason than readers in a more sheltered age may see. His hatred of Spain flies barbed with angry sarcasm:

But sure I am, that there is no kingdom or commonwealth in all Europe, but, if they be reformed, they then invade it for religion's sake: if it be, as they term, Catholic, they pretend title; as if the Kings of Castile were the natural heirs of all the world. And so, between both, no kingdom is un-sought.

The story, written out of a white heat of indignation, is direct and vigorous, almost unique amid the lumbering Elizabethan prose. It inspired Tennyson's ballad, and retains independent value of its own.

He pushed on steadily with his main business, privateering. Hume, analyzing the disposition of the plunder brought by one of his captains in 1591:

Value of merchandise, etc., captured, £31,150. One-third for the mariners, £10,383; for my Lord his tenth, £3015; for the Queen's customs, £1600; cost of bringing the goods, £1200 = £16,198. Rest unto the owners and victuallers, to be divided amongst twelve, £14,952.

—observes, "It will be seen that the business of plunder was organized on a thoroughly commercial system."[1]

His supplanting by a younger showier rival made Ralegh a greater man. Hitherto, "he had vicariously explored, colonized, plundered and fought. Henceforth he was to do a substantial part of his own work. . . . From 1587, as the star of Essex rose, and his was supposed to be waning, his orbit can be seen widening. It became more independent."[2] Sometimes he almost seemed half-released from attendance on the aging Queen.

Then he was brought back to a brief spell of influence, by the Earl of Essex's marriage to Sir Philip Sidney's widow, Frances, in 1590. Elizabeth, having remained single herself, thought those whom she selected for personal favor should do the same. Her hatred of everything sexual was pathological. Those curious enough, or fair-minded enough, to care to understand this feeling, as deserving more respect than a smart ribaldry, can find its roots and reason in her dreadful childhood, and the playful brutalities of her semi-stepfather, Thomas Lord Seymour. At the age of fifteen she had been alleged to be with child by him, and had had to clear herself officially. The episode explains why she wanted the romantic fondnesses of love, without its heats and ardors.

Her rancor toward Lady Essex was almost insane, and Essex himself ultimately won forgiveness only on condition that his accomplice lived "very retired" in the country. He went out for a time; and Ralegh

1. *Ralegh,* pp. 123–124.   2. Stebbing, p. 63.

came in, and was able to get Spenser a pension, and to assist others. "When will you cease to be a beggar?" the Queen once asked him. "When your gracious Majesty ceases to be a benefactor."

In January, 1592, she made the Bishop and Chapter of Salisbury lease Sherborne to her, and passed it on to Ralegh—her last and greatest gift. He held it at a rent of £360 a year. St. Osmund, Bishop of Sarum, was believed to have laid a curse on anyone who alienated Sherborne; and the lease was made, only after the see had lain vacant for three years (because Elizabeth was insisting that Sherborne Castle must be surrendered, as a condition of appointment). When at last an accommodating cleric was found, Ralegh gave the Queen a jewel worth £250 for making this gentleman Bishop. The estate was soon rounded off by the lease of Wilscombe manor from the Bishop of Bath and Wells, who had the misfortune to marry again in his gouty old age. The marriage of the clergy was notoriously felt by Elizabeth as peculiarly degrading, and in her disgust she shook the place out of him as a ransom. The action, from first to finish, was high-handed, even for her, and St. Osmund's curse was to prove effective. Three of Ralegh's lay successors at Sherborne died on the scaffold (as he did); two in prison; another was murdered.

Sherborne became the place he regarded as home. It seems likely that he sought it because he now wanted to possess a home. In March, 1592, whispers were abroad that he had secretly married, or secretly debauched, Elizabeth Throckmorton, a maid of honor. The rumor came at an inconvenient time, when Ralegh, undeterred by the *Revenge* disaster, had persuaded other adventurers to join with him in fitting out thirteen vessels, to capture the silver fleet and sack Panama. It was to sail under him, an Admiral at last. But the Queen finally ordered him to start the voyage only, and, when it was well under way, to give place to Frobisher and return, a decision which deeply discontented him. He was being used at all only because Frobisher, like Gilbert, had a bad name with seamen, while he himself, detested by the country at large, was loved by them. He dared not come to London to press his protests. So he sailed, May 6, 1592, to be overtaken next day by Frobisher with orders for his return. He took his time about obeying, going on to Cape Finisterre, through a tempest on May 11; then went back, and was at once sent to the Tower.

When first confronted with his enemies' assertion that, once on shipboard, he would stay away until the Queen had forgotten the offense now alleged against him, to Robert Cecil Ralegh lied with Elizabethan decision:

I mean not to come away, as they say I will, for fear of a marriage and I know not what. If any such thing were, I would have imparted it unto yourself before any man living; and therefore I pray believe it not, and I beseech you to suppress what you can any such malicious report. For I protest before God, there is no one on the face of the earth that I would be fastened unto.[3]

But by June he could no longer deny what had happened. Elizabeth Throckmorton was known to be with child, and by him—or so it is generally said, following Camden's statement: "*honoraria Reginae virgine vitiata, quam postea in uxorem duxit.*" But the matter, even yet, does not seem so entirely decided against him. Gosse suggests[4] that the mysterious child of a mysterious letter supposed to have been written under sentence of death, in 1603—"my poor daughter, to whom I have given nothing"—was the love-child of this intrigue. But there is no other reference anywhere, or in any authority, to this "poor daughter." She was not Lady Ralegh's daughter. No child came of this alleged seduction, and there is not the slightest ground to imagine any miscarriage. All that is certain is that Ralegh and the maid of honor were found to be compromised together, and that their contemporaries gleefully did as contemporaries do, assumed the worst construction possible. Elizabeth sent them both to the Tower, into a "domestic punishment within her own fortress-palace, inflicted by the Queen as head of her own household."[5] Very properly," observes Professor Neale austerely:

Elizabeth was *in loco parentis* to her maids of honour, and for them to belie their name was an offence like the lapse of a Vestal Virgin. They enjoyed a coveted position, in daily contact with the Queen, with the chance of earning her intimate, lasting friendship, and with unequalled facilities for making a brilliant marriage. Like their manners and morals, their marriage was a royal responsibility, and it was a breach of duty as well as a gross personal affront to their sovereign to marry without her leave.[6]

3. Letter of March 10, 1592.   4. *Ralegh.* But see Appendix B.
5. Stebbing, *Ralegh*, p. 88.   6. *Queen Elizabeth*, p. 327.

"Intimate lasting friendship," however, it was not in Elizabeth's power to give, least of all to her maids of honor: their "unequalled facilities for making a brilliant marriage" were nil, unless they did it by stealth followed by flight from the Court forever: and the last thing that the Queen would ever have sanctioned was a marriage of one of her servants with one of her favorites, particularly with Sir Walter Ralegh. Storms broke when Essex married, when Ralegh married, when Southampton (even) married. Her Court had reached, in so far as she could manage it, the condition of Gonzalo's ideal commonwealth, in Shakespeare's *Tempest*:

> *Sebastian*. No marrying 'mong her subjects?
> *Antonio*. None, man; all idle; whores and knaves.

Her "known displeasure to open and honourable engagements" directly "led to the clandestine and dishonourable connections";[7] and this somewhat offsets what we may admit, gladly, that she "had a sincerer love for purity of manners than posterity has commonly believed."[8] It was "marry without her leave" (that "breach of duty as well as gross personal affront") or marry not at all. There was something to be said for her indignation with Ralegh. But it was less than people suppose, marriage or seduction being almost equally obnoxious to her. Now, raging because a lover who had kept his heart free till he had reached the mature age of forty had secretly condescended to one of her attendants, she was assured that all right-thinking persons shared her horror.

Scandal gives delight in a wide circle, and particularly scandal about a man eminent and detested. Ralegh, who had pretended to solely intellectual interests, who had been so proud and assumed such superior airs, was humanly sensual after all! Essex came back to favor, and the glee of his partisans is preserved in Sir Edward Stafford's message to Anthony Bacon (July 30, 1592):[9] "If you have anything to do with Sir Walter Ralegh, or any love to make to Mrs. Throckmorton, at the Tower to-morrow you may speak with them." It is still more vividly preserved in a ribald anonymous letter:

7. *Calendar of Carew MSS.*, 1515–1574, ed. Brewer and Bullen, p. xxxvi.
8. Stebbing, *Ralegh*, p. 94.
9. Birch, *Memoirs of Queen Elizabeth*, i, 79.

S.W.R., as it seemeth, have been too inward with one of her Majesty's
maids; I fear to say who, but if you should guess at E.T., you may not be
far wrong. The matter hath only now been apparent to all eyes, and the
lady hath been sent away, but nobody believes it can end there. S.W.R. hath
escaped from London for a time; he will be speedily sent for, and brought
back, where what awaiteth him nobody knoweth, save by conjecture. All
think the Tower will be his dwelling, like hermit poor in pensive place,
where he may spend his endless days in doubt. It is affirmed that they are
married; but the Queen is most fiercely incensed, and, as the bruit goes,
threateneth the most bitter punishment to both the offenders. S.W.R. will
lose, it is thought, all his places and preferments at Court, with the Queen's
favour; such will be the end of his speedy rising, and now he must fall as
low as he was high, at the which many will rejoice. I can write no more at
this time, and do not care to send this, only you will hear it from others.
All is alarm and confusion at this discovery of the discoverer, and not indeed of a new continent, but of a new incontinent.

Cecil, cautious son of a cautious father, had been warned by that
father: "seek not to be Essex, shun to be Rawleigh." "Robert Cecil,
awkward and deformed, was in no danger"[10] of being either. He
dazzled nobody, but won and kept success by a scrupulous avoidance
of risk, and by a steady undeviating mediocrity which was his by gift
of nature. He was a humbug, carefully trained as such by his father,
whose *Ten Precepts,* "addressed to his son Robert as a supplement to
the Ten Commandments, will keep anyone prosperous to the end of
his days and the world laughing till the end of time."[11] Shakespeare's
Polonius, far more than (as some have suggested) Milton's Beelzebub
majestically rising to address his demon peers, is modelled on Elizabeth's chief of statesmen, whose calculating servility would have been
applauded by the Reverend Mr. Collins:

Be sure to keep some great man thy friend, but trouble him not for
trifles. Compliment him often with many, yet small, gifts of *little* charge.
And if thou hast cause to bestow any great gratuity, let it be something
which may be daily in sight. . . .

Lord Burghley had become a parent, somewhat precociously, at the

10. Stebbing, p. 57.
11. A. Cecil, *A Life of Robert Cecil, First Earl of Salisbury,* p. 9.

age of fourteen, and the experience left him with a low opinion of the young of both sexes, which he packs into three pithy sentences: "Marry thy daughters in time, lest they marry themselves. And suffer not thy sons to pass the Alps. For there they shall learn nothing but pride, blasphemy and atheism." The son he was addressing had "no facility in the cultivation of wild oats,"[12] but could on occasion show himself broad-minded in assessing others' harvests. In February, 1601, when the Earl of Pembroke and Mary Fitton (posterity's favorite candidate for the rôle of Shakespeare's "Dark Lady") were detected in an intrigue which (unlike Ralegh's and Miss Throckmorton's) did not end in marriage, Robert Cecil took it as a jest, gaily noting that both sinners "will dwell in the Tower a while." But now, in 1592, he wisely took his cue from the Queen, whose wrath burned against Ralegh as it never burned against men who had made a lesser dent on her susceptibilities, and he expressed himself as appalled by Ralegh's precipitate sensuality. A letter by Lady Ralegh, written from her imprisonment ("Never were written more charming letters" than hers, "in more unembarrassed phonetic spelling"[13]), has been discovered, which with dignity protests against his misrepresentation. It is signed, not "E. T.," but "E. R.," "thus pointing to a secret marriage before the imprisonment":[14]

I asur you trewly I never desiared nor never wolde desiar my lebbarte with out the good likeing ne advising of Sur W:R: hit is not this inprisonment if I bought hit with my life that shuld make me thinke hit long if hit should doo him harme to speke of my delivery: but Sur R. S. was somewhat deceved in his Jugement in that and hit may be hee findeth his error.[15]

Sir Robert Cecil ("Sur R. S."), who has put the worst possible construction on her relations with Sir Walter Ralegh, gratifying the Queen thereby, has (she indicates very gently) been somewhat mistaken, and may so realize soon, if he is not realizing it already. That is, she and Ralegh were husband and wife. In later years, though a false and

12. *Life of Robert Cecil*, p. 15. There is evidence that this judgment may do Robert Cecil wrong.
13. Stebbing, p. 89. Ralegh's own spelling was turbulent. In a letter to the Lord Admiral at this very time, he writes of the "manhangled trobles" of Continental nations.
14. V. T. Harlow, *The Discoverie of Guiana*, p. xxi.
15. Letter to Sir Moyle Finch (*Historical MSS. Commission*, Allan George Finch MSS., i, 33–34).

treacherous friend to Ralegh, Robert Cecil was consistently respectful, almost remorseful, to Ralegh's wife. Is it unreasonable to detect some fulfilment of her prophecy that he would find he had misjudged her? It is not of first importance—or would not be, if critics had not brought to Ralegh standards different from those they use with his contemporaries—but it is not proven that he and his wife committed the offense against morals alleged against them.

For the rest, Lady Ralegh's married life was so entirely in the shadowed part of her husband's career, and was crowded with so many miseries, borne with unsurpassable nobleness, that as a result we are tempted to think of her as the suffering wife, a creature meek and subdued. She was nothing of the kind. She was charming in person, tall, slender, golden-haired and blue-eyed; and she inherited all the courage and energy of her father, Nicholas Throckmorton, "a busy intriguing man,"[16] prominent through four reigns. In Mary's, accused of high treason, he achieved a miracle; "by his own wary pleading, and the Jury's upright verdict" he "hardly escaped." His superb defense stood in men's memories as a landmark, until Ralegh's own eclipsed it.

Lady Ralegh was permanently banished from Court, whatever pardon might some day be extended to her husband; and began her married life at Sherborne. Their shelter in these first shadowed days, Sherborne meant everything to her, even more than to him. Yet for him also, "it is questionable whether this period was not really the happiest in his life."[17] Their elder son was born here in 1594. How deeply they cherished Sherborne we shall see later. Ralegh so labored to beautify and enrich it, building and rebuilding, guiding a stream into new channels, planting cedars from Virginia and shrubs which his captains brought him from tropic islands, that "to-day his very spirit hovers there among the bricks he laid."[18]

No man ever had a nobler mate, and the deepest and loveliest strands in his experience were woven by his wife's affection. In death's presence he was to give her the assurance: "I chose you and I loved you in my happiest times." Those wonderful words were true in all the depth of emotion that still lives in them. Before life entered on its long slow

16. Strype.   17. Hume, pp. 137–138.
18. Waldman, *Ralegh*, p. 53.

depression into the valleys of humiliation and disaster—Ralegh chose and loved his wife.

Meanwhile, the old pretenses were kept up—very vainly. He was under surveillance of Sir George Carew, who was Master of Ordnance in the Tower. Carew was ready to help a kinsman, and on July 26, 1592, he wrote Robert Cecil a fairy tale that his prisoner, hearing that the Queen was about to take an airing on the Thames, had begged to be rowed near enough to at least look on Divinity. Refused, he had gone temporarily out of his mind, and had resisted, frantic with frustrate passion. Sir Arthur Gorges (another kinsman), had been slashed across the hand with his dagger, while trying to save him from himself! "Sir Walter Ralegh will shortly grow to be 'Orlando Furioso' if the bright Angelica persevere against him a little longer. Thus wrote Carew, rising to unwonted heights of what Andrew Lang used to call "poestry," striving to attune his prosaic key to these brave desperate doings. In all this there could be no word of Elizabeth Throckmorton; the feminine partner in such guilt must be left in silence, lest the bright Angelica, suddenly recollecting, should receive her suppliant's penitence with reserves. She so received it now, being deeply and beyond forgiveness angry. Robert Devereux, Earl of Essex, had been little more than a boy when he offended by marrying; Ralegh might have been supposed to know better.

In the Tower he could conduct his business only by proxy; and, writing to Robert Cecil about the paying for the coats of the Yeomen of the Guard, whose Captain he still nominally was, he indulged in his famous description of the Queen, now no longer the girl who recalled her mother's vivacity, but a weather-beaten lady of nearly sixty. Such documents add a welcome touch of comedy to the often gruesome and rarely exhilarating narrative with which the biographer must trouble his readers.[19] Ralegh, of course, knew that the Queen would see the letter, after the eyes of Cecil had overrun it. She only, of all possible readers, might take it seriously—or half-seriously.

My heart was never broken till this day that I hear the Queen goes so far

19. Yet I believe Schomburgk is right (Introduction to *The Discoverie of Guiana*) in saying that Ralegh's "theatrical deportment" in the Tower permanently lowered his prestige. Like many intensely imaginative men, he often overdid what was a current convention.

off, whom I have followed so many years with so great love and desire in so many journeys, and am now left behind her in a dark prison all alone. While she was yet near at hand, that I might hear of her once in two or three days, my sorrows were less, but even now my heart is cast into the depth of all misery. I that was wont to behold her riding like Alexander, hunting like Diana, walking like Venus, the gentle wind blowing her fair hair about her pure cheeks like a nymph! sometimes sitting in the shade like a goddess! sometimes singing like an angel, sometimes playing like Orpheus! Behold the sorrow of this world! Once amiss hath bereaved me of all. O glory that only shineth in misfortune! what is become of thy assurance? All wounds have scars but that of fantasy; all affections their relenting, but that of womankind. Who is the judge of friendship but adversity? or when is grace witnessed but in offences? There were no divinity but by reason of compassion, for revenges are brutish and mortal. All those times past—the loves, the sighs, the sorrows, the desires, can they not weigh down one frail misfortune? Cannot one drop of gall be hidden in so great heaps of sweetness? I may then conclude, *Spes et fortuna, valete.* She is gone, in whom I trusted, and of me hath not one thought of mercy, nor any respect of that that was. Do with me therefore what you list. I am more weary of life than they are desirous I should perish, which if it had been for her, as it is by her, I had been too happily born. Yours, not worthy any name or title —W.R.[20]

Ralegh's over-delicate reference to what had happened ("one frail misfortune"—to Lord Howard he called it "this unfortunate accident")[21] did not impress Elizabeth. His disgrace was to be in essentials permanent. Too able, too useful, to be kept always in prison, he was to serve her again, both near her person and in her fleets. But his fortune was over. Something had happened which was not to be forgiven.

Presently he himself was forced to accept his imprisonment as likely to last some time; and chafed because everything was (naturally) going wrong with his affairs, especially in Ireland. He wrote to Robert Cecil (July, 1592), with a zoological confusion that has frequently caused comment:

It is a sign how my disgraces have past the seas, and have been highly commended to that wise Governor, who hath used me accordingly. So I

20. W. Murdin, *State Papers,* etc., ii, 657.
21. August, 1592.

leave to trouble you at this time, being become like a fish cast on dry land, gasping for breath, with lame legs and lamer lungs.

Then his release came, accidentally, out of a capture made by the fleet in which he should have been.

It had divided after he had left it; Frobisher watched the Spanish coast, and the Vice-Admiral, Sir John Burrough, in Ralegh's *Roebuck,* sailed off to prowl about the Azores. Burrough fell in with the Portuguese East Indian carracks, heavily laden and bound for Lisbon. One was run ashore and burnt by her crew. But the largest of all, the *Madre de Dios,* "a floating castle, with nearly 800 inhabitants,"[22] 7 decks high and 165 feet long, was cut away from the others. For hours she fought desperately, and while still struggling to escape was stopped by an independent fleet belonging to the Earl of Cumberland—an interference which exacerbated the ensuing quarrel over booty. She was the richest single prize ever taken, her capture "the most brilliant feat of privateering ever accomplished by Englishmen, even in the days of Queen Elizabeth."[23] "Traditions have lingered even to our own days of the excitement in the west country"[24] when she was towed into Dartmouth, September 8. Her cargo was staggeringly valuable, including, according to her purser, 537 tons of spices—8500 quintals[25] of pepper, 900 quintals of cloves, 700 quintals of cinnamon, 500 quintals of cochineal, 59 quintals of mace, 59 quintals of nutmegs, 50 quintals of benjamin"—also 400,000 crusados' worth of musk, precious stones, pearls, amber. The pepper Lord Burghley estimated as worth £102,000. Among the jewels were "two great crosses and one other great jewel of diamonds which the Viceroy sent for a present to the King." There were 15 tons of ebony; and satins, tapestries, silks. Nothing that our own orderly age has ever seen can convey the fire which flamed up in the Devon populace; to imagine it, we must visualize the rushing down of some tribe on India's north-western border, when news comes of a wealthy caravan, stranded and lying ready for the looting. Sir John Hawkins, Treasurer and Controller of the Navy, wrote to the Lord High Admiral that the value was probably £500,000. It was not as much as that, but it took ten ships to carry the cargo to London, and

22. Edwards, ii, 61. Strype (*Annals*) says she carried 600 men.
23. Edwards, ii, 59.   24. Hume, *Ralegh,* p. 129.
25. Hundredweights.

this was worth over £150,000, apart from the precious stones and the ship herself.

Robert Cecil, sent down to save as much as possible, found the West Country had gone mad: "for jewels, pearls, and amber," he told his father, "I fear that the birds be flown." In the possession of one sailor were "a chain of orient pearls, two chains of gold, four great pearls of the bigness of a fair pea, four forks of crystal, and four spoons of crystal set with gold and stones, and two cords of musk." A corporal had a large bag of rubies; another plunderer had over three hundred diamonds; a third a bag of diamonds as big as his fist. An eyewitness testified that the Devon ports looked like a St. Bartholomew's Fair. Putting suspected plunderers on their oath was "a mere offence to God." Cecil wrote from Exeter that he stopped on the road every man "which did smell of the prizes"; he searched "every bag and mail coming from the west"; and he clapped some in prison, whereby "I have left an impression with the Mayor and the rest." The excitement caught even him.

My Lord, there never was such spoil.[26] I will suppress the confluence of these buyers, of which there are above two thousand. My sending down hath made many stagger. Fouler ways, desperate ways, no more obstinate people did I ever meet with. . . . Her Majesty's captive comes after me, but I have outrid him, and will be at Dartmouth before him.[27]

"Her Majesty's captive" was Ralegh. The sailors, coming in with their prize, had been indignant to learn that he was in prison. Sir John Hawkins, after him the chief adventurer in the expedition which had been so spectacularly successful, wrote that he was "the especial man" to settle the vast confusion. Accordingly, under guard of a keeper, Ralegh was allowed to follow Cecil. He came filled with a fervor to stop plunderers, even at this late hour. "If I meet any of them coming up, if it be upon the wildest Heath in all the way, I mean to strip them as naked as ever they were born!"

26. Cf. the Countess of Bath's apology (her husband was Lord Lieutenant of Devon) to Julius Caesar, Judge of the Admiralty, several months later, for sending his lady a gift of insufficient value: "I send your wife a small token, in show of thankful remembrance; but, had I anything by this rich carrick, she should have perceived it by my token. But my Lord's house is far off, and so lighted of nothing."

27. Letter of September 17, 1592, to Lord Burghley.

He reached Dartmouth, to a reception which astounded and cha-grined Cecil, who had not dreamt that he was such a power among his own.

I assure you, sir, his poor servants, to the number of 140 goodly men, and all the mariners came to him with such shouts of joy, as I never saw a man more troubled to quiet them in my life. But his heart is broken; for he is very extreme pensive, longer than he is busied, in which he can toil ter-ribly. The meeting between him and Sir John Gilbert was with tears on Sir John's part. Whensoever he is saluted with congratulations for liberty, he doth answer, "No, I am still the Queen of England's poor captive." I wished him to conceal it, because here it doth diminish his credit, which I do vow to you before God is greater amongst the mariners than I thought for. I do grace him as much as I may, for I find him marvellously greedy to do anything to recover the conceit of his brutish offence.[28]

At this time, Cecil and Ralegh were still—with reservations—allies, and this letter, like most of its kind, was of course written to be shown to Elizabeth.

Ralegh was meanwhile making overtures of his own. He had no in-tention of enriching the Queen by his influence, and then returning to prison. He wrote to the Lord Treasurer (Burghley),[29] to ask

in particular how Her Majesty might be profited by the Carrack, according to the offer I made. My promise was not to buy my bondage, but my lib-erty, and, I hope, of Her Majesty's favour. . . . Fourscore thousand pounds is more than ever a man presented Her Majesty as yet. If God have sent it for my ransom, I hope Her Majesty will accept it.

She was entitled to one tenth of the booty, which after all possible sal-vage had been effected amounted to £141,000 (or about £750,000 in present values): she had risked £1800 of a total joint stock of £18,000 and had provided 1150 tons out of 5000 tons. Ralegh, it will be seen, offered her £80,000, with a touch of excusable hauteur. This touch, with lapses in times of extreme humiliation and peril, was to remain with him.

The settlement was complicated by the assistance given by the Earl of Cumberland's privateers in the capture. They maintained that Sir

28. Cecil to Sir Thomas Heneage.   29. September, 1592.

John Burrough's flagship, the *Roebuck,* and the Queen's ship, the *Fore-sight,* had been disabled, and that they themselves had done the actual boarding. The final division left Ralegh dissatisfied and bitter, but, under the circumstances, helpless. He had put his whole fortune into the enterprise, and had besides borrowed £11,000 at interest; and his elder brother, Carew Ralegh, had contributed the *Galleon,* of 250 tons and carrying 160 men. Cumberland, who had spent £19,000, got £36,-000; the City of London merchants, who had ventured £6000, got £12,000; and of the whole booty Elizabeth took half:

and we that served the Queen, and assisted her service, have not our own again. . . . I that adventured all my estate lose of my principal, and they have double. I took all the care and pains; carried the ships from hence to Falmouth, and from thence to the north cape of Spain; and they only sate still.[30]

But the Queen clutched all she could, grimly thinking that a man who had protested such devotion for over a decade had got off lightly with his gigantic fine for strayed affections.

From now, until his life's end, Ralegh is an unsuccessful man. But his loss, though he thought it heavy, was less than it seemed. His high place had encompassed him with continual envy but with little genuine esteem. His early military achievements, in personal quality striking enough, had never been scrutinized nor much admired; they had been in campaigns whose participants, then and now, can stir no more interest than belongs to wild beasts raging together, and they had almost at once dropped into obscurity. His ceaseless and uniquely effective war against Spain he had been allowed to wage only with his purse and patronage, while the Queen kept him dangling at her elbow. Had he so continued, he could have won little more respect or attention from us than we give to Sir Christopher Hatton. Of him, as Themistocles said of himself, we may say that, "had he not been undone he had remained undone for ever." The courtier is now finished, or all but finished; a very different and nobler man takes the stage.

30. Letter to Lord Burghley, December, 1592.

CHAPTER XI

Guiana

All the vessels of his home, table, and kitchen were of gold and silver, and the meanest of silver and copper for strength and hardness of the metal. He had in his wardroppe hollow statues of gold which seemed giants, and the figures in proportion and bigness of all the beasts, birds, trees and herbs, that the earth bringeth forth, and of all the fishes that the sea or waters of his kingdom breedeth. He had also ropes, budgets, chests and troughs of gold and silver, heaps of billets of gold that seemed wood marked out to burn. Finally, there was nothing in his country, whereof he had not the counterfeit in gold. Yea, and they say, The *Ingas* had a garden of pleasure in an island near Puna, where they went to recreate themselves, when they would take the air of the sea, which had all kind of garden herbs, flowers and trees of Gold and Silver, an invention and magnificence till then never seen. RALEGH's translation of Spanish accounts of the household of the Emperor of Guiana.

The account, which he published after his return, proves him to have been a master in the art of puffing. JOHN LINGARD.

Every page, nay, almost every sentence, awakened past recollections, and I felt in imagination transported once more into the midst of the stupendous scenery of the Tropics. . . . My chief object was to prove, from circumstances which fell within my own experience, the general correctness of Ralegh's descriptions, and to exculpate him from ungenerous reproaches. SIR ROBERT SCHOMBURGK.

RALEGH was still installed in Durham House, still engaged in Irish and parliamentary business. But the Queen had extorted a sum amounting to a quarter of her ordinary revenue, and in return tossed him the worst of both worlds—heavy and continuous expense to preserve splendor without the advantages that accompany splendor. For five years he was not allowed at Court, and his duties as Captain of the Guard were performed by deputy.

This was not an arrangement in which he was prepared to acquiesce. He tried hard to remind the Privy Council that he was an authority on important matters. Ireland was one, and he pursued his colonizing work there, though more languidly than formerly. But Ireland was beating him, as he deserved to be beaten by it. Despondent and exasperated, he burst out to Robert Cecil (May 10, 1593), that it was "no small dishonour" for England "to be vexed with so beggarly a nation, that have neither arms nor fortifications."

He was out, and his enemies meant that he should stay out. In January, 1594, when there was some veering or weakening of the adverse winds that had blown him from his course, Nicholas Faint[1] wrote: "it is now feared of all honest men that he shall presently come to the court; yet it is well withstood. God grant him some further resistance."[2] The prayer was heard. In May, Ralegh had to protest to the Lord Keeper, Egerton, against Star Chamber encroachment on his Stannary jurisdiction.

Blocked and baffled in his old lines of approach, Ralegh found a new one,

going aside, thereby to teach envy a new way of forgetfulness, and not so much as to think of him; howsoever, he had it always in mind never to forget himself, and his device took so well, that at his return he came in (as rams do, by going backward) with the greater strength, and so continued to her last, great in the Queen's grace, and captain of the guard.[3]

The *Madre de Dios* had freed him, when the Queen's wrath was at its most raging; this should bring him back, and win him his place in her council. Gold was what rulers dreamed of; gold they should have, and at his hands.

The assumption of David Hume and others, that Ralegh from beginning to end deliberately lied and invented about Guiana, does not deserve separate dismissal. It will disappear during our narrative. For the exaggerations in his account, these were set down by him in good faith and on the best contemporary evidence. His most extravagant details were copied from the mere facts of the astonishing civilization the Spaniards had found in Peru. We cannot demand that any man should

1. Formerly Walsingham's private secretary.
2. To Anthony Bacon (Birch, *Queen Elizabeth,* i, 151).
3. *Fragmenta Regalia.* But Naunton's memory has telescoped several years together; the Guiana voyage did nothing for Ralegh, it was only after Cadiz that he "came in . . . with the greater strength."

be wiser in his knowledge of the material world than his own generation at their wisest are.

It was known that when Pizarro conquered Peru, many of the people
fled inland. There was a tradition—which, when Ralegh lived, only a
fool would have doubted—that they had refounded their empire. Later,
better informed (and more careful) writers than David Hume accept

the probability that the Incas actually did succeed in prolonging their civ-
ilisation, apart from Spanish contamination, in the vast plains to the east-
ward of the Andes, for one or two centuries after the time of Pizarro. The
same story was told to me, when I was on the shores of the Purus in 1853,
and my informant pointed to the forests which stretched away to the hori-
zon, at the same time describing a lake, on the banks of which Ynti (the
Peruvian deity) still found adorers. It is a pleasant reflection that this story
may possibly be true.[4]

For seventy years Spaniards made successive thrusts into South America's heart, as mysterious then as Africa's in Livingstone's youth. They
slew ruthlessly, and were slain; and at last a handful with sun-black-
ened faces would stagger into the safety of Quito or Lima, bringing
little but tales of intolerable hardship. But one and all brought circumstantial report of a mighty realm whose magnificence recalled the
tales told of Peru by sober historians. When Ralegh read these stories,
they no more seemed incredible to him than they would have done to
us had we lived then and been steeped in the literature of the Americas
as he was. It was a *fact,* blazoned as hardly any fact ever had been, that
Spain had been gorged with gold from Peru. That gold must have come
from somewhere. The natural conclusion was that "Peru had a heart of
gold," which lay inland; "through the veins of Guiana flowed its
wealth."[5]

We may make a present at the outset of those few wilder reports
which Ralegh, in his almost feverish enthusiasm, set down; the cursory
reference to the

nation of people whose heads appear not above their shoulders; which,
though it may be thought a mere fable, yet for mine own part I am resolved

4. Sir Clements Markham, *Expeditions into the Valley of the Amazons* (Hakluyt Society, 1859), Introduction, p. xlv.

5. Irvin Anthony, *Ralegh,* p. 145.

it is true, because every child in the provinces of Arromaia and Canuri affirm the same. They are called Ewaipanoma; they are reported to have their eyes in their shoulders, and their mouths in the middle of their breasts, and that a long train of hair groweth backward between the shoulders.

Shakespeare has remembered this passage as part of Othello's enchantment of Desdemona by narrative:

> the Cannibals that each other eat,
> The Anthropophagi, and men whose heads
> Do grow beneath their shoulders;[6]

and remembered it more seriously, in another play, which is not friendly or respectful to so great a man as Ralegh. But Shakespeare was an enthusiastic member of the faction of Essex. In *The Tempest,* therefore, he sneers at those who bring Indians for London to gape at;[7] and at promoters of wild enterprises, with their yarns of

> mountaineers
> Dewlapped like bulls, whose throats had hanging at them
> Wallets of flesh . . . such men
> Whose heads stood in their breasts—which now we find
> Each putter-out of five for one will bring us
> Good warrant of.[8]

These were the stories which justified him, David Hume considered, in stigmatizing Ralegh as author of "the grossest and most palpable lies that were ever attempted to be imposed on the credulity of mankind."[9] The eighteenth century, which inhabited a neat Vauxhall Gardens of a world, before explorers had presented men's vision with the duckbill platypus and the okapi, was shocked by sober willingness to consider what had come with abundant serious testimony. All we need do is note how tiny a space these marvels fill in Ralegh's account—there set down apologetically, because they came in his story, and a conscientious narrator could not dismiss them summarily. Schomburgk testifies to having heard the same stories, centuries later, told circumstantially by tribes that believed them.[10]

6. *Othello,* I, iii, 143–145.   7. *The Tempest,* II, ii, 55.
8. *Ibid.,* III, iii, 44–48.   9. *History of England* (under year 1596), v, 377.
10. In 1844. See his edition of *The Discoverie of Guiana,* pp. xliv and 212.

As regards the ethics of trying to win for England a share in the immense New World that Columbus had discovered, Ralegh's attitude was very like that of some Germans toward the British Empire in 1914. He intensely admired the Spaniards' constancy, courage, and enterprise, but thought it preposterous that they should claim to hold what was far beyond their resources of man-power, and should refuse other countries any "place in the sun." This was his specific charge against them. He made others also. Enthralled by the astonishing history of the Conquistadores, he was repelled by their fiendish and incredible cruelty. His pity for the Indians whom they had burnt alive and torn to pieces with dogs, inflicting tortures hardly paralleled elsewhere, even in mankind's miserable annals, was deep and genuine, as pity is with an imaginative mind. The bullion that he seized from Spanish ships he took without qualms; he considered it had been stolen. He considered it more useful to mankind, as well as to his own country, in his hands. England, he believed (conveniently forgetting Ireland, as all Englishmen did), was a better and more merciful master, a thousand times, than the gallant brutes who had inflicted such suffering and wrung such treasures from America.

We can trace the settling down of his gaze on Guiana and its fabled hinterland of El Dorado, in a letter written by his wife, February 8, 1594. She was expecting the birth of their first son; and she turns to Robert Cecil, whose kindness was assumed by them both (and in her case seems to have existed), and pleads with him to use his influence against Guiana:

I hope for my sake you will rather draw sur watar towardes the est than heulp hyme forward toward the soonsett, if ani respecke to me or love to him be not forgotten. But everi monthe hath his flower and everi season his contentment, and you greate counselares ar so full of new councels, as you ar steddi in nothing; but wee poore soules that hath bought sorrow at a high price desiar, and can be plesed with, the same misfortun wee hold, fering alltarracions will but multiply misseri, of wich we have allredi felt sufficiant. I knoo unly your parswadcions ar of efecke with him, and hild as orrekeles tied to them by Love; therfore I humbelle besiech you rathar stay him then furdar him. By the wich you shall bind me for ever . . .[11]

11. Edwards, *Ralegh*, ii, 397–398.

But her husband had found that which drives the earnest spirit forward—a comrade who shared his belief. Laurence Kemys, at the age of twenty or less, while still an undergraduate, had been made Fellow of Balliol, in 1583. He had proceeded to B.A. and M.A., had become Notary and Bursar, and remained a Fellow until 1591.[12] He has left Latin verses on Guiana, an unusual accomplishment for a "rough sailor";[13] more ordinary qualifications for the rôle forced on him by Ralegh's unfriendliest critic were those which Anthony à Wood says[14] he possessed, skill in geography and mathematics. He left his comfortable and honored place, and sacrificed all to follow Ralegh.

The royal patent, by a precedent grimly repeated in his last voyage, was addressed to "our servant Sir Walter Ralegh," neither "trusty" nor "well beloved," but plainly still under the cloud of his Queen's anger. The usual sanction, "to discover and subdue heathen lands not in possession of any Christian prince, or inhabited by any Christian people," was wider than the later sanction, and authorized him "to offend and enfeeble the King of Spain," and "to resist and expel" anyone who tried to settle within 200 leagues of the place he chose for his colony. He and Kemys sailed, February 6, 1595. Of their five ships, two somehow missed the others, and another small galley was lost sight of near Spain. Only Ralegh's own ship and one other reached Trinidad (March 22).

Trinidad was under a Governor, Antonio de Berreo, who was partly responsible for Ralegh's arrival now. In April, 1593, he had sent thirty-five men up the Orinoco, to annex it, and find its fabled capital, Manoa. A copy of his official report had fallen into the hands of Ralegh's privateers, and in 1594 Ralegh had sent his old servant, Captain Jacob Whiddon,[15] to make a reconnaissance of Guiana. Berreo invited some of Whiddon's men ashore, and murdered them. This action was merely his way of signifying that the Englishmen's presence in that part of the world was distasteful to him. A wide latitude of conduct was allowed and expected in America, and Ralegh speaks highly of Berreo, as "a

12. Information supplied from College records, by the present Master of Balliol.
13. S. R. Gardiner's description of him. Wood says (*Athenae Oxonienses*, i, 433) that Kemys was "born of sufficient (and, I think, genteel) parents."
14. *Athenae Oxonienses*, i, 433.
15. "A man most honest and valiant." Ralegh, *The Discoverie of Guiana* (Hakluyt's *Voyages*, "Everyman's Library," vii, 282).

gentleman well descended . . . very valiant and liberal . . . of great assuredness and of a great heart. I used him according to his estate and worth in all things I could." That, however, was presently.

It was a race between England and Spain. Ralegh began with an enthralled survey of Trinidad, missing nothing, from the oysters on the mangroves ("very salt and well tasted") to the lake of pitch, now a tourists' show place, but then new and mysterious. Berreo was hanging and quartering Indians who showed the newcomers friendliness. But under cover of darkness some began to visit Ralegh. Owing Berreo somewhat for his reception of Whiddon, he remarks that to have alarmed Spain by explorations and have then gone away would have been silly. "I should have savoured very much of the Ass." So he surprised the new Spanish settlement of San Joseph, capturing Berreo. The action cannot have been liked by the Spaniards. But it is humbug to call it treachery, as Lingard does.[16] "That he might not savour of the ass, he became a murderer." England and Spain were officially, as well as actually, at war. "Less particular"[17] than Lingard, Berreo and the Spanish Government

saw nothing in his conduct adverse to the laws of war and nations. If their soldiers had arrived in time, they would have anticipated him in the aggression. Throughout this whole period Spaniards and Englishmen, on the ocean and in the Indies, fought or fought not, as suited not merely their mutual, but their several, convenience. Neither side held it treachery to be assailed without a solemn declaration of war.

Ralegh merely did exactly what Berreo would have liked to do.

Berreo had fiendishly executed Indians; and Ralegh freed from a den five caciques bound together, "almost dead of famine and wasted with torments." Then he took Berreo off as an honored guest, with whom he soon set up relations of mutual if guarded esteem. He was queerly tolerant of this accomplished brute, far more so than Berreo would have been of him. But his pity for the Indians is plain in his narrative, and his own behavior toward them was centuries in advance of his age. He gathered their tribes, and showed them his Queen's portrait, "which they so much admired and honoured as it had been easy to have brought them idolatrous thereof"; and explained that he was

16. *History of England,* ix, 227–228.   17. Stebbing, p. 113.

the servant of a Queen who was the great cacique of the north and a virgin, who had more caciques under her than there were trees in the island, that she was an enemy of the Castellanos in respect of their tyranny and oppression, and that she delivered all such nations about her as were by them oppressed, and having freed all the coast of the northern world from their servitude had sent me to free them also, and withal to defend the country of Guiana from their invasion and conquest.

Berreo's cruelties had so roused the Indians that Spain had been compelled to evacuate Guiana, except for a mere garrison left on an eastern branch of the Orinoco delta, which did not trouble Ralegh when he presently made his way up the western channel. Internecine hostility also threatened the Spanish hold on the country, such as it was. Wherever they went, the Conquistadores quarrelled and fought among themselves. Berreo, whose ambition to annex Guiana had not been supported, and over whom another man had been put, was excessively bitter. Both pique and a humorous willingness to mislead the Englishman probably contributed to his communicativeness. But when he understood that his host was not merely showing curiosity, but meant to explore and take the land, "he was stricken with great melancholy and sadness, and used all the arguments he could to dissuade me, and also assured the gentlemen of my company that it would be labour lost, and that they should suffer many miseries if they proceeded." His pleadings failed, and Ralegh entered on a course of unspeakably arduous exploration, from which his mind took in pictures transmitted to us in prose that keeps the stormy threatening outline of his experience:

in the bottom of an old Galego which I caused to be fashioned like a galley, and in one barge, two whirries, and a shipboat of *The Lion's Whelp,* we carried 100 persons and their victuals for a month . . . being all driven to lie in the rain and weather, in the open air, in the burning Sun, and upon the hard boards, and to dress our meat, and to carry all manner of furniture in them, wherewith they were so pestered and unsavoury, that, what with victuals being most fish, with wet clothes of so many men thrust together, and the heat of the Sun, I will undertake there was never any prison in England, that could be found more unsavoury and loathsome, especially to myself, who had for many years before been dieted and cared for in a sort far more differing.

They explored "the great river of Orenoque or Baraquan"—which Kemys renamed, and ever after scrupulously called, Raleana—"that disemboqueth by sixteen arms in all," between islands "very great, many of them as big as the Isle of Wight, and bigger, and many less." They had reached a point 300 miles from the sea, when Ralegh was visited by Topiawari,

the king of Aromaia, uncle to Morequito, slain by Berreo . . . he came to us on foot from his house, which was 14 English miles, (himself being 110 years old), and returned on foot the same day, and with him many of the borderers, with many women and children, that came to wonder at our nation, and to bring us down victual, which they did in great plenty, as venison, pork, hens, chickens, fowl, fish, with divers sorts of excellent fruits, and roots, and great abundance of *Pinas,* the princess of fruits.

In that last judgment King James afterwards agreed with Ralegh, after his first taste of a pineapple remarking that it was too good for a subject to eat. The Indians brought also bread, wine, parakeets, "and one of them gave me a beast called by the Spaniards *Armadilla,* which they called *Cassacam,* which seemeth to be all barred over with small plates somewhat like to a Renocero." Ralegh ate the armadillo.

Asking Topiawari of his predecessor, Ralegh opened afresh deep wounds. The old man, who was "every day called for by death, which was also his own phrase," expanded to his eager interest and sympathy, and talked freely yet with dignity. Ralegh knew a man when he met one, and he gave as well as won respect. Topiawari, who had been dragged in a chain by Berreo for seventeen days, until he ransomed himself with a hundred plates of gold and strings of spleenstones, was anxious for a coalition against the Spaniards. It was now that Ralegh's mind took the impress of an idea it never lost: he saw an English protectorate which should make life and possessions safe for these gentle savages, and provide a shadow under which they could grow into the arts of civilization. He saw England stepping into the place of Spain, which had been weighed in the balance and found wanting.

The English went altogether 400 miles up-river from the sea. They trusted themselves to the kindness of the natives, walking across the Guiana plains in tiny bands, Ralegh with less than a dozen companions, Kemys with half a dozen. To the timid persecuted people they were a new kind of European; and, dreading the inevitable coming of the Spaniards from the coast, the chiefs everywhere eagerly offered their allegiance to Ralegh's Queen. He accepted it, and his heart was to endure a long-drawn bitterness in later years, when he was a prisoner and compelled to betray the confidence he had encouraged. His noble courtesy won a forlorn loyalty. "I am assured now that they will all die even to the last man against the Spaniards, in hope of our succour and return." Topiawari said that, if fifty Englishmen were left to defend his province against Spanish vengeance, he would himself lead the others to Manoa the Golden. Ralegh could not do this, but promised to return next year; and was given young Indian men to take to England, to show them its marvels and bring them back. When finally the strangers who had been so powerful, yet so trustful and unfailingly gentle, vanished down Orinoco's ways, they left a memory as of some apparition of gods. As late as 1769, Bancroft found that the Guianans retained a tradition of an English cacique who had come "and encouraged them to persevere in enmity to the Spaniards," promising return and assistance and to settle among them. It was said that they still preserved "an English Jack, which he left there, that they might distinguish his countrymen."[18]

After seeing Topiawari, the English tried to force their way up the Caroni. But the current was so overmastering that "we were not able with a barge of eight oars to row one stone's cast in an hour." They disembarked therefore, and Ralegh and a few others walked inland until they could see a waterfall, now famous:

When we were come to the tops of the first hills of the plains adjoining to the river, we beheld that wonderful breach of waters, which ran down Caroli: and might from that mountain see the river, how it ran in three parts, above twenty miles off; and there appeared some ten or twelve overfalls in sight, every one as high over the other as a Church tower, which fell with that fury, that the rebound of water made it seem as if it had been all covered over with a great shower of rain: and in some places we took it at the first for a smoke that had risen over some great town. For mine own part, I was well persuaded from thence to have returned, being a very ill footman; but the rest were all so desirous to go near the said strange thunder of waters, as they drew me on by little and little, till we came into the next

18. *Essay on the Natural History of Guiana*, p. 258.

valley where we might better discern the same. I never saw a more beautiful country, nor more lively prospects, hills so raised here and there over the valleys, the river winding into divers branches, the plains adjoining without bush or stubble, all fair green grass, the ground of hard sand easy to march on, either for horse or foot, the deer crossing in every path, the birds towards the evening singing on every tree with a thousand several tunes, cranes and herons of white, crimson, and carnation perching in the river's side, the air fresh with a gentle Easterly wind, and every stone that we stooped to take up promised either gold or silver by his complexion . . . and yet we had no means but with our daggers and fingers to tear them out here and there, the rocks being most hard of that mineral Spar aforesaid, which is like a flint and is altogether as hard or harder, and besides, the veins lie a fathom or two deep in the rocks.

Orinoco had risen. "All the night it was stormy and dark, and full of thunder and great showers . . . we were heartily afraid both of the billow and terrible current." Hearts "grew cold" to see "the great rage and increase" of the river. They abandoned the expedition to Manoa, the reported capital of the Guianan Empire, whose king and court in annual solemn feast so picturesquely disported themselves:

first stripped naked, and their bodies anointed all over with a kind of white balsamum . . . when certain servants of the Emperor, having prepared gold made into fine powder, blow it thorow hollow canes upon their naked bodies, until they be all shining from the foot to the head; and in this sort they sit drinking by twenties, and hundreds, and continue in drunkenness sometimes six or seven days together.[19]

Of this and similar stories the Spanish narratives, flowering wildly (yet in the light of what was known to have been true of the empires of the Aztecs and Incas, it could hardly have seemed extravagantly), were full.[20] Berreo had told Ralegh a tale whose mystic quality never ceased to haunt him, as it haunted also the minds of the next generation. It was of one Martinez, a Spanish officer condemned to death for negligence, but spared to the extent of being marooned on Orinoco's

19. For Ralegh's Guianan customs anthropologists can find adequate foundation. But his inland sea, his "Lake of Parima," we now know was nothing but Orinoco's vast inundations.

20. The story was heard by Sir Robert Dudley, earlier in this year of Ralegh's own voyage (1595). See Dudley's account in Hakluyt.

current, where Guianans found and took him off as a curiosity, to the "great city of Manoa, the seat and residence of Inga the emperor." Well treated, he was kept strict prisoner for seven months, and then conducted out of the country blindfold as he had been brought. Martinez, Berreo told Ralegh, was the person who invented the name *El Dorado*, from the gilded men who feasted together; and this was his account of the fourteen or fifteen days of hooded journeying by which he first reached Manoa:

He avowed at his death that he entered the city at Noon, and then they uncovered his face, and that he travelled all that day till night through the city, and the next day, from Sun rising to Sun setting, ere he came to the palace of Inga.

Prevented by storms from going on to Virginia from Guiana, Ralegh reached England in August, after seven months' absence. His explorations had so little rehabilitated him, that the jesting at his tall stories, which was to continue so long after his death, began immediately. He had been merely hiding in Cornwall, and had found his gold and silver ores in that county! He defended himself in his fervent *Discoverie of Guiana,* not in the least the farrago of legend which many have alleged, but a storehouse of first-hand impressions and of information of every kind, for the most part astoundingly accurate as well as vivid. He scornfully waved aside the charge that he had sailed in hope of getting money. He could have achieved that better, by privateering! But

it became not the former fortune in which I once lived, to go journeys of picory. It had sorted ill with the offices of Honour which by Her Majesty's grace I hold this day in England, to run from Cape to Cape, and from place to place, for the pillage of ordinary prizes.

Guiana promised England renown, as well as resources. The Americas' wealth had lifted the King of Spain "in a few years, from a poor king of Castile, to the greatest monarch of this part of the world, and likely every day to increase, if other princes forslow the good occasions offered." Spain was now all set to enter Guiana, "the Magazine of all rich metals." Peru and Mexico had been sacked and ransacked. But here was a country that hath yet her maidenhead, never sacked, turned, nor wrought, the face of the earth hath not been torn, nor the virtue and salt of the soil spent by manurance; the graves have not been opened for gold, the mines not broken with sledges, nor their Images pulled down out of their temples. It hath never been entered by any army of strength, and never conquered or possessed by any Christian Prince.

His pleadings met with no response. Elizabeth had grown old, and her Government was long sunk in the shoals of hesitation and nervelessness which mark its dragging last years. One by one Ralegh's own peers in courage were passing from the scene: Gilbert had gone long ago, Frobisher died of wounds, 1594, Sir John Hawkins died in 1595, and Drake in 1596. Ralegh, who had been a marked man for many years, was left alone, in perilous eminence. In November, 1595, the Spanish Government heard how the notorious English pirate Guatteral, "after having caused much trouble and injury to the Isle of Trinidad and its inhabitants," had entered the Orinoco. He was now exposed to Spanish enmity and English courtier derision alike.

He urged in vain an alternative plan—not of conquest, but of alliance with Manoa's emperor—merely to send a few hundred armorers, artificers, soldiers—a protectorate, with colonization and mining in certain districts. The Guianans should be on an equality with the English, some of them annually brought to England for education and given English wives. They should be civilized and Christianized. In a few years, London would have "a contraction house of more receipt for Guiana than that of Seville for the West Indies." The scheme looks absurd, only because his freedom from racial feeling is not ours. He felt distress that England should lose so fair an opportunity; should falter, and then deliberately leave so plain a path to greatness.

He was unable to keep his promise to return next year. But he strained his resources, despite the Cadiz expedition, and in January, 1596, sent Kemys on a third voyage, with two ships, one lent by Robert Cecil—"bravely furnisht, the very Hull stands in £800."[21] Lord Burghley also helped, with £500. Kemys found the Indians dreading and hating the Spaniards, whose habit was "to borrow some of their wives." Living "betwixt hope and fear" they had "earnestly expected

21. Rowland Whyte to Sir Robert Sidney, December 13, 1595 (Collins, *Letters and Memorials of State,* ii, 1698).

our return . . . these four or five months." He reminded them that "at our departure we left no Spaniards alive to annoy them" (possibly a reference to Ralegh's supposed extirpation of Berreo's—again, supposi- tional—first feeble foundation of San Thomé in 1591 or 1592); and, everywhere moving freely among them (as no Spaniard would have dared), he strengthened them in their resolution to remain free and to join themselves to the English. Ralegh's annexation of the country and acceptance of its people's allegiance in Elizabeth's name was completed by Kemys, who made the first chart of the coast,[22] and list of rivers sighted along it.

On his return, he published a report[23] as pleading as Ralegh's own, desiring "to remove all fig-leaves from our unbelief" and "to shake off the colourable pretences of ignorance." "Myself, and the remain of my few years, I have bequeathed wholly to Raleana, and all my thoughts live only in that action." He is full of sturdy loyalty and outspoken praise of his patron: "of all men living in his days, most industrious in seeking, most fortunate in attaining to the fulness of an inestimable public good." Passionately, even desperately, eager, he stressed the ac- tivity to which Spain had been spurred of a sudden. Immediately after Ralegh had left in the previous year, Berreo had placed a lock on the confluence of Orinoco and Caroni, in a battery commanding it, and a tiny settlement, San Thomé, "a Rancheria of some twenty or thirty houses." The Spaniards had further fortified a "high rocky Island" in mid-Orinoco, opposite the infall of the Caroni, and had placed

a secret ambush, to defend the passage to those mines, from whence your rare and white stones were taken the last winter. We all, not without grief to see ourselves thus defeated and our hungry hopes made void, were wit- nesses of this their remove.

Those "rare and white stones," wrenched out with daggers and fin- gers, had not particularly impressed Ralegh at the time. But he believed that genuine veins lay a fathom or two deeper down. This was his original "mine," and its reality seemed now confirmed by Berreo's elabo- rate measures to defend the way to it. But Ralegh and Kemys had learnt of a second mine, in their 1595 visit. Ralegh's Indian guide had

22. J. A. Williamson, *English Colonies in Guiana*, p. 25.
23. See also Thomas Masham's account, Hakluyt, viii, 1–13.

then persuaded him to walk some distance inland, from a point twenty miles lower. He was shown more stones, which again did not seem much to him. Being a poor walker, he had gone back to his ships, leaving Kemys with six musketeers to walk parallel to the river, and rejoin him. Kemys afterwards recollected that at one place his guide became excited, and signed to him to follow; he had refused, supposing that it was another waterfall. It was merely "an ordinary incident of travel,"[24] and probably slipped out only casually when he was talking to Ralegh afterwards. Kemys learnt later, however, that the guide had wanted to show him where gold existed; and on his return, in 1596, thought he would inquire further. He could not find his former guide; but his Indian pilot told the same story at the same place, offering to guide him to wonderful gold deposits, under Mt. Aio, a day's march from where they lay at anchor. But Kemys would not risk plunging into the forest, now that Spanish troops were in Guiana. He calculated, from appearances, that Mt. Aio was about fifteen miles from the river. This second "mine" (which even Kemys never actually saw), from its double confirmation took on in after-years, as he and Ralegh talked together, a significance which was to put the first mine—that near San Thomé, and near the meeting of Caroni and Orinoco—entirely in the background of their thought. It was the cause of their destruction, twenty years later.

Ralegh and Guiana left the Queen and her Councillors cold, with the exception of the Cecils. But his *Discoverie of the large and bewtiful Empire of Guiana* was at once successful, being republished in the year of its appearance, 1596. There have been at least half a dozen reprints since. There were numerous translations, some in Ralegh's own lifetime. Between 1598 and 1747, six Dutch editions appeared. There were Latin and French translations also.

The book came home most of all to the imagination of Ralegh's own intellectual peers. I have thrown out hints of the way in which Shakespeare's *Tempest* is haunted by it, even if the references are tinged with hostility. Mr. Harlow points out that Caliban, "half-man, half-beast, is surely a representation of the primitive races spoken of by Ralegh. The grotesque monster bears no relation to the Red Indian of Virginia or

24. Gardiner, *History of England,* 1603–1642, ii, 375.

the negro of the Guinea Coast."[25] With the Puritans of the next two generations Ralegh was a heroic memory, consecrated by his sacrifice to Spain by a dastardly king; and I never read Milton's descriptions of Eden or Bunyan's description of the Land of Beulah, without being sure that behind them shakes the remembered tapestry of Ralegh's pictures of the kindly plains of Guiana. His Gilded Man has had an apotheosis in the Shining Ones who inhabit a City yet more splendid than Manoa.

But it is on Milton that his influence was strongest and most pervading. It is clear on many a page of Milton's prose works; and no one can read Ralegh's many and crowded lists of strange and sounding names, without seeing how Milton must have delighted in them and lingered over them. There are no such lists of names in literature anywhere, outside *Paradise Lost,* as we find in Raleigh's *Discoverie of Guiana.* The poet takes over the latter's name for the unfortunate Peruvian king, *Atabalipa.* I do not quote Ralegh's most sonorous list of all, that beginning "In the Port towns of the Province of Venezuela," for there is a more direct connection between Ralegh's

Guiana, and that great and golden City, which the Spaniards call El Dorado, and the naturals Manoa, which City was conquered, re-edified, and enlarged by a younger son of Guainacapa, Emperor of Peru, at such time as Francisco Pizarro and others conquered the said Empire from his two elder brethren, Guascar and Atabalipa, both then contending for the same, the one being favoured by the Orejones of Cuzco,

and Milton's

> Rich Mexico, the seat of Montezume,
> And Cuzco in Peru, the richer seat
> Of Atabalipa, and yet unspoiled[26]
> Guiana, whose great City Geryon's sons
> Call El Dorado.

Ralegh solaced himself as he might, by keeping in touch with the Orinoco tribes, while he and Kemys watched until God should grant a day for their dream's fulfilment. He remained in shadow, unforgiven

25. *The Discoverie of Guiana,* p. xcix.
26. Cf. Guiana, "that hath yet her maidenhead," etc.

and uninfluential. Not even the jewels he had brought to appeal to Elizabeth's passion for finery—his stone "which I think is amatist, and hath the strange blush of carnation" and his other stone, which, "if it be no diamond, yet it is exceeding any diamond in beauty"—won him a return to favor. He says angrily (November 13, 1595), that he is "not in haste" to let them

go out of my fingers. But these stones bear witness of better, and there is enough for all the world, if we have the grace. . . . If the Spaniards had bin so blockish and slothful, we had not feared now their power, who by their gold from thence vex and endanger all the estates of kings.

The Queen understood what he wanted; and she did not believe in Guiana.

Nor was a letter to the Privy Council, a fortnight later (November 25, 1595), discussing defense measures for Devon and Cornwall against a rumored Spanish attack, and considering minutely the nature of the coast and country, given much attention. He had to stay fretting his heart out at Sherborne—sometimes taking the waters at Bath, sometimes visiting Weymouth for sea-bathing. There was no employment for him, other than he could find for himself, and that which was left to him in his own two western counties. He was definitely relegated to helplessness and obscurity. In Chapman's verses, prefixed to Kemys' account, Guiana appealed to the "thronèd Vestal of the West":

> Guiana, whose rich seat are mines of gold,
> Whose forehead knocks against the roof of stars,
> Stands on her tiptoes, at fair England looking,
> Kissing her hand, bowing her mighty breast,
> And every sign of all submission making,
> To be her sister and her daughter both,
> Of our most sacred maid . . .

The English Queen was urged to send out bands of young colonists, who would

> take Hymen's lights in hand
> And fill each roof with honoured progeny.

And there do palaces and temples rise
Out of the earth and kiss enamoured skies,
Where New Britannia humbly kneels to heaven—
The world to her—and both at her blest feet,
In whom the circles of all empires meet.

Hymen's lights stirred no enthusiasm in the lady addressed. The mention reminded her of how the discoverer of Guiana had rekindled them, in her own chaste court.

Colonization schemes were too far ahead of the age to be taken seriously. But there was another concept included in the name *Guiana* that had more chance—the one expressed in Chapman's naïve picture of the welcome awaiting those who went thither:

A world of savages fall tame before them,
Storing their theft-free treasuries with gold.[27]

Ralegh accordingly had to talk of gold, and to talk of it increasingly—baiting prospectuses with it, bidding his surveyors waste time hunting for ore that would prove its existence. This, although he had early come to a clear perception of its relative and comparatively unimportant usefulness! Thinking of families, now leading a pent-down pestered existence, expanding elsewhere to a released and vigorous one as free nations linked to England by gratitude and common blood, he saw that gold was merely a medium of trade, and in itself nothing; and that Spain, flooding the Old World with precious metals, had deflated currencies and raised the cost of living. His own resources, not only in his brief day of opulence but throughout his long evening of disgrace and powerlessness, were poured out on enterprises whose ends, as he well knew, were far out of sight and beyond the finish of his own life. But, since everyone else—the exceptions, Hariot, Kemys, and a few others, were men working under his inspiration, and directed by him—dreamed of gold, and demanded gold, to win any support at all he *must* drag in the metal:

it was futile to discuss any aspect of discovery . . . save that of gold discovery. Many . . . seemed to think gold was found in mines piled up in convenient bars.[28]

27. Chapman, *Works*, iii, 50.   28. W. McFee, *Sir Martin Frobisher*, p. 31.

He sent out to Guiana yet a fourth expedition—a pinnace, the *Wat* (named after himself, or, more probably, after his son). It sailed, December 27, 1596, and reached Guiana, February 27, 1597. Its crew were everywhere enthusiastically received by the Indians, for their master's sake. But this was all he was to achieve; events that shook Spain in her center of power now occupied all his energies, and then his life of voyaging was ended by his enemies.

CHAPTER XII

Sea Exploits. The Taking of Cadiz

Now all the youth of England are on fire,
And silken dalliance in the wardrobe lies. *Henry V*.

He . . . called upon to face
Some awful moment to which Heaven has joined
Great issues, good or bad for human kind,
Is happy as a Lover, and attired
With sudden brightness, like a Man inspired.

The Happy Warrior.

AS long ago as December, 1587, Sir John Hawkins had urged an attack on Cadiz, the naval base of Spain. Ralegh eagerly supported him: the thing could have been easily achieved, "if the Queen would have hearkened to reason."[1] But she refused to hearken to it till, ten years after, her Government was frightened by defeats in Ireland and by Spain's alliance with the Earl of Tyrone and her reappearance off the coast, in the Breton ports possessed by the Catholic League. Then the one home-thrust of the Elizabethan sea-struggle was made.

Early in 1596, Essex and Ralegh, whom events were temporarily drawing together, were told to advise jointly on coast defense. Drake and Hawkins were dead; their successors were a man whom the Queen had hitherto denied actual participation in what his brain planned, and a nobleman who was a courageous blunderer. Partisans did their best to mar their coöperation. Ralegh, collecting crews to attack Spain at home, wrote to Cecil (May 4, 1596): "as fast as we press men one day they come away another, and say they will not serve. . . . I cannot write to our generals at this time; for the poursevant found me in a country village, a mile from Gravesend, hunting after runaway mariners, and dragging in the mire from alehouse to alehouse, and could get no paper, but that the poursevant had this piece." The sycophants

1. Ralegh, *A Discourse of the Marriage of Princess Elizabeth* (*Works*, viii, 246).

who crowded round Essex, ignorant of these dreary activities in remote
Thames estuary hamlets, explained Ralegh's absence in their own fashion. His "slackness and stay by the way," observed that generous member of a generous family, Anthony Bacon, "is not thought to be upon
sloth or negligence, but upon pregnant design."[2] Bacon's friend, Sir
Anthony Standen, wrote back from Exeter, May 18:

There was no speech of the departure of the fleet, there being no kind of
news of Sir Walter Ralegh, whose stay seemed to stay all and to put the
Earl of Essex to insupportable charges.

These suspicions were resented by Ralegh's young brother-in-law,
Arthur Throckmorton. He quarrelled publicly with Essex, after having
drunk too much (an enemy version, possibly true), and was ordered
away from table.

Presently Ralegh arrived. He took in the state of affairs, and was extremely tactful, determined not to lose his chance, which had come
after so long waiting. The squabble, so far as he had been involved in
it, was officially settled. Arthur Throckmorton was dismissed (it can
only have been temporarily) from the Army, and remained under
arrest. Ralegh's politeness his enemies interpreted as cunning mock
humility.

The expedition proceeded to gather itself together; and as a proof
that this was to be a campaign in earnest, the usual mutinies and desertions were sternly handled, and at once. Essex solemnly hanged two
offenders, "on a very fair pleasant green called the Ho."[3] Then everyone was ready to sail. A Dutch squadron (24 ships and 2600 men) accompanied 96 English ships of all sorts, carrying 14,000 men (including a thousand gentlemen volunteers). The English sailed in four
squadrons, one[4] being under Ralegh as Lord Warden. Essex and Lord
Howard were in joint supreme responsibility, supported by a Council
of Five—Ralegh and Lord Thomas Howard as possessing special sea
experience, Sir Francis Vere and Sir Conyers Clifford as soldiers, Sir
George Carew as Master of the Ordnance. Sir Anthony Ashley was

2. Birch, *Memoirs of Queen Elizabeth*, i, 486.
3. *Purchas his Pilgrimes* (James MacLehose & Sons, 1907), xx, 7.
4. 22 ships, 1353 sailors, 1875 soldiers.

Secretary of the Council. The Queen had written a special prayer. They sailed, June 1.

Every captain had sealed instructions—not to be opened unless the fleet were scattered by storms—to be flung into the sea if he fell into the enemy's hands. On the 18th, an Irishman who had come directly from Cadiz was captured, and from him it was learnt that it was full of shipping, including 18 or 19 galleys, among them "divers of the King's best." Two days later the inhabitants of the doomed city through the early dimness saw, anchored a league away, the terrifying apparition that had come softly out of the north. The town's President wrote to King Philip that they inferred they were about to be attacked by a combined French, English and Dutch fleet—such was the uncertainty as to what quarter of the sky might rain tempest in those days. With detached artistic appreciation, he testified that the enemy formed "the most beautiful armada that was ever seen." "A very fair Dove" alighted, "very timely," on the Lord Admiral's mainyard, and sat there "very quietly for the space of three or four hours."[5] Heaven and all strong angels were prospering the enterprise, as they had prospered none before it.

A line of Spanish ships ran out of harbor, and stood on guard. The sea being rough, attempts to land troops failed, so a Council of War was held, from which Ralegh, who had been sent to scour the coast for fugitive vessels trying to slip by, was absent. It decided to attack the city before attacking the galleons, "my Lord Admiral being careful of Her Majesty's ships."[6] Elizabethan commanders had to keep close watch on the national budget, even in moments of extreme urgency, and ships were more important than men were. There was no lavish expenditure on side-shows; we can guess with what horror they would have regarded a proposal to send into submarine-infested straits comparatively old vessels to find out what hostile strength was lurking there! Every penny had to be saved, every ship kept from everything except absolutely unavoidable peril. The enemy *looked* too safe, having "a wonderful advantage of us, all circumstances being well weighed,

5. *Purchas*, xx, 8.
6. Sir Walter Ralegh's narrative, Edwards, ii, 146.

but especially the straitness of the place, and the natural form and situation of the Bay itself."[7]

When Ralegh arrived, disembarkation was in process, in a wild sea where boats were sinking, crews and all. In dismay, he went to Essex and

protested against the resolution, giving him reasons, and making apparent demonstrations that he hereby ran the way of our general ruin, to the utter overthrow of the whole armies, their own lives, and Her Majesty's future safety. The Earl excused himself, and laid it to the Lord Admiral, who (he said) "would not consent to enter with the fleet till the town were first possessed." All the commanders and gentlemen present besought me to dissuade the attempt; for they all perceived the danger and were resolved that the most part could not but perish in the sea, ere they came to set foot on ground; and if any arrived on shore, yet were they sure to have their boats cast on their heads; and that twenty men in so desperate a descent would have defeated them all. The Earl hereupon prayed me to persuade my Lord Admiral.

This was Ralegh's highest point of greatness, his by reason of outstanding ability, acknowledged when the crisis had become desperate. A bigoted stupidity in the highest commands was working to make the Cadiz triumph into just one of the wretched scatterings of life and resources, a Walcheren or Passchendaele. The moment was his, but only the moment; for "it was only for a moment, at Cadiz or Fayal, that by a doubtful breach of prerogative he struggled to the surface, to sink again directly the achievement was accomplished."[8] He now hurried from Essex to the Lord Admiral, whom he found embarrassed by the plain ruin to which all was tending. Lord Howard consented to countermand the disembarkation. As Ralegh returned and his boat swung rocking by, Essex and his officers crowded to the rails of their ship to hear his news. He shouted in Spanish, *Entramos;* and the Earl answered the schoolboy joyousness of this anouncement with the gesture ever since famous. He flung his hat into the sea.

The day was growing late (another circumstance making for destruction if the attempt had been persisted in); and it proved a hard job to recover the scattered and sometimes half-swamped boatloads.

7. *Purchas,* xx, 9.   8. Edmund Gosse, *Raleigh,* p. 131.

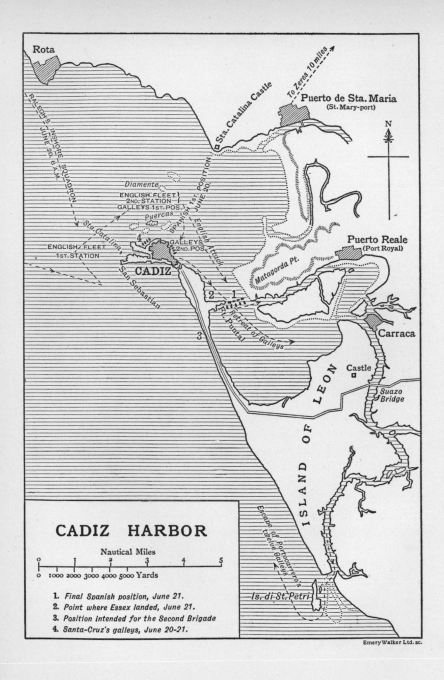

Rota

To Zeres 10 miles

Sta. Catalina Castle

Puerto de Sta. Maria
(St. Mary-port)

N

RALEGH'S INSHORE SQUADRON JUNE 20. 6 A.M.

Diamente
ENGLISH FLEET
2ND. STATION
GALLEYS 1ST. POS.
Puercas

Sta. Catalina

SPANISH 1ST. POSITION JUNE 20.

English Attack

ENGLISH FLEET
1ST. STATION

4

GALLEYS
2ND. POS.

CADIZ

San Sebastian

2   1

Fr. Puntal

Retreat of Galleys

Matagorda Pt.

Puerto Reale
(Port Royal)

Carraca

3

Castle

Suazo
Bridge

ISLAND OF LEON

Escape of Portocarrero's twelve Galleys

Is. di St. Petri

CADIZ HARBOR

Nautical Miles

0   1   2   3   4   5

0 1000 2000 3000 4000 5000 Yards

1. *Final Spanish position, June 21.*
2. *Point where Essex landed, June 21.*
3. *Position intended for the Second Brigade*
4. *Santa-Cruz's galleys, June 20-21.*

Emery Walker Ltd. sc.

The attack had been decided on without plans of any sort; and now "many (seeming desperately valiant)," says Ralegh, in the story whose justified exultation is so engaging, criticized him because it was postponed till next day. All evening he was kept busy seeing Lords Howard and Essex. By his advice the fleet moved up to the mouth of the harbor. Then, at ten o'clock at night, he wrote out his plan of action and sent it to Lord Howard. It urged that two big flyboats should be appointed to board each galleon as soon as it was sufficiently battered—for they would burn rather than yield, and if the fleet returned to England with some of its own vessels lost and no compensating captures, "it would be termed but a lamentable victory." Women are often said to be realists more than men: the belief is supported by Elizabeth's attitude. Of "glory" she made little account; it was the actual cash balance she demanded to be shown.

Ralegh's dispositions accepted, the leading of the assault was trusted to him, though Lord Thomas Howard challenged this post of honor, and, according to an anonymous writer (believed to be Sir William Monson), was granted it. Ralegh partly admits this; Lord Thomas left his own flagship, the *Mer-Honour,* and entered the *Nonpareil,* a ship allotted to Ralegh's advance. Ralegh, willing to render deference to his rival's rank and position in the navy, was nevertheless not going to be surpassed by anyone, in this supreme chance. "With the first peep of day, therefore, I weighed anchor"; and his squadron swung arrogantly toward the seventeen galleons "ranged under the wall of Cales,[9] on which the sea beateth." These stood ready "to flank our entrance," as the English swooped toward the galleons in the inner shelter. "There was also a fort called the *Philip,* which beat and commanded the harbour. There were also ordnance, which lay all alongst the curtain upon the wall towards the sea. There were also divers other pieces of culverin, which also scoured the channel."[10] So the chief actor relates, in a piece of prose that keeps the excited happiness of that day, his unique vitality rising as it always does when he has the opportunity of writing of great action in which he had been *pars magna.* Under his command

9. Cadiz.

10. It must be unique for the word *also* to play so effective a part in literature, as if expressing the very magnanimity of exultation which tosses obstacles together and hardly deigns to notice them!

were names that are themselves radiant poetry: the *Warspite,* the *Mary Rose* (under his friend George Carew), the *Lion,* the *Rainbow,* the *Swiftsure,* the *Dreadnought,* the *Nonpareil,* "the twelve ships of London" also, with the flyboats for boarding. Against this pagan assemblage the Spaniards moved their array of apostolic guardians: the *St. Philip, St. Matthew, St. Thomas, St. Andrew;* and a vast swarm of frigates, argosies ("very strong in artillery"), flagships of the Admiral, Vice-Admiral and Rear-Admiral of Nueva Espagna, with forty other great ships bound for Mexico. Amazement must have been intense as the assailing force sailed into their massed fire, the leading ship, Ralegh's own *Warspite,* replying contemptuously, "to each piece a blurr[11] with a trumpet . . . disdaining to shoot one piece at any one or all of those esteemed dreadful monsters." The defenders took to their oars and fled to the galleons in the straits. Doing this, they had no choice but to offer a full-side target. "I bestowed a benediction amongst them."

The galleys were "mere wasps." He pulled up alongside "the *St. Philip,* the great and famous Admiral of Spain . . . the mark I shot at . . . resolved to be revenged for the *Revenge,* or to second her with mine own life." The melee's crash and fury called in others. "Towards ten of the clock, my Lord General Essex, being impatient to abide far off, hearing so great thunder of ordnance, thrust up through the fleet." He entered the *Swiftsure,* and came close to Ralegh. However, "always I must, without glory, say for myself, that I held single in the head of all."

"Now, after we had beat, as two butts, one upon another almost three hours (assuring your Honour that the volleys of cannon and culverin came as thick as if it had been a skirmish of musketeers), and finding myself in danger to be sunk in the place," Ralegh went in his skiff to Essex, to ask for the flyboats. If they did not come, he must risk a Queen's ship by thrusting her close enough for boarding—a serious matter, with a mistress who demanded her every ship safe, from the fiercest battle whatsoever. Yet board he must. It was the only way to save the *Warspite.* "It was the same loss, to burn or sink, for I must endure the one." The ardors of this struggle drew Essex and Ralegh very close in comradeship and esteem; and when he failed to dissuade

11. Blare.

Ralegh, by representing the danger of attacking such superior numbers as inhabited the *St. Philip,* Essex promised "he would second me in person, upon his honour." The Lord Admiral wanted to come up also, in his flagship the *Ark Ralegh,* but the bay was too choked with shipping. The day's excitements had so infected him, however, that he too left his ship and joined his son, Lord Thomas Howard, in the *Nonpareil.*

Ralegh was away, talking with Essex, for a quarter of an hour, during which Sir Francis Vere thrust his ship, the *Rainbow,* ahead of the *Warspite,* and Lord Thomas Howard pushed the *Nonpareil* ahead of both. Ralegh on return, "finding myself from being the first to be but the third," slipped anchor, nosed between his rivals and then swung "athwart the channel, so as I was sure none should outstart me again, for that day." Then Essex managed to get ahead of all but Ralegh and Lord Thomas. The latter, therefore,

while we had no leisure to look behind us, secretly fastened a rope on my ship's side towards him, to draw himself up equally with me. But some of my company advertising me thereof, I caused it to be cut off, and so he fell back into his place,

where (as Ralegh says, wild with delight at his prominence in the day's glory and peril) he was "guarded, all but his very prow, from the sight of the enemy."

The flyboats could not get through the crowded channel; Ralegh "laid out a warp by the side of the *Philip,* to shake hands with her." The Spaniards did not wait to be ejected, but ran the ship aground. Seeing she could escape no further, they fled,

tumbling into the sea heaps of soldiers, so thick as if coals had been poured out of a sack in many ports at once, some drowned and some sticking in the mud.

The *St. Matthew* and *St. Andrew* were caught in time. But the *St. Philip* and *St. Thomas* were fired by their crews. The victors now saw a spectacle "very lamentable":

for many drowned themselves; many, half burnt, leapt into the water; very many hanging by the ropes' ends by the ships' side, under the water even to the lips; many swimming with grievous wounds, strucken under water, and put out of their pain; and withal so huge a fire, and such tearing of the ordnance in the great *Philip,* and the rest, when the fire came to them, as, if any man had a desire to see Hell itself, it was there most lively figured. Ourselves spared the lives of all, after the victory; but the Flemings, who did little or nothing in the fight, used merciless slaughter, till they were by myself, and afterward by my Lord Admiral, beaten off.

Surely there cannot be in our language, or in any language, a more vivid and wonderful story of a battle, by one of its participants!

The time came for the army to storm the town. Spanish cavalry sallied out, and attempted a half-hearted defense, but the place "was carried with a sudden fury, and with little loss." Here Ralegh's story loses its first-hand quality, for toward the end of the naval fight he was severely wounded, his leg being "interlaced and deformed with splinters." He had himself carried ashore on men's shoulders, and even tried to ride a horse. But the agony proved too much; and there was, besides, the peril from "the tumultuous disordered soldiers that, being then given to spoil and rapine, had no respect." He returned to the fleet, which that night was without any Admiral, and almost without personnel at all—"all running headlong to the sack."

At daybreak he sent Sir John Gilbert and Arthur Throckmorton to beg leave to go into Puerto Real roads and seize the Indies fleet, said to be worth twelve million crowns and lying there helpless. But the Supreme Command were overwhelmed by their victory's embarrassing completeness. "The confusion was great; it was almost impossible for them to order many things at once." Permission was refused. It was characteristic of Ralegh's ill-luck throughout life that Essex afterwards blamed him because "they did not assail the enemy in their other ports" —an ungenerous criticism of an exceedingly sick man, destined to permanent lameness, and now unable to move—a man whose advice, moreover, had been put by.

Nevertheless Ralegh, as the sentimental tragedians put it, had "had his moment." His achievement had been towering—a superhuman recklessness overleaping contention of enemy and rival alike in this assault (as it must have seemed to the foe) of demons from the deep. Henceforward his countrymen could never quite forget the hero of Cadiz. There was instant, if passing, revulsion from his unpopularity. "If our sovereign mistress had seen," wrote a gentleman in the fleet, "it would, I think, have been a sufficient expiation of all his faults whatsoever."[12] "Sir Walter Ralegh was exceedingly commended for his judgment, discretion and valour in the sea-service, and much attributed to him," especially by the Lord Admiral. George Carew wrote to Robert Cecil, June 30: "Sir Walter Ralegh's service was so much praiseworthy as those which were formerly his enemies do now hold him in great estimation. For that which he did in the sea-service could not be bettered." His contemporary reputation as an admiral, which has so vexed some modern critics, was firmly established on this day, and never again eclipsed. Even the ranks of Tuscany were—temporarily—moved to cheer. That dour Essexite, Sir Anthony Standen, wrote from Cadiz, July 5, to Lord Burghley:

Sir Walter Ralegh did in my judgment, no man better; and his artillery most effect. I never knew the gentleman until this time, and I am sorry for it, for there are in him excellent things beside his valour; and the observation he hath in this voyage used with my Lord of Essex hath made me love him.

That was amends for this same writer's former interpretation of Ralegh's courtesy to Essex as "the cunningest respect and deepest humility that ever I saw."

"The fury now being past," proclamation was published that "all men should surcease from all manner of blood and cruel dealing."[13] The town was given over to pillage for a limited space, but violence to any civilian was forbidden, under pain of death. The chroniclers decline to say as much for their Dutch allies—between whom and the Spaniards "there is an implacable heart-burning"[14]—but the English, by even enemy testimony, did mercifully. The Lord Admiral was able to boast: "No aged or cold blood was touched; nor woman defiled; but were all with great care embarked, and sent to St. Mary's Port." "Even Philip the Second repeated the praises of the English commanders on this score. But he was very far indeed from making their conduct a precedent for that of his own commanders."[15]

The merchants of Seville and Cadiz offered two million ducats to

12. Birch, *Memoirs of Queen Elizabeth*, ii, 97.
13. *Purchas*, xx, 14.   14. *Ibid.*, xx, 15.
15. Edwards, *Ralegh*, i, 220.

save their Indies fleet. But the fervor of conflict, with its accompanying generosities, was over, and the calculating huckster mood had taken charge. Ralegh wanted to seize first, and sell afterwards: Essex, a land soldier who wanted to stand well with his followers, wished the Army to have this valuable spoil, while Ralegh and the sailors stood aside. Lord Howard was bluffly professional, "the senior service" in its stickiest and most correct attitude. "We came to consume them, and not to compound with them." While this none too wise debating was delaying action, time and the enemy swept the chance away for ever. The Duke of Medina Sidonia, whom fate had set in responsibility over the luckless Spaniards here (as well as in the Armada of 1588), could be as proud and professional as the English Admiral. Heretics should not profit by impertinence. Rather let the fleet be lost to its owners! He ordered everything to be burnt, therefore; and all that wealth flared into ashes, the English having gained only the *St. Matthew* and the *St. Andrew,* Ralegh noting philosophically that these "two Apostles" were "well furnished" with artillery, "which (God willing) we purpose to bring into England."

Commanders-in-Chief had then a delegated power of granting knighthoods, as in the Great War they had of granting "immediate M.C.'s," that coveted honor. Between 1914 and 1918 men talked freely of divisions that were lucky in generous leaders; Essex was such a leader, and his lavishness on this occasion passed into a popular rhyme:

A Gentlemen of Wales,
With a Knight of Cales,
    And a Lord of the North Countree—
A Yeoman of Kent
Upon a racked rent
    Will buy them out all three.[16]

Making knights was a passion with him. On Saturday, June 26, Army and Navy together buried with great pomp Sir John Winkfield, the most important of their few dead; and next day, after knighting sixty gentlemen, Essex attended a ceremonial service in Cadiz Abbey, where his chaplain, Master Hopkins ("a man of sweet utterance"), delivered

16. Osborne, *Traditional Memoirs,* etc., p. 25. "Cales," rhyming with "Wales," is Cadiz.

a "learned Sermon."[17] One of the knights was Lady Ralegh's brother, Arthur Throckmorton, Essex thereby signifying that all was at peace between him and the Raleghs.

Much plunder was gained in Cadiz, and those who were energetic after the battle got valuable prisoners. Providence had incapacitated Ralegh from doing this:

What the Generals have gotten, I know least; they protest it is little. For my own part, I have gotten a lame leg and a deformed. For the rest, either I spake too late, or it was otherwise resolved. I have not wanted good words, and exceeding kind and regardful usance. But I have possession of naught but poverty and pain. If God had spared me that blow, I had possessed myself of some House—

i.e., of some prisoner worth a thumping ransom.

Having behaved themselves, not only with outstanding valor but with as much humanity as is compatible with war, the English went away again, well content. They left Spain with a lurking terror of destruction suddenly coming, all unheralded. Her decline "dates from that day when Ralegh" passed the "wasps" with his "blare of trumpets," "making straight for the two great galleons, some of whose crews had heard Richard Grenville's dying words."[18] Though Essex would have kept it, an earlier Gibraltar, the town was laid in ruins, and its forts were dismantled. Cadiz was one of the three keys of Spanish strength, and in his *History of the World* Ralegh says, "We stayed not to pick any lock, but brake open the doors, and, having rifled all, threw the key into the fire."

The people of England rose to the triumph of their returning warriors. But the Queen saw only that unexampled opportunities for pillage had been wasted, or when used had been used by private persons. The Lord Admiral's wife, who had been told that her husband was going to receive five thousand pounds prize-money, and Ralegh three thousand, learnt to her indignation "that the Queen claimed *all!* and my Lord of Essex, it is thought, will yield his right to Her Majesty." Essex despised loot beside honor; King Philip testified of him, "such a nobleman is not to be seen among heretics." But others fought for their

---

17. *Purchas*, xx, 18.   18. Edwards, i, 220.

share, and Burghley supported them, supporting Essex's just claims also, only to be called "miscreant" and "coward" by the angry old woman. She had the excuse that (as always) individuals had intercepted all they could, of what should have come to the treasury. The Privy Council tried hard to find out how much this was, and to recover some of it. At her farewell, when the expedition sailed, Elizabeth had told Essex

that he should use her men like a match that, once set on fire, burns to the end. Her purpose then was, that what he should get, she would keep for her debts.[19]

In her disappointment, she "resolved that the service at Cadiz should be no matter for reward or distinction to anybody."[20] She sulked or flared out at those, like Essex, whom she compelled to attend her. Ralegh, who wrote to Robert Cecil, "I hope Her most excellent Majesty will take my labours and endeavours in good part. Other riches than the hope thereof, I have none," was bidden still to keep his distance. He had preferred Elizabeth Throckmorton to Elizabeth Tudor, and should stay with his choice.

The Privy Council inventory finally showed that he had done somewhat better out of Cadiz fight than he alleged. His booty was listed as worth £1769, and it was not taken from him. But the Lord Marshal (Sir Francis Vere), who had not been hampered by a game leg, got £3628; and the ill feeling that had shown periodically in the expedition was renewed when Ralegh and other naval officers demanded on their sailors' behalf that the soldiers' chests should be searched, and all plunder shared equably. Enmities were made, which might be lulled to slumber, but would reawaken.

The most unexpected beneficiary was the University of Oxford. The victors had varied the quiet tenor of their return by swooping on Faro; and Bishop Osorius' fine library was carried off, to become the nucleus of the Bodleian Library.

19. Logan Pearsall Smith, *The Life and Letters of Sir Henry Wotton,* ii, 493.
20. Edwards, i, 225.

CHAPTER XIII

The Islands Voyage

His bold trespass, in landing without his Lordship's leave.
Reliquiae Wottonianae.

ELIZABETH'S reign could not last much longer. To gain or keep power, men must ingratiate themselves with her successor; they jealously watched each other. There seemed three chief parties, those of Essex, Robert Cecil, Ralegh. The last two had long been nominally allies, and between their families had passed what, with anyone less cold-blooded than Cecil, would have been friendship. When Lady Cecil died, Ralegh wrote a letter (January 24, 1597) whose beauty and sincere grief only a fool could miss. It is "conventional"—inevitably, since for death there is nothing to say but "I am sorry," and to add such religious comfort as the age and our own belief permits. But the essence of such letters is their sympathetic effort to draw the mourner's mind away from sorrow, that time may have a chance to work with healing:

. . . you have lost a good and virtuous wife, and my self an honourable friend and kinswoman. But there was a time when she was unknown to you, for whom you then lamented not. She is now no more yours, nor of your acquaintance, but immortal, and not needing or knowing your love or sorrow. Therefore you shall but grieve for that which now is as then it was, when not yours; only bettered by the difference in this, that she hath passed the wearisome journey of this dark world, and hath possession of her inheritance. . . .

I believe that sorrows are dangerous companions, converting bad into evil[1] and evil in worse, and do no other service than multiply harms. They are the treasures of weak hearts and of the foolish. The mind that entertaineth them is as the earth and dust whereon sorrows and adversities of the world do, as the beasts of the field, tread, trample, and defile. The mind of man is that part of God which is in us, which, by how much it is subject to

---

1. Ralegh's spelling of such words as "evil" and "earth" is "yevil" and "yearth," no doubt representing his pronunciation. Perhaps this spelling should have been kept.

passion, by so much it is farther from Him that gave it us. Sorrows draw not the dead to life, but the living to death. . . .

Yours ever, beyond the power of words to utter.

After Lady Cecil's death, the Raleghs showed special kindness to her son Will, who stayed at Sherborne, recovering his health in the country air and studying under Sir Walter's guidance. Ralegh kept his father posted of his condition ("Because I know that you can receive no pleasinger news from hence than to hear of your beloved creature"):

. . . His stomach, that was heretofore weak, is altogether amended, and he doth now eat well and digest rightly. I hope this air will agree exceedingly with him. He is also better kept to his book than anywhere else.[2]

This boy afterwards became the second Earl of Salisbury, to whom Ralegh, then a prisoner losing health and time and hope, dedicated ("I intend, by the help of God and your furtherance, right noble Earl of Salisbury, to write a *Brief History of the World*") all that was ever completed of the mighty task that solaced his captivity.

Between Ralegh and Cecil was no open suspicion as yet, and the two were to draw together and to draw in Essex with them. The latter had learnt respect for Ralegh, by what he had seen happen at Cadiz; in February, 1597, he and Ralegh are noted as constantly in conference. Ralegh acted as intermediary to reconcile his new friend with Cecil, and presently all three were in association.

"On the same day on which Essex sailed from Cadiz something of the highest moment was done in England: Elizabeth made Robert Cecil her Secretary, in name as well as in fact."[3] Cecil decided to use his power to win forgiveness for Ralegh's old offense. Little by little, the long banishment was mitigated, and then ended. On April 9, 1597, Rowland Whyte ("at this time the most observant and acute of the courtly writers of news-letters"),[4] noted that Ralegh was "daily in court,"[5] and hoping to resume his former nearness to the Queen. His

2. Letter of March 27, 1600.
3. Lytton Strachey, *Essex and Elizabeth*, p. 106.
4. Edwards, i, 226.
5. Thomas Birch, *Memoirs of Queen Elizabeth*, ii, 345; Arthur Collins, *Letters and Memorials of State in the Reigns of Queen Mary, Queen Elizabeth, King James*, etc., ii, 37.

friends were powerful and Essex neutral ("he gives it no opposition").
Weary of a life so subject to caprice, with a mistress sick in mind and
body and lost to her old human kindness, Essex was dreaming of what
Ralegh was dreaming of, a life of action. Ralegh was given the contract
to provision a new expedition, six thousand men to serve three months;
he did it efficiently, at ninepence a head *per diem,* and "let the Earl of
Essex have much" (that is, free of cost) "for his private provision."[6]
Essex sanctioned Cecil's taking him (June 1) to the Queen, "who used
him graciously, and gave him full authority to execute his place as Captain of the Guard, which immediately he undertook, and swore many
men into the places void." That evening he rode at her side again; and
he began to come "boldly into the Privy-chamber, as he was wont."

The three rivals grew "exceedingly great" together, constantly going
"very private" to Robert Cecil's house.[7] "None but Cecil and Ralegh
enjoy the Earl of Essex; they carry him away as they list." A "treaty of
peace" was "confirmed" among them.[8] Ralegh wrote Cecil (July 6) a
mysterious letter about Essex's

kind acceptance of your entertainment. He was also wonderful merry at
your conceit of Richard the Second. I hope it shall never alter, and thereof I
shall be most glad of, as the true way to all our good, quiet, and advancement, and most of all for Her sake whose affairs shall hereby find better
progression.

"Sir," he concludes, "I will ever be yours. It is all I can say, and I will
perform it with my life, and with my fortune."

Cecil's "conceit of Richard the Second" is one of the time's most
teasing problems. It was in August, 1597, that Andrew Wyse entered at
Stationers' Hall his copyright in Shakespeare's play of that name. If—
as seems the irresistible conclusion—the temporary triumvirate had
been watching an early performance of this, we have our one certain
connection of Ralegh and Shakespeare, who were of opposed factions,
from their different opinion of Essex. Nearly four years later, on the
eve of Essex's rebellion, his henchman, Sir Gilly Merrick, asked Shakespeare's company to perform *Richard II*. There was hesitation, on the
ostensible grounds that it was "so old and so long out of use, that they

6. Collins, ii, 42 (April 19).   7. *Ibid.*, ii, 44 (April 23).
8. Birch, ii, 341.

should have small or no company at it"; but Merrick persuaded them, by a gift of forty shillings, and Essex at his trial was charged (among graver crimes) with having watched in acted show what he was plotting himself, a sovereign's deposition.

This must have been on the eve of what is known as "the Islands Voyage," of which we have an excellent account by Sir Arthur Gorges, captain of Ralegh's flagship. Philip was believed to have sworn to avenge Cadiz, if it drained his resources;[9] and Ralegh, though doubting his ability to do anything adequate "in so short time, considering his late losses," was in favor of striking hard again, before he could stir. On July 10, 120 vessels, volunteers except for ten Dutch ships and twenty of the Queen's, sailed from Plymouth. Essex was Commander-in-Chief, with Lord Thomas Howard as Vice-Admiral and Ralegh Rear-Admiral. Sir George Carew was in his usual post as Master of the Ordnance; Sir Francis Vere was again Marshal. Essex made Ralegh and Vere shake hands, to forget their quarrels after Cadiz, and this, says Vere, "we both did, the more willingly because there had nothing passed between us that might blemish reputation." Ralegh, long after, returned the magnanimity, in a generous reference in his *History of the World*.

It is over what happened at the outset of this voyage that the strongest attacks have been made on Ralegh's seamanship. The squadrons were scattered by storm, and most of the ships under Ralegh, as well as those directly under Essex, were driven back to Falmouth and Plymouth. "Ralegh's premature retreat and his extravagant account of the gale" have "a look that is little to his credit."[10] "Lord Thomas Howard, that weather-beaten sailor, fought out the gale with his squadron and reached Coruña in triumph."[11] Since I have never sailed in such vessels as the Elizabethans had to use, I do not feel entitled to speak so confidently; but Ralegh's story does not read to me as if it had come out of an overheated imagination:

the Thursday, Friday, and Saturday, the storm so increased, the ships being weighty, the ordnance great, and the billows so raised and enraged, as we

9. He swore to be avenged if it wasted his kingdom to a candelabra (*Calendar of State Papers, Venetian*, 1592–1603, p. 223).
10. Sir J. S. Corbett, *The Successors of Drake*, p. 177.
11. V. T. Harlow, *The Discoverie of Guiana*, pp. xviii–xix.

could carry out no sail which to our judgment would not have been rent off the yards by the wind. . . . In my ship it hath shaken all her beams, knees, and stanchions well nigh asunder, insomuch as on Saturday night last we made account to have yielded ourselves up to God . . . our men being wasted with labour and watchings, and our ship so open everywhere, all her bulk-head rent, and her very cookroom of brick shaken down into powder.[12]

The Dutch Admiral also limped back, and so did Essex, whose failure is condoned by Ralegh with a generosity never extended to himself:

This Wednesday morning my Lord General is expected here at Plymouth, being on Tuesday night put into Falmouth in great extremity and imminent peril of sinking in the sea. . . . Most of these ships have cracked their masts and are marvellous leaky, especially my Lord General's own ship. . . . The most of the long boats are lost, and all the barges. . . . Sir, I beseech you to work from Her Majesty some comfort to my Lord General, who, I know, is dismayed by these mischances, even to death, although there could not be more done by any man upon the earth, God having turned the heavens with that fury against us, a matter beyond the power, or valour, or will, of man to resist.[13]

The age was in its mellow autumn. The strain had lifted from the Spanish warfare, the initiative had definitely passed to England. Elizabeth herself was growing "old and full of sleep," though with fiery intervals; in the love-making which surrounded her was nothing more than courtliness. Ralegh was officially back in favor, but "the saturnine old woman had no longer any tenderness for her Captain of the Guard . . . her pulses had ceased to thrill at his coming."[14] He might go on as many voyages, and as often, as he pleased. He knew this, and the ancient pretense was practically dropped between them.

It was still kept up between Essex and Elizabeth; but even here it was now a convention. In his demands on her forbearance, making drains on a treasury of affection which did not go anything like as deep as he imagined, Essex was playing the fool, as everyone but his own besotted followers realized. However, there *was* a convention; and in his letters to Cecil, Ralegh observed it. In the last stages of the first preparation, Essex had been his guest on the *Warspite,* and Ralegh sent

12. Letter to R. Cecil, July 18, 1597.   13. Letter of July 20.
14. Gosse, *Ralegh,* p. 111.

the Queen a courtly assurance which indicated his complete acceptance of his own favor as definitely in the past: "Her Majesty may now be sure his Lordship shall sleep the sounder, though he fare the worse, by being with me, for I am an excellent watchman at sea." Cecil worked on the same convention. After its return, as the fleet waited wind-bound, he wrote to Essex, "The Queen is now so disposed to have us all love you, as she and I do talk every night, like angels, of you." But to the old woman who had passed through a life of such vicissitudes, men must have begun to seem remote and dim, shadows moving beside her, uttering the same old insincerities, now hardly heard or heeded. The names that still seem living on the page of history, and to carry to eternal ages the sense of that period's flesh-and-blood vigor, the Drakes, Gilberts, Frobishers, Sidneys, were almost all a memory now. Gloriana was surrounded by tradition and habit, by such foolery as she was presently to tell her silly godson, Sir John Harington, he himself would not waste time over when he heard Death knocking at his gate.

The ships, refitted, started again, August 17, to encounter a repetition of storms. Carew's ship, the *St. Matthew,* was disabled, and driven back. Ralegh, who for ten days was unable to enter either bed or cabin, was severed with his squadron from the others. Thus weakened, the remaining commanders held a council, and abandoned the original plan of attacking Ferrol, also that of attacking Terceira. Timidity took hold; all that was thought possible was to intercept the Mexican fleet. Even this seemed too frightening when a ship joined them with Ralegh's message that the Spanish Admiral had sailed out to convoy it home. Halting and vacillating, Essex sailed "for the island of Flowers."[15]

Here, ten days later, Ralegh joined him, and Essex "seemed" (said Gorges)[16] "to be the joyfullest man living for our arrival." Without Ralegh's proved skill and experience, the courtier folk who were nominally in charge were very unhappy. They found their ships unmanageable, and wrestled with the unknown elements, as a bad horseman with a restive mount. "A great many of our young gentlemen . . . seeing that the boisterous winds and merciless Seas had neither affinity with London delicacy nor Court bravery," had already taken "their high

15. Flores.
16. *A Larger Relation of the said Iland Voyage*—a first-rate piece of writing—*Purchas,* xx, 34 ff.

Plumes and imbroydered Cassocks" back to England. Another trouble
came from these amateur sailors' ignorance of shipbuilding. Anything
that could float seemed good enough, and the bigger the better. Many
of the gay popinjays must have wondered if Ralegh, after all, *was* so
mad with his experiments and eager interest in shipbuilding, and his
insistence that new methods of fighting needed new vessels, and not
endless repetition:

some began to taste the inconvenience and peril of high cargoed ships drawing little water, and overcharged with mighty ordnance in a furious high-
wrought sea. And now also others found and felt the mischief of weak-built
vessels and of rotten tackle.[17]

It is impossible to understand the depth of conviction behind Ralegh's
comments on naval matters, and his wish, in the evening of his life, to
write a treatise on the whole Art of Warfare at Sea, unless we put our
imagination into these so often repeated experiences.

Ralegh's detractors had been using their time. Essex, however, in his
relief at seeing him again, protested "that he never believed that we
would leave him, although divers persuaded him the contrary; and acknowledged that he was sorry for a Letter which he had written by
Master Robert Knolles into England against us." Ralegh and his principal officers dined with the Lord General, who acquainted him "with
the many conjectures and surmises of our absence." Essex named some
of the unkindly imaginative ones, insisting that (despite the letter he
had precipitately sent off to England) he had all along seen through
their "scandalous and cankered dispositions." One thing that makes the
story of Essex's ruin so deeply tragic is that it was so unnecessary, and
not least in Ralegh's participation in it. For Essex and Ralegh were
fitted for friendship. Gorges, speaking of the very great kindness "and
inward familiarity" with which Essex, "to the great dislike and heart-
burning" of some of his flatterers, received them, testifies to that "liking
which of his own disposition our General" bore to Ralegh:

For, albeit the Earl had many doubts and jealousies buzzed into his ears
against the other, yet I have often observed, that both in his greatest actions
of service and in his times of chiefest recreations, he would ever accept of

17. *Ibid.*

his counsel and company, before many others that thought themselves more in his favour.

But their stars were mutually hostile. Essex sailed to the capture of Fayal. Ralegh, starting after him, got there first, and for two days watched its inhabitants streaming away into the interior, with all their goods. He waited a third day, while the Fort fired at him and hung out a red flag of defiance. The English had to look on while intrenchments were dug. At last he held a Council of War, at which Essex's violent partisan, Sir Gilly Merrick, was almost alone in insisting that they must wait for the Commander-in-Chief; the other officers, ashamed to seem afraid to assault the enemy, urged him not to let the chance slip altogether. Ralegh felt he could wait no longer, merely "to reserve the title of such an exploit (though it were not great) for a greater person." Merrick thereupon took off his half-dozen ships, and "would not budge." Ralegh, not choosing that the Dutch auxiliaries should think that he "was driven to turn tail" because of this desertion, or that he needed their help, gathered together under 500 picked men, among them a few gentlemen volunteers "whom I could not refuse"[18]—Gorges and Kemys among them—and, declining to take the storming of an Azores town over-seriously, went pell-mell at it. "As for the *working of the Sea, the steepness of the Cliffs,*" these "were not new to us" (he says contemptuously, with a glance at the queer collection of courtiers that were somewhere wasting time with their idol Essex). He took sailors only, for the soldiers were reckoned particularly the Lord General's followers. He rallied his men when they faltered under a severe fire at landing, and "bade as many as were not afraid" to follow him, clambering and wading. The shore's defenders, who were Portuguese ("a people very swift and nimble of foot") fled. Ralegh collected his men and marched straight for the fort in front of the town, four miles away, himself leading, staff in hand, with no armor except a collar ("a bravery in a chief commander not to be commended").[19] The enemy "very shrewdly pelted" them, and many skulked to shelter. Ralegh, ignoring these, went steadily on, Gorges ("out of the love of a kinsman") accompanying him, though disapproving of such subalternlike reckless-

18. *History of the World*, Part I, Book 5, chap. 1, §9.
19. Gorges.

ness. The former received bullets through his clothes, and the latter was shot in the leg. However, both town and fort were reached, and both found evacuated. Having achieved a feat whose importance he lightly rated, Ralegh then made strict dispositions against surprise. The Azores had "of late years become very watchful," and it was felt that the ejected garrison could not be trusted to keep the peace.

Dawn next morning (September 22) showed off shore Essex's ships, which had been vainly beating up and down, hunting for the Mexican fleet. Sir Gilly Merrick took opportunity by the forelock, and rushed to his patron and misrepresented Ralegh's perfectly natural action, as "played by the Rear-Admiral only to steal honour and reputation from him, and to set his own forwardness to the view of the world." He knew his man, one "that did affect nothing in the world so much as Fame, and to be reputed matchless for magnanimity, and could hardly endure any that should obscure his glory in that kind." Essex was the spoilt child of Elizabeth's Court; and in the determined folly which brought him to destruction finally he was seconded by the populace. He was moreover surrounded by a pernicious entourage, many of them indebted to him for their knighthoods. They now urged that for his "presumption and scorn," Ralegh should be called before a court-martial,[20] and beheaded (as Doughty was by Drake). Essex had enough sense to refuse; he "let fall a Noble word": "I would if he were my friend."[21]

Ralegh "found all men's countenances estranged, as he passed through them" to pay his respects. In the Lord General's cabin, after faint welcome he was taxed with breach of orders. He answered boldly that he knew of none. Essex reminded him of the order that no one should land troops without permission. Ralegh was able to show that the order was that *no Captain or military officer*,[22] if severed from the rest, should land anywhere, without directions from the General, "or some other principal Commander." "But I take myself to be a principal Commander, under your Lordship, and therefore not subject to that Article, nor under the power of the law martial, because a successive commander of the whole fleet in Her Majesty's Letters Patents, your Lordship and my Lord Thomas Howard failing." He added that he

20. Birch, *Memoirs of Queen Elizabeth*, ii, 360.
21. *Reliquiae Wottonianae*, p. 180.
22. My italics, as no doubt they were Ralegh's also.

had waited four days, and naturally assumed that the Commander-in-Chief must think him strong enough to take a paltry island without assistance; and while he had delayed thus, at Sir Gilly Merrick's insistence, his own men were murmuring that he was afraid. Essex was courteously but plainly reminded that others besides himself had to consider what was known as "honour."

The defense was too strong to gainsay. Essex seemed to accept it, and visited his Rear-Admiral. But he would not sup with him, though Ralegh urged that the meal should be without prejudice to any further action or question that he desired to take. The most insolent of Essex's following, Sir Christopher Blount, a young man who was in the interesting position of being the Lord General's stepfather, took it upon himself to answer for Essex, "that he thought my Lord would not sup at all." To which Ralegh fired up, that when he invited Sir Christopher Blount "he might disable his own appetite," but that Lord Essex would be very welcome. Lord Thomas Howard, like Ralegh (and unlike Essex) a seaman, stepped in to save Ralegh from further impertinence; and by next day was able to assure him that all that was necessary was an apology, without which "the rest would think" the General "a very weak and tame Commander." Perhaps nothing in the whole Elizabethan story so brings out the childishness of the men who were making its greatness—or, on occasion, throwing away its opportunities for greatness. It is a record we might think out of fashion, if the commanders of the Great War had not published memoirs. We can sympathize with Elizabeth's often peremptory handling of generals and admirals; they needed to be sent about their business, with sharp words of scorn.

Ralegh demurred—not from the apology, which he was willing to present as a sacrifice to the Earl's insatiate self-esteem, but from the risk of putting himself in his power again. He proposed to stay in his own squadron, and fight against being arrested, or else leave Essex. Howard persuaded him otherwise, promising to take his side if he were offered any wrong. Ralegh then apologized, and the affair simmered down to an apparent reconciliation. After a day or two, Essex and Howard and other officers dined with Ralegh; and Ralegh, whose generous defense of his subordinates never failed, insisted that he must take responsibility for whatever had been done by certain captains whom Essex had arrested and was keeping under arrest.

While the English were wasting precious days in this foolery, the enemy decamped out of reach with their possessions. Essex's followers, aware that a wasted expedition had put them completely in the wrong, accused Ralegh's four hundred and sixty of remissness. This charge also apparently died down, and Essex, finding Ralegh's continual advice necessary, grew again into "very kind terms"[23] with him. In his magnanimity in not having his Rear-Admiral beheaded, but merely disciplined "with a wise and noble admonition,"[24] his friends assured him he had behaved like himself. He subsided into some complacency.

The fleet now betook itself to prize-hunting. Of three Spanish ships that it caught, Ralegh in his *Warspite* captured the largest, which Essex insisted must be given over to his own boats to board. It proved full of cochineal and indigo, enough to serve England for many years, and held valuable prisoners besides. From these Essex learnt of forty Portuguese Indiamen near by, which he and his friends swarmed off to find. Some of the gaily named ships of the "temporary seamen," the *Rainbow,* the *Garland* (commanded by that brilliant young gentleman, the Earl of Southampton), the *Marigold*—in company with that shadow of a great name to fall centuries after, the *Dreadnought*—came across sixteen vessels, of which they sunk one and lost all the rest. The indignation felt by Ralegh and his officers still burns in the account written down by Gorges, and published long after, in 1607, at the request of Henry, Prince of Wales (when Ralegh was a prisoner under sentence of death).

The other Indiamen escaped to the shelter of the strong defenses of Terceira. At a Council of War held before this fort, Essex's colonels boasted that with fifteen hundred men they could storm it. Howard and Ralegh pointed out the immense difficulties, but offered to support them with three thousand seamen, if they persisted. But the scene was near to Grenville's last fight, which has come down to us (thanks to Tennyson) as a very splendid feat, but to contemporaries seemed a horrid example of headstrong folly insisting on its own punishment. Grenville was looked upon as a magnificent Ass (to use a word the Elizabethans were fond of), which indeed he was; and moreover, as an Ass by whose action the Spaniards had gained their solitary English ship of war—a great disgrace. Finding their boasts likely to be taken

23. Gorges.   24. Sir Francis Vere.

up, the fire-eaters abated in zeal—which was just as well, thought Gorges, and no doubt Ralegh and Howard also; for, if the Spanish fleet which they had failed to find had come upon them while attacking this powerful fortress, they would have been caught as between nut-crackers. The fleet therefore left Terceira, and continued to pounce here and there, without striking effectively anywhere. A landing was made at St. Michael's, but the people of Villa Franca entertained the English with wine and fruit for six continuous days, a feasting too pleasant to leave. So the island's capital escaped. The story of this "Islands Voyage" reads closely like that of the *Voyage of Maeldune*.

Presently a carrack was spied, and chased, not wisely but precipitately. She ran herself ashore, and her crew burnt her—an 1800-ton ship "of infinite wealth," whose sea-wet smoldering spices and sugar flung out fumes for hours. On October 9 the whole expedition turned homewards, and, on reaching Cornwall, found that the enemy whom they had failed to meet had been raiding the county, terrifying the populace. Ralegh, being Lieutenant for Cornwall, got off at St. Ives, and with characteristic promptness took hold of the panic and arranged measures against an Armada (of which rumor was again talking).

Ralegh expressed his disgust at these futile expeditions, many years afterwards, when he was a voice crying out of the Elizabethan age and muffled by imprisonment—still vainly urging a vigorous war policy, to end the Spanish menace once for all. He used to quote a Spanish proverb, "The lion is not so fierce as he is painted." The King of Spain's forces (he was telling England in the pacific reign of King James),

in all parts of the world but the Low Countries, are far under the fame. If the late Queen would have believed her men of war as she did her scribes, we had, in her time, beaten that great empire in pieces, and made their kings kings of figs and oranges, as in old times. But her Majesty did all by halves, and by petty invasions taught the Spaniard how to defend himself, and to see his own weakness, which, till our attempts taught him, was hardly known to himself. Four thousand men would have taken from him all the ports of his Indies—I mean, all his ports by which his treasure doth or can pass. He is more hated in that part of the world by the sons of the conquered, than the English are by the Irish.[25]

25. Ralegh, *Discourse Touching a Marriage between Prince Henry of England and a Daughter of Savoy (Works,* viii, 246).

Talk in England buzzed of the rancor between the Lord General and his Rear-Admiral; many heard the opinion which Sir William Monson voices in his account, that if Essex, who was "by nature timorous and flexible, had not feared how it would be taken in England, Sir Walter Ralegh would have smarted" for his superior skill and presence of mind. What would the Queen have said, men speculated, if the expedition had returned without its third officer, beheaded by martial law under his rival's authority? However, Essex had not, as it happened, openly committed himself to the indecent threatenings of his Merricks and Blounts, and he satisfied his inordinate sense of what was due to his dignity by merely ignoring Ralegh's services in his official report. Even official reports, however, do not always hide the facts. Ralegh's friends were jubilant, and Essex's conduct, Rowland Whyte said, "is greatly misliked."[26] The Queen made it plain that she thought ill of the way he had squandered his chances, and particularly ill of his treatment of an abler man than himself.

In this winter of 1597 she made Lord Howard of Effingham, her Lord Admiral, Earl of Nottingham. By virtue of his headship of the Navy, he now took precedence of all other Earls. Thereupon Essex declined to attend either Court or Privy Council, with the insulting excuse that they gave him a pain in the head; he had a "violent throbbing in the temples, when exposed either to cold or to long speeches."[27] Ralegh set himself to heal the breach[28] and the Queen restored to Essex his precedence, by making him Earl-Marshal. Thereupon, Howard was aggrieved, and Ralegh was commanded (December, 1597) to reconcile the two. He merely estranged them both from himself. His adroit solution of the trouble had failed, and had lost him the friendship of the Lord Admiral, an old if tepid ally, who remained neutral when Ralegh's day of tempest burst. Meanwhile, Elizabeth was growing very weary of Lord Essex.

26. Collins, *Letters and Memorials of State,* ii, 68, 74.

27. Malingering was an old trick of Essex. In February, 1597, he kept his bed, "yet did one of his Chamber tell me, he could not weep for it, for he knew his Lord was not sick" (Collins, ii, 10).

28. Birch, *Memoirs of Queen Elizabeth,* ii, 365.

CHAPTER XIV

The Death of Essex

This Court Leviathan (too deeply strook with the harping Irons of malice) was removed from the Ocean of Favour he lay in. OSBORNE, *Traditional Memoirs.*

He was grown so popular, that he was too dangerous for the Times, and the Times for him. *Epistolae Ho-Elianae.*

The last Act, which was written in the Book of Necessity. SIR HENRY WOTTON.

RALEGH'S health was flagging. He took the waters at Bath, and the Privy Council sent him word that they were sorry to hear of his troubles, and wished him speedy restoration. Apart from his sickness, luck was turning his way; far more than when Wotton said it,[1] "the sea, and earth, and all the elements" were "for him." The tempests which had ravaged the gentlemen of the Islands Voyage saved him some of his tasks, scattering those still worse sailors, the Spaniards, and preventing their appearance, except as single ships, in English waters. Storms continued, and wrapt the island up from invaders.

He was by now, apparently all unconscious of it, singled out by Spain for an individual preëminence of detestation. All the resentment built up by the decades of Elizabethan rapine and raiding descended to him as by bequest, for no other outstanding privateer remained. Ralegh not only remained; he was active at every hour of his waking existence. Now he was commending to friendly offices a spy with a pass from King Philip, enabling him "safely" to "look into" Spanish ports; now he was urging the strengthening of Cornish points, or the sending of a flight of swift ships to harass the Mexican Plate Fleet.

All through the sessions of late 1597 and 1598 he was energetic in Parliament. He spoke on beggars who pretended that the wars had

1. At the time of the *Madre de Dios* capture, December 3, 1592 (L. P. Smith, *Life and Letters of Wotton,* i, 295).

been their ruin; on the Queen's debts; on the rights of the Commons against the Peers in points of respect and ceremony. He urged a drastic policy in Ireland, whose Deputy it was rumored in 1598 he was about to be—a prospect Rowland Whyte considered "a fair way to destruction." In October, 1598, he wrote a note to Robert Cecil on the question whether Irish rebels might be assassinated:

It can be no disgrace if it were known that the killing of a rebel were practised; for you see that the lives of anointed Princes are daily sought, and we have always in Ireland given head-money for the killing of rebels, who are evermore proclaimed at a price. So was the Earl of Desmond, and so have all rebels, been practised against. . . .

This policy would save Elizabeth expense, when her Irish wars were insupportably costly and it was plain that she had no one competent to conduct them. It was not unprecedented (nor unfollowed) that civilized men should regard "rebels" as vermin and frankly buy their heads. But in his *History of the World,* Ralegh "condemned lying in wait privily for blood as wilful murder."

He was kept busy also by his duties with West Country fishermen and merchants, and troubles with the Duchy's land-tenures. He supported the tin-miners in a struggle against the powerful Corporation of Plymouth. The case had been wrongly taken out of his Stannary jurisdiction, to that of the Star Chamber, where "a great purse or procuring extraordinary means" would undo the tin-miners. He begged that the decision might be postponed until he could be present; or else "dismissed to the place and nature of the proper trial."

He was building at Sherborne. In October, 1601, he tells Mr. Secretary Cecil: "My wife says that you came hither in an unseasonable time, and had no leisure to look abroad; and that every day this place amends, and London, to her, grows worse and worse." These messages from Lady Ralegh give his letters a shot-silk sudden gaiety, which she squandered most of all on Cecil—a charming brightness, which distresses the reader, by reminder (as Macaulay said of Milton's praise of "sad Electra's poet") of the beautiful queen of fairyland kissing Bottom's ass-ears. She sends a pair of gloves, and (September 25, 1601): "Bess says she must envy any fingers whosesoever, that shall wear her gloves but your own." "Bess returns you her best wishes, notwithstanding all quarrels."

As Cecil's brother-in-law, Lord Cobham came within the favored circle of Lady Ralegh's kindness. In August, 1601, he is warned that her oysters will be spoilt and her partridge stale if he does not come soon. "Bess remembers herself to your Lordship, and says your breach of promise shall make you fare accordingly." Another time: "Bess remembers herself to your Lordship, with a challenge that she never heard from you. I beseech your Lordship to favour this poor man"—now "preparing my miserable journey into Cornwall" (it was October)—"who is worthy estimation."

He never forgot either Virginia or Guiana; both called out his unsleeping experimentation in commodities for trade and in trees that might be naturalized. In August, 1602, he had from Virginia a ton of sassafras wood and 26 cedars, the former an inconveniently rich freight, which will "cloy the market" and bring down the price—"sarsephraze was worth 10s., 12s., and 20s. a pound before Gilbert returned" with this glut of it. "And it were pity to overthrow the enterprise; for I shall yet live to see it" (Virginia) "an English nation." He was the first to import mahogany from Guiana; and, in October, 1598, he meditated a voyage thither with Sir John Gilbert the younger, a kinsman guilty of impertinent and unfriendly conduct in the previous year, for which he received a severe dressing-down, in a letter of which only fragments have survived.

He tries to get a Government debt paid to a sea-captain: he writes (April 21, 1600) to have a kinsman's son released from prison, where he was for some unknown reason (probably, as Edwards suggests, for religious nonconformity, since he was one of the Catholic Carews). He acts as Press Censor, on a translation of a book on the Wars in Portugal and Africa; and gives it his *nil obstat,* after correcting some errors.

With all this, his main effort was toward a lasting peace with Essex. On return from the Islands Voyage, he magnanimously passed on to Cecil (October, 1597) a Plymouth captain's report that

the Earl our General hath as much fame and reputation in Spain and Italy as ever, and more than, any of our nation had; and that for an enemy he is the most honoured man in Europe.

His overtures may have met with some success, for in January, 1598, we hear of him and another playing primero with the Earl of Southampton, Shakespeare's patron and Essex's friend. The Queen having retired to rest, "the esquire of the body, Master Willoughby," asked them to go also. "Sir Walter Ralegh put up his money, and went his ways." But the Earl resented the request as an impertinence; there was a scuffle, in which "the esquire polled off some of" his "locks." Next day, the Queen had something to say, pleasant to Master Willoughby but not pleasant to Southampton. Presently Southampton was found to have committed what was even now, in this waning evening of Gloriana's day, a crime. It was repetition of Ralegh's and Elizabeth Throckmorton's offense: perhaps a secret marriage,[2] perhaps an anticipation of marriage—in either case, an insupportable insult to the Queen, who continually exhorted "all her women to remain in a virgin state as much as may be." Elizabeth Vernon, the "new-coined Countess," was driven from Court, and the honeymoon began in the usual place, a prison: "the Queen hath commanded the *novizia* countess the sweetest and best appointed lodging in the Fleet; her Lord is by commandment to return upon his allegiance."

Chamberlain adds, with that haunting note of mystery and prevision which contemporaries felt and expressed in all the stages of the tragic Essex business, "these are but *initiae malorum.*" An accomplice in his friend's guilt, Essex shared his disgrace. He grew ever more reckless and "temperamental." He was always in pecuniary distress, despite the Queen's generous gifts to him[3] (and, in her long reign, to him only). Ralegh offered him one third of his prizes. At the same time Elizabeth made Cecil a £7000 grant from the proceeds of the Crown cochineal taken in the Islands Voyage. Cecil and Essex must have regarded Ralegh's high-seas activities as very useful. All three met from time to time as if still allies, and the two former promised to have Ralegh made Privy Councillor at last, and, if possible, Vice-Chamberlain. He had often exercised a Councillor's functions, and at this period did so constantly. In August, 1598, he and Cobham were "in speech to be sworn

2. See John Chamberlain, *Letters Written during the Reign of Queen Elizabeth,* ed. Sarah Williams (Camden Society, 1861), p. 18.

3. Amounting to £300,000 (or nearly a whole year's revenue), in addition to positions of great profit.

shortly of the Council."[4] Essex was much with Ralegh and Cecil; "none but they enjoy him."[5]

But the pact had no underlying sincerity, though Ralegh, who had been fighting a losing battle all his life, would have been glad to have it hold. Had he cared, Essex had opportunity enough to settle down into a statesman; the grim depressing pages on which his and Ralegh's names were hereafter written together need never have come into existence. But he did not care; and his fortunes clouded fast toward their stormy setting. He was a pall-bearer at Lord Burghley's funeral in August, 1598, and it was noticed that he "carried the heaviest countenance of the company (whether it were upon consideration of the present occasion, or for his own disfavors)."[6] He sued afterwards for the highly lucrative post of Master of the Wards, one vacated by Burghley's death. The Queen refused him, and proposed to discharge the duties herself, whereupon he told her she would be doing what none of her predecessors had done, and "the world may judge, and I must believe, that you overthrow the office because I should not be the officer." In the course of English history, many men have been executed for "high treason" on the flimsiest of charges. None ever earned it so thoroughly and so often as Essex did; none was so much forgiven, or given such warning on warning. The Queen told him: "He would do well to content himself with displeasing her on all occasions and despising her person so insolently. But he should beware of touching her sceptre."

The break came over Ireland, where things were going excessively ill. That "miserable Nation . . . wanted not only wisdom and virtue to purchase her own Freedom, but a competency of patience to submit to the English civility."[7] In Hugh O'Neill, Earl of Tyrone, the Irish found a leader, one in close association with Spain. In August, 1598, he routed a royal force on the Blackwater, "the greatest loss and dishonour the Queen hath had in her time."[8] Of the vague menace of Spanish invasion which hung over England's western coasts continually, there

4. Chamberlain to Carleton, August 30, 1598 (*Letters, etc.,* p. 16.)
5. Rowland Whyte, January 3, 1598 (Collins, *Letters, etc.,* ii, 79).
6. Chamberlain to Carleton.
7. Osborne, *Some Traditional Memoirs of the Reign of Queen Elizabeth,* p. 87.
8. Chamberlain to Carleton, *Letters,* p. 17.

was some lifting when Philip II died, on September 13. But there was no lifting of the Irish menace. The Queen resolved on a policy ruthlessly vigorous. Ralegh saw to it that his own name was withdrawn from nomination to the Lord Deputyship, and in any case was too much needed in the exposed counties of Devon and Cornwall. But Essex thought Ireland the right place for his rival's partisans, and wanted Carew, now President of Munster, to be promoted Lord Deputy.[9] The Queen refusing, he turned his back on her with a movement of scorn, and she boxed his ears. He put his hand on his swordhilt, swore that he would not have taken such treatment from Henry VIII, had he been alive, called her "a King in petticoats," and rushed from the room. He had been treated like the child he was.

He sulked in retirement at Wanstead, Epping Forest. "But the Queen says he hath played long enough upon her, and that she means to play awhile upon him, and to stand as much upon her greatness, as he hath done upon stomach." His personal charm must have been immense, for even in that age of little trust and keeping of faith he had friends as well as sycophants. Even Ralegh persisted, after rebuff on rebuff, in trying to come to an understanding. "You are not so far gone," Lord Keeper Egerton advised Essex, "but you may well return. The return is safe, but the progress dangerous and desperate in this course you hold." He answered proudly that he "had been content to do Her Majesty the service of a clerk; but can never serve her as villein or slave." He owed her "the duty of an Earl and of Lord Marshal of England" (but not, apparently, of a gentleman and quiet subject). "What! Cannot princes err? Cannot subjects receive wrong? Is an earthly power or authority infinite?" The Queen could be handled only by bullying; he had "a settled opinion" that she "could be brought to nothing but by a kind of necessity or authority."[10]

"After a time, with sulky lip-submission, he returned, ready to quarrel with anyone."[11] His followers were determined it should be first with Ralegh. There was to be a tournament on the Queen's birthday, November 17, 1598. Essex learnt that Ralegh meant to bring his train in orange-plumed hats and with orange favors; he did the same, and his huge private army of two thousand swamped and swallowed up his

9. E. P. Statham, *A Jacobean Letter-writer*, p. 16.
10. Francis Bacon.   11. Hume, p. 213.

rival's company.[12] Doubtless his flatterers told him he had done a brilliant thing, and put Ralegh in his place. But the Queen's honor had been turned into ridicule, a mere scene of faction, and herself ignored. No one would have dared such insolence ten years previously. She knew now that only a sharp lesson would check the contempt that had gone so far. She made her resentment obvious, and Essex "ran very ill." The festivities broke up in the atmosphere of gathering storm.

Popular opinion demanded Essex for Ireland, the biggest task that loomed, asking a giant's powers. He had blocked everyone else's appointment. At the end of March, accordingly, he was sent over as Lord Deputy, with a mischievous display of general exultation. Shakespeare shared it, and we can imagine how his Globe audience rose to his expression of it!

> Were now the general of our gracious empress
> (As in good time he may) from Ireland coming,
> Bringing rebellion broachèd on his sword,
> How many would the peaceful city quit
> To welcome him![13]

Essex had ridden through the cheering City, with a large band of nobles and gentlemen accompanying him. He was to come riding through London streets again—but as the demented leader of a rising which had no chance of bringing anything but the gallows.

He took to Ireland an army such as no English general had had before, and unprecedented authority: "so ample a Commission as might give his Ambition full power and room to expatiate in, by which he was most likely to be tugged aground."[14] But he had no policy and no plans—only a brain seething with fancied wrongs and savage suspicions. Arrived in Ireland, he loitered, while his followers talked more wildly than ever. It was caustically noted that he was at his favorite game of knight-making: "My Lord hath lately made sixteen new knights, for what service I know not, but belike it is *de bene esse,* in

12. *Reliquiae Wottonianae,* p. 190: "two thousand Orange-tawny Feathers, in despite of Sir Walter Ralegh."
13. *Henry V,* Prologue, Act V, ll. 30–34.
14. Osborne, p. 34. The "tugged aground" refers to him as the "Court Leviathan." See p. 144.

hope they will deserve it hereafter."[15] That was written on August 1, 1599. Eight days later a fleet was being put in readiness—against possible Spanish attacks, *of course*. But a common belief was that it was against an attack Essex was planning from Ireland. Ralegh and Lord Thomas Howard, the Vice-Admiral and Admiral, "took leave at Court of all the ladies." London was barricaded for a fortnight. Two years later, when Essex's life had finally gone down in ruins, his lieutenant Sir Christopher Blount on the scaffold confessed to Ralegh that there *had* been plans considered to bring forces back to Milford Haven, and thence march on London.

Elizabeth remarked that she was spending a thousand pounds a day, merely to let Essex go on progress. Going on progress was a splendor she reserved for herself. By August 23 she knew that he had made threescore knights. "It is much marvelled that this humour should so possess him, that, not content with his first dozens and scores, he should thus fall, to huddle them up by half hundreds." Men were beginning to ask themselves, after all what *had* Essex ever achieved, for all his immense vogue? A subject who had not "been six months together in any one action" had "upon so little service and small desert" made "more knights than are in all the realm besides, and it is doubted that if he continue this course he will shortly bring in tag and rag, cut and long tail, and so draw the order into contempt."[16] On the other hand, he had by court-martial sentenced to decimation a body of soldiers who had been defeated, after showing cowardice under incompetent leaders. Such drastic discipline was resented. Elizabeth, watching angrily and impatiently, must have wondered where this young man's courses would end, when he was exercising such powers of reward and military execution, in a campaign which he had made into mere foolery.

Meanwhile he was wavering toward a gentler method with the now triumphing Irish—an excellent thing if he had not been so nerveless that his wavering never came to resolution. The Queen, aging rapidly and waxing wrathful with the thwarted exacerbation of old tired imperiousness, wanted simply swift and complete crushing of all rebels. When overruling instructions came from London, checking the mod-

15. Chamberlain to Carleton, *Letters*, p. 57.
16. *Ibid.*, p. 63.

eration he half intended, Essex assumed that Ralegh was mainly responsible. He dared not openly abuse Robert Cecil and great noblemen like the Earl of Nottingham, but he hinted that others were in a plot against him. He wrote (June 25, 1599):

Is it not lamented by your Majesty's faithfullest subjects, both here and there, that a Cobham and Ralegh—I will forbear others for their places' sakes—should have such credit and favour with your Majesty, when they wish the ill success of your Majesty's most important action, the decay of your greatest strength, and the destruction of your faithfullest servants?

As Stebbing urges, we may sympathize "with his general tendencies in Irish administration," rather than with Ralegh's policies there. "He would detect the voice and hand of Ralegh in all the hindrances to, and in every criticism upon, his measures."[17] He would in imagination hear that persuasive voice "arguing adversely at sittings of the Council, to which he was informally admitted, and in the Queen's chamber"; and arguing, with all the weight of long Irish experience. But Essex's interest in Ireland and the Irish was very slight; his heart was only in regaining his former ascendancy at Court. He was bemoaning continually his "banishment and proscription into the cursedest of all islands." He wrote to the Council that he was "armed on the breast, but not on the back"—against Ralegh and Cobham and Cecil.

While he negotiated and intrigued with Tyrone, and procrastinated and plotted, he received from the Queen "an express letter all written with her own hand," forbidding him ever to make another knight. In September followed a scathing analysis of his actions, or rather, his determined inaction. On his allegiance he had been *absolutely commanded not to presume to come over* (for those were her words),"[18] until he had affairs in a satisfactory condition, and had permission to return. But on September 3 he astounded the Irish Privy Council with the announcement that he was immediately going. He took a hundred gentlemen who were closely knit to his cause; and on the 28th he burst into the chamber where Elizabeth was dressing, her hair tumbled about her face. He had always been notoriously careless about his ap-

17. *Ralegh*, p. 147.
18. Robert Cecil to Sir H. N. Neville, October 8, 1599 (*Memoirs . . . from the Papers of Sir Ralph Winwood*, i, 118).

pearance, and he now came mired from furious travelling. His reception seems to have been mixed. "God's death, my lord! what do you here, your presence hateful, without Tyrone's head?"[19] She then controlled her anger (or else it came later, and now she was genuinely touched with something of the old kindness), until he fell "more to a dispute than to any excuse," and "she, in disdain to be taught but what she pleased to do, bid him be gone, his boots stunk." Yet he seems to have gone momentarily happier, as if things had not been so bad as he dreaded. He "thanked God, though he had suffered much trouble and storms abroad, he found a sweet calm at home."[20] Next day, however, he had to see the Council, and on October 1 was committed to the Lord Keeper's custody at York House. Four days later he was again examined by the Lord Keeper, the Lord Treasurer and Cecil. The Queen spoke scornfully to the French Ambassador of "Monsieur d'Essex," who had intended to pardon her Irish rebels for her, which she meant to show him was out of his power.

The Court was in a ferment, for his followers had swarmed over, leaving Elizabeth's affairs in Ireland to get on as best they might. The populace grew excited. Its hero was being abominably treated, all because of base enemies, and of that knave Ralegh in particular, and he was being held under constraint without cause even pretended. Elizabeth, not for the first time in her life, had to think hard and quickly, and to hide her thoughts. On November 28, accompanied by the Earl of Worcester and the Countess of Warwick, she visited Essex at York House, and next day the Court of Star Chamber prepared a public statement of the "Causes of the Imprisonment of the Earl of Essex." In his strange popularity things seemed touch and go, so much had Elizabeth lost her hold on her people. It was rumored that the Earl was about to be sent to real imprisonment, the precursor of real trial and real condemnation, "and some of the Guard that gave out they must wait on my Lord to the Tower had their coats plucked off."

We must now consider "a shocking but sagacious letter"[21] written by Ralegh to Cecil.[22] It must have fallen in this period, and few documents of a deeper or more complex psychological interest exist.

19. William Sanderson, *The Lives and Reigns of Mary Queen of Scotland and James the Sixth, King of Scotland* (1656), p. 236.
20. Rowland Whyte.   21. Neale, *Queen Elizabeth*, p. 366.
22. Printed, R. Murdin, *State Papers,* etc., ii, 811.

Sir,

I am not wise enough to give you advice; but if you take it for a good counsel to relent towards this tyrant, you will repent it when it shall be too late. His malice is fixed, and will not evaporate by any your mild courses. For he will ascribe the alteration to Her Majesty's pusillanimity, and not to your good nature; knowing that you work but upon her humour, and not out of any love towards him. The less you make him, the less he shall be able to harm you and yours. And if Her Majesty's favour fail him, he will again decline to a common person.

For after-revenges, fear them not; for your own father that was esteemed to be the contriver of Norfolk's ruin, yet his son followeth your father's son, and loveth him. Humours of men succeed[23] not; but grow by occasions and accidents of time and power. Somerset made no revenge on the Duke of Northumberland's heirs. Northumberland, that now is, thinks not of Hatton's issue. Kelloway lives, that murdered the brother of Horsey; and Horsey let him go by, all his lifetime.

I could name you a thousand of those; and therefore after-fears are but prophecies—or rather, conjectures—from causes remote. Look to the present, and you do wisely. His son shall be the youngest Earl of England but one, and, if his father be now kept down, Will Cecil[24] shall be able to keep as many men at his heels as he, and more too. He may also match in a better house than his; and so that fear is not worth the fearing. But if the father continue, he will be able to break the branches, and pull up the tree, root and all. Lose not your advantage; if you do, I read your destiny.

Yours to the end,

W. R.

Let the Q. hold Bothwell while she hath him. He will ever be the canker of her estate and safety. Princes are lost by security; and preserved by prevention. I have seen the last of her good days, and all ours, after his liberty.

Biographers, with Stebbing wavering, have nearly all interpreted this as Ralegh's determination that his rival should be brought to the scaffold. It is nevertheless plain that this is just what it is not:

this Letter—whatever its other faults—is *not* an incitement to the raising of a political scaffold, in order to avenge personal injuries sustained by its writer, or to remove a stumbling-block from his onward path.[25]

23. i.e., are not passed on.   24. Robert Cecil's heir.
25. Edwards, ii, 221.

Those "other faults" are obvious, and need not be justified. It is calculating, Machiavellian, cold-blooded. Does anyone suppose that high
affairs have ever been otherwise? But it is *not* pitiless, as Ralegh's own
enemies were when his hour came. There is pity in it, though shrouded
with contempt and ineradicable distrust. It is plainly written in direct
reply to a request for advice. It is no objection to this theory that we do
not possess Cecil's request; it is implied in the opening of Ralegh's letter, and the man never lived who covered up his own tracks more carefully than Robert Cecil, First Earl of Salisbury. He

was of a nature to discuss questions of policy with his confidants, and extract
their views, while he revealed only half his own. . . . He may have requested Ralegh to repeat in writing objections urged orally by him. . . . At
all events, it would be convenient for Cecil to have the document if in future it should be doubted which of the confederates had been the more
vindictive.[26]

The letter was carefully preserved at Hatfield, and among the eyes
which later looked over it may have been those of King James, who
called Essex "his martyr."

The letter, then, in my judgment was written during this first period
of Essex's more or less informal imprisonment. His mad egoism had
been convulsing England. His following of young energetic noblemen
and gentlemen was large, influential, insolent. His intrigues were not
all known, but were known to run out very far and widely, with the
chance of a Scots intervention to back him. His enmities were vigorously blazed abroad, and his often expressed intention was to cut away
those cankers of the State, Ralegh and Cecil, the threatened men who
were now taking counsel together. The question agitating inner political circles was: Ought Elizabeth to be encouraged to free her prisoner?
If she did, he would strain every nerve to regain his old ascendancy.
Ralegh says that his malice is now fixed, and it will not evaporate
because of gentle treatment. Then he considers the problem of Essex's
son, when he comes of age. Will he not seek vengeance? And, discussing this, all unintentionally he reveals what was true, that in the Elizabethans natural affection was rarely seen. The age presents a spectacle
like that of the Punjab border tribes during the Sikh anarchy a century

26. Stebbing, *Ralegh*, pp. 153–154.

ago, when the Neapolitan Avitabile could put to death with torments too terrible to relate, and yet always had an enthusiastic following, among them many who were near akin to men he had sent shrieking out of life. In the deep steadfast love and loyalty which the Raleghs showed always, they were almost alone in their generation. Ralegh was historically and exactly right in pointing out to Cecil that the son of that Thomas Howard, Duke of Norfolk, who had died by Elizabeth's first political execution, when Cecil's father was her chief minister, now jackalled the second Cecil. Indeed, the Howards were now all strongly anti-Essex and strongly pro-Cecil, very well aware in what camp their chances lay. His other instances are all historically correct and personally interesting.

That Ralegh is not thinking of execution is plain from the sentence: "And if Her Majesty's favour fail him, he will again decline to a common person." By no racking of the words can they be made to mean: "If Her Majesty behead him, he will again decline to a common person." Moreover, execution involved loss of rank and wealth, and Essex's son would not "be the youngest Earl of England but one"—he would not be an earl at all. Stebbing finds that statement equally puzzling either way, and wavers toward the usual (though untenable) interpretation of the letter because of it. Those who treat

the letter as a plea for imprisonment and disqualification for office have to show how he could have been kept a State prisoner for life for offences he had committed before the rising of February, and moreover, how the imprisoned living father was to make way in his peerage for the son. On the other theory, which presumes it to have been an argument for sending Essex to the scaffold, it is as unintelligible how the father's fate, with its necessary attainder of blood, could legally transmit his dignity.[27]

But it has been generally overlooked that Essex for some time had been a very sick man, suffering from the stone and other troubles (which is some explanation of conduct hardly approaching sanity for a week together). Ralegh was thinking of imprisonment, or banishment from Court. In the course of nature this could not last many years, and would leave a boy Earl of Essex. There was precedent enough (if a Tudor was going to bother about precedent) for keeping Essex, not exactly "a

27. Stebbing, *Ralegh*, p. 153.

State prisoner," but a man under rigid restrictions of movement and abode. "Let the Q. hold Bothwell," this creature of incessant turbulence, "while she hath him." The reference is to Francis Stuart Hepburn, fifth Earl of Bothwell, son of a natural son of James V; Bothwell was sometimes an invader of Scotland, sometimes a fugitive in England or on the Continent. To conclude Ralegh's argument, if Robert Cecil saw to it that Essex ceased, once for all, to matter, then his own son, Will Cecil, would one day be great enough and greatly enough allied to laugh at fears of reprisal from Essex's son, even if he should think of any. All of which came true.

We must return to Essex. Aware of praises exciting him from his earliest days and of the noisy admiration of the mob, he was furious at any hesitation in restoring him to all his old position. He and his friends were busy intriguing with James VI, were meeting incessantly and talking and plotting wildly, were wondering why they had not pushed home the precedent of Bolingbroke's landing to depose Richard II. Meanwhile the Queen had taken deeper and more lasting offense than Essex could believe; he thought of her as an old and ailing woman, her hand shaking on her scepter, who could be frightened into the mood he desired. His monopoly of sweet wines ran out; she did not hurry to renew it. She kept him at a distance. On February 22, 1600, John Chamberlain wrote to his friend:

You left us with so fair weather, and with so confident an opinion that all should go well with my Lord of Essex, and that we should see him a-cock-horse again, that I know it will be strange news to you to hear that all was but a kind of dream, and a false paradise that his friends have feigned to themselves, giving their hopes and discourses liberty to outrun their wit, for the bright sunshine that seemed so to dazzle them was indeed but a glimmering light that was suddenly overshadowed again, and the sky as full of clouds as before.[28]

The same correspondent was assured that "the Earl of Essex hath been somewhat crazy this week." Indeed it is as plain as any past event can be that for long before his death he was a pathological case, a man out of his normal wits, highly strung as those were at mildest. "His humours grew Tart, as being now in the Lees of favour."[29]

28. Chamberlain to Carleton, *Letters*, p. 65.   29. *Reliquiae Wottonianae*, p. 166.

Twice in the spring of 1600 Ralegh tried approaches of conciliation by writing to Lady Essex. Lady Ralegh sighed her wish that there were "love and concord amongst all," and he joined in emphatically. But the State was infected with a poison which only life could let out. Essex, forbidden to approach the Queen, was brooding on violent courses: sometimes these took the form of only a roughly unconventional loyalty, as when he wrote: "I sometimes think of running; and then remember what it will be to come in armour, triumphing, into that presence, out of which by your own voice I was commanded, and by your hands thrust out." It is hard for us to believe that we are not what we once were; and he thought, if he entered unannounced—the beloved and admired warrior who was to sweep from her Court the crew of Raleghs and Cecils and Cobhams who were misleading her—the ancient kindness would leap into flame again. At other times he indulged in such tirades that even his friends were frightened. "His speeches of the Queen," wrote Sir John Harington, "become no man who hath *mens sana in corpore sano.*" There is reason to believe that he achieved what his mind was brooding on, an audience with Elizabeth; how and where we do not know, but it was an unauthorized and violently obtained one. It was probably in this last appalling interview that he leapt into the words of mad insult which Ralegh has recorded,[30] with his judgment of their effect:

the late Earl of Essex told Queen Elizabeth that her conditions was as crooked as her carcass: but it cost him his head, which his insurrection had not cost him, but for that speech. *Who will say unto a King* (saith Job) *Thou art wicked?* Certainly it is the same thing to say unto a Lady, Thou art crooked,[31] (and perchance more), as to say unto a King that he is wicked.

It was a cruel speech to an old woman who knew that everyone was waiting for her death, and who could not be unaware of the picture she presented, her long gaunt features grotesquely capped with a reddish wig, her teeth yellow and few and irregular.

Essex, repulsed, intrigued hard with the King of Scots, whose whole

30. *Prerogative of Parliaments* (1657 ed.), p. 81. See also Osborne (p. 93) and other nearly contemporary authorities.

31. "There was a little unevenness in her shoulders" (Sir Henry Wotton, *Reliquiae Wottonianae,* p. 192).

existence had for many years been concentrated on merging his turbulent and mountainous kingdom in the rich and peaceful larger one to the south. He

aspired to the English crown from his youth, and they say that his ambition helps him to swallow the shedding of his mother's blood, and has caused him to avoid irritating the Queen of England, by displaying the greatest regard and subservience towards her.[32]

After Essex's death, James wrote to Robert Cecil, in spelling which (as with Lady Ralegh's) no hand would be so sacrilegious as to change:

Saint george surelie rydes upon a towardlie rydding horse, quhaire I am daylie burstin in daunting a wylde unreulie coalte.[33]

Not yet on terms with Cecil, to favor him with these equestrian comparisons, he was being frightened by Essex with an alleged scheme to leave him astride his untidy garron to the end, and to mount the Infanta of Spain on St. George's charger. Essex designated as the plot's leaders the Cecils, powerful in London and the north (of which Lord Burghley, Robert Cecil's elder brother, was President); Ralegh, strong in the west and the Channel Islands (in September, 1600, he was made Governor of Jersey); Cobham, Warden of the Cinque Ports; George Carew, President of Munster; the Lord Treasurer and the Lord Admiral. It was a formidable combination, had it existed. But James, though alarmed and angry, hesitated to demand the open acknowledgment of his title that Essex urged. Essex therefore moved rapidly to the thought of insurrection, having "come to regard himself as necessary to the Queen and to the country."[34] Elizabeth needed saving from herself and her evil counsellors, by whose machinations he was "sure his chance had gone, not by his own folly." His rising "had no intelligible object, and appealed to nothing in men's minds: it was an outburst of childish vanity."[35] When it came (Sunday, February 8, 1601), it found the Government warned and ready.

32. *Calendar of State Papers, Venetian,* 1592–1603, p. 540. For an exceedingly unflattering foreign picture of King James see p. 604 of the same volume.
33. *Correspondence of King James VI of Scotland with Sir Robert Cecil and Others during the Reign of Queen Elizabeth,* ed. John Bruce (Camden Society, 1861), no. xi, 31–32.
34. Mandell Creighton, *Elizabeth,* p. 290.   35. *Ibid.,* p. 292.

One of Essex's fellow-conspirators was Ralegh's kinsman, Sir Ferdinando Gorges,[36] Governor of Plymouth Fort, the most important post in Ralegh's own special responsibility. Ralegh sought to draw him back, and asked him to come by river to see him at Durham House. Probably the message was a direct order, as from his superior officer. The action precipitated the insurrection. Ralegh was seeking to disintegrate their fellowship! Essex consented to let Gorges go, but advised him to meet Ralegh, not at Durham House but on the river itself. Ralegh accepted this condition; he came in a boat, alone, while Gorges brought two gentlemen to secure him from violence. When the rebellion had collapsed and its participators were being examined, Gorges said that Sir Christopher Blount had pressed him to either kill or capture Ralegh as a hostage; but he refused, having still some loyalty to his old commander, "unless Sir Walter had given me the first occasion by violent deeds or unkind words, for either of which I was both resolved and prepared." The "intent was particular against Sir Walter Ralegh and others," which "was no matter of treason against Her Majesty, but rather a manifestation of the contrary." Blount took four shots at Ralegh with a musket during the interview, but missed him.

Ralegh warned Gorges that a warrant was out for him, and sternly bade him return immediately to his post at Plymouth. Gorges said he was too deeply committed, and it was too late. Asked what the conspirators expected to do, he said

there were two thousand gentlemen who had resolved that day to live or die free men. Sir Walter protested unto me he heard not of it, until that morning; but did not see what they were able to do against the Queen's authority. My answer was, it was the abuse of that, by him and others, which made so many honest men resolve to seek a reformation thereof. His reply was, that no man is without a colour for his intent; and advised me to look to myself and to remember my duty and allegiance.

In the exaltation of his persecution-complex, Gorges exclaimed, "This is like to be the bloodiest day's work that ever was!" Then the two parted, "he to the Court, and I to Essex House."

The rebellion flared up, and was over. Alleging that Ralegh and

36. Cousin of Sir Arthur Gorges.

Cobham had laid an ambuscade of muskets for him on the river,[37] Essex led his gentlemen through London, crying that they were for the Queen, that his life was threatened, that England was sold to Spain. The Government sent out a herald proclaiming him a traitor; gates clanged behind him, and the train-bands presently blocked escape. As he sank in the terrors of failure, his countenance grew "ghast" and he sweated with dread. Not even men he knew would help him. In one place there were no arms for him ("Not for me, Pickering?"); there were none from the Sheriff either, though he had thought the Sheriff his friend. When they tried to retreat to Essex House, to sell their lives dearly there or with resistance to buy their pardon, they found Lud Gate locked, and guarded with chains across the street and soldiers. He galloped to the river-side, and got by boat to Essex House. It was already besieged on the Strand front, and very quickly it was besieged by water also. All the great captains were out against them, Ralegh and Lord Thomas Howard among them. The conspirators held out for a few hours, and then surrendered.

The collapse was as hysterical as the uprising. The accused wallowed in an orgy of confession and (still more) counter-accusations. Each one, it appeared, had been egged on and misled by someone else. The Earl of Southampton, when condemned, begged for life in a way that was censured as ill befitting his rank. Sir Christopher Blount, Essex's father-in-law, behaved better, admitting that neither he nor Essex had believed that Ralegh and Cobham had plotted to kill Essex. "It was a word cast out, to colour other matters."

The executions were few, and Southampton, who in any other reign would have died, was spared. Blount on the scaffold had the grace to ask: "Is Sir Walter Ralegh here?" When Ralegh, officially present as Captain of the Guard, came nearer, he said:

Sir Walter Ralegh, I thank God that you are present. I had an infinite desire to speak with you, to ask your forgiveness ere I died. Both for the wrong done you and for my particular ill intent towards you, I beseech you forgive me.

Ralegh replied: "I most willingly forgive you, and I beseech God to

37. Sanderson, p. 239. See also Birch, *Memoirs of Queen Elizabeth*, p. 465; and Robert Cecil, *Letters from R. C. to Sir George Carew*, ed. John Maclean, p. 68.

forgive you, and to give you His divine comfort." To the spectators he added: "I protest before God that, whatever Sir Christopher Blount meant towards me, I, for my part, never bore him any ill intent." He interfered when Blount's dying words were about to be cut short, and procured for him the decency of full leisure in going hence.

Essex's demeanor at his trial had been that of insolence trying to be witty. "Superb disdain," Professor Neale strangely calls it.[38] When Ralegh was about to be sworn as a witness, he bawled out, "What booteth it to swear this fox?" and that a small Testament was insufficient, a folio was needed. When sentence was pronounced he said: "I think it fitting that my poor quarters, which have done Her Majesty true service in divers parts of the world, should now at the last be sacrificed and disposed of at Her Majesty's pleasure." He was a playboy, and one who witnessed the trial wrote down as his judgment: "A man might easily perceive that, as he had lived popularly, so his chief care was to leave a good opinion in the people's minds now at parting." But when he was back in the Tower, the deeply religious side of his nature, the Puritanism which had been in earlier days conspicuous in his thought though not in his conduct, and which was to be present in his son,[39] took control of his disordered brain. The chaplain he had asked for showed him his guilt. Essex exhorted his secretary, Henry Cuff (who was to die a far unpleasanter death than the easy one allotted to one of his own quality), to "call to God for mercy, and to the Queen, and deserve it by declaring truth"; and "accused the man of being the greatest instigator of his actions."[40] He made a confession whose unnecessary thoroughness appalled even his greatest admirers, who had never dreamt how far a turgid penitence could go. The folly into which "the preacher" beguiled him was constantly referred to, for years afterwards. Ralegh's own betrayer to death, Sir Lewis Stukeley, in 1618 desperately trying to justify conduct which had covered him with abhorrence, thought it worth while going back to this surpassingly wretched episode to stir up feeling against Ralegh. He said that Ralegh spoke of "the great boy" dying "like a calf," and that to one who asked if in the Islands Voyage the Earl had not brought him to his mercy, he replied that he trusted they were now quits. There can be

38. *Elizabeth*, p. 374.
39. Commander-in-Chief for the Parliament against King Charles I.
40. Neale, *Elizabeth*, p. 375.

little worse testimony than Sir Lewis Stukeley's, but the remark about the "great boy" bears so individual a ring of scorn that it leaves an unpleasant fear that it may not have been invented. Others thought similar thoughts at the time. When Essex had dragged in his own sister's liaison with Lord Mountjoy, the Lord Admiral had a word of indignant comfort for the latter. "Would your Lordship have thought this weakness and this unnaturalness in this man?" No one would have thought it, until it happened.

The fervor of conviction continued to the end. Having learned that "all popularity and trust in man" was vain, he sought a private death, for "the acclamation of the people might have been a temptation." When he was beheaded, February 25, 1601, he "acknowledged, with thankfulness to God, that he was thus justly spewed out of the realm." Admitting that "he knew no other than that" Ralegh and Cobham "were true servants to the Queen and the State,"[41] in his last moments he asked for the former. Present as Captain of the Guard, Ralegh had at first stood near, hoping Essex might want to speak to him, as Blount had done. But seeing that spectators were murmuring, he withdrew to the Armory, where he could see, himself unnoticed. So he was not able to come forward when the dying man desired to be reconciled, a matter of lasting regret to him.

After the execution, people noted that Ralegh's face was filled with gloom. Most things come too late; and his preëminence came when it was worthless. The Queen's capricious choice had now nothing of personal feeling in it, and little of kindness. His own gains from it amounted to comparatively little; no first-rate position ever came his way.

Essex had just died miserably at the age of thirty-four; and, as he rowed back to Durham House, Ralegh must have felt that with him more than one excited life had passed away. The Elizabethan Age was over, with all its ardors of reckless spirit squandering itself, not wisely, not righteously, but generously and madly and brightly. The Age of Robert Cecil and of James had begun; and in that Age there could be nothing for him but the unhappiness of striving against rivals without one spark of the magnanimous mind that had burnt fitfully in Essex, and had sometimes been fanned to sudden fulness.

41. *Winwood Papers*, i, 301. See also *Letters from Robert Cecil to Sir George Carew*, ed. John Maclean (Camden Society, 1854), p. 72.

CHAPTER XV

Elizabeth's Last Years

Authority forgets a dying King. TENNYSON.

AFTER Essex's death, all care for living left the Queen. "Nothing pleased her. She stamped and swore violently at the ladies of the Court, whom she tormented beyond measure,"[1] beating and cuffing them, in paroxysms that recalled her father's. Meanwhile Essex's popularity with the nation grew, till it was unofficial canonization, without parallel before or since. Anger at those who were believed to have trapped him to his ruin went deep, and was without bounds. "Sweet England's pride," who "ne'er did ill," had been foully done to death by slanderous tongues, whose punishment was eagerly prophesied and awaited. Most detested of all were "little Cecil," now "tripping up and down," who had issued the long proclamation declaring that the Government's drastic action had saved London, a statement received with complete disbelief, and Ralegh, who had rid himself of his rival.[2] Trouble was coming for him also; of this the ballad-makers and lampoonists were sure:

> Ralegh doth time bestride:
> He sits 'twixt wind and tide:
> Yet uphill he cannot ride,
> For all his bloody pride.
> He seeks taxes in the tin:
> He polls the poor to the skin:
> Yet he swears 'tis no sin.
> Lord, for thy pity!

The dismayed perplexity of Essex's comrades that the Queen's kindness should have permitted such a finish was touchingly expressed by Sir

1. Sir John Harington, October, 1601.
2. To this time belongs the well-known incident of the Queen playing the virginals (with Ralegh as Captain of the Guard beside her), and, noticing a meaning smile on the Earl of Oxford's face, asking the reason, to be given the answer: "I see that when jacks go up heads go down"—a reference to Ralegh's survival when Essex had fallen.

Henry Wotton, writing to a friend (July 5, 1602) from Florence: "I am not deep enough to judge of great actions; and therefore let princes do what they will, and we will love one another."

In 1599 there had been peace negotiations with Spain at Boulogne, in which Ralegh had wanted to be a Commissioner. The Queen refused, for it would have made it hard to keep him out of her Council, the reward he was desiring so passionately that Lord Henry Howard said he now "found no view for Paradise out of a Council board." Many witnesses testify that he was a Councillor in all but name: "he was often called to counsel . . . but never sworn."[3] In June, 1601, he seemed certain to be sworn at last, but was not. Then, after Essex fell, rumor had it that he was to be raised to the peerage as Earl of Pembroke. Cecil saw to it that he remained as he was; and at this time managed to detach from Ralegh George Carew, who was wearying of long Irish exile. Cecil wrote to him that he would never consent to Ralegh joining the Council, unless he surrendered to Carew the Captaincy of the Guard.

For ornamental and laborious jobs, however, Ralegh might serve. His fluency in several Continental tongues kept him in constant request when distinguished foreigners visited London; and he became to them personally, as well as by report, one of the best known of Englishmen. In March, 1600, he "carries up and down" in London a Spanish envoy, "to see sights and rareties hereabout." A little later in the year, Henri IV sent over his celebrated minister, the Duke of Sully. Sully came, he imagined, incognito. But he had been expected, and was recognized at Dover:

I had scarcely entered my room, and was in the act of speaking to my attendants, when I found myself approached, behind my back, by some one who said to me, "I arrest you as my prisoner, in the Queen's name." It was the Captain of her Guard, whose embrace I returned, telling him I should consider such an imprisonment as a great honour.[4]

Delighted to enter into the courtly custody of the least insular of Eng-

3. Sanderson, p. 292.
4. *Mémoires* (1814), iii, 29. See also A. Jamieson, *Memoirs of the Duke of Sully* (1822), i, 264.

lishmen, Sully was taken at once to the Queen, who scolded him for trying to come in unsuspected. "It is well, Monsieur de Rosny! Do you break our fences thus, and pass on without coming to see me? I am greatly surprised at it, for I thought you bore me more affection than any of my servants, and I am persuaded I have given you no cause to change those sentiments."

In September the Duke of Biron, Constable of France, came. Essex's execution was still the talk, and Sully tells us that Biron asked the Queen about her treatment of him. Unperturbed by this impertinence, Elizabeth discussed the Earl's continued treasons, and said that when all was known he refused to sue for the pardon which she would have granted. Another French writer, Eudes de Mezerai, "for the information of his compatriots on our domestic manners has improved upon"[5] Sully's account; he tells how Biron entered London with Elizabeth, and that she drew his attention to Essex's head, adorning Temple Bar. This story, often repeated as true and sometimes told in the variant form that she opened a box and showed Essex's skull to the Frenchman, is incredible to those who realize how terrible was her grief. To return to solid ground of known fact—Biron was already in treasonable intrigues against his own King, and closely watched. Sully comments:

I know not whether the Queen saw in the French Ambassador certain points of resemblance with the English favourite. The just reflections on the functions of crowned heads and on the duties of subjects with which she wound up her recital leads one to think so. But Biron turned the conversation to no profit.

Ten months later Biron went to the scaffold, a tragedy startling France as Essex's had startled England, and setting the London dramatists writing. Now, however, the shadow of the headman's axe, to him at least, was nowhere visible. He brought a retinue of four hundred, an embarrassing and costly train. The Queen being absent in Hampshire, Ralegh received them and showed them London. The Privy Council had issued orders for their entertainment; but such was the general disintegration of the public services that nothing was ready. Ralegh wrote to Cecil:[6]

5. Edwards, *Ralegh*, ii, 232.   6. Sept. 7, 1601.

I am glad I came hither, for I never saw so great a person so neglected . . . not one nobleman nor gentleman to accompany them nor to guide them. . . . We have carried them to Westminster to see the Monuments; and this Monday we entertained them at the Bear Garden, which they had great pleasure to see. . . .

I sent to and fro, and have laboured like a moyle.[7] . . .

He took them on to the Queen, at Basing, where he noted[8] their plainness, against "that outward magnificence which had become almost a second nature to the courtiers of Queen Elizabeth":[9]

The French wear all black and no kind of bravery at all, so as I have only made me a black taffeta suit to be in, and leave all my other suits.

This letter was written late on the Saturday night (he often worked right through the dark hours); and a postscript says he is immediately journeying to London, "to provide me a plain taffeta suit and a plain black saddle, and will be here again"—at Basing House—"Tuesday night."

Ralegh remained "still underwood, cut and yet growing";[10] even his presence was a matter of indifference to the Queen. In September, 1600, he had been made Governor of Jersey,[11] partly to get him away from London, where his existence was a constant provocation to Essex. He went; and shortly after his sailing, "that rotten houes,"[12] Durham House, suffered a fire, mentioned by Lady Ralegh in a letter to Robert Cecil:[13]

Hit is trew that your packet brought me the newes of the miscchans of feeiar at Durram Houes, wher, I thanke God, hit went noo fardar. Other wies, hit had rid ous of all our poour substans of plat and other thinges. Unly now the loos is of your cumpani and my Lord Cobham's, wich I thinke by this menes wee cannot injoy this wintar. . . .

She urged Cecil to get them something better than a mere lease interest. As matters stood, it was not worth while to repair Durham House, which must fall to ruin, ultimately entailing expense on the Crown:

7. Mule.   8. Letter to Lord Cobham, Sept. 12, 1601.
9. Edwards, i, 278.   10. Sanderson, p. 283.
11. See *Egerton Papers*, p. 313, for his Patent.
12. Lady Ralegh.   13. October, 1600.

I knoo none so un wies that will besto so mani hundred pounes as Sur Wattar hath dun, without fardar intrest or asurans of hit. I besuch remembar hit now, soo shall not the Quine be trobled to bild the Bushope's ould stabels.

I ded heer from Sur Wattar within too dayes after he landed at Jarsi: wher he was safly landed and rioly intertaned with joye. But he was too dayes and too nites on the see, with contrari windes; not withstanding hee went from Wamouthe in so fayer a wind and weether, as littell Wat and my selfe brought him abord the ship. Hee wrytteth to me hee never saw a pleasanttar iland; but protesteth unfannedly hit tis not, in valew, the veri third part that was reported, or inded hee beliffed. My cossin Will is heer, very will,[14] and louketh will and fat with his batheing. This,[15] wishing you all honnar and the full contentements of your hart, I ever rest

Your asured poure frind,

E. Ralegh.

I am glad this mischans of feeiar cam not by ani neckelegans of ani sarvant of mine, but by me cossin Darci's sarvant—a woman that delleth[16] just under our logging, and anoyeth ous infenitly. . . .

The Will whose bathing has done him such good is Cecil's son, mentioned earlier. His health gave anxiety, and he was a constant guest of the Raleghs.

Cecil, however, had his own ideas about Durham House; he had determined to get the Raleghs out of it. The fire usefully spread a belief that its present tenants were careless about its upkeep, which was partly true.

As Lady Ralegh's letter indicates, the Jersey governorship proved financially disappointing. The Crown docked Ralegh of three hundred pounds a year, to compensate a rival for the post, Lord Henry Seymour. But here, as everywhere, he did his job unsparingly. "He shrank from no accumulation of pluralities. But he had no love for sinecures."[17] He opened up a profitable trade of the island with Newfoundland. He abolished an irksome compulsory service system in the Mont Orgueil district, the *Corps-de-Garde*. He refused to carry through an order issued for economy's sake, to dismantle Mont Orgueil:

14. Well.
16. Dwelleth.

15. Thus.
17. Edwards, *Ralegh,* i, 263.

to say true, it is a stately fort of great capacity, both as to maintenance and comfort, to all that part of the island next unto Normandy, which stands in view thereof; so as, until I knew further Her Majesty's pleasure, I have left at mine own charge some men in it. And, if a small matter may defend it, it were pity to cast it down, having cost Her Majesty's father, brother, and sister—without her own charge—20,000 marks the erecting.[18]

He at once took up the completion of another fort, "for the name's sake" (he told Elizabeth through Cecil), *Isabella Bellissima,* "which I have presumed to christen it by—being before without any denomination at all." He instituted public registration of real estate.

The only task he pulled out from was Ireland, which in September, 1601, had a second and more serious Spanish invasion, that landed at Kinsale. Ralegh told Cecil he thought Kinsale was not where the enemy meant to land, unless seeking Florence McCarthy. They *were* seeking him; and were disappointed, on landing, to learn he was a prisoner in the Tower (where he and Ralegh, a little later, were fellow-captives). The Lord Deputy of Munster (now George Carew) and the Lord President of Ireland were optimistic that they would make "short work" of the visitors, as once at Smerwick. Ralegh disagreed: his cool prognostication was that Spain would meet with a disappointing response from the Irish, and would be dilatory in sending reinforcements. "I do not think that Spain will supply them in haste; neither will those Spaniards already there find such a party as they hoped." Spain accordingly would linger out her help, neither withdrawing nor strengthening it. Then he seems to have wearied suddenly of his share in the Irish business, in December, 1602, selling off his property for £1000, to Robert Boyle (afterwards first Earl of Cork[19]). He kept only Inchiquin Ralegh, a castle of which Katharine, Dowager Countess of Desmond, was life tenant. She was believed to have been born in 1464, when Edward IV was King; and she died, a hundred and forty years old, in 1604, as the result (tradition affirms) of falling from a tree which she had climbed for apples.

Despite his Jersey governorship, and more duties than any other man can ever have accomplished with like efficiency, he was busy improving Sherborne, his half-brother Adrian Gilbert acting as his agent. Lady

18. Letter of Oct. 15, 1600.
19. The "great Earl," largely responsible for bringing Strafford to his death.

Ralegh cannot have felt much interest in a rumor that she was to be re-called to Court. But it alarmed Cecil's party. Lord Henry Howard to King James called her (April, 1602) "a most dangerous woman, and full of her father's inventions." "A very strong league" existed between Lady Ralegh and Lady Shrewsbury.

Ralegh continued to remind the Government how much the buc-caneer he was—superbly serviceable when the intention was to keep Spain exasperated and timid, but embarrassing when the drift was toward peace. Cecil's mind was all toward peace, with a King coming whose ambition was to win the Peacemaker's garland; and one cause of his final resolution to wreck Ralegh once for all, was this deep divi-sion of aims. On February 29, 1600, we find the Venetians complaining of "a prize taken by Sir John Gilbert to Sir Walter Ralegh's use."[20] They did more than complain; they held up English shipping. Few men had crueller luck in life than Ralegh. But ill-luck is rarely *all* luck. His intellectual gifts went with stupidities which lesser men never fell to. He never readjusted himself to shifting times, but remained the magnificent Elizabethan when all but the name of that epoch was dead, and indeed, long after it *had* died. Europe was passing into its modern phase. He, the historian, living through this momentous change, could not see it when others could.

The Elizabethans were a generation highly developed imaginatively —capable of high and deep speculation, of moments of magnanimity and sudden radiances of self-giving. But their personal relationships were shot through with treachery. Not once, but repeatedly, those who had worked in intimate comradeship and shared experiences which (one would have thought) had left some tenderness too genuine to be forsaken, turned to the basest and most unscrupulous enmity, in which the more powerful or more lucky engineered a friend's ruin, and fre-quently his death. Neither old association nor mental affinity and es-teem caused Cecil or Francis Bacon to pause one moment from be-trayals. Cecil now laid murderous plots for Ralegh.

In his defense something, as always, can be said. In 1603, we are told, "Cecyll doth bear no love to Ralegh, as you well understand, in the matter of Essex."[21] That statement, which is made by Sir John Haring-

20. Chamberlain, *Letters,* p. 69.   21. *Nugae Antiquae,* ii, 342.

ton, Essex's follower, may not mean more than that Cecil was at pains to dissociate himself from the immense and growing obloquy attaching to those held responsible for the hero's ruin. He saw, as Ralegh failed to see, that this was no ordinary resentment felt by an executed politician's immediate friends, but something which was going to exact blood for blood. He had not had all Ralegh's reasons for troubling about Essex's rivalry. Their grotesque disparity in personal grace of appearance made his father's advice, "seek not to be Essex," cruelly superfluous; and his own place, secure because of cautious steady sagacity, Essex could not challenge, even had he wished it. He may, therefore, have felt qualms over a course drastic beyond his desires, and have transferred to Ralegh the resentment we always feel when we have been sharers in some act which we shrank from even when it was doing.

Whatever his own personal feelings about Essex, that Cecil was now bending all his energies to disentangling himself from the hatred left by that tragedy is clearer to us than it was even to his contemporaries (and it was fairly clear to them). His thoughts all turned north, beyond the border. For forty years statesmen of both countries had dreamed of union, a fact which is the greatest example of political wisdom in history. Union lifted England and Scotland out of the position of Balkan States eternally watching or assaulting each other; it is amazing that both nations should have been able to suppress memories as deep and recent as Flodden and Pinkie and the border raidings (which of course continued throughout Elizabeth's reign), and plan an act of oblivion and amalgamation. But the actual wish for union was stronger in Scotland than in England, and strongest of all in King James. From childhood he looked with distaste on his rugged land and people; in England he saw a paradise of comfortable greatness. He kept continual watch on his chances.

In February, 1601, at the request of Essex, James sent secret agents to sound English statesmen. They had instructions to threaten the anti-Essex faction with trouble if they did not join King James's cause betimes:

Ye shall plainly declare to Mr. Secretary and his followers, that since now, when they are in their kingdom, they will thus misknow me, when the chances shall turn I shall cast a deaf ear to their requests; and whereas now I would have been content to have given them, by your means, a preassur-

ance of my favour—if at this time they had pressed to deserve the same—
so, they now contemning it, may be assured never hereafter to be heard.

Essex was dead when they reached London, and they learnt how
completely the political situation had been misconceived in Edinburgh.
In particular, one episode in Essex's trial, tragically hurtful to him, had
made a deep impression on Scots who witnessed it. Questioned as to his
wild cry, when he rode through London streets, "The Crown of England is sold to the Spaniard," he had nothing better to say than "I
spake it not of myself, for it was told me that Mr. Secretary should say
to one of his fellow-councillors, 'The Infanta's title comparatively is as
good in Succession as any other.'" The random vague hearsay sprang
instantly into drama. Cecil, who was hiding behind an arras, stepped
out, and on bended knee besought the Lord High Steward to let him
"answer this false and foul report." He beat down the confused Earl,
who could claim as a witness only Sir William Knollys, Comptroller of
the Queen's Household. Cecil flung his whole case on Knollys' agreement or disagreement, and insisted that he be sent for. Knollys, in
words that must have sounded to Essex like the bell tolling for his
death, said:

> I never heard Master Secretary speak any words to that effect. Only there
> was a seditious book, written by one Doleman, which very corruptly dis-
> puted the title of the Succession, inferring it as lawful to the Infanta of
> Spain as to any other; and Mr. Secretary and I being in talk about the book
> Mr. Secretary spake to this effect: "Is it not a strange impudence in that
> Doleman to give as equal right in the Succession of the Crown to the In-
> fanta of Spain as any other?" Hereupon was grounded the slander upon
> Mr. Secretary, whereof he is as clear as any man here present.

Cecil drove home his victory by a fierce "slating" of Essex, who stood
there trapped by his own folly, the noises of his own self-deception at
last drowned by the plashing of Charon's oars. James had agents present, who drew their own conclusions as to Essex's political value. A
little later James himself came to admit that in him he had lost a "noble
gentleman" but "no great friend."

Essex being dead, James's agents turned to "Mr. Secretary and his
followers," by the latter meaning Ralegh, Cobham and the Earl of
Northumberland. At this juncture Ralegh's conduct was incredibly un-

wise. Under Robert Cecil's betrayal of him lurks a wounded feeling. He complains of "ingratitude," which has puzzled biographers. But if the reader will look back, there is no perplexity. It was Cecil who finally smoothed the way back to favor for Ralegh, and ended the long banishment from Court. The Essex tragedy had followed, clouding all spirits with despondency and leaving men sensitive and "nervy." And now Ralegh, whose vitality was as inexhaustible as Cecil's was low, deserted Cecil and ran off with Cecil's brother-in-law, Henry Brooke, Lord Cobham. Cecil was hurt, and his isolation was intensified.

Cobham was "a most silly lord, but one degree from a fool."[22] What attracted Ralegh to him? Apparently, that he was a lively and reckless talker. He must have had some superficial charm, for Lady Ralegh liked him, and so did the Queen, with whom in her last days he almost attained the status of a "favourite." Elizabeth in 1597 made him Warden of the Cinque Ports, a post which Essex had wanted; and "his greatness with the Queen"[23] hid his dangerous character from Ralegh, who passed into irresponsibility of mood, more than ever responding to wild untrammelled speech, a *hubris* bound to bring down punishment. He took no heed of the fact that the spacious days of Queen Elizabeth were over in all but name and had given place to days when careful men would gather up and assess by standards of rigid literalness every word uttered "in the mad pride of intellectuality."[24]

It is now that he is supposed to have founded that most renowned of literary clubs, at the Mermaid Tavern:

> What things have we seen
> Done at the Mermaid! heard words that have been
> So nimble and so full of subtle flame,
> As if that every one from whence they came
> Had meant to put his whole wit in a jest,
> And had resolved to live a fool the rest
> Of his dull life.[25]

At the Mermaid were men—Shakespeare was one—who cherished resentment for Essex's death. And the man whose brilliance flashes out

22. Sir Anthony Welldon, *The Court and Character of King James* (1650), p. 30.
23. *Ibid.*, p. 17.   24. Edgar Allan Poe.
25. Francis Beaumont.

unrestrainedly, as Ralegh's did, gives himself bound to his enemies, by a thousand strings suddenly tightened when his evil day comes. His contemporaries called him a "Machiavel." But it was Cecil who schemed with a thorough-paced lack of scruples, haunting dimness for all he did, while Ralegh and his silly ally did everything openly, discussing most of all what was matter of intense excitement, the question of Elizabeth's successor. No one was paying much attention to the dying Queen. But it was no time for the holiday mood in which Cobham and Ralegh now met at Durham House, and now flitted over to France, to look at war again at close quarters:

finding the Queen is so resolved to have Peace (if good conditions could be had), they obtained leave with importunity to see this one Action, before they should become desperate of seeing any more of that kind in Her Majesty's time.

So Cecil wrote;[26] and the madcap trip was ascribed by many to some deep Continental intrigue, kept to themselves by these two because "we be not worthy to know it."

Cecil detached from Ralegh his oldest and best friend, George Carew, and laid on him strict injunctions that both should keep secret any complaints which either made about Ralegh or Cobham, for those two "shew all men's letters to every man."[27] Cecil showed letters to no man, and liked to have his own destroyed. Carew, perhaps offended by the headlong fashion in which the Raleghs gave themselves to an irresponsible fool like Cobham, accepted an exchange of hidden counsels. Cecil was "a great lover and rewarder of virtue and able parts in others, so they did not aspire too high in place, or look too narrowly into his actions";[28] and to this strictly limited virtue and ability Carew (but not Ralegh) attained, and

being a very wise man, contented himself with a mean place, that was worthy of a much greater; and, although very active formerly, called to mind this saying: *Felix quem faciunt,* &c., and meddled with no State business, his

26. July 14, 1600. Sawyer, *Memoirs of Affairs,* etc. (*Winwood Papers*), i, 215.
27. See *Calendar of State Papers, Domestic,* Elizabeth, 1515–1574, pp. liii–liv, for Cecil's letter of November 4, 1602; also *Correspondence of Robert Cecil and George Carew* (Camden Society).
28. Welldon, *Court and Character of King James,* p. 14.

wisdom foretelling his Fate, if he had done otherwise. For he did see one better headpiece than his own sit tottering at that time, and fell off afterwards, which made him think it was good sleeping in a whole skin.[29]

So long as Lady Cecil was alive she kept her husband and brother friendly, and she remembered the steady kindness her son had received at Sherborne. But she died in 1597. Then Cobham, whose own wife was dead, in 1602 married Lady Kildare, the Lord Admiral's daughter. Between her and Lady Ralegh was "an ancient acquaintance," which had settled into mutual detestation. The new Lady Cobham warped her own family also into hostility to the Raleghs.

King James's eyes had long been angrily fixed on Ralegh. As far back as 1585, John Peirson, scrivener, examined by Walsingham concerning political books of which he had made copies, confessed that of one, *Reasons why the King of Scots is Unacceptable to the People of England,* he had made "five or six copies, whereof he delivered one to Sir Walter Rawley his master." Yet there was a time when James seemed willing to seek an understanding with Ralegh, whose power, and the importance of the discussions he and Cobham were openly holding at Durham House, were much exaggerated. In November, 1601, his kinsman the Duke of Lennox was sent to London and saw Ralegh.

Unfortunately there was already a triple correspondence in active being between James, Robert Cecil and Lord Henry Howard. The last, of a branch collateral to the Lord Admiral's family, was the basest man of a time rich in despicable characters—"of so venomous and cankered a disposition, that indeed he hated all men of noble parts":[30]

of all who gathered round the new King, this man was, beyond all comparison, the most undeserving of the favours which he received . . . in an age when what we should call the grossest flattery was used as frequently as phrases of common civility are by us, he easily bore away the palm for suppleness and flattery.[31]

His character is set out beyond defense, in his own prolix letters, which

29. *Ibid.,* pp. 17–18.
30. William Sanderson, *The Lives and Reigns of Mary Queen of Scotland and James the Sixth, King of Scotland* (1656), p. 22.
31. S. R. Gardiner, *History of England,* 1603–1642, i, 93–94.

James, himself the reverse of taciturn, styled "ample, Asiatic and endless"; and, after a career of unchecked success in the next reign, he was *felix opportunitate mortis,* dying just before the discovery of the poisoning of Sir Thomas Overbury, with his own hand revealed as stained with murder. He hated Ralegh almost to insanity. Nothing in literature so breathes almost incoherent malignity as his letters, the moment Ralegh's name enters them:

Rawlie, that in pride exceedeth all men alive . . . holding absolutely lost to him what others gain, inspireth Cobham with his own passions . . . and cares not at what rate he purchase opportunity to vex others, having no great hope of ascending to his own altitude. His wife, as furious as Proserpina with failing of that restitution in Court which flattery had moved her to expect, bends her whole wits and industry to the disturbance of all motions, by counsel and encouragement, that may disturb the possibility of others' hopes, since her own cannot be secured . . . these two gallants . . . divide their provinces at this day, touching traffic of the State, with so great artifice, as, *if the Peace go forward, Cobham prospers by his industry; if it do not, Rawlie by his opposition.* In matter of intelligence Cobham is commended as most secret; in matter of action Rawlie blazed as most sufficient. *Cobham in discoursing hath holden a kind of privilege to vent his passions; Rawly, to temporize.* Cobham must have the rough hand of Esau, in execution of rigour; Rawlie, the soft voice of Jacob, in courtly hypocrisy. Cobham must delight, second, inveigle, and possess the Queen's opinion, by improving dangers, casting figures, and contriving invectives against the Scottish hopes, pretensions, and actions. *Rawly must insinuate his own affection, and applaud their expectations, and concur with them.* Cobham must in all things tender the conservation of the present State, to maintain his own tenure. Rawlie must persuade anticipation, for proof of known destiny. Cobham must exclaim against the small account and reckoning that is made of noblemen. Rawlie must in all discourses hold them to be fools, and thereby insufficient for charge; or cowards, and therefore incapable of lieutenancy. Cobham must relate, and gain the credit of the Queen's satisfaction. Rawly must inspire and romance, secure from justification. Cobham must be the block almighty, that gives oracles; Rawlie must be the cogging spirit that still prompteth it. . . .[32]

From that rabid endless running-on of fury, emerge the facts that

32. Letter to Robert Cecil (? 1602). The sentences I have italicized are of importance hereafter.

Cobham and Ralegh, all unsuspecting, were enjoying themselves by talk at large, but that Ralegh was infinitely the saner and more restrained of the two: and that Ralegh had the constancy to oppose Spain still, and the wisdom to see, and admit openly, that James must be the next ruler of England. But facts were not going to hamper the conspirators. There never was a snake that hissed so loudly, that had so ample a corresponding store of venom, as Howard had. For a while he played with the idea of entrapping Elizabeth into executing Ralegh, as she had executed her other favorite:

Her Majesty must know the rage of their discontent for want of being called to that height which they affect; and made to taste the peril that grows out of discontented minds, untamed by due reverence of loyalty . . . roundly Her Majesty must daily, and by divers means, be let to know the world's apprehending her deep wisdom in discerning the secret flaws of their affections. . . . She must be taught to see the peril that grows into princes by protecting, countenancing, or entertaining persons odious to multitudes.

(Here Howard cites the precedents of Empson and Dudley, put to death by Henry VIII because they were unpopular.) "She must be told what canons are concluded in the Chapter of Durham, where Rawly's wife" (her own unforgiven former Maid of Honor) "is President." Cecil is frantically exhorted to begin by pushing Cobham, the fool, into some high position where he might come to grief. "I account it unpossible for him to scape the snares which wit may set, and weakness is apt to fall into. The Queen did never yet love man that failed in a project of importance put into his hand" (probably a glance back, such as is in Howard's mind continually, at Essex, e.g., his failure in Ireland). By using *everything,* therefore—the Queen's susceptibility to flattery, Cobham's inadequacy to any great service, Ralegh's bad name with the common people and with foreigners (that is, Spaniards)— Howard and Cecil might bring in the day when they would gloat over Ralegh's agony in ruin:

the greatest Lucifer that hath lived in our age . . . shall run himself on ground in rage, and make the Queen more sensitive in scorning so great sauciness in so great infirmity. Besides the sparks and flabs of fire that will break out of conflict, assure yourself it will enflame him with some violent desire upon the sudden to shuffle the Stoic; and, finding that his rest is set upon so slender cards, look all the ways and wrinches that he can, for a better gain—which will bring him into that snare which he would shun otherwise.

Would it not be a good idea to get King James to consent that Elizabeth should be informed that his own agents had spoken to Ralegh and Cobham? "It were not possible to make shorter nor surer work, than by this overture." But Howard rejects this proposition with a sigh. Ralegh and Cobham had declined to correspond with James unless he would first promise them that it should be kept confidential. A base untrustful attitude, and unfortunate. James could hardly commit himself on paper, and then betray them:

after such a warrant is awarded by the King, he will not willingly permit the cancelling or defacer of his own workmanship. . . . Besides, it may be that the King will be afraid that such a scandal may discourage others from embarking, out of fear that there is intelligence between the scouts and the enemy. . . .

Cecil knew both Ralegh and Elizabeth too well to think that the Essex tragedy could be reënacted. He therefore let the suggestion of ruining his friend with the Queen go, and concentrated on poisoning James's mind. Cecil, James and Howard made a secret treaty, at Duchy House, in the Strand, close to where Ralegh and Cobham were squandering their chances in idle talk. The Scots Commissioners agreed[33] that all intercourse should be inviolably secret, and ciphers used instead of names. Cecil was 10, Howard 3, the King 30, Queen Elizabeth 24. Ralegh 2, Cobham 7. These identifications are placed beyond doubt, by a paper in Cecil's own hand, at Hatfield. Cecil took further precautions. He interlarded his letters with protestations of passionate hope that Elizabeth's death might be very far off, and with flattery of her. Even so, he had some narrow escapes. Once he was with her, as minister in attendance, when a post went by the royal carriage. Learning that it was from Scotland, she sent him to get the mail-bag. He did so in trepidation, for it contained a letter to him from James; but, thinking hard, he had the presence of mind to simulate eagerness, crying out to the menials for a knife to open the packet. Bringing it up with pretended alacrity, he played on the Queen's horror of bad smells—held it

33. John Bruce, *Correspondence of King James VI of Scotland with Sir Robert Cecil and Others, during the Reign of Queen Elizabeth* (Camden Society, 1861), p. xxxv.

off from him, and declared that it stunk too much to be opened in her presence. By this subterfuge he escaped what would have been an appallingly unpleasant discovery for him.[34]

This correspondence began in the summer of 1601. When Lennox made furtive half-approaches to Ralegh and Cobham in 1602, Cecil was jealous at once, and pressed to be told who had acted as go-between. The King with some reluctance told Lord Henry Howard that it was a former comrade-in-arms of Ralegh:

I doe also persave by youre letters to Bruce that Sir Robert Cecil is verrie desyrouse to knowe the knichtis name that delt betuixt the Duike of Lennox and Raulie; and thairfore, althoch the knicht him self be a verrie honest plaine gentleman for so farre as I can learne, yett knowing that confident trust can no more be severid from trew freindshippe than the shaddow can be cutte from the boddie, I will give to Sir Robert Cecil this further proofe of my confident truste in him by discoverie of this gentlemanne's name unto him—quhiche is Sir Airthoure Savage—not doubting but that Sir Robert Cecil will conserve this as a freind's secreate, without suffering the gentleman to receave any hairme hearby, quhiche more volde interest me in honoure that him in person; especiallie since the gentlemannis nature appearis to be farre different from Raulie's, thoch oute of zeale to me and affection to his freinde he could not refuse to be trucheman unto him.[35]

Over this mission of Lennox, Ralegh behaved with characteristic unwisdom. Howard chucklingly wrote to King James that "the very next day" he went to Cecil, as to a friend,

with the same brave flourishes of confidence and love, but—touching the main point—more reservedly. For he denied any kind of proffer of devotion or kind affection to have been made to King James from him by the Duke. But he protested that the Duke had sent earnestly to crave conference with him privately, which he had denied, with a gallant answer that he had been over-deeply engaged and obliged to his own mistress to seek favour anywhere else, that he should either divert his eye or diminish his sole respect to his own sovereign.

Cecil gravely commended him. "You did well, and as I myself would have made answer, if the like offer had been made to me." After all

34. Sanderson, *The Lives, etc., of Mary and James*, p. 225. See also *Reliquiae Wottonianae*, p. 169; and Goodman, *Court of King James*, i, 32.
35. Ciphers are changed to names. Trucheman, ambassador.

these years a child in statecraft, Ralegh asked Mr. Secretary to let the Queen know. But Mr. Secretary, who did not want this matter to be probed and perchance his own deep share in it dragged to light, "dissuaded him by many reasons—as, that the Queen would rather mark a weakness that gave the Duke encouragement, than praise his resolution—and, again, that it would be thought a motive to pick a thank."

James, when the intrigue began, was desperate with impatience, determined not to be jockeyed out of the succession. He began it with bitter prejudice against Cecil,[36] "a very wise man, but much hated in England, by reason of the fresh bleeding of that universally beloved Earl of Essex."[37] Cecil knew himself forlorn and threatened, "in his own, and all men's opinions, so under the Hatches, as not ever to appear above board again"; and he took measures cautious, prompt and unpitying. Yet he must be given credit for statesmanship; he achieved a quiet succession after Elizabeth. The gloomy picture of general misgiving when her long and glorious reign was plainly finishing, given in the Dedication of the Bible's Authorized Version, is not overdrawn. James himself had subjects who thought a timely invasion of England might be the best way out; in April, 1602, a Border laird told him he had forty muskets ready (which no doubt could have got their owners as far as Carlisle jail). But James was schooled and quieted by Cecil, who dissuaded him from precipitate action, and assured him the Queen was "not inclined to cut off the natural branch, and graft upon the wild stock."[38] All would be well if he stayed quiet and trusted his friend, keeping his pretensions in abeyance. James soon trusted him absolutely. "Cecil's solid business qualities" won him over, "until from intense dislike the King passed to the most ardent admiration,"[39] observing that

it were wery small wisdome, by clymming of diches and hegges for pulling of unrype fruite to haserd the brekeing of my necke, when by a litle patience, and abyding the seasone, I may wyth far more ease and safetie enter at the gette of the garding, and injoy the fruittes at my pleasur, in thaire greatest maturitie.[40]

36. Part of it went back to his mother's execution, when Lord Burghley was Elizabeth's chief minister.

37. Welldon, *Court and Character of King James,* pp. 10–11: "nor did any of the counterfaction to Essex, besides himself, ever attain to the King's favour."

38. Bruce, *Correspondence of James,* etc., no. ii, p. 5.

39. *Ibid.,* p. xxxviii.   40. *Ibid.,* p. 62.

Master and man understood each other, and thoroughly approved; both had "safety first" as their motto in all things.

The one rival whom Cecil feared was Ralegh, whose reputation was therefore unscrupulously wrecked, whose thoughts and actions were misrepresented with the utmost hardihood. His somewhat lukewarm friend, the Earl of Northumberland, who made his own occasional isolated efforts to set up good relations with his future King, gave him a certificate (of a strictly qualified kind), assuring James:

I must needs affirm Ralegh's ever allowance of your right, and although I know him insolent, extremely heated, a man that desires to seem to be able to sway all men's courses, and a man that out of himself, when your time shall come, shall never be able to do you much good nor harm, yet must I needs confess what I know, that there is excellent good parts of nature in him, a man whose love is disadvantageous to me in some sort, which I cherish rather out of constancy than policy, and one whom I wish your Majesty not to lose, because I would not that one hair of a man's head should be against you, that might be for you.

Cecil, however, made no bones about lying (with the usual prefatory blasphemy). Ralegh did not, he admits, actually in so many words *say* he was against King James; but he *was,* and it was only Cecil who checked him and Cobham from speaking out:

I do profess in the presence of Him that knoweth and searcheth all men's hearts, that if I did not sometimes cast a stone into the mouth of these gaping crabs when they are in their prodigal humour of discourses, they would not stick to confess daily how contrary it is to their nature to resolve to be under your sovereignty; though they confess—Ralegh especially—that, *rebus sic stantibus,* natural policy forceth them to keep on foot such a trade against the great day of mart. In all which light and sudden humours of his, though I do no way check him, because he shall not think I reject his freedom or his affection, but always *(sub sigillo confessionis)* use contestation with him . . . yet, under pretext of extraordinary care of his well-doing, I have seemed to dissuade him from engaging himself too far, even for himself.[41]

Baseness, it might seem, could hardly go further. Terror lest Ralegh should come to know what was happening thrusts in the reminder that all this is under "seal of confession," while he brags of holding back

41. *Ibid.,* p. 18.

Ralegh, under pretense of doing this *for his own sake,* from making James his friend. But baseness does go further, and in the words immediately following. Cecil begs the King, if Ralegh, whose outflowings of extreme generosity he knows, should ever speak well of him, Cecil, not to be misled into thinking they are on good terms; and he throws out the charge which of all charges will prejudice beyond conversion the bigoted King, stressing Ralegh's notorious want of "religion":

> Let me, therefore, presume thus far upon your Majesty's favour that, whatsoever he shall take upon him to say for me, upon any new humour of kindness—whereof sometimes he will be replete, upon the receipt of private benefit—you will no more believe it . . . be it never so much in my commendation. . . . Would God I were as free from offence towards God in seeking, for private affection, to support a person whom most religious men do hold anathema.

The same mud of atheism is flung by Howard. "Hell," he tells James, "cannot afford such a like triplicity, that denies the Trinity"—the "triplicity" being Ralegh, Cobham and Northumberland. In another place, "this fool" (i.e., Northumberland) is alleged to be trying to win the King's "favour towards that accursed duality," Ralegh and Cobham. James's agent Lord Mar is assured that

> my Lord Admiral, the other day, wished from his soul that he had but the same commission to carry the cannon to Durham House, that he had this time twelve months to carry it to Essex House, to prove what sport he could make in that fellowship,

that is, the fellowship of Ralegh and Cobham. "Your Lordship may believe that Hell did never show up such a couple."

James promised Cecil, "Your suspicion, and your disgracing, shall be mine." Howard's exultation grew prophetic.[42] "The glass of time being very far run, the day of the Queen's death may be the day of their doom, if they do not agree with their adversary upon the way, lest he deliver them to the judge, and the judge to prison—*unde non exibunt, donec ultimum quadrantem solverint.*" Howard was reputed the most learned nobleman of his day, and his learning was particularly deep in the Scriptures; he had versified the Psalms. He quotes sacred words ac-

42. June 4, 1602.

cordingly. But he has left it exceedingly hard to see what chance Ralegh and Cobham had "to agree with their adversaries" betimes. He begged the Earls of Mar and Kinross to prevent Lennox's offices bringing about any understanding between James and Ralegh and Cobham. Only let himself and Cecil know what Lennox was doing; and out of it "if we make not good use for the King, and with as good workmanship as you can wish, then conclude that you deal with bunglers." The King's references to the doomed couple, and above all, to Ralegh, were soon crammed with loathing. "We are exceeding far inamorat of them."

Meanwhile Cecil continued Ralegh's faithful friend, and Cobham's loving relative. He sends them greetings, July 20, 1602, "both in one letter," and pledges himself "to do you both service with all I have, and my life to boot." The pledge, in the autumn of this year, to Carew takes a scriptural form. "Our two old friends do use me unkindly. But I have covenanted with my heart not to know it. . . . In show we are great. All my revenge shall be to heap coals on their heads." "He carried out his promise, and his coals scorched."[43] Always collecting all the money he could—though no one has ever accused him of such a vice as greed (of which everyone accuses Ralegh)—he continued in partnership with Ralegh, the acknowledged king of privateers. The Lord Admiral joined also, having two strings to his bow of profit: by virtue of his official position, he sold "protective passports, against rovers," and, by being "part-owner or part-outfitter" of rovers, saw to it that his passports were worth buying. Sir John Gilbert writes to Cecil, December 21, 1601, about sharing the cost of a privateering venture Ralegh had mentioned. And in January, 1603, Cecil writes to Ralegh, of another venture:

I will be contented to be half-victualler, and the rest may be borne between my Lord Cobham and you. . . . But now, Sir, that you know all these particulars, I pray you, as much as may be, conceal our adventure, or at the least my name, above any other.

That was "the Cecil touch," to do good by stealth. Spoiling the Spaniard, under Ralegh's experienced supervision, was profitable, and no doubt built up England; but King James might have misunderstood

43. Stebbing, p. 179.

it. "For though, I thank God, I have no other meaning than becometh an honest man in any of my actions, yet that which were another man's *Pater Noster* would be accounted, in me, a charm"—i.e., a wicked charm. Open association with privateering was all right for Ralegh, who was not a Privy Councillor. This was less than ten weeks before the Queen's death.

CHAPTER XVI

James, by the Grace of God, King

Upon the twenty-fourth of March, 1603, did set the most glorious Sun that ever shined in our Firmament of England. SIR ANTHONY WELLDON.

Great and manifold were the blessings, most dread Sovereign, which Almighty God, the Father of all mercies, bestowed upon us the people of *England,* when first He sent Your Majesty's Royal Person to rule and reign over us. For whereas it was the expectation of many, who wished not well unto our *Sion,* that upon the setting of that bright *Occidental Star,* Queen *Elizabeth* of most happy memory, some thick and palpable clouds of darkness would so have overshadowed this Land, that men should have been in doubt which way they were to walk, the appearance of Your Majesty, as of the *Sun* in his strength, instantly dispelled those supposed and surmised mists, and gave unto all that were well affected exceeding cause of comfort. Dedication of the Authorized Version.

IN December, 1602, the Queen's godson, Sir John Harington (who had been in trouble for taking a knighthood from Essex), ventured to Court again, and with the genuine affection that wins forgiveness for all his coxcombries, told his wife: "Our dear Queen doth now bear show of human infirmity—too fast for that evil which we shall get by her death, and too slow for that good which she shall get by her releasement from pains and misery." He could not "blot from my memory's table the goodness of our Sovereign Lady to me." Their conversation turned on Ireland, and she remembered Essex. "Oh! now it mindeth me that you was one who saw this man elsewhere," and for a moment she wept, and smote her breast. Harington, at a loss how to help her, read some of his verses. She smiled once, and said, not unkindly: "When thou dost feel creeping time at thy gate, these fooleries will please thee less. I am past my relish for such matters. Thou seest my bodily meat doth not suit me well. I have eaten but one ill-tasted cake since yesternight." In March, 1603, Sir Robert Cary was called to her presence, and "found her in one of her withdrawing chambers, sitting low upon her cushions. . . . She took me by the hand, and wrung it hard, and said, 'No, Robin, I am not well' . . . and in her discourse she fetched not so few as forty or fifty great sighs . . . in all my life-time before, I never knew her fetch a sigh, but when the Queen of Scots was beheaded." "From that day forwards, she grew worse and worse." "Hereupon I wrote to the King of Scots . . . and certified him in what state Her Majesty was. I desired him not to stir from Edinburgh; if of that sickness she should die, I would be the first man that should bring him news of it."[1]

The Queen died about three in the morning, March 24, 1603. At six o'clock, sunrise, the Privy Council assembled, and Cecil read a Proclamation of James as King. For long there had been no serious question of his accession, despite desultory talk of Arabella Stuart. Before ten, Cary, who had horses ready along the route, posted north, and, incredible to relate, reached Holyrood late at night, March 26, went in, and kissed the King's hands. For all this officious kindness he was rewarded in due course, but not (as he thought) adequately.

The Privy Council called into consultation eminent men outside their number. Ralegh was in the west. But he posted to London, and was included in a company which assembled to draw up an address of welcome, signed by all. He is said to have suggested making England a republic. "Let us keep the staff in our own hands, and set up a commonwealth, and not remain subject to a needy beggarly nation."[2] He and Cobham and others debated forcing terms on James, as to the number of Scots he was to bring south. Everyone, however, was thinking of himself, and afraid to offend the new King.

On March 28 George Carew reaped the first fruits of his subservience to Cecil, being sent with Thomas Lake to take James the official news of Elizabeth's death. James left Edinburgh, April 5, and came junketing and feasting, scattering knighthoods (as he was presently to scatter peerages) "with a profusion which astonished those who remembered the sober days of Elizabeth."[3] He would be thriftier soon, when he had realized the cash value of titles in a remarkably open market. Everyone has heard how at Newark he hanged a thief without trial. But not everyone remembers with what a flourish and through what incessant

1. *Memoirs of Robert Cary, Earl of Monmouth,* pp. 115 ff.
2. Aubrey, ii, 186.
3. S. R. Gardiner, *History of England,* 1603–1642, i, 87.

festivating (to borrow a word from the Duke of Wellington) he moved into his kingdom.

Cecil, "having, after a struggle, clambered on board the new ship of State," "could not afford to identify himself with wrecked comrades known to be distasteful to his present master."[4] He set himself to prevent these comrades from laying hold of the vessel on which he now was. The French Ambassador told his King (May 2, 1603): "It was said at Court that Cecil had procured Ralegh's disgrace, because he was unable to support the weight of his unpopularity." This was one reason, an excellent one. Carew had accepted a post under his command: Ralegh, that incorrigible freelance, "wanting strength, though not wit, to be the Treasurer's co-rival, perished because not thought to own humility enough to be his servant."[5] A Proclamation was issued, forbidding persons holding public offices to resort to the King while on his journey, lest State business suffer and his Court be inconveniently crowded. It was known to be particularly aimed at Ralegh, who ignored it. James is said to have greeted him with "Rawly! Rawly! true enough, for I think of thee very rawly, mon."[6] It is now usual to reject any such picturesque stories. This seems to me probable enough. Nor would I dismiss as absurd Aubrey's other report that, when James was bragging how he could have won the throne by force, Ralegh replied, "Would God that had been put to the trial!" and, when asked *why,* had the wit, if not the tact, to say, "Because Your Majesty would then have known your friends from your foes"—an explanation "never forgotten or forgiven." Ralegh's sharp tongue had a share in costing him his head. If he said what Aubrey relates, it was enough to set the King brooding on so two-edged and oracular a sentence.

He saw he was unwelcome, and lamely justified his coming by the plea that he had to ask for the renewal of his Stannaries Wardenship and his Lieutenancy of Cornwall, where the royal parks and woods were being wasted. James promised him a letter of continuance of process, and another letter forbidding any meddling with the Duchy estates, until he himself had "determined what to do with it"; and ordered Lake (who was acting as Cecil's spy and the King's Secretary): "Let them be delivered speedily, that Rawly may be gone again." Lake,

4. Stebbing, p. 204.   5. Osborne, *Memoirs.*
6. Aubrey, *Brief Lives,* ii, 186.

sending regular minutes to Cecil, next day told him what had happened, with satisfaction concluding: "To my seeming he hath taken no great root here."

Aubrey does not finish a sentence (whose completion we can guess): "Sir Walter Ralegh had that awfulness and ascendancy over other mortals that the K— . . ." Cecil and James, the uncouth with the uncouth, must have felt more comfortable together than with Ralegh. James was "of a middle stature, more corpulent through his clothes than in his body, yet fat enough—his clothes ever being made large and easy, the Doublets quilted for stiletto-proof, his Breeches in plates and full stuffed." He hated the "sight of a soldier or any valiant man," had a horror of steel and lived in constant dread of assassination. He had an almost equal horror of water, never washing but merely occasionally rubbing his fingers' ends on wet napkins. His skin was "soft as taffeta sarsnet." His legs were weak (at the age of seven he had been unable to stand), and he preferred to walk leaning on some favorite's shoulder. His walk (into which he always broke sooner or later, for sitting still was intolerable to him—he could never be brought to sit for his picture) was a circular waddle, with his hands all the time busily engaged where they should not have been. Timorous, he would roll his eyes after any stranger, so that many left his presence from very shame, being put out of countenance. He had a steady cough. His beard was thin, his tongue too large for his mouth, lolling out; because of this defect, he spoke in a full "mouthing" fashion, and drank in "very uncomely" manner, "as if he were eating his drink." He was neither abstemious nor very intemperate. He swore much, and his blasphemy sometimes horrified even himself (but he hoped God would see that it proceeded from passion). He never willingly changed his clothes till they were in rags, and "his fashion" he changed not at all. One of his courtiers said that, if he slept for seven years and then waked, he could tell where the King had been every day of the interim, and what dishes he had had at table. He was exceedingly crafty in small things, a fool in all that mattered. Everyone has heard Henri IV's description of him as "the wittiest" (most learned) "fool in Christendom." The same monarch allowed also his claim to be called "the modern Solomon," on the grounds that he was "the son of David, who played on the harp" (a reference to Mary of Scotland's favor to David Rizzio, her Italian music-master and private secretary). He was liberal with others' money. His merits were that he really loved peace, and was witty, having the gift of "a poker face" when making his jests. One of the earliest and best settled the common discussion as to whether his Scots subjects merited the epithet "beggarly." "Content yourselves. I will shortly make the English as beggarly as you, and so end that controversy."

On May 3 he was a guest at Cecil's house at Theobalds, within easy reach of London. Here he issued orders releasing the Earl of Southampton and the rest of those imprisoned for Essex's rebellion. On the 7th, he called in all monopolies, until such time as the Council could be satisfied that they were not harmful to his people. This held up Ralegh's wines-licensing patent; it was later decided not to be a monopoly, but by then his ruin had been achieved. On May 13 Cecil became Baron Cecil of Essendon, one of four new peers, the harbingers of a spring of royal favor that "raised the numbers of the House of Lords with a rapidity that would have astonished Elizabeth."[7] James presently struck another blow at Ralegh, who was summoned to the Council Chamber at Whitehall, where the Lord President notified him that he was replaced as Captain of the Guard by a Scotsman, Sir Thomas Erskine. "Sir Walter, in very humble manner, did submit himself." As some compensation, he was told, through Cecil, that the three hundred pounds a year hitherto reserved from his salary as Governor of Jersey was excused. "His Majesty is pleased to remit the same unto Sir Walter."

Like many men of genius, Ralegh had no "common sense." No man was ever a greater master of the theory of life; few were worse at its practice. He showed this conspicuously now. The Dutch, helped by an English contingent, were trying to save Ostend, which the Spaniards had besieged for three years. While James, on his first triumphal progress, was the guest, at Beddington Park, Surrey, of Lady Ralegh's uncle, Sir Nicholas Carew, Ralegh forced an interview on him, and presented him with a *Discourse touching a War with Spain, and of the Protecting of the Netherlands*[8]—a grave, "forcible, and, from its own point of view, sagacious disquisition"[9] ("promising the West Indies," says his

7. Gardiner, *History of England*, 1603–1642, i, 101.
8. *Works*, viii, 299 ff.   9. Stebbing, p. 183.

own son,[10] with a touch of slightly scornful amusement). "As a controversial pamphlet it evinces none of the want of judgment with which Hallam charges Ralegh." The want of judgment resided rather in his having written it at all and having written it for James, who in season and out of season, rated the Dutch as rebels, who should get no countenance from him. Carew Ralegh, looking back almost half a century later, says that the new monarch had not been entirely unfriendly to his father until, "finding him (as he said himself) a martial man, addicted to foreign affairs and great actions, he feared lest he should engage him in a war, a thing most hated and contrary to the King's nature." James was bent on peace, and Cecil was going to see that he obtained it; Ralegh's "inclination went with the humour of those times of War, but now his counsel came out of season."[11] The age had changed, but he had not changed with it. Sublimely irrelevant, he offered to raise two thousand men and invade Spanish territory at his own charges. "To the King, who could hardly see a sword drawn without shivering, such an offhand readiness to face perils . . . would naturally seem to carry within it some germ of possible treason."[12]

The day of Ralegh's enemies had come. Tobias Matthew, Bishop of Durham, met James at Berwick, when he had barely touched English soil, and asked for Durham House back.[13] In 1594, when the King was twenty-eight and his particular qualities might have been taken as mature, Matthew, then Dean of Durham, had written to Lord Burghley in a tone of surprise, that he was "a deeper dissembler than is thought possible for his years," adding the caveat, "I pray God the King's protestations be not too well believed." He did not allow such private opinions to impair the cordiality of his loyal greetings now. James received these kindly, and on May 31 issued orders to evict Ralegh, within a reasonable time-limit. That limit seemed to the Bishop to be about a week. On June 7 he wrote the Lord Keeper a rancorous letter[14] demanding immediate possession, "the supposed tenants seeking nothing else but to gain time to deface the house more than is justifiable by law, or to

10. Petition to the Long Parliament, 1648, by Carew Ralegh.
11. Sanderson, p. 283.   12. Edwards, i, 365.
13. The Crown had held it, except for a short space in Mary's reign, ever since Henry VIII had taken it away.
14. Edwards, ii, 264. See also *Egerton Papers,* pp. 377 ff.

shuffle in some noble or otherwise gracious[15] person thereinto (if not more than one), whom to remove it may be harder for me than I am willing to assay." He takes it for granted that Ralegh is defenseless, unless he can put up as screen some influential sub-tenant; and he is not going to give him a chance to remove "tenant's fixtures."

It is probable that Ralegh did not mind overmuch his ejection from Durham House, but he did resent the inconsiderate way it was done. He was ordered to be out by midsummer (June 22), which he told the "Commissioners Appointed by King James to Inquire into the Tenure of Durham House" seemed to him

very strange, seeing I have had possession of the house almost xx years, and have bestowed well nigh £2,000 upon the same out of mine own purse. I am of opinion that if the King's Majesty had recovered this house, or the like, from the meanest gentleman and servant he had in England, that His Majesty would have given six months time for the avoidance, and I do not know but that the poorest artificer in London hath a quarter's warning given him by his landlord.

He had laid in the year's provisions for forty persons and nearly twenty horses. "Now to cast out my hay and oats into the streets, at an hour's warning, and to remove my family and stuff in 14 days after, is such a severe expulsion as hath not bin offered to any man before this day . . . the course taken with me is both contrary to honour, to custom, and to civility." The Commissioners, in certain matters, had gone beyond their instructions. The Bishop had enough on his side without this partiality; for, as Ralegh despairingly concludes: "if I do anything contrary to law the Bishop may take his remedy, and I perceive cannot want good friends."

He still had Sherborne left, and his work and place in the West. These, however, were not going to be left to him. The real reason for the prosecution which ruined him, as he himself said afterwards, was his enemies' conviction that, having been visited with insult upon insult, despoiled and thrust down, he could not possibly be contented but *must*[16] be thinking thoughts unfriendly to Cecil and the King. At his

15. i.e., in grace with the new Powers that were.
16. Cf. "a syllogism" which "my Lord Harry" (Henry Howard) "had made against" Cobham: "Because you were discontented, therefore you were likely to enter into an

trial, it was stressed as a proof of his treason that he was discontented *"in conspectu omnium."*

Cobham, meanwhile, had been behaving more foolishly than ever. He had been "one of the most bitter and most persistent of the enemies of Essex. He had shown at the crisis, and after it, neither relenting nor remorse";[17] and his terror, when James was moving south, was ludicrous. In April, 1603, he begged Cecil to tell him if it were true that the King had invited "young Essex to come unto him." He was anxious for leave to go abroad, yet he wanted to go without any sort of "imputation" hanging over him. Another time, he wanted advice as to whether "it were not fit for me to invite His Majesty to my house"; and he asked how the King treated Lady Cobham ("my Lady of Kildare"), "and whether the King have spoken of me unto yourself, and what the reports be of the speeches between the King and me. In London they be very strange and falsely reported." At the same time as he was seeking all this information from Cecil, according to the French Ambassador he hardly ever mentioned Cecil's name without calling him "traitor": *"le Sieur Coban . . . est ulcéré contre le dit Sieur Cecil avec une telle violence que, quant il parle de luy, il ne le nomme point autrement que traistre."* In every way he behaved like a man with an exceedingly guilty conscience, ready to fly at a hint.

Not James only, his Queen—Anne of Denmark—also arrived keenly interested in the inner story of the Essex business, and entirely pro-Essex and anti-Cobham and anti-Ralegh. She had scarcely reached Windsor when she asked the released Earl of Southampton, now in high favor, why, when it came to fighting, Essex's party had put up such a poor show; why "so many great men did so little for themselves." Southampton answered that they had been paralyzed by the other side's dishonest representations. But for the false color of treason put on their proceedings, their enemies durst not have opposed them. Lord Grey of Wilton flared up at the word "durst"; he and Southampton gave each other the lie, and narrowly escaped being sent to the Tower (June 30), for violating the sanctities of the palace. The inci-

action of treason": i.e., "discontented men plot treason; Cobham is discontented; Cobham is therefore plotting treason."

17. Edwards, i, 354.

dent shows how alive the Essex affair still was, and how wisely Cecil had betimes ostentatiously separated himself from Ralegh.

Part of the tragedy of Ralegh's falling through his intimacy with Cobham is that it is plain the intimacy had greatly lessened. But he had not the Cecil sense to abandon a friend who was obviously bound for trouble. He was so little aware of what was happening that, after his dismissal from the Captaincy of the Guard, he put before the King a written protest against the way (he declared) Cecil had prejudiced James against him. He had so slight suspicion of how deep his enemies had gone, mining to destroy him, that, as late as the month of his arrest (July, 1603), writing to his wife he referred to the privateering partnership between him and Cecil as still in existence.

Some day between the 12th and 16th of July he made his last appearance as anything but a prisoner. He was waiting on the terrace at Windsor, to attend the King when he rode out hunting. Cecil came up and told him, "as from the King," that he was not to go, but was to attend on the Privy Council, in the Council Chamber. "They have some questions to ask you." These were about a plot to surprise the King's person, and about communications between Cobham and the Spanish Minister in the Low Countries, Count d'Arenberg. Ralegh said he knew nothing about these matters. He was dismissed and told that he was confined to his own house. Here, perhaps to clear himself, perhaps because he considered the matter of no real importance (as, indeed, it was of none), he wrote Cecil a letter in which he pointed out that he *had* noticed that sometimes, after visiting him, Cobham, being rowed back, had gone past his own house and called on La Renzi, an agent of Arenberg. Thinking this over, he thought perhaps Cobham and Arenberg might be in communication about something or other. His writing this letter must be admitted as an act "of not very friendly officiousness."[18] On the other hand, having said before many important persons that he knew nothing of Cobham having communications with Arenberg, he had made a statement which they all knew was far too sweeping; he wanted to correct it before it was twisted to his prejudice. Cobham was one of those fussy creatures who are always rushing about engaged in trivial intrigues. He was an old acquaintance of Arenberg,

18. Stebbing, *Ralegh*, p. 189.

who was just then in England, trying to negotiate a peace. In November, 1602, Arenberg, absurdly over-assessing his influence, had asked Cobham to run over to the Low Countries to continue talks they had previously had. Just before Elizabeth died he had written again, and Cobham sent the letter on to Cecil, asking what he should say. After her death, feeling very important, as about to arrange terms of peace (a self-appointed Commissioner), Cobham asked the King: "What answer shall I make to Arenberg?" Getting no reply, he reminded the King, as he was coming south, and got an angry snub, that "I was more busy in it than I need to be"; he would get his answer after the Privy Council had met. This is the context of Ralegh's letter admitting he had surmised that Cobham had dealings with Arenberg—a fact notorious and open. Cecil, however, showed the letter to Cobham, who had already been arrested: Cobham flew into a passion and assumed that Ralegh had accused him of treason. That accusation had been made against him already (Cecil did not think it necessary to tell him this) by his own brother, George Brooke, who was under arrest.

Ralegh had made a fatal slip. Had he really been plotting, he would have been an utter fool to provoke his one accomplice by accusing him. As a matter of fact, Ralegh often *was* a fool, and this was one of the worst occasions. Cobham, terrified and indignant, was prepared to accuse Ralegh of anything, for revenge and to save himself. Ralegh seems to have seen that he had been foolish, for he sent Kemys to tell Cobham (who, of course, was under close surveillance, as a prisoner) that he had "cleared him" in his actual interview with the Council. This (like so much else) was pressed against him at his trial, to prove that he was in a conspiracy with Cobham. And Kemys, either from Ralegh (which Ralegh denied) or on his own account, was alleged to have told Cobham to cheer up, as "one witness could not condemn for treason," there had to be two.[19] This, Ralegh himself was to find, was an error.

19. Kemys was not brought into Court to testify concerning this remark. Ralegh primarily sent Kemys to Cobham about some ordinary business, being unable to go himself, as under restraint.

CHAPTER XVII

Trial and Condemnation

Though his Judges were willing enough to destroy him there, yet they did rather tire him out of his life, by the brawling of the King's Counsel on one side, and the Benches insisting on a Confession extorted from the Lord Cobham out of fear . . . than convince him.[1] Osborne.

His trial, which is the opprobrium of forensic and judicial annals, makes a bright page in national history for the unique personality it reveals, with all its wealth of subtlety, courage, and versatility. . . . The Ralegh who has stamped himself upon English history, who has fascinated English imagination, is not so much the favourite of Elizabeth, the soldier and sailor; it is the baited prey of Coke and Popham, the browbeaten convict of Winchester, the attainted prisoner of the Tower. Stebbing.

JAMES'S quiet accession had been accepted with relief; England, growing up, was wearying of the contests of dynasties. But a "flux of moody speech and angry threat"[2] remained; the settlement was not safe until confused and disappointed groups had been dispersed.

During Elizabeth's last years, when every group was holding discussions, the Catholics had held theirs at Enfield House (afterwards used in the Gunpowder Treason). Garnet, Provincial of the English Jesuits, had instructions from Rome to see that, "if possible, no one should be allowed to succeed except one who would not only grant toleration, but would directly favour the Catholic religion."[3] Two priests, Watson and Clerke, in 1602 interviewed James, son of the martyred Queen Mary, and asked for a promise of toleration. The possibility that they might be satisfied pained Cecil, who wrote to the Archbishop of York: "I love not to yield to any toleration. . . . I will be much less than I am, or rather, nothing at all, before I shall ever become an instrument of such a miserable change." He let James know he would feel hurt and humiliated if he temporized as to "how you should deal with the messengers from Antichrist." "It would be a hor-

---

1. i.e., convict him.   2. Edwards, i, 342.
3. Gardiner, *History of England*, 1603–1642, i, 98.

ror to my heart to imagine that they that are enemies to the Gospel should be held by you worthy to be friends to your fortune."

Here there was a divergence between Cecil and Lord Henry Howard. The latter—a concealed Catholic, who died an avowed one—urged that England was well worth permitting "a mass in a corner"; and James cannily and characteristically allowed both sides to think he was with them. While scolding the English Government for their mildness to "Jesuits, seminary priests, and that rabble," he exchanged friendly letters with the Pope. The Catholics had some reason to hope they were in for a season of gentler weather when Elizabeth died. James, however, when his accession came so easily, swept aside any suggestion of granting tolerance, remarking: "Na, na, we'll no need the Papists noo."

In the time's bad temper, Catholics delated Catholics, and Cecil learnt from them, as well as by his spies, that Watson and Clerke were consorting with George Brooke (Cobham's brother and Cecil's brother-in-law), Sir Griffin Markham, and others, in what was afterwards called the "Bye" or "surprising" Plot. Brooke's grievance was against Robert Cecil; he had been for years one of the latter's secret agents, and felt disgruntled at his treatment by him. He had written Cecil grumbling letters (which Cobham probably knew of), and Cecil had his eye on him. The conspirators drew in for a time Lord Grey of Wilton, a rigid Puritan who detested Catholicism and did not at first realize exactly with what colleagues, or for what purposes, he was engaging himself. He was disquieted by the flood of southward-pouring Scots, with prospect of more to follow, and he wanted fuller religious and civil liberty. But his main reason for playing with treason seems to have been that he was vaguely angry. The plot was framed on Scottish analogy: the King was to be surprised and taken into honorable custody, and freed when he had given promises of toleration and a general pardon to those who had put this violence upon him.

One of the plotters, Anthony Copley, was arrested, July 6. In the course of the next few days the arrests of Brooke, Lord Grey, Sir Griffin Markham, Watson, Clerke and others followed, then Cobham's; then Ralegh's restraint to his house. With the horrible doom of treason over them, those arrested poured out a flood of wild tales. Their examiners plied them separately; held out hopes of pardon if they inculpated others; led them up to suggestions; told them that their guilt was plain from what their colleagues had confessed. Sir William Waad was in charge of the investigation. He was one of the meanest men of a time exceptionally rich in such. He had broken into Mary of Scotland's cabinet when papers convicting her were wanted; he had had his nose down to plot after plot, real or invented, which had brought Catholics to the gallows. It was not concealed that the main aim was to catch Ralegh. It proved heart-breakingly hard. However, on July 17, Brooke, before his examiners, deposed that "the conspirators, amongst themselves, thought Sir Walter Ralegh a fit man to be of the action." That thought was one bound to occur to any conspirators, looking round for a mind and spirit that could be trusted in any peril. Browbeaten further and further, the wretched man, a month or so later, suddenly remembered that Cobham, and then, later still, that Ralegh had said, it would be a good idea to destroy the King "with all his cubs." As the "Bye" treason was one of merely kidnapping, not even this brought Ralegh into it.

Ralegh knew well that the purpose of a treason trial was to get a conviction. Cecil scored the first point when he showed Cobham Ralegh's silly letter about his communications with Arenberg. Cobham fell into the pit, and cried out, "Oh, traitor! oh, villain! I will now tell all the truth!" "He had never entered into these courses but by the instigation of Ralegh, who would never let him alone." He had hardly said this when he saw he had been trapped; before he reached the stairs leading back to his chamber, he withdrew all he had said about Ralegh. He had said what was to bring his friend to the scaffold, however. Ralegh was definitely arrested, and, foreseeing the end, tried to kill himself, to save his property (which would be forfeited if he were convicted). He merely wounded himself in the breast. Possibly the action was only a theatrical gesture of despair.

The despair, at least, was genuine. Early in August he wrote to Cecil, and the Earls of Nottingham[4] and Suffolk[4] and Devonshire, Commissioners to try the alleged conspirators, begging them not to send him "to the cruelty of the law of England." He was accused of having been privy to a trip which Cobham, long eagerly working for peace with that country, had made into Spain; by necessary conclusion, he was accused of being privy to all Cobham's intrigues. Ralegh, who had taken Cobham's pro-Spanish activities light-heartedly, as part of the man's

4. Two old comrades-in-arms, Lord Howard of Effingham and Lord Thomas Howard.

amusing endless busyness, showed the absurdity of this charge, in words he was to repeat memorably at his trial:

God doth know, and I can give an account of it, that I have spent forty thousand pounds of mine own against that King and nation; that I never reserved so much of all my fortune as to purchase forty pounds *per. ann.* land; that I have been a violent persecutor and furtherer of all enterprises against that nation. I have served against them in person; and how, [he cries out proudly] my Lord Admiral and my Lord of Suffolk can witness. I discovered, myself, the richest part of all his Indies: I have planted in his territories: I offered His Majesty, at my uncle Carew's, to carry two thousand men to invade him, without the King's charge.

As to the other accusation made against him, that money had been offered him by Count d'Arenberg, nominally for his offices in bringing about a peace, but really for helping in "His Majesty's Surprise," he claimed confidently that they knew he was guiltless.

Waad and Howard, however, managed to shake out of some of the accused what they hoped would settle Ralegh's chances. Waad wrote to Cecil, August 24: "It may please your good Lordship, by my Lord Henry Howard I was bold to trouble you with the short collection of these last labours, which have greatly entangled Sir Walter Rawley—or, rather, disclosed him out of his covert." Kemys was arrested, and threatened with the rack unless he produced evidence against his master. Helpless as he was, he stood out; and this iniquity produced one of the most dramatic of the many dramatic episodes of Ralegh's trial, which I reproduce here:

Coke. Cobham saith that Kemishe came to him with a letter, torn; and did wish him not to be dismayed, for one witness could not hurt him.
Ralegh. This poor man hath been close prisoner these eighteen weeks. He was offered the rack, to make him confess. I never sent any such message by him. I only did write to Cobham, to tell him what I had done with Mr. Attorney, I having of his at that time the great pearl and a diamond.
Lord Henry Howard. No circumstance moveth me more than this! Kemishe was never at the rack. The King gave charge that no rigour should be used.
The Other Commissioners. We protest, before God, there was no such matter, to our knowledge.

Ralegh. Was not the Keeper of the Rack sent for; and he threatened with it?

Sir William Waad. When Mr. Solicitor and myself came to examine Kemishe, we told him he "deserved the rack," but did not threaten him with it.

The Other Commisioners. It was more than we knew.

That interlude stands out, after all this lapse of time, more tellingly than any dramatist could invent it. Howard's hypocrisy, as he protests against the mere notion of Kemys having been threatened with anything cruel and illegal: his fellow-Commissioners making the usual disclaimer ("before God") that this never happened, "to our knowledge." Ralegh, alone before ruthless and all-powerful enemies, nevertheless compelling Waad, by direct address to him, into that moment of embarrassment, all eyes upon him, from which he slowly escapes by that distinction without a difference. "We told him he '*deserved* the rack,' but did not threaten him with it."

France was watching with deep interest. On James's accession Sully had been sent to congratulate him, and had tried to find out exactly what *was* happening under the surface, between Spain and England. Cecil he found *"tout mystère,"* interested only in his own fortunes. He found one party which was merely dissatisfied—without cohesion, its leaders (if such a term could be applied to those who did not act together) Northumberland, Cobham, Ralegh, Sir Griffin Markham, Southampton. All these together made up a discontented clan, such as you find only in England (*"gens seditieux, de caractère purement Anglais"*), ready to look at any new suggestions, particularly if against the Government. He sounded "Milords Cobham and Raleich" with his own ideas of what Spain was up to, and they gave him a noncommittal answer (*"conformement à cet avis"*). Now that these Milords had been arrested, the French Ambassador in England, the Count of Beaumont, told his King (August 3) of the difficulty Cecil was finding in entangling his old friend. Neither Lord Grey nor Sir Griffin Markham would budge from their statement that they had had nothing to do with the detested Ralegh, and that if they had even suspected that he was in their plot, however slightly, that would have been enough to make them abandon it utterly. As for Cobham, having denied as he did what it is alleged that he charged upon Sir Walter Ralegh, the Lords of the Council find it difficult to sustain Ralegh's prosecution.

Ralegh was making a magnificent fight against the hearsay drivel which was all that had been collected against him, and his inconsiderate behavior was distressing the Government:

This untoward and ill-boding affair infinitely harasses the King's mind. But it afflicts and troubles the mind of Sir Robert Cecil far more, as he has to bear the whole weight of it. And he undertakes and conducts it with so much enthusiasm, that it is said he acts more from interest and passion than for the good of the State.

Ralegh, Beaumont says, declared that his attempt at suicide arose not from fear, but to cheat his enemies of their triumph; their "power to put him to death, despite his innocency, he well knows." A week later, August 10, he reports that Watson had not yet accused either Ralegh or Cobham. "According to their friends, they look rather to be acquitted than condemned." On October 10 Beaumont wrote to the French Secretary of State that Lady Ralegh told him her husband had been examined about dealings with France.

The only evidence against Ralegh, of anything whatsoever, was Cobham's reckless outburst of rage, when shown the former's letter. As evidence, this was vitiated by Cobham's extraordinary (but for him, characteristic) behavior afterwards. He told the son of the Lieutenant of the Tower (Sir John Peyton) that he had from his window seen him talking with Ralegh. "God forgive him! He hath accused me, but I cannot accuse him!" Why, answered young Peyton, "he doth say the like of you! You have accused him, but he cannot accuse you!"[5] Cobham told the vicar of Cobham parish, who visited him, "Ralegh had done him no hurt, but he had done Ralegh a great deal."[6] Sir John Peyton, since his family were falling under Ralegh's fascination, was removed, and Sir George Harvey took his place. But Harvey's son also saw immediately through the plot—the new generation were going to do Ralegh's greatness justice! Cobham wrote a letter expressing remorse for having wrongly charged Ralegh. "God is my witness, it doth

5. Cobham to his examiners, Aug. 10.   6. Goodman, *Court of King James*, i, 65.

trouble my conscience." This letter he gave to the Lieutenant of the Tower, who suppressed it. But young Harvey let Ralegh know how unhappy Cobham was, and as a result soon found himself in prison. Here his cautious father left him, until a month after Ralegh had been convicted and it had become plain that the King was not going to execute him. He then thought he might with safety to himself try to help his son, so he wrote Cecil the following magnanimous letter:

MY SINGULAR GOOD LORD,

Knowing how easily a man might be limed in matters of treason, I did heretofore leave my son to himself, without making of any apology for him (because I knew not the quality of his offence). But now that the law and His Majesty's mercies have had their course, I am bold to acquaint your Lordship with these enclosed, written unto me by the Lord Cobham, the 24 of October last, whereby he hath, under his own hand, manifested the great desire he had, of himself (without any instigation of my son), to justify Sir W. R.; which course of his being by me then stopped (as was fit), he diverted it,[7] as I conceive and as is very likely, unto Sir W. himself —which I leave unto your honourable considerations. And do humbly crave pardon to entreat your honourable commiserations towards my unworthy son, in releasing his restraint. . . .

Ralegh, when he learnt that Cobham's conscience was working, sent him two appeals, afterwards used to condemn him, but—as he pointed out at his trial—perfectly justifiable ("It was not ill of me to beg him to say truth"). He inclosed the first in an apple, which was thrown through Cobham's window. "You or I must go to trial. If I first, then your accusation is the only evidence against me." Cobham responded:

Seeing myself so near my end—for the discharge of my own conscience and freeing myself from your blood, which else will cry vengeance against me—I protest, upon my salvation, I never practised with Spain by your procurement. God so comfort me in this my affliction, as you are a true subject, for anything that I know. I will say as Daniel, *Purus sum a sanguine hujus.* So God have mercy on my soul as I know no treason by you.

Cobham, as by now the reader must understand and as his contemporaries perfectly well knew, was the type that wallows in emotional experiences. He could be wildly inventive and deeply contrite, with

7. That is, young Harvey was told by Cobham, and let Ralegh know.

exasperating alternation. This letter, in tone satisfactorily religious, was not categorical enough, as Ralegh saw ("was not to my contenting"). Ralegh therefore begged him to come down from penitential clouds to solid helpful earth. "And then he writ me a very good letter":

> Now that the arraignment draws near; not knowing which should be first, I or you; to clear my conscience, satisfy the world, and free myself from the cry of your blood, I protest upon my soul, and before God and his angels, I never had conference with you in any treason; nor was ever moved by you to the things I heretofore accused you of. And, for anything I know, you are as innocent and as clear from any treasons against the King, as is any subject living. Therefore I wash my hands, and pronounce, *Purus sum a sanguine hujus.* And so God deal with me and have mercy on my soul, as this is true.

This letter Ralegh carefully put away, to be used in his hour of extremity.

Meanwhile James and Cecil were not hindered by any pedantry from acting as if Ralegh had been found guilty. In August the Jersey Governorship, "forfeited to us" by Sir Walter Ralegh's "grievous treason intended against us," was bestowed on Sir John Peyton. In September Sir Francis Godolphin, High Sheriff of Cornwall, was authorized to take that county's musters, "the Commission of Lieutenancy granted to Sir Walter Ralegh being become void and determined."[8]

On September 21 Ralegh was indicted at Staines, for conspiring to deprive the King of his sovereignty, to alter the true religion, and to levy war. This blossomed into definite charges that he and others were plotting to make Arabella Stuart Queen; that Cobham had been offered 600,000 crowns by Count d'Arenberg, and had planned a journey to Spain, to get help for Arabella's cause; that Ralegh and Cobham had promised that Arabella should be persuaded to make peace with Spain, tolerate Catholicism, and be guided in marrying by the King of Spain and his two dependents, the Archduke of Austria and the Duke of Savoy; that Ralegh had given Cobham a treasonable book against the King's title; and that Cobham had promised to let him have 8000 (or perhaps 10,000) crowns of his "peace-money," when he got it. Only part of this farrago of nonsense was seriously pressed when it came to

8. i.e., ended.

the trial. Why Spain should be expected to help Arabella when its own Infanta claimed the English throne, no one ever troubled to explain. Nor was it explained why Ralegh should be willing to risk his life for a sum so paltry, and how it came about that the other conspirators all had important posts allotted to them in the new régime they hoped to bring about, while he, the notoriously ambitious, asked for nothing except a very little money.

The Plague was ravaging London, so the King's Bench kept the next term at Winchester, whither Ralegh was taken, November 10. Passing through London, "it was hob or nob," Waad told Cecil, whether he "should have been brought alive through such multitudes of unruly people as did exclaim against him." "If one hare-brain fellow" had started an attack, he would have been lynched. At Winchester the even greater perils of the King's justice awaited him. Sir John Harington wrote: "I doubt the dice not fairly thrown, if Ralegh's life be the losing stake."

The trial took place, November 17, in Wolvesey Castle, palace of the former Bishops of Winchester. The two Chief Justices, Sir John Popham and Sir Edmund Anderson, were in charge. The former was an ugly mountainous creature. Said to have been stolen by gipsies as a child, he had grown up a precocious ruffian; when thirty years old and a barrister, he still joined bands who took purses. Then he decided to join the safe side of roguery, that which condemned rather than associated with malefactors. He became a Member of Parliament, and a judge notorious for severity, which did not disdain even mean victims. ("Sir John Popham hath played rex of late among whores and bawds, and persecutes poor pretty wenches out of all pity and mercy.")[9] Anderson's brutality had been for many years displayed chiefly in what we may call religious trials (a field where Popham had also exercised his gifts). His favorite prey was the noblest, such men as Udal and Campion. Popham and Anderson were assisted by judges sitting by special commission: Waad, who had concocted the reports on the preliminary examinations; Cecil and Howard, who had arranged, before ever James came to the throne, that Ralegh should be trapped into the law's grip; the Earls of Suffolk and Devonshire, Lord Wotton, Edward Wotton,

9. John Chamberlain, October 20, 1598, *Letters*, p. 23.

Sir John Stanhope,[10] and two puisne judges, Gaudy and Warburton. The prosecution was begun by Serjeant Hele, a renowned brawler and usurer, and then taken on by Edward Coke, a dapper little savage.

"One of the most salient characteristics of this memorable trial"—a trial which, for power to grip the mind with pity and admiration, has only one equal among English trials, that of King Charles—"is that, from its beginning to its end, it was a long dialogue, with many and impassioned interlocutors. . . . Not even under the Lord High Chancellor Jeffreys was law ever more openly bent beneath prerogative."[11] The day-long battle of one friendless man for his life was a fierce main struggle, never relaxed until the inevitable finish came, but with countless subsidiary skirmishes—sheer irrelevances, "quite apart from the real issue then depending, yet plainly influential upon the result."

There was no pretense at fairness. A conviction was what was desired, and a conviction was going to be obtained, whatever the evidence, however grandly the great accused broke wave after wave of foolish lying. Before ever proceedings started, the jury were sounded, and changed overnight as unsatisfactory. James himself said afterwards, referring to this trial, that he would be sorry to be tried before a Middlesex jury.[12] Then, at every point, and in every way, the accused was told the King's supposed rights must take precedence of his mere wish to escape the gallows. He asked that he might answer Coke's charges one by one, as they were brought. No, replied Coke: the majestic work of art on which he was engaged must not be marred by interruption. "The King's evidence ought not to be broken or dismembered, whereby it might lose much of its grace and vigour." Ralegh showed a disconcerting knowledge of the law, and pointed out that *two* witnesses were needed, whereas against him there was only crazy terrified self-contradicting Cobham. But the Lord Chief Justice said that this requirement "in cases of treason was found to be inconvenient," and so such cases had been put under the Common Law. The accusation of a person who "by his accusation first accuseth himself" (as Cobham had done) met

10. Who has his niche in history for having signed the warrant to torture the clergyman Peacham, in 1615.

11. Edwards, i, 387.

12. Carew Ralegh, *Observations* (on Sanderson's *Lives and Reigns of Mary and James*), p. 8.

all possible requirements, for it had "the force of a verdict of twelve men." This dictum another judge, Mr. Justice Warburton, reinforced, asking the accused, more in surprise and grief than anger, how he could be so pedantic as to want to hamper his own conviction. "I marvel, Sir Walter, that you, being of such experience and wit, should stand on this point. For many horse-stealers should escape, if they may not be condemned without witnesses. By law, a man may be condemned upon presumption and circumstances, without any witness to the main fact." When Ralegh urged that "your Lordships, as ministers of the King, are bound to administer the law in equity," Popham denied this. "Equity must proceed from the King. You can only have justice from us."[13] Later still, Popham again emphasized the King's safety (which apparently required a victim) as the overriding necessity, Ralegh having asserted that the common trial of England "is by jury and witnesses":

There must not be such a gulf opened for the destruction of the King, which would be, if we should grant this. You plead hard for yourself. But the laws plead as hard for the safety of the King.

He was pelted with any mud available, including (of course) his irreligion. "I doubt not but this day," prophesied Coke, "God shall have as great a conquest by this traitor, and the Son of God shall be as much glorified, as when it was said, *'Vicisti, Galilaee!'*" "O damnable Atheist! . . . Essex died the child of God.[14] God honoured him at his death. Thou wast by. *Et lupus et turpes instant morientibus ursae!*" Coke, early on, stressed "rebellion in the heart of the realm—yea, in the heart of the heart, that is, the Court"—that is, the "Bye" Treason, to "hastily surprise the King's Court." This made listeners' flesh creep; but Ralegh, imperturbable, reminded them it was irrelevant. "I pray you, Gentlemen of the Jury, to remember that I am not charged with the 'Bye,' which was the treason of the priests." Coke retorted furiously that "their Lordships will see that all these treasons, though they consisted

13. Cf. Cecil's letter to Winwood (his own italics), before the trial: *"Always he shall be left to the Law,* which is the Right all men are born unto." *Memoirs of Affairs,* etc. (*Winwood Papers,* ii, 8).

14. Coke had been almost equally virulent at Essex's trial. He had not thought him the child of God then.

of several points, closed in together—like Samson's foxes, which were joined in the tails, though the heads were severed." By way of warming himself up to his argument, he went through some major treasons of English history, following them with a philosophical (and heavily pedantic) disquisition on the different kinds of treason: *"in corde,* which is the root of the tree"; *"in ore,* which is the bud"; *"in manu,* which is the blossom"; *"in consummatione,* which is the fruit." He leapt forward to the statement ascribed to the priests, but no longer seriously alleged against Ralegh, that there "would be no safety in England until the fox and his cubs were taken away." "But to whom, Sir Walter, did you bear malice? To the royal children?"

This astounding day still stands out as if photographed, in the superhuman, supernatural coolness of one man, towering over a contemptible rabble, their immeasurable superior in character and intellect both. Ralegh quietly asked, what had all this to do with him?

Master Attorney, I pray you to whom, or to what end, speak you all this; I protest I do not understand what a word of this means, except it be to tell me news. What is the treason of Markham and the priests to me?

Coke. I will then come close to you. I will prove you to be the most notorious traitor that ever came to the bar. You, indeed, are upon the "Main"; but you followed them of the "Bye" in imitation. I will charge you with the words.

Ralegh. Your words cannot condemn me. My innocency is my defence. *Prove* against me any one thing of the many that you have broken, and I will confess all the Indictment, and that I am the most horrible traitor that ever lived, and worthy to be crucified with a thousand torments.

Coke. Nay, I will prove all. Thou art a monster! Thou hast an English face, but a Spanish heart. You would have stirred England and Scotland both. . . .

"Yes," Ralegh admitted later on, he *had* said that the best way of troubling England was by starting with Scotland; he had always accepted so elementary and obvious a point of strategy and international politics.[15]

The accused's ability was made heavy testimony against him. Cobham's business needed a swordsman and a politician; he was notoriously neither, whereas Ralegh was notoriously and superlatively both,

15. Sanderson, *Lives and Reigns of Mary and James,* p. 285.

therefore "a man fitting" for what Cobham had in mind. Cobham had not yet been tried, but his guilt was assumed, as a vantage-ground from which to bring down Ralegh. It was in vain that the latter asked, when confronted with some wild statement attributed to Cobham, "Could I stop my Lord Cobham's mouth?" or reminded the Court of what everyone knew, that no one took Cobham's prattle seriously. Coke invited everyone to "lament and rejoice" for that (as yet unconvicted) traitor—"lament, in that his ancient and noble house which hath stood so long unspotted is now ruinated; rejoice, in that his treasons are revealed." The very fact that, except for Cobham, there was no witness against Ralegh was the most damaging witness of all, showing up his devilish cunning. "Such was Ralegh's secrecy and machiavellian policy in these courses, that . . . he would talk with none but Cobham; because, saith he, 'one witness can never condemn me.' "

So far flung was the net dredging for treason (which yet brought up such emptiness), that a book written against the King's title, over twenty-six years ago, which had been found among Cobham's effects, picked up (he said) from Ralegh's library, was part of the accusation. Ralegh here, as so often in this trial, was frankly contemptuous. "Here is a book supposed to be treasonable. I never read it, nor commended it, nor urged it. I will tell your Lordships how I came to it, and what little account I made of it. I had it out of a Councillor's library long since." What Councillor? Why, "My Lord Treasurer Burghley." This brought up Cecil, embarrassed and rebuking:

Cecil. You may remember that, after the death of my father, you desired the having of some cosmographical maps and books of that kind, concerning discoveries of the Indies and Western parts. I allowed you a search; but if, under colour of this, you extended the liberty to other things I meant not, you abused my trust. To find a book of that kind there was not hard. For no book that touched the State, nay, scarce a libel that in the Queen's time had been spread against the State, but amongst those papers it might have been found—he being a Councillor of State—and so, perhaps, may be yet found with me. Therefore let it not seem strange to any that such a book was found there. But you did wrong, Sir Walter Ralegh, to take it thence—

a point of view righteously approved by Sanderson—"though justifiable in Cecils to keep all important books against Elizabeth and James, yet was it a crime in Ralegh,[16] who never was" a Councillor of State. Let us, however, hear Ralegh in his own defense:

There was no purpose in taking that book. But amongst other books and maps it seems it was cast in. Upon sorting of the papers afterwards, it came to my hand. It was a manuscript, written upon by my Lord Treasurer, "This book had I of Robert Snagge." The scope of the book is to justify the late Queen's proceedings against the Queen of Scots. But I marvel it should be now urged as a matter so treasonable in me to have such books, when it is well known that there came out nothing in those times but I had them, and might as freely have them as another. How my Lord Cobham came by this book I know not, but I remember that it lay upon my board at a time when he was with me . . . but at this time I knew of no discontentment he was troubled with.

Lord Henry Howard. I remember well that I, being sent to take the Lord Cobham's confession, pressed him about that book. He suddenly brake out into a great passion, and said: "A man is unhappy that must accuse his friend. I had the book of Sir Walter Ralegh. He made no account of it, but said it was against the King's title."

The "book" episode occupied much wrangling, but Lord Henry Howard had the grace to admit that Cobham afterwards retracted (as, given a chance, he retracted most things) what he had said, "and now said that it contained nothing against the King's title, and that he had it not from Sir Walter Ralegh, but took it from his table, when he was sleeping."

Ralegh then scored that other point, over the threatening of Kemys with the rack. It was no wonder that many began to think he would be acquitted, despite the determination to find him guilty. He laughed about Cobham's vaporings of the "great sums of money" ("his fashion is to utter things easily") that "would be given to some Councillors for making the Peace, and named my Lord Cecil and the Earl of Mar" (James's "Jocky o' Sclaittis").[17] It may be remarked in passing that it embarrassed the prosecution that the only real charge against Ralegh was that Cobham had been negotiating with Count d'Arenberg to get 600,000 crowns to bribe supporters of a Peace. Arenberg had just left

16. *Lives and Reigns of Mary and James.* It must be remembered that, as Carew Ralegh convincingly showed, Sanderson's book is full of slanders against Ralegh.
17. "Jocky of Slates" (he had been the King's schoolfellow).

England, and it was awkward to say too much about his offering money to be used (it was alleged) to dethrone his host. The minor (yet perhaps not so minor) absurdity of asking people to believe that the King of Spain's servant was anxious to pay money to support Arabella Stuart against his own Infanta has been referred to earlier. Ralegh answered:

Now if, after this, my Lord Cobham changed his mind as to the use to be made of the money, and joining with the Lord Grey and the others, had any such treasonable intent as is alleged, what is that to me? They must answer it, not I. The offer of the money to me is nothing; for it was made to me before Count Arenberg's coming. The offer made to the others was afterwards.

Another piece of "evidence" was that "one Dyer, a pilot" had been told in Lisbon by "a Portugal gentleman" that the King of England would never be crowned, "for his throat will be cut by Don Ralegh and Don Cobham, before he be crowned." Mr. Dyer being called, affirmed that this was so—he had heard this in a conversation at Lisbon (presumably in Portuguese; we do not know how expert Mr. Dyer was in that tongue). Whereupon Ralegh, who certainly *enjoyed* some parts of this amazing day—he answered, says an eyewitness, "with that temper, wit, learning, courage, and judgment, that, save it went with the hazard of his life, it was the happiest day that ever he spent"[18]—asked derisively and drily:

What infer you upon that?
Coke. That your treason hath wings.

Cecil and Lord Nottingham had prepared a dramatic scene. Lady Arabella Stuart, "being in a standing with" the latter, through him protested, "upon her salvation, that she never dealt in any of these things." Cobham, she said, had written to her, asking for an interview, "and gave her to understand that there were some about the King who laboured to disgrace her." Mistrusting that "it was but a trick," she had not answered. Ralegh here, as often, passionately begged that Cobham might be brought face to face with him:

18. Carleton to Chamberlain. "And so well he shifted all advantages that were taken against him, that, were not *fama malum gravius quam res,* and an ill name half hanged, in the opinion of all men he had been acquitted. In one word, never was a man so hated and so popular in so short a time."

The Lord Cobham hath accused me—you see in what manner he hath forsworn it. Were it not for his accusations, all this were nothing. Let him be asked if I knew of the letters which Renzy brought to him from Arenberg. Let me speak for my life. It can be no hurt for him to be brought. He dareth not accuse me. If you grant me not this favour, I am strangely used. Campion was not denied to have his accusers face to face.

The Lord Chief Justice demurred. If Cobham's "old friend" should be acquitted, Cobham also, when his time came to be tried, might "speak otherwise than the truth" (in hope of similar luck—therefore no risk of Ralegh's being acquitted should be taken now). Ralegh broke out:

I—have been "the infuser of these treasons into him!" You, Gentlemen of the Jury, mark this! He said, I have been the cause of all his miseries and the destruction of his house, and that all the evil hath happened to him by my wicked counsel! If this be truth, whom hath he cause to accuse and to be revenged on, but on me? And I know him to be as revengeful as any man on earth.

Cobham would hardly lie to let off the author of his ruin, whom Coke had already addressed in that classic of legal gutter-vituperation: "All that Lord Cobham did was by thy instigation, thou viper! for I *thou* thee, thou traitor! I will prove thee the rankest traitor in all England."

Even Cobham's confession, extorted out of him with such difficulty, was one he had long refused to sign. The Lord Chief Justice, however, had seen to this formality; and now offered himself as witness as well as judge:

I came to the Lord Cobham, and told him he ought to subscribe, which presently after the Lord Cobham did. And he said of Sir Walter Ralegh, in the doing of it, "That wretch! That traitor Ralegh!"—

words which referred to what he had been told, that Ralegh had accused him, so that it was all up with him and a case of *sauve qui peut* (by accusing Ralegh back). Popham interpreted otherwise. "And surely the countenance and action of my Lord Cobham much satisfied me that what he had confessed was true; and that"—there is much virtue in "and that," coming back, so unobtrusively as not to be noticed, to the real meaning of Cobham's exclamation—"he surely thought that Sir Walter Ralegh had betrayed him."

Fifteen years afterwards, when soon to go to the scaffold, Ralegh asked (and received no answer) why, if he had been justly convicted of plotting with Spain to invade England, the Spanish Ambassador, who had been so anxious to stop his voyage to Guiana, did not do so by the simple expedient of "discovering the great practices I had with his Master against the King, in the first year of His Majesty's reign." His prosecutors tried to pack his trial with surprises, to his discredit. But he himself provided the most effective surprise, in exposure of the nonsense of saying that *he,* of all men, had plotted to bring Spain into England! No other Englishman has ever broken into majestic utterance with his ease and readiness; and this protest, spoken extempore, is such prose as Milton might have written when his passion was flying its clearest course and steadiest wing:

Master Attorney, whether to favour or to disable my Lord Cobham, you speak as you will of him; yet he is not such a babe as you make him! He hath dispositions of such violence, which his best friends could never temper. But it is very strange that I, at this time, should be thought to plot with the Lord Cobham, knowing him a man that hath neither love nor following, and myself at this time having resigned a place of my best command, in an office I had in Cornwall.[19] I was not so bare of sense but I saw that, if ever this State was strong, it was now that we have the kingdom of Scotland united, whence we were wont to fear all our troubles—Ireland quieted, where our forces were wont to be divided—Denmark assured, whom before we were always wont to have in jealousy—the Low Countries our nearest neighbour. And instead of a Lady whom Time had surprised, we had now an active King, who would be present at his own businesses. For me, at this time, to make myself a Robin Hood, a Wat Tyler, a Kett, or a Jack Cade! I was not so mad! I knew the State of Spain well—his weakness, his poorness, his humbleness, at this time. I knew that six times we had repulsed his forces: thrice in Ireland, thrice at sea—once upon our coast, and twice upon his own. Thrice had I served against him myself at sea—wherein, for my Country's sake, I had expended of my own property forty thousand marks. I knew that where aforetime he was wont to have forty great sail, at the least, in his ports, now he hath not past six or seven. And for sending to his Indies he was driven to have strange vessels—a thing contrary to the institutions of his ancestors, who straitly forbade that, even in case of necessity, they should make their case known to strangers. I knew

19. The Wardenship of the Stannaries.

that, of twenty-five millions which he had from his Indies, he had scarce any left. Nay, I knew his poorness to be such at this time, as the Jesuits, his imps, begged at his church doors—his pride so abated that, notwithstanding his former high terms, he was become glad to congratulate His Majesty and send unto him. Whoso knew what great assurances[20] he stood upon with other States, for smaller sums, would not think he would so freely disburse to my Lord Cobham six hundred thousand crowns! And if I had minded to set my Lord Cobham awork in such a case, I would have given him some instructions how to persuade the King! For I knew Cobham no such minion[21] that could persuade a King that was in want to disburse so great a sum, without great reason and some assurance for his money! I knew the Queen of England lent not her money to the States, without she had Flushing, Brill, and other towns in assurance for it. She lent not money to the King of France, without she had Newhaven for it. Nay, her own subjects, the merchants of London, did not lend her money, without they had her lands in pawn for it! And to show I am not "Spanish"—as you term me— at this time I had writ a treatise to the King's Majesty of the present state of Spain, and reasons against the Peace!

To this analysis of the flimsy charges against him—a defense surely unparalleled, with its close reasoning, its pride of experience and of appeal to experience, its scornful ironic commentary on the "treasons" ascribed to a mind like his—Coke could reply but with the sneer, "Methinks it would have been better for you to have stayed in Guiana, than to be so well acquainted with the state of Spain!" This trial was Ralegh's victory—a turning-point in more than his career. In that Court crowded with men who loathed and reviled him, he swept away, once for all, his countrymen's opinion of him. He went to judgment the best hated man in England; he came from it with life forfeited and liberty lost, but with reputation won back triumphantly and forever.

Some have strangely seen sarcasm[22] in the wonderful reference to his dead dear Mistress: "a Lady whom Time had surprised." But surely Mr. Waldman is right: "there must have been a complete hush in that solemn medieval hall as the poet uttered this lovely reference to the old queen."[23] This speech was the passage which struck home with the most thrilling effect, in a trial which again and again shook men whose

20. i.e., security.   21. i.e., person gifted with persuasive graces.
22. Algernon Cecil, *Life of Robert Cecil*, p. 189: "as Ralegh caustically phrased it."
23. *Ralegh*, p. 164.

wills were fixed never to be stirred by this man. It changed—and, for once, *dramatically* is the right word—the prejudice of many even from that nation whose coming south he had dreaded, who for many years had heard of him as one opposed to their King's succession. It was a Scot[24] who reported to James that, "whereas, when he saw Sir Walter Ralegh first, he was so led with the common hatred that he would have gone a hundred miles to see him hanged, he would, ere they parted, have gone a thousand to save his life." Another witness, Roger Ashton, told the King, "Never man spake so well in the time past, nor would in the time to come." I have no doubt that the traditions of this trial left their impress on Bunyan's account of Faithful's passion at the hands of the men of Vanity Fair.

Even Cecil seems to have had qualms during the trial he had engineered. Once he mildly remonstrated against Coke's vileness of temper: "Be not so impatient, good Master Attorney. Give him leave to speak." Coke took this as an outrage, exclaiming, "If I may not be patiently heard, you will encourage traitors and discourage us. I am the King's sworn servant, and must speak. If he be guilty, he is an odious traitor; if not, deliver him." Good Master Attorney sat down, and had to be long and earnestly coaxed before he would continue his patriotic orations. At another point, when Ralegh (as he had done all along) urged that Cobham should confront him, and offered to risk his case on the latter's witness, Cecil wavered, protesting, "My affection to you, Sir Walter Ralegh, was not extinguished but slacked, in regard of your faults"; and then supported the request. Ralegh taking advantage of this to offer, as unreservedly as possible, to stand or die by what Cobham said, Cecil tried to warn him in time. Anticipating another triumph like that he had gained when he called Knollys as a witness against Essex, he cried out: "Then call to God, Sir Walter, and prepare yourself, for I do verily believe my Lord will prove this! Excepting your fault, I am your friend. The great passion in you, and the Attorney's zeal for the King, make me speak thus." He had previously sworn by God that he loved Ralegh, "and had a great conflict in himself, that so compleat a member had fallen from the State"[25] (the

24. Lord Hay, who was afterwards Ralegh's friend.
25. So elsewhere in the trial: "I am in great dispute with myself to speak in the case of this gentleman; a former dearness between me and him tied so firm a knot of my conceit of his virtues, now broken by a discovery of his imperfections."

reader will again notice that there was none of our modern nonsense of assuming a man innocent until you have proved his guilt—Cecil was one of the judges). But the Court were afraid of Ralegh; they simply dared not accept his challenge and produce the unstable Cobham.

There was still one trick up the sleeve of the prosecution with which they meant to finish the game. The end came when, after Coke had asserted, "The King's safety and your clearing cannot agree," Ralegh's exchange of letters with Cobham was related, and a subsequent letter from that miserable creature was produced, in which, "in duty to my Sovereign, and in discharge of my conscience," he affirmed that Ralegh had tried to get him to procure for him a pension of £1500 from Spain, for which "he would always tell and advertise what was intended against Spain." "And so hath he bin the only cause of my discontentment." At this appalling disclosure "Sir Walter Ralegh was much amazed," as he well might be. Even so, "by and by he seemed to gather his spirits again," and he produced his own two letters. It was in vain. The jury, after retiring for fifteen minutes, found him guilty, and the Lord Chief Justice was able to fill in the little that Coke had overlooked. "Coke had forgotten to apply the word 'devil' to the prisoner. Popham was able so to apply it to the prisoner's friend," the mathematician Hariot, "as to carry an insinuation that the man whom a Jury had just found guilty of betraying his King had previously denied his God."[26] He exhorted Ralegh to repent while he had the chance. "Let not any devil Hariot, nor any such doctor, persuade you there is no eternity in Heaven. If you think thus, you shall find eternity in Hell fire!" He ended with a shudder: "I never saw the like Trial, and hope I shall never see the like again!" Then he pronounced the fiendish formula of condemnation:

Since you have been found guilty of these horrible Treasons, the judgment of this Court is, That you shall be had from hence to the place whence you came, there to remain until the day of execution; and from thence you shall be drawn upon a hurdle through the open streets to the place of execution, there to be hanged and cut down alive, and your body shall be opened, your heart and bowels plucked out, and your privy members cut off and thrown into the fire before your eyes; then your head to be stricken off

26. Edwards, i, 436.

By courtesy of The Walpole Society and the Oxford University Press.

SIR WALTER RALEGH AND HIS ELDER SON

PORTRAIT AT WICKHAM COURT, KENT

from your body, and your body shall be divided into four quarters, to be disposed of at the King's pleasure. And God have mercy upon your soul!

Dignified to the last, Ralegh briefly said he hoped the jury might never have to answer for their verdict, and "only craved pardon for having concealed Lord Cobham's offer to him, which he did through a confidence that he had diverted him from those humours." Then he stepped up to some of his judges, and quietly asked them to intercede that he might die honorably, and not by the proper mangling process. They promised, Cecil with tears. He asked also that, if Cobham too were convicted, he might die first (for he knew he could not face "either death or me without recanting"). After this, he accompanied the High Sheriff to prison, "with admirable erection, yet in such sort as a condemned man should."[27]

A crop of stories sprang up immediately, and continued to increase, showing how well popular opinion understood who had been really convicted. One of Ralegh's judges, Sir Francis Gaudy, on his deathbed said that "never before had the justice of England been so depraved and injured as in this Trial."[28] Before it, practically everyone had believed Ralegh guilty of plotting, though expecting there might be trouble in proving it. Afterwards, no one believed it. Even Coke, "in a garden resting his brazen lungs and his venomous temper,"[29] is said to have been astounded when a messenger told him Ralegh had been found guilty of treason. "Surely thou art mistaken. For I myself accused him but of misprision of treason."[30] "Some of the jury," says Francis Osborne, "were, after he was cast, so far touched in conscience as to demand of him pardon on their knees."[31] No one who has studied the reports of the trial has ever thought Ralegh in any degree guilty, except Hallam, and perhaps Gardiner. Lingard, "in whose Catholic eyes Ralegh was simply an unscrupulous flatterer of Elizabeth, and immoral adventurer," begs the issue ("not pledging his own judgment to the righteousness of the verdict"),[32] by asserting that "the guilt

27. Sir Thomas Overbury, *The Arraignment of Sir Walter Rawleigh*, p. 25.

28. Ralegh himself confidently appealed to this, as a well-known fact.

29. Stebbing, p. 230.

30. This is probably on Carew Ralegh's authority (in *Observations*, on Sanderson's *Lives and Reigns of Mary and James*, by "A Lover of the Truth," p. 9).

31. *Traditional Memoirs*, p. 18.   32. Stebbing, *Ralegh*, p. 225.

of Ralegh was no longer doubted after the solemn asseveration of Cobham on the scaffold"—a statement whose ridiculous falsity will emerge often enough in the rest of this story. Gardiner, while admitting that "with unerring judgment posterity has reversed the verdict of the Winchester jury," thinks that "the whole trial resolves itself into a question of character"[33] (apparently as to whether Ralegh or Cobham was the bigger liar). He is very shocked by what he calls Ralegh's "unlucky falsehood," his saying that he had not authorized Kemys to comfort Cobham with the reflection that it needed two witnesses to condemn a man; and seems to think the Government may have had proofs, which for political reasons they did not care to use, of Ralegh's guilt. Hallam recognizes the grotesquely illegal conclusion of the trial, but palliates it by some truly extraordinary reflections. He reproves Cayley for writing his *Life of Ralegh* "too much in the spirit of an advocate, which, with so faulty a client, must tend to an erroneous representation of facts."[34] Ralegh, it seems, among his eminently honest contemporaries was noticeable for dishonesty. He was also "far too intent on aggrandizement." The King's prejudice, and Cecil's hostility, were practically certain to drive "a man of his rash and impetuous courage to desperate courses." Hallam makes one good point only, when, after admitting the preposterous nature of the charges, he adds: "If Ralegh had ever shown a discretion bearing the least proportion to his genius, we might reject the whole story as improbable." It is unfortunately true that, even among men of genius, few have been less wise than Ralegh. But the question of his guilt or innocence is one of evidence, not of character, though character (as he interprets it) leads Hallam to observe that it is "very probable that the charge of plotting to raise Arabella to the throne was partly at least founded in truth."

To which we must say, that not a scrap of evidence was ever produced. The judges, with the ruthless machinery of power behind them, extorted none. Long afterwards the accused's son drily remarked, "I would fain know what it was that ever Cobham accused Ralegh of; for never I could. Likewise, whether ever any man was condemned by a single witness, and he not present either."[35] As to the charge of plotting

33. *History of England, 1603–1642*, i, 136.
34. *The Constitutional History of England* (1881 edition), i, 354.
35. *Observations*, on Sanderson's *Lives and Reigns*, etc., p. 8.

to elevate Arabella to the throne, no evidence was even pretended except her story that Cobham (not Ralegh) had written to her. Ralegh himself says, "I never liked her."[36] Cobham, perhaps, played for a time with the idea of her as Queen. He says she "sought my friendship"; and she may have been willing to know a man who was in high favor, and moreover represented himself as with fingers in all sorts of pies and as generally important and influential. Even so, all this was while Elizabeth was alive, so could not be held treason to James. Ralegh, who may have done Arabella some injustice as a woman, did her none as a possible ruler, and certainly never encouraged Cobham in this particular silliness. Not the least absurdity in his condemnation was that he was, among other offenses, "convicted of plotting to put on the English throne an empty-headed girl whom he had never seen, save as a child-guest in the house of an early patron, or as a sort of animated and over-dressed doll in an occasional Court pageant."[37] Even Cobham, after interviewing her, woke up into sanity. After his conviction, he told Cecil, in a letter which, as Edwards observes, carries conviction that for once Cobham spoke with truth and sincerity: "When I saw her, I resolved never to hazard my estate for her."

Cobham's trial followed, a perfect contrast. "Never was there so poor and abject a spirit," said an eyewitness[38] of both trials. Ralegh, Cobham said, had told Arenberg of Privy Council discussions at Greenwich, and had hoped to get a retaining salary of 1500 crowns for reporting such. (Ralegh could not betray what he did not know; Arenberg had no need to go to an outside source—he could get information from Privy Councillors themselves.) He had also planned the disembarkation of a Spanish army at Milford Haven. We do not know how, but *that* particular invention was presently blown sky-high, after Cobham

36. We know of only one occasion when they had met, in 1587, as fellow-guests of Lord Burghley. She was then a girl of twelve, and came to them greatly impressed from having dined with her awe-inspiring kinswoman—particularly happy because the Queen, whose standards of scholarship were exacting ones, "examined her nothing touching her book." As they supped Lord Burghley praised "Lady Arbell" to Sir Walter, no doubt assuring her that if the Queen *had* examined her, she would have shown up creditably, for "she had the French and the Italian: played of instruments: danced: and writ very fair." Then he wished "she were fifteen years old," and roguishly whispered something to Sir Walter, who replied, "it would be a very happy thing."

37. Edwards, p. xli.   38. Sir Dudley Carleton.

had been condemned, for in November Ralegh wrote to the Lords Commissioners:

The first accusation, for which I was committed, indicted, and arraigned, your Lordships do know to be false, and yet it was by your Lordships most constantly believed. And my Lord Chief Justice avowed that it could not be otherwise, because the Lord Cobham accused himself also therein. Then, my Lords, if I had perished, you all find that I had perished innocent; and that the presumption of the money was also inferred against me, and yet neither true. . . . If this matter of Milford had been true, what needed the Lord Cobham to have invented a treason against me, which was not true?

In conclusion, something should be said of Arenberg, whose "knavery . . . underlies, of necessity, the treason charged against Cobham." As Edwards says, one of two things must have happened in 1603: either Arenberg betrayed "every duty of an ambassador," or else "the character given" to his intercourse with Cobham, with Ralegh abetting, was "a piece of deliberate political falsehood of the most infamous sort."[39] Which was it? The reader shall judge. Next year, in August 1604, Spain and England made peace; and James then wrote to the Archduke Albert, thanking him for using such a "worthy and eminent instrument" as "our Cousin, the Prince Count of Arenbergh," who by his "sufficiency, prudence, and integrity" had "so conducted this important affair that we have received therein very great satisfaction." So, apparently, Cobham and Ralegh were guilty, and Arenberg noble, in one and the same transaction!

Lastly, when peace was made, the new resident Spanish Ambassador secretly allotted Henry Howard (then Earl of Northampton) a pension of £1000 a year; similar pensions to Lady Suffolk and Lords Dorset and Devonshire; £350 to Sir William Monson, the Admiral commanding in the Channel, and to Mrs. Drummond, the first Lady of the Queen's Bedchamber. Three of these beneficiaries had sat as Ralegh's judges! A fourth judge, Robert Cecil, also received £1000, which next year was raised to £1500. His position, as James's supreme minister, made him assess his services highly, and he saw that his *douceur* was paid punctually.

39. *Ralegh*, i, 486.

Of the persistence with which he exacted payment there can be no doubt whatever. Five years later, when the opposition between the two Governments became more decided, he asked for an increase of his payments, and demanded that they should be made in large sums as each piece of information was given.[40]

One of the Spanish ambassadors "pronounced him to be a venal traitor, who was ready to sell his soul for money." These were the men who condemned Ralegh.

40. Gardiner, *History,* etc., i, 215.

CHAPTER XVIII

The King's Mercy

When he [James] gave himself up to the Devil he often did it sincerely from the noblest motives, but it is hardly possible to believe that he did not enjoy doing it. He sipped the rich wine of cruelty, and was never drunk. CHARLES WILLIAMS, *James I.*

TO the present age, disillusioned beyond precedent, its ancestors seem less luridly iniquitous than perhaps they sometimes were. It is rather the excessive *childishness* of men's thoughts and motives and actions—angry and aimless and futile—that depresses.

Howard and Cecil had broken Ralegh utterly, and might send him to a death as terrible as malignity might wish. The Court had secured its verdict. Yet somehow things had gone not according to plan. The intended victim had shown himself too fine to be cast away casually, as other victims constantly were. The whole thick-spun web of "treason" was seen, and by everyone, to be a sham. After a trial packed with hatred and determination to close every way of escape, lassitude came on the victors, and instead of working the tragedy out exultantly to the end, they hesitated. James, the French Ambassador reported, December 8,

has been occupied for some days past, in hearing and considering the indictments and trials, having ordered, for the satisfaction of his conscience, that the whole should be reported to him, point by point, to the end that he might fully inform himself of the matter. The motives to mercy, and the reasons which urge a strict execution of the law, have kept him long in perplexity.

The Queen, who had at first, naturally, taken his view of Ralegh, and had snubbed Lady Ralegh, had been won over to an admiration she never lost, and was interceding. Privy Councillors were pressing for mercy. "Sidney's sister, Pembroke's mother," whose relations with Ralegh, apart from this one tantalizing half-gleam, are absolutely obscure, made her son, the King's host at Wilton, do the same. "I do call to mind," Dudley Carleton wrote to Chamberlain, November 27,

a pretty secret, that the Lady of Pembroke hath written to her son Philip, and charged him of all her blessing to employ his own credit and his friends, and all he can do for Ralegh's pardon; and though she does little good, yet she is to be commended for doing her best in showing *veteris vestigia flammae.*

Even open enemies were chivalrously anxious to prevent grotesqueness ending in grimness. The French Ambassador reported of a colleague:

The Spanish ambassador has spoken strongly to some members of the Council on Sir Walter Ralegh's behalf. Whether it be by mere artifice, or out of shameless impertinence, he makes show of an earnest wish to see all the conspirators saved from death, fearing (in my opinion) that their execution may serve to increase the disaffection of the English towards Spain, and may become an obstacle to the conclusion of the Treaty of Peace. The Ambassador makes no scruple to bargain for the Treaty openly, offering pensions and money to the grandees of this kingdom, for the purpose of promoting it.

Spain's credit was deeply involved at an awkward moment, Ralegh having been condemned for listening to intrigues alleged to have been those of their trusted envoy in England.

Ralegh, meanwhile, who had borne himself so superbly when face to face with enemies and odds that he could not possibly hope to conquer, was writing letters which are a distress to remember. To the Lords Commissioners, after argument masterly in his own unique manner, exposing the absurdity of the stories on which he had been condemned, he writes despairingly:

But the law is past against me. The mercy of my Sovereign is all that remaineth for my comfort. . . . And I desire your Lordships, for the mercy of God, not to doubt to move so merciful a prince to compassion, and that the extremity of all extremities be not laid on me. Let the offence be esteemed as your Lordships shall please in charity to believe it and value it, yet it is but the first offence; and my service to my country, and my love so many years to my supreme Lord, I trust may move so great and good a King, who was never esteemed cruel, and I trust will never prove so to be.

And, if I may not beg a pardon or a life, yet let me beg a time at the

King's merciful hands. Let me have one year to give to God in a prison and to serve Him. I trust his pitiful nature will have compassion on my soul; and it is my soul that beggeth a time of the King.

Had he been a man altogether unstained by ambition, as Socrates was, he might have left to us a second memory as noble as that of the sophist's farewell to his judges: "We go our ways, I to death and you to life. Which is better, God only knows." He would then have probably perished, killed for his unbending pride, for refusing to render the tribute his enemies passionately desired—of humility which seemed to justify the monstrous wrong they had done him. And there would have fallen a silence, when

> in calm peace the appointed Victim slept,
> As he had fallen in magnanimity—
> Of spirit too capacious to require
> That Destiny her course should change; too just
> To his own native greatness to desire
> That wretched boon, days lengthened by mistrust.

But he was not a man of such moral greatness.

Yet we must see that he was suffering intensely from the knowledge that he, a man known to be innocent and supremely gifted, had been deliberately and cynically trapped by creatures contemptible. He had no possible chance of escape except in submission. "There was no prospect of rescue through the machinery of the law," says Stebbing:[1]

As soon as the law with its automatic violence had possession of his case, he felt himself held in a grasp not to be relaxed. He knew he must look outside law for justice as well as mercy. . . . It had the right to pursue him to the death, whether innocent or criminal, so long as the rules of the art were observed. Its point of honour was not to let the accused escape.

The law "had assumed a scientific shape from which morality and common sense alike were absent." It was useless to insist that the whole trial had been a fraud; that would merely precipitate his destruction. James was in the position of the King in *Valentinian*, confronting his victim's threat to appeal to "Justice":

> Justice will never hear you! *I* am Justice!

1. *Ralegh*, pp. 234 ff.

The English law, once it had set afoot a prosecution, cared nothing about justice, but only about justifying itself.

About the meaner victims, at any rate, there was no vacillation. After all this elaborate paraphernalia of judgment, someone must die, and the priests accordingly "led the dance."[2] It was the usual horrid one, both Watson and Clerke being cut down alive, and the latter "both strove to help himself, and spake"[3] during castration and disembowelling. He had exasperated the Government by declining to play the game according to the established rules, by which the condemned meekly acknowledged that he had been justly convicted. But this ferocity continued the case's undoing; this poor wretch "was most miserably tortured, to the great discontent of the people, who now think that matters were not so heinous as were made show of."[4] A week later, George Brooke was beheaded, his family connection with Cecil helping him to a humane death. On the scaffold he withdrew as an invention his statement about "killing the fox and his cubs,"[5] and uttered a sphinxlike remark which threw everyone into turmoil for a few days afterwards: "There is somewhat yet hidden, which will one day appear for my justification." He said something else also, which stirred his brother-in-law to an outburst of fury. We do not know what it was, but it moved Cecil strangely. He called it "a base and viperous accusation—unpleasant for many respects—but not divulged." Possibly he mentioned that Cecil, no less than Cobham, had been busy trying to get money out of Spain. "As Brooke lived, so he died. God forgive his soul!" shuddered Cecil.[6]

Thomas Bilson, Bishop of Winchester, was sent to act as Ralegh's confessor and prepare him for death. Of this remarkable and versatile man, notable even in the Jacobean episcopal galaxy, we shall hear again. He found Ralegh, to his surprise, satisfyingly orthodox and devout. But he got no confession.

2. Dudley Carleton to Chamberlain, Nov. 27, 1603 (Birch, *Court and Times of King James,* i, 24).

3. Goodman, December 5 (*The Court of King James,* ii, 88).

4. *Ibid.*   5. Robert Cecil (*Winwood Papers,* ii, 11).

6. It is an interesting commentary on political executions, that Brooke's son did not allow his father's fate to depress him. He became "a great reveller at Court in the masques where the Queen and greatest ladies were" (Goodman, *Court of King James,* i, 70).

The King signed warrants for the execution—on December 10—of Cobham, Grey and Markham at Winchester. Ralegh was to die three days later, and on December 9 wrote his wonderful farewell to his wife:

You shall receive, dear wife, my last words in these my last lines. My love I send you, that you may keep it when I am dead; and my counsel, that you may remember it, when I am no more. I would not, with my last Will, present you with sorrows, dear Bess. Let them go to the grave with me, and be buried in the dust. And, seeing it is not the will of God that ever I shall see you in this life, bear my destruction gently, and with a heart like yourself.

First, I send you all the thanks my heart can conceive, or my pen express, for your many troubles and cares taken for me, which—though they have not taken effect as you wished—yet my debt is to you never the less. But pay it I never shall in this world.

Secondly, I beseech you, for the love you bare me living, that you do not hide yourself many days, but by your travail seek to help your miserable fortunes, and the right of your poor child. Your mourning cannot avail me, that am but dust. . . .

And I trust my blood will quench their malice that desire my slaughter, and that they will not also seek to kill you and yours with extreme poverty. To what friend to direct thee I know not, for all mine have left me in the true time of trial; and I plainly perceive that my death was determined from the first day. Most sorry I am (as God knoweth) that, being thus surprised with death, I can leave you no better estate. . . . But God hath prevented all my determinations, the great God that worketh all in all. If you can live free from want, care for no more; for the rest is but vanity. Love God, and begin betimes to repose yourself on Him; therein shall you find true and lasting riches, and endless comfort. For the rest, when you have travailed and wearied your thoughts on all sorts of worldly cogitacions, you shall sit down by Sorrow in the end. Teach your son also to serve and fear God, while he is young, that the fear of God may grow up in him. Then will God be a husband unto you, and a father unto him; a husband and a father which can never be taken from you. . . .

Remember your poor child for his father's sake, that chose you and loved you in his happiest times. Get those letters (if it be possible) which I writ to the Lords, wherein I sued for my life, but God knoweth that it was for you and yours that I desired it, but it is true that I disdain myself for begging it. And know it (dear wife) that your son is the child of a true man, and who, in his own respect, despiseth Death and all his misshapen and ouglie forms.

I cannot write much. God knows how hardly I stole this time, when all sleep. And it is time to separate my thoughts from the world. Beg my dead body, which living was denied you; and either lay it at Sherborne, if the land continue, or in Exeter church, by my father and mother. I can write no more. Time and Death call me away.

The everlasting, infinite, powerful, and inscrutable God, that Almighty God that is goodness itself, mercy itself, the true life and light, keep you and yours, and have mercy on me, and teach me to forgive my persecutors and false accusers; and send us to meet in His glorious kingdom. My true wife, farewell. Bless my poor boy; pray for me. My true God hold you both in His arms!

That his religious faith was deeper, sincerer, than that of the multitudinous orthodox who never exchanged speculation with men like Marlowe and Hariot, no one who has read Ralegh's letters in his times of anguish can doubt. The reality of his faith shines no less conspicuously in his great dirge, *The Pilgrimage,* written during these days when he was awaiting death:

> Give me my scallop-shell of quiet,
>   My staff of faith to walk upon,
> My scrip of joy, immortal diet,
>   My bottle of salvation,
> My gown of glory, hope's true gage!
> And thus I'll take my pilgrimage.
>
> Blood must be my body's balmer;
>   No other balm will there be given;
> Whilst my soul, like quiet palmer,
>   Travelleth towards the land of heaven,
>   Over the silver mountains,
>   Where spring the nectar fountains—
>   There will I kiss
>   The bowl of bliss,
>   And drink mine everlasting fill
>   Upon every milken hill.
>   My soul will be adry before,
>   But after, it will thirst no more!

He is going, he rejoicingly reminds himself,

> to Heaven's bribeless hall,
> Where no corrupted voices brawl;
> No conscience molten into gold;
> No forged accuser bought or sold;
> No cause deferred, no vain-spent journey;
> For there Christ is the King's Attorney;
> And when the grand twelve-million jury
> Of our sins, with direful fury,
> Against our souls black verdicts give
> Christ pleads his death, and then we live!

Gardiner calls these verses "a strange medley, in which faith and confidence in God appear side by side with sarcasms upon the lawyers and courtiers."[7] Mr. Harlow is severer yet. "After a grotesque description of heaven" (incidentally, *every* description of heaven in literature—not excepting the sublimities of the Apocalypse and of Socrates' account of the country where "the gods themselves are visible to men"[8]—is grotesque after exactly the same manner) "he descends to a furious attack upon his judges."[9] It is of course deplorable that Ralegh should for a moment glancingly remember how far short of fairness Coke's indecent fury (which arouses little comment in historians) came. "A temperament thus curiously compacted excited widespread antagonism." "A temperament curiously compacted" always does that. What are we to feel about critics who contemplate with such portentous disapproval Ralegh's mild reflections on the iniquitous travesty of "justice" of which he had been the victim?

James, meanwhile, in Lord Pembroke's hospitality at Wilton, had been elaborating a little play of which he was to be the hero. He kept it absolutely to himself and to a favorite Scots page, John Gibb, and produced his drama so cunningly that its *dénouement* came very close to being missed, owing to this important actor not getting on to the stage in time for his cue. The execution warrants were sent to the Sheriff, and on December 10, at ten in the morning, Sir Griffin Markham was brought on to a scaffold erected in Winchester Castle yard. He had

7. *History of England*, 1603–1642, iii, 152.
8. In the *Phaedo*.
9. *The Discoverie of Guiana*, p. xxiii.

made his adieus and prayers and was expecting the axe, when John
Gibb was seen excitedly trying to force a way through the spectators.
He had to shout to the Sheriff to save Markham's neck. Ralegh, watching all from a window, must have had "hammers working in his head
to beat out the meaning of the stratagem."[10] The French Ambassador
was told that he "beheld the comedy played out by his companions
with a smiling face."[11] If this is true, it was only because he knew he
was being watched. Gibb managed to get a paper into the hands of the
Sheriff, who read it, and then gravely told Markham, "You say you
are ill prepared to die. You shall have two hours' respite." Markham
was removed, and locked up in the hall where "Arthur's Round Table"
hangs. Grey came next, with a troop of friends, reminding spectators
of a bridal rather than a dying. He was a popular man, and his demeanor was a contrast of cheerfulness. Nevertheless it was noticed that
he turned over the straw with his foot, to see if there was blood there.
A famous Puritan divine, Dr. Richard Field, made a long prayer,
which Lord Grey outdid with a longer. The play (as revised by King
James) began to prove trying, with no actual beheadings to enliven it.
Sir Dudley Carleton, that connoisseur of executions, complained that
the condemned man's devotions "held us in the rain more than half an
hour."[12] But Grey also was at last ready for the headsman, when the
Sheriff—a man after King James's heart, thoroughly enjoying this protracted solemnity—stopped proceedings by telling him that by royal
command the order of execution had been changed; Cobham was to
come first. Grey, utterly bewildered, went to join Markham; "he had
no more hope given him than of an hour's respite." Now came Cobham, bold, and almost swaggering. Watchers who knew the man, and
remembered how craven he had been throughout, told the Comte de
Beaumont that they were sure he was in the secret of what was happening. He too prayed fervently. But his auditors felt the affair was passing
beyond a joke, and began to barrack. His petitionary duet with the
minister was spoiled by the criticism: "He has a good mouth in a cry,
but he is nothing single" (i.e., by himself). However, orisons ended,

10. Dudley Carleton (L. Aikin, *Memoirs of the Court of King James the First*, i,
174).
11. *"Était à la fenêtre, regardant la comédie de ses compagnons avec un visage riant."*
12. Letter to Chamberlain, Dec. 11, 1603.

and Cobham came to what the Government considered the real point. Observing that it was "no time to dissemble," he "therefore protested, before God and His Angels, that all and every part of his accusation of Sir Walter Ralegh was substantially true . . . as I have hope of my soul's resurrection." "But he had said of Ralegh, as of his own soul, far too much . . . affirmation had followed affirmation . . . the statement deposed to in one week,—'as I hope to be saved'—had next week been contradicted, flatly, by another statement, upon which, in turn, damnation was invoked if it were false."[13]

Cobham, too, was taken away. Then all three were gathered together, and the Sheriff asked them, collectively and severally, "Are not your offenses heinous? Have you not been justly tried, and lawfully condemned? Is not each of you subject to due execution, now to be performed?" They all replied affirmatively, and were then called on to "see the mercy of your Prince, who of himself hath sent hither a countermand, and hath given you your lives!" James, three days previously, had drawn up the reprieves, with explanation: "The two prestis and George Brooke vaire the principall plotteris and intisairs[14] of all the rest to the embracing of the saiddis treasonabill machinations," "a suggestive and pregnant statement, whether true or false."[15] It shows how little seriously was taken Ralegh's share in plots of which Coke alleged he had been the mainspring.

The reprieved made enthusiastic acknowledgment of the King's clemency, and everyone assembled about the condemned expressed wild admiration of the mind which had plotted so delightful a tragi-comedy. While the crowd was dispersing with cries and shouts, the drama's author was collecting congratulations in person, at Wilton. He had gathered Privy Councillors and favorites, and an antechamber was thronged with lesser persons to swell the song of praise. He expatiated on his difficulties, and, taking the condemned in pairs, showed there were reasons for and against mercy in each case. Was it kingly to kill fearless Grey and spare a worm like Cobham? On the other hand, Grey had been arrogant, refusing to beg for life, while Cobham had been deeply penitent, gratifyingly humble. He held this strain to his triumphant conclusion: "And therefore I have saved the lives of all." The applause

13. Edwards, i, 453.   14. Enticers.
15. Edwards, i, 448.

which broke out was continued by Cecil and others, in imbecilely extravagant letters. Ralegh also, with infinitely more excuse, in the depths of wretchedness lest he only should be left to die, wrote to the Commissioners:

> We have this day beheld a work of so great mercy, and for so great offences, as the like hath bin seldom if ever known; not after the manner of men, or of kings, *"sed coelestis judicis, eternique regis more."* And although my self have not yet bin brought so near the very brink of the grave, yet I trust that so great a compassion will extend itself towards me also. . . . Only the memory of mine own unworthiness made me to despair of so great grace, who otherwise beheld Pity in the face, the voice, the writing, and life of my Sovereign.

How long the King, in the despicable cruelty which he and his sycophants called mercy, kept Ralegh still expecting death, we do not know, but it was not long. He was told he was reprieved, and on December 16 he left Winchester for London.

Outside England James's mercy was looked upon with more suspicious and cynical eyes. Henri IV surmised that Spanish bribery had been at work, to save Spain's detected agents from punishment; or that Ralegh's money had proved effective. "The faith in Ralegh's endless resources and skill prevailed in France as in England."[16]

16. Stebbing, p. 240.

CHAPTER XIX

First Years in the Tower

The best of men are but the spoils of Time, and certain images wherewith childish Fortune useth to play—kiss them to-day and break them to-morrow —and therefore I can lament in myself but a common destiny . . . having forgotten that happiness which found too much too little. RALEGH, to Robert Cecil, 1604.

I have only a penitent soul, in a body of iron, which moveth towards the lodestone of Death, and cannot be withheld from touching it, unless your Majesty's mercy turn the point towards it which repelleth. RALEGH, to King James, 1604.

THAT Ralegh's life was spared we may set down to Cecil, all-powerful with James in these first days of gratitude and of uncertainty amid the intricacies of the English scene. He was now steadily and consistently kind. With characteristic caution disguising his handwriting, he had sent words of comfort, which Ralegh acknowledged with deeply sincere thankfulness ("I knew the phrase"). The broken yet dignified humility of Ralegh's letters to the companion who had risen so high above him, and was showing himself the only effective helper, is very touching. It was to Cecil that Lady Ralegh addressed her appeals. Had he stayed implacable, nothing could have saved them from that penury whose crushing results Ralegh realized so strongly. He had nothing of illusion about the supposed beneficial effects of "honest Poverty, that hangs his head and a' that." "Poverty is a shame, an imprisonment of the mind. Poverty provokes a man to do infamous and detested deeds."[1] His relief was immense when, in December, 1603, the King promised Lady Ralegh her personal possessions. And early in 1604 he wrote to Cecil:

My wife told me that she spake with your Lordship yesterday about my poor estate and hers, and that it pleased your Lordship to tell her that you would be pleased to deal for the assurance of my land unto some Feoffees,

1. *Instructions to his Son and to Posterity.*

of trust to the use of her and my child. But that for my pardon, it could not yet be done.

To a convicted traitor Cecil was unexpectedly kind, the King unprecedentedly generous.

In all this, as in the ferocity of his persecution, there was something personal. Hated as he was, distrusted and marked down for ruin, Ralegh wrung from his enemies recognition of some individual importance which secured him separate treatment. The others paid their fines to the uttermost. Markham was presently exiled, so pillaged that he had to sell the silver inlaid hilt of his sword for bread. He became a soldier of fortune and a spy for Cecil on the Continent. Grey and Cobham lost their lands. The former died in the Tower, 1614; Cobham stayed there till released on leave in 1617, a dying man permitted to visit Bath for the waters.

We may dismiss Cobham's subsequent history here. His wife, one of the fine unscrupulous Howards, had bewildered people by her passion for one "whom never woman loved, or will love, beside herself."[2] But his ruin quite cured her, and she left him utterly alone thereafter. The Crown, after ransacking his possessions, flung him back £500 a year for maintenance; even this was not paid toward the end. Probably, in the wave of immense admiration and pity for Ralegh, whose execution (October 29, 1618) had been turned by him into a surpassing triumph, it was felt that Cobham might as well share in the misery which even the King was beginning to feel was the proper lot of all who had brought Ralegh to his death. Cobham returned from Bath half paralyzed, too ill to be again imprisoned, and lingered on until his death (January 12, 1619), in a hovel,

lousy for want of Apparel and Linen; and had starved, had not a Trencher-scraper, some time his Servant in Court, relieved him with scraps—in whose house he died, being so poor a house as he was forced to creep up a Ladder into a little hole to his chamber.[3]

This story, often doubted, rests on Lord Pembroke's authority.

Why was Ralegh treated as a case apart? The answer is, even legal

2. Goodman, *The Court of King James*, i, 69.
3. Welldon, *Court and Character of King James*, p. 37.

humbug and fury could not disguise the fact that he *was* a case apart. The rest took what little they were given, and were thankful; they had all, in different degrees, been guilty of treason sufficient to bring them within the law's wide and merciless cruelty, and they knew they were lucky to have escaped being tortured out of life. Ralegh was innocent, and knew that the Government knew this. He received comparatively much, and continually pressed for more. We can see how hard he found it to get reconciled to the fact that he was definitely and finally ruined—until he found he had to die it is doubtful if he ever did get reconciled to it. We can see how monstrous it seemed to him and his devoted wife that *he* should have been condemned, on *such* evidence and on such a charge—intrigue with Spain. He could confidently claim before the nation at large that the verdict was an insult to intelligence. His enemies, he felt, were *bound* to release him; the State, which had found him of such service so often in England's vulnerable West, at Cadiz and in the Islands, in Virginia and Guiana, on the high seas everywhere, in person or by proxy of his ubiquitous privateers, in unofficial council in London, would surely presently awake to the fact that such powers and experience as his must not rust unused!

Nevertheless things would have gone desperately hard with the Raleghs but for Cecil. The vultures swarmed down, before the carcass was even technically dead. A special swoop was made on Sherborne. In October, 1603, before Ralegh was condemned, Cecil told a Scots applicant that a dozen others had preceded him. Ralegh had made the estate over to his son while Queen Elizabeth was alive, so that only his own life interest could legally be forfeited. But no one supposed that in this generous hour of nuptials to his new kingdom such pedantry would bind James, the bridegroom who had come accompanied by such a host of joyous friends. The common supposition proved right, though not immediately.

Most rapacious of all who profited by Ralegh's fall were the Howards. Before he was condemned his wine patent was obtained by the Lord Admiral. It had been in abeyance until the Council decided if it came under the new prohibition of monopolies. When it was decided that it did not, Ralegh was at least entitled to the arrears of payment. Lord Nottingham, however, thought otherwise, and claimed them. A ruined man, in his judgment, was entitled to nothing; and the strong were entitled to all they could collect. This despicable meanness where, if anywhere, they might have expected some consideration, hurt to the quick. Lady Ralegh wrote to Cecil:

I might have hoped that my Lord Admiral (if we might hope for anything from any living man) would rather have given us something back again of his great portion. His Lordship hath six thousand pounds, and three thousand pound a year, by my husband's fall. And, since it pleaseth God that his Lordship shall build upon our ruins, which we never suspected, yet the portion is great and I trust sufficient, out of one poor gentleman's fortune to take all that remains, and not to look back before his Majesty's grant, and take from us the debts past, which your Lordship knows were stayed from us by a proclamation, before my husband was suspected of any offence. . . .

God knows that our debts are above three thousand pound, and the bread and food taken from me and my children will never augment my Lord's table, though it famish us. . . .[4]

She besought Cecil, "both in compassion and justice, to speak one word to my Lord Admiral not to take from us by strong hand that which his Majesty hath given us for our relief."

Cecil spoke the word, and the spoiler was checked. He must have spoken many words. Ralegh's Rangership of Gillingham Forest and his Lieutenancy of Portland, though taken from him, were left with his brother, Sir Carew Ralegh, who had been joint tenant of them with him. This must have been a great cause of hopefulness; a time would come when all these troubles were a memory, and he would enjoy again that double life of sport and duty which no man fulfilled with more zest. Cecil's greatest kindness of all saved Sherborne. It had been attached, and Commissioners had descended on it, and begun at once to sell stock, fell timber, dismantle the castle, and do any destruction which might bring in a little quick cash and give the feeling (so dear to public bodies) that the landscape would always bear the gashes left by their visit. In every way Lady Ralegh was distressed: servants and beneficiaries repudiated obligations, tenants refused to pay rents, all who wished to be dishonest were dishonest. Cecil stopped all this. On July 30, 1604, the Crown made over to trustees, on Lady Ralegh's and

4. For once, I have modernized Lady Ralegh's spelling, which in this one letter is far less individual than usually.

her son's behalf, a sixty years' grant of Sherborne and ten other Dorset and Somerset manors. Cecil then felt he had done enough, and began to grow weary of receiving continual applications, as a letter written by Ralegh, probably in the late spring of 1604, shows.

It was about his health. When brought back from Winchester he remained in the Tower only a short time, and was then removed to the Fleet. Here he fell ill, so was taken back to the Tower. But only to be reëjected. The King had arranged Easter junketings for the Venetian Ambassador: two mastiffs were to be put on to a lion, and bulls were to be baited. In seeing animals suffer James took "a great but unmanly pleasure."[5] On March 26, 1604, the royal family, "together with the Council and the whole Court, went down the river to the Tower, in long and gay procession."[6] Then the King rode to the place of the revels, "on a white gennet under a rich canopy borne by six members of the Privy Council" (Cabinet ministers exercised a wider range of functions then than they do now). The quality, who followed, had difficulty in pushing through the crowd of humbler spectators packing the approaches. Prison enlargements were part of the religious games; so the Tower opened its doors to all but Ralegh, Grey, Cobham and Markham, whom His Majesty "did not deem worthy of his grace." These worst offenders were sent elsewhere for the period of the festivities, lest they mar them by their vicinity. When they returned, the Tower, a damp place because of the river mists and water oozing through its walls, was full of the Plague (possibly a legacy from the recent incursion of the populace). Lady Ralegh and her son had been living in it; they now fled precipitately. Ralegh wrote to Cecil, asking to be removed also, and incidentally complaining of his old friend's altered countenance:

. . . whatsoever your Lordship hath conceived, I cannot think myself to have bin either an enemy, or such a viper, but that this great downfall of mine, this shame, loss and sorrow, may seem to your Lordship's heart and soul a sufficient punishment and revenge. And, if there be nothing of so many years' love and familiarity to lay in the other scale, O my God! how have my thoughts betrayed me in your Lordship's nature, compassion, and

5. John Bayley, *History and Antiquities of the Tower of London,* p. 94.

6. Venetian Archives, *Consiglio di X.: England;* quoted Duffus Hardy, in report on the V.A. (1866).

piety. For to die in perpetual prison I did not think that your Lordship could have wished to your strongest and most malicious enemies. . . .

I have presumed at this time to remember your Lordship of my miserable estate—daily in danger of death by the palsy, nightly of suffocation by wasted and obstructed lungs. And now the plague being come at the next door unto me, only the narrow passage of the way between. My poor child having lien this 14 days next to a woman with a running plague sore, and but a paper wall between, and whose child is also this Thursday dead of the plague. . . .

My most humble desire is to be removed elsewhere, even to what place which God's goodness, and Charity, shall move your Lordship's heart. . . .

His prayer was not granted. Lady Ralegh, however, took a house on Tower Hill, where in 1605 their second son, Carew, was born.

In his hour of helplessness Ralegh found friends, faithful even if they could effect little. Laurence Kemys was imprisoned with him until December 31, 1603, at a cost of 11s. a week added to £5 for Ralegh and his servants. All this was a charge against the prisoner, equal to nearly £30 by the present standards. Kemys paid his own costs, but Ralegh had to meet the rest, selling his "rich hangings" for £500 to the Lord Admiral and putting his plate in pawn with Cheynes, a London goldsmith, where it became "lost, or eaten out with interest." Kemys' name, although the last bill for 1603 states that he was now discharged from the Tower, reappears after Ralegh's on the Fleet prison bills of early 1604. Both as prisoner and voluntarily he kept close to his master.

Ralegh saw other friends. He had the attendance of a surgeon and a physician. Shelbury, the steward of Sherborne, "a man whom I can better entreat than know how to reward," was allowed to visit him. The Indians he had brought from Guiana were living in England, baptized Christians; they lodged in or close to the Tower, and helped to enrich the romantic legend which was flowering fast about him. Sir George Harvey, the Tower Lieutenant, became friendly, and Ralegh often dined with him. In every way imprisonment was made as easy as possible, the Bloody Tower door standing unlocked and open, so that he might use the Lieutenant's private garden.

But in August, 1605, Sir William Waad superseded Harvey. The strings were now twitched, and Ralegh reminded that he was a prisoner. Waad brought the official mind at its meanest, suspicious of all that it could not bring under some regulation. A week after his arrival he wrote to Cecil (now Earl of Salisbury):

Sir Walter Ralegh hath converted a little hen-house in the garden into a still, where he doth spend his time all the day in his distillations. I desire not to remove him, though I want, by that means, the garden. . . . If a brick wall were built, it would be more safe and convenient.[7]

The wall was built.

But it needed more than a brick wall to cover up the man about whom the wildest beliefs were spreading. He was Ralegh the magician, Ralegh the mighty chemist, whose experiments in that mysterious laboratory where he worked all day were producing wonderful elixirs. One day in 1605, the Comtesse de Beaumont, wife of the French Ambassador, visited the Tower with Lady Effingham, to see the lions. She happened to see the most renowned lion of all, and must speak to him. Could Sir Walter let her have a little "Balsam of Guiana"? In her train was a Captain Whitelocke, a dependent of Ralegh's friend the Earl of Northumberland; Ralegh asked him to see to the delivery of the balsam. Waad, who had been one of Ralegh's judges, was humiliated to see how much less account was taken of the Tower's Lieutenant than of the Tower's captive; it looked as if his fame were sinking into that of being Ralegh's jailer. Because of his harmless act of compliance with a lady's request, when the Gunpowder Plot was discovered later in this year Ralegh was questioned before the Privy Council.[8] Even they had to see that he could not have had the remotest contact with the plot. So in their disappointment they strove to justify themselves by curtailing his liberties. He was closely confined, and as a result, in 1606 (his physician, Dr. Peter Turner, reported) his left arm and left side were growing palsied, the fingers of his left hand were contracting, his tongue was losing the power of speech. He was therefore allowed to build a small room on to his hen-house laboratory, and to live there, away from the river.

Waad remained dissatisfied and angry. Lady Ralegh, refusing to accept her position as the wife of a man legally dead, used to drive into the courtyard. His prisoners "were adapting themselves to circum-

7. Cayley, *Life of Sir Walter Raleigh*, ii, 84.
8. See Edwards, ii, 387 ff.

stances, and giving to their daily life something of the aspect of home."[9] The beadle's mind set to work, and produced just such a set of "Ordinances for Government of the Tower" as gratified its sense of power and intelligence. A bell was to be rung at 5 P.M., whereupon "all the prisoners, with their servants, are to withdraw themselves into their chambers, and not to go forth again for that night. None of the servants of the lords, or other prisoners, are to be permitted to lodge out of their lords' or masters' chambers." Prisoners were to dine by themselves, and the Tower was to cease to be regarded as an "ordinary."[10] Doors were to be kept shut henceforward, day and night. Lady Ralegh's coach was to stop outside. These regulations, admittedly aimed specially at Ralegh, came into force, July, 1607. But they neither quelled the prisoner nor pacified his keeper. In December, 1608, Waad wrote to Cecil:

Sir Walter Ralegh doth show himself upon the wall in his garden to the view of the people, who gaze upon him, and he stareth on them—which he doeth in his cunning humour, that it might be thought his being before the Council [i.e., about the Gunpowder Plot]—was rather to clear than to charge him.[11]

It was awkward, the way this convicted man had of making his judges feel that they, and not he, had been condemned! Waad commends himself for daring to draw tight the bonds: this conduct "made me bold, in discretion and conveniency, to restrain him again."

Everything done by Ralegh, everyone spoken to by him, was made matter for suspicion—even such a circumstance as that Lady Ralegh, visiting Sherborne in September, 1605, had the old armor in the castle burnished. And presently there was reason enough for the dread that this man, legally done with, was in fact very much living. Queen Anne, long ago won over to romantic admiration, pushed for his pardon untiringly. George Carew, rewarded for his discretion and support of Cecil, by being brought definitely and finally from Ireland, 1604, and made Baron Carew, 1605, became her Councillor (August 9, 1604) and Vice-Chamberlain. His brief estrangement from Ralegh was over, and he was again his unfortunate kinsman's champion. Perhaps at his in-

9. *Ibid.,* i, 490. 10. Inn.
11. Cayley, *Raleigh,* ii, 86.

stigation, during a deadly sickness the Queen sent for Ralegh's "balsam"; she believed it saved her life. Sanderson (who set himself, long after Ralegh's death, to slander him all he could) reports[12] that her waiting women said "she was never cured of her disease, but by death, that ends all Maladies." But the story rests on good evidence, and is intrinsically likely, from the way the far-famed cordial continued to be sought (by Anne herself again, especially when her son was dying).

Sir Anthony Welldon says[13] that for curing her Ralegh asked the Queen, as his reward, that certain Lords might be sent "to examine Cobham, whether he had accused Sir Walter Rawleigh of Treason at any time under his hand," and that she persuaded the King to consent, and to send the Duke of Lennox, Lords Salisbury, Worcester, Suffolk and Carew, and Sir Julius Cæsar. Cobham, questioned by them, protested: "Never! but that Villain Waad did often solicit me, and not prevailing, got me by a trick to write my name upon a piece of white paper, which I, thinking nothing, did, so that if any charges came under my hand, it was forced by that Villain Waad, by writing something above my hand without my consent or knowledge." Whereupon Lord Salisbury gravely reported to the King that Cobham "hath made good all that ever he wrote." We may think what we like of Lord Salisbury, and run little risk of doing him injustice. But the acquiescence of Carew (if he were told what Cecil was going to say) in a piece of abominable sharp practice throws an air of improbability over the story. Yet I do not believe it is all legend.[14]

What was this cordial? Le Febre, physician of Charles II, prepared some of it by royal command, out of forty vegetable substances (roots, seeds, etc.) pounded in spirits of wine and distilled, and then mixed with pearls, red coral, deer's horn, ambergris, powdered bezoar stone, white sugar, musk, antimony, several sorts of earth and other ingredients—to which Sir Kenelm Digby, to "make the gruel thick and slab," had added "mineral unicorn" and viper's flesh with the heart and liver. Ralegh, however, kept his secret here, as in so many things; we need not ascribe this fantastic iniquity of the druggist's art to him. My own

12. *Lives and Reigns of Mary and James,* p. 462.
13. *Court and Character of King James,* pp. 39–40.
14. If it is, how did James come to his belief that Raleigh's condemnation (which was solely on Cobham's evidence) was a miscarriage of justice?

belief is that his cordial was largely quinine, brought by him from Guiana, and that the Queen's sickness was mainly malarial.

Ralegh's cordial, his immense reputation as a physician, his consultation by the Queen, did nothing to rehabilitate him with the King. Nor did the fact that it was *his* example that had popularized the habit of smoking, for which sovereign medicinal qualities were claimed (as was natural when its leading exponent was so renowned a scientist). In 1604 James exploded in his *Counterblast against Tobacco*. "The treasure of our land" was being wasted on smoking (he could not foresee how much this vice was going to contribute to the exchequers of his immediate descendants). It was

an inconsiderate and childish affectation of Novelty . . . first found out by some of the barbarous Indians, to be a Preservative or Antidote against the Pox, a filthy disease, whereunto those barbarous people are (as all men know) very much subject, what through the uncleanly and a-dust constitution of their bodies . . . a stinking and unsavoury Antidote, for so corrupted and execrable a Malady, the stinking suffumigation whereof they yet use against that disease, making so one canker or vermin to eat out another . . . a smoke, all smoke and vapour, being of itself humid, a drawing near to the nature of the air and easy to be resolved again into water—as meteors and exhalations. . . . It makes a kitchen of the inward parts of men, soiling and infecting them with an unctuous and oily kind of soot, as hath been found in some great tobacco takers, that after their death were opened. . . . Is it not a great vanity, that a man cannot heartily welcome his friend now, but straight they must be in hand with Tobacco? . . . that the sweetness of man's breath, being a good gift of God, should be wilfully corrupted by this stinking smoke?

Men made their wives, those "delicate wholesome and clean-complexioned" companions, "live in a perpetual stinking torment." In brief, the King did not like smoking, and was quite sure of its malodorousness—he falls back on that, whenever other vituperation temporarily runs out:

a custom loathsome to the eye, hateful to the Nose, harmful to the brain, dangerous to the lungs, and in the black stinking fume thereof nearest resembling the horrible Stygian smoke of the pit that is bottomless . . . an incurable stink.

It was directly connected with atheism; and Ralegh, perusing this effusion in the Tower, could learn what was the fountain that had spouted forth all this wickedness. Smoking in England was the off-spring of "a father generally hated," who learnt it from

beastly Indians, slaves to the Spaniards, refuse to the world, and as yet aliens from the holy Covenant of God. . . . Why not walk naked, prefer-ring glasses, feathers and such toys, to gold and precious stones, as they do? and deny God and adore the Devil?

In the English Marcellus (whose death was to darken the winter of 1612), Henry, Prince of Wales, Ralegh found an eager and affectionate friend. Born in 1594, Henry was physically and mentally advanced, and "ceremonious beyond his years." The Venetian Ambassador reports, of an interview with him, in 1603: "The Prince is ten years old, little of body and quick of spirit . . . with great gravity he covered and bade me be covered."[15] That suggests something of priggishness, which the flattery that surrounds princes must (one imagines) induce early, and almost inevitably. But all testimony concurs as to the promise of this noble boy, in all things his father's opposite. He never swore, and used to say, "He knew no Game, or Value, to be won or lost, that could be worth an Oath."[16] He was very courteous, very constant in his resolves, very secret of confidences intrusted to him, very brave and enthusiastic and able in all sports, especially riding, tennis and swimming. His great desire was "to compose differences in Religion." He cared less than nothing for the Court's incessant revels; all his eagerness went out to affairs of State, and most of all, to shipbuilding and seamanship.

He found in Ralegh a mood of kindred seriousness and tolerance. He procured the evidence put forward at the notorious trial, and de-cided that both charges and condemnation were an unexampled trav-esty of decency and sense. He became Ralegh's frequent visitor; every-one has heard of his exclamation, "No one but my father would keep such a bird in a cage!" Ralegh, among whose passions was the making and study of ships, made one for him, of such a kind as he would see adopted for the British fleet.

15. *Calendar of State Papers and MSS. relating to English Affairs, existing in the Archives and Collections of Venice and in other Libraries of Northern Italy*, x (1603–1607), ed. Horatio F. Brown, p. 74.
16. *Aulicus Coquinariae*, p. 157.

These proofs of inextinguishable vitality and power to fascinate were the worst crimes Ralegh could have committed. In July, 1610, Cecil, who was now Lord Treasurer and Earl of Salisbury, visited him after long neglect, and soundly rated him. For the presumption he had shown, Ralegh was closely confined for three months, and a notice was served on his wife: "The Lady Raleighe must understand his Majesty's express will and commandment that she resort to her house on Tower Hill or elsewhere, with her women and sons, to remain there, and not to lodge hereafter within the Tower." On October 9 Ralegh, in a letter to an old acquaintance, showed how this unkindness still rankled, while he tried to save the remnants of his self-respect:

For whatsoever terms it hath pleased his Lordship to use towards me, which might utterly despair anybody else, yet I know that he spake them as a Councillor, sitting in Council, and in company of such as would not otherwise have bin satisfied. But, as God liveth, I would have bought his presence at a far dearer rate than those sharp words and these three months close imprisonment, for it is in his Lordship's face and countenance that I behold all that remains to me of comfort and all the hope I have, and from which I shall never be beaten till I see the last of evils and the despair which hath no help.

He begged his correspondent to "move my Lord Treasurer in my behalf, that by his grace my wife might again be made a prisoner with me, as she hath bin for six years last past, she being now divided from me, and thereby, to my great impoverishing, I am driven to keep two houses."

Now, and for the next dozen years and more, the most urgent political interest was the marriage of the King's son. Proposals in 1611 to marry James's daughter Elizabeth to the Prince Palatine, a Protestant, were countered by Spain and the Spanish party, with proposals for her marriage to a son of the Catholic Duke of Savoy, and also a marriage of the Prince of Wales to the Duke's daughter. The Prince, disliking the proposals, consulted Ralegh, who wrote for him two excellent political papers[17] against them. They convinced the Prince, who made his often-

17. *Discourse Touching a Marriage between Prince Henry of England and a Daughter of Savoy*, and *Discourse Touching a Match Propounded by the Savoyard between Lady Elizabeth and the Prince of Piedmont* (*Works*, viii, 223 ff. and 237 ff.).

quoted observation that "two religions should never lie in *his* bed." But they infuriated the King. "All parties knew that the things really to be bargained for with Spain were not bridals . . . but props to Romanism, and weapons of war against the Dutch."[18] James had received proposals for his son from France also, in the very first year of his reign, when Prince Henry was only nine—a State secret which he mortified the Duke of Sully by mentioning casually over the wine-cups. Sully tried to check him into sense of the serious issues at stake by whispering that Spain had made an offer of its Infanta for the Dauphin. "I, too, have had the like," James answered carelessly. "They offer their Infanta to everybody."

Despite this affectation of indifference he longed for a Spanish alliance, and secular jealousy of a Franco-Scottish *entente* made many of his English advisers also want it. The English feared "that the Scots would profit most by a French alliance"; they were "always ready to snap at the Scots," a French Ambassador wrote in 1616 (*"ont toujours une dent de laie sur les Écossois"*). Into this turmoil of angry suspicions and thwarted schemings Ralegh rushed, ignorant of the way the Court, and the King especially, were moving; and analyzed with masterly impersonal decision the folly of a deal with Spain. He asked: What if there should be no heir of the proposed Savoy marriage? We might easily see again a foreign ruler in England, a Savoyard of Spanish blood. Yet there could be no reciprocity; no English King could acquire Savoy, "all France being interjacent." Savoy itself, always and necessarily dependent on France or Spain, would be no source of strength. Nothing but ill could come of this alliance: either a terribly difficult war on behalf of a Piedmontese son-in-law, or a disgraceful abandonment of him. His abundant historical knowledge strews Ralegh's argument with apposite instances, such as the bandying and bartering of kingdoms which had come by the betrothals and weddings of Charles V's family. Princess Elizabeth, "one of the precious jewels of this kingdom," would be exiled "into a country as far estranged from our nation as any part of Christendom, and as far differing from us in religion as in climate." She must choose between seeing her children brought up in a faith that opposed hers and sacrificing her own beliefs.

His argument against a Spanish marriage for the Prince of Wales is

18. Edwards, i, 495.

equally cogent, a series of hammer-blows. Savoy is, and always has been, servant to Spain, and "Whatsoever is pretended to the contrary, it is Spain that we ought to suspect. Savoy from Spain is inseparable. Spain to England is irreconcilable." Those critics who have denied his sole authorship of *The History of the World,* because they consider its immense background of knowledge something inconceivable in a man irregularly educated (mainly by himself) and now in a prison, not a library, cannot have studied the ease and swiftness with which he sketches the recent past of Europe, and of Piedmont in particular. He comes home to two considerations not yet obsolete: the necessity to England of a free people in those European ports that confront her, and the equal necessity of controlling the sale of weapons that may be used against her. We forgot the former, he says, when we deserted the Dutch, with no hurt to them but much to us:

They were the last that put down arms; and, though they compounded with the greatest disadvantage (France and England having first compounded), yet they made a far more noble Peace with Spain than we did. Since that time, they have neglected us by degrees. Let us look to it with all the eyes we have. For to which of the three those people fasten themselves—whether to England, France, or Spain—he that hath them will become the greatest, and give the law to the rest. If any man doubt it, he knows not much.[19]

For the second consideration, Spain, which Elizabeth's sailors had met with unfaltering certainty and proof of superiority, was now England's naval equal, through

our own fault, and the detested covetousness of some great ones of ours: for whereas, in my time, I have known one of her Majesty's ships command forty of theirs to strike sail, they will now take us one to one, and not give us a good morrow. They master us both in their number and in their mariners; and they have our own ordnance to break our own bones withal.

The reader cannot too often remind himself of the astounding situation of this man who wrote so confidently and firmly, as if he were an elder statesman for whose views all were waiting. He appeals, as no other living man could have done with equal composure and assurance,

19. *Works,* viii, 248.

to what used to happen "in my time," and with "her Majesty's ships" when they met the galleons. He advises the heir-apparent "to keep his own ground for a while, and no way to engage or entangle himself" with any marriage or proposals of marriage. As to Spain, "the wounds" we have given her and her allies "are too many and too deep . . . to be healed with the plaister of a peace." Herein he was one more example of a doctor who could see the case of others, but not his own. These pamphlets, so masterly and far-seeing, were but another item laid up against him, in his long account with Spain. He was to find that no "plaister of a peace" was going to be of any use to him.

How these pamphlets and his growing influence with the Prince of Wales exasperated the King we can guess, and partly know. The states-men who surrounded James regarded England as a third-rate Power on the edge of Europe and existing by the kindness of two great coun-tries whom she must be careful not to provoke. They could not under-stand this calm assumption that there were *three* great Powers, among whom Great Britain (not mere England any longer—not that Ralegh ever considered mere England anything but a Power of first rank) held the balance and controlling hand. He was a ghost that refuses to know it is a ghost—a voice crying out of the vanished age of Drake and Sid-ney and Elizabeth. His refusal to accept the fact that he was a felon, whose only safety lay in keeping very still and trusting that justice would forget his existence, maddened the *canaille* who were now rul-ing. They were reminded (June 26, 1611) by Lord Grey, one of Ral-egh's fellow-prisoners, of how much he had been allowed to rise above his station: "Northumberland hath liberty to walk on the hill; Cobham, to walk freely in the garden; Sir Walter Ralegh hath a garden and gal-lery to himself. I only am shut up." Accordingly Cecil (as we have seen) visited him, and sternly commanded him to keep his place. He had visits from other Privy Councillors also; and to Henry Howard, though he knew well that in the terrible days of 1603 this enemy had exhausted neither his will nor his power to hurt, Ralegh showed that he understood perfectly, and knew that the other understood perfectly, the difference between himself, even in misfortune, and the man who was the meanest spirit then alive. Howard reported, in a letter of sav-age chagrin, to Robert Kerr, Lord Rochester:

We had a bout with Sir Walter Ralegh, in whom we find no change, but the same boldness, pride and passion, that heretofore hath wrought more violently, but never expended itself in a stronger passion. Hereof his Majesty shall hear when the Lords come to him. The lawless liberty of the Tower, so long cockered and fostered with hopes exorbitant, hath bred suitable desires and affections.

It was magnificent, but it was not war; for Howard had all the weapons, and they were promptly used. It would be tedious to relate all the occasions when Ralegh was driven back into his den, and the door tightly sealed—how often he was cross-examined, and bullied on one pretext or another. He did not take it meekly, but told his friend the Queen of his failing strength,

with the despair of obtaining so much grace to walk with my keeper up the hill within the Tower . . . who, after eight years' imprisonment, am as straitly lockt up as I was the first day, and the punishment due to other men's extreme negligence laid altogether upon my patience and obedience.

Neither to her nor to anyone else did he make any pretense of considering himself a criminal. "Subject every day to suffer for other men's offences," he desired "to die, once for all, and thereby to give end to the miseries of this life," rather than "to strive against the ordinance of God, who is a true judge of my innocency towards the King, and doth know me."

CHAPTER XX

Sherborne; and *The History of the World*

The malice of the world doth exceed the wisdom thereof. RALEGH to Queen Anne, 1611.

As for Rawly, none ever employed Enlargement worse, that knew so well how to advantage himself and his country in Imprisonment. For, during his tedious Lying in the Tower (under the jealousy rather than Justice of King James, who did so far participate of the humour of a pusillanimous Prince, as to pardon any sooner than those injured by himself) he was delivered of that Minerva, the History of the Old World. FRANCIS OSBORNE.

> Here writ was the World's History by his hand
> Whose steps knew all the earth; albeit his world
> In these few piteous paces then was furl'd.
> Here daily, hourly, have his proud feet spann'd
> This smaller speck than the receding land
> Had ever shown his ships. . . .
>
> D. G. ROSSETTI, *Raleigh's Cell in the Tower.*

I venerate that villainous adventurer, for his views on universal history. LORD ACTON, May 21, 1869.

JAMES, who was not uxorious, had other passions, notorious long before he came to London. Since these passions would be satisfied, and the person in whom he found their satisfaction would become the channel of royal bounty, English statesmen hoped that some young gentleman of their own nation would find favor in his eyes. The Howards took this important matter in hand, and the Countess of Suffolk conducted a school for favorites; she "did look out choyse young men, whom she daily curled and perfumed their heads."[1] Unfortunately, these efforts were overthrown when Robert Kerr, one of the ancient family of the Kerrs of Ferniehurst, had the good luck to break his leg tilting before the King. We know that Pity

1. Osborne, *Traditional Memoirs of the Reign of King James,* p. 7.

in Love's service dwells,
A porter at the rosy temple's gate.

James saw how delightful the boy was, as he lay before him helpless. Kerr had all his master lacked, abounding spirits, animal vitality. He was advanced swiftly and steadily; knighted in 1607, in 1613 he became K.G. and an earl.

The Countess of Suffolk, seeing her patriotic labors wrecked by a piece of bad riding, was wrathful. But the Howards soon realized that wisdom lay in courting the new minion. Robert Cecil, Earl of Salisbury, had realized it at once, and he gave his realization practical expression. In 1607 it became known that Kerr wanted Sherborne, and that the Earl of Salisbury was going to see that he got it.

In 1604 Cecil had promised Sherborne to Lady Ralegh, who had passed his assurance on to her husband. The Raleghs "might have reckoned" it "indefeasibly safe."[2] But their anxiety for it was extreme, and Ralegh determined to make it lawyer-proof, having found a flaw in the conveyance drawn up in Elizabeth's time; the clerk who had drawn it up had omitted ten words, "shall and will from henceforth stand and be thereof seized." Coke and Popham were consulted, at Ralegh's request, and reported to Cecil (June 7, 1605) that the omission invalidated the transference. The Letters Patent (granted July 30, 1604) which placed Sherborne in trustees' hands for Lady Ralegh were consequently no protection.

During the suspense, while they were waiting for the lawyers' decision, Lady Ralegh's self-control and affection gave way. The Tower and the threat of plague had broken her down, and she had the sole care of a new-born infant as well as of a young child. She rated her husband hysterically: he had saved himself from the gallows, and cared nothing about anything else! Ralegh appealed once more to Cecil:

I shall be made more than weary of my life by her crying and bewailing, who will return in post when she hears of your Lordship's departure, and nothing done. She hath already brought her eldest son in one hand, and her sucking child in another, crying out of her and their destruction, charging me with unnatural negligence, and that, having provided for mine own life, I am without sense and compassion of theirs.

2. Stebbing, p. 260.

But Cecil had tired of the Raleghs. Lady Ralegh (whom James was getting to know by sight rather well) then sought an audience with the King, whom she begged to overlook a clerk's slackness. In a mood of expansive generosity he consented, and told Cecil to have a proper grant made out. This Cecil never troubled to do. He had his hands full, and the most harassing business of all was that of finding funds for the King's lavishness to favorites and for their rapacity. It is doing him no injustice to suppose his inaction was deliberate. Presently James was insisting that an estate must be found for Kerr, whom he was about to make a peer. Cecil, who knew it well, suggested Sherborne, throwing the King into transports of delight and gratitude:[3]

The more I think of your remembrance of Robert Kerr for yon manor of Sherborne, the more cause I have to conclude that your mind ever watcheth to seek out all advantages for my honour and contentment; for as it is only your duty and affection to me that makes you careful for them that serve me, so must I confess that he is the only young man whom, as I brought with me and brought up of a child, that was now left unprovided for, I mean, according to that rank whereunto I have promoved him, besides that the thing itself, when I have now considered it will prove excellent fit for him, and withal that 3[4] before my parting requested me for him in it. . . .

Accordingly the Crown commenced proceedings, late in 1607, to establish its claim on Sherborne. Lady Ralegh waylaid the King at Hampton Court—an incident which, forty years later, when he was trying hard to recover Sherborne from the Long Parliament,[5] still moved her son Carew to resentful indignation. James passed her by in silence, then returning that way and finding her still there, said only, "he mun have the land, he mun have it for Carr";[6] whereupon

she, being a woman of a very high spirit and noble birth and breeding, fell down upon her knees, with her hands heaved up to Heaven, and in the

3. Hatfield MSS. 134, fol. 149.
4. "3" is Lord Northampton (Lord Henry Howard). James and he and Cecil still conducted the more shady of their business, such as this theft of Sherborne, in cipher, as if they were still conspirators.
5. Carew Ralegh's appeal is printed in vol. viii of the *Collected Works* of Ralegh (Oxford University Press, 1826) as an appendix.
6. Carew Ralegh, though a child of about three years old, may have been with his mother.

bitterness of her spirit beseeched God Almighty to look upon the justness of her cause, and punish those who had so wrongfully exposed her and her poor children to ruin and beggary.

The appeal was futile. In January, 1608, the Court of Exchequer decided that Sherborne's conveyance was invalid, and Chamberlain wrote to Dudley Carleton, January 10:

Sir Walter Ralegh's estate is fallen into the King's hands by reason of a flaw in the conveyance. He hath bestowed it on Sir Robert Carr. And though the Lady Ralegh hath been an importunate suitor all these holidays in her husband's behalf, yet it is past recall, so that he may say, with Job, Naked I came into the world, and naked shall I go out. But, above all, one thing is to be noticed: the error of oversight is said to be so gross that men do merely ascribe it to God's own hand, that blinded him and his counsel.

Ralegh was allowed lawyers to fight his case. But the King, naturally, was not going to waste time over formalities. His conscience was salved by the compulsory purchase for £5000 from Lady Ralegh, of the grant he himself had made her in 1604. A writ for payment of the first instalment was issued, March 13, 1608, actual payment to be made in June. Nothing was actually paid yet, however, for the family were most reluctant to do anything (such as accepting money) that finished their hopes. The legal proceedings ended, October 27, and the Crown stood possessed of everything. Ralegh tried a last desperate throw, writing direct to Kerr:

it is come to my knowledge that yourself (whom I know not, but by an honourable fame) have been persuaded to give me and mine our last fatal blow, by obtaining from his Majesty the inheritance of my children and nephews, lost in law for want of words. This done, there remaineth nothing with me but the bare name of life. . . . His Majesty, whom I never offended . . . stayed me at the grave's brink; not, as I hope, that his Majesty thought me worthy of many deaths and to behold all mine cast out of the world with myself, but as a King who, judging the poor in truth, hath retained a promise from God that his throne shall be established for ever.

And for yourself, Sir, seeing your day is but now in the dawn, and mine come to the evening . . . I beseech you not to begin your first buildings upon the ruins of the innocent, and that their griefs and sorrows do not attend your first plantation. I have been bounden to your nation, as well for many other graces as for the true report of my trial to the King's Majesty—

an extraordinarily interesting statement, an example of the way in which study of Ralegh's own words confirms the truth of stories which are usually rejected because they are picturesque and only the drab and undeviatingly ordinary *can* be true[7]—

against whom, had I been found malignant, the hearing of my cause would not have changed enemies into friends, malice into compassion, and the greatest number present into commiseration. . . . I therefore trust, Sir, that you will not be the first that will kill us outright, cut down the tree with the fruit, and undergo the curse of them that enter into the fields of the fatherless. . . .

Appeals to fairness or to magnanimity were lost on Kerr. James, however, acted with some consideration. He put in Commissioners, one being Kemys, to survey the land, after which Sir Arthur Throckmorton, Lady Ralegh's brother, one of the trustees, with his fellow-trustees had to accept an agreement by which, in place of the proposed £5000, the Raleghs received £8000, and Lady Ralegh a pension of £400 a year, to be continued to her elder son if he survived her. Part of the £8000 was paid, and the dowager Countess of Bedford borrowed it. For the rest, the Crown paid interest not very regularly. Lady Ralegh's pension also was paid irregularly and reluctantly.[8]

That is the story of a wrong which deeply impressed contemporaries, who soon had reason to believe that to its other curse Sherborne carried another, laid on it by Lady Ralegh. It has been maintained that the King did not treat his prisoner harshly. "In order to judge the extent of the wrong done to Ralegh, it is necessary to know what was the precise money value of the land which was taken from him."[9] It is necessary to know more than that—to remember that it was wrested from him by legal high-handedness, against the King's own promise. The Prince of Wales, "hearing the King had given Sherburn to Sir Robert Carr, came with some anger to his father,"[10] protesting that a place of such strength and beauty should not be given away from the Crown, and demanded it for himself. Prince Henry's wishes "were commonly delivered in such language as sounded rather like a demand than an

7. He is referring to Lord Hay's special report, at His Majesty's request.
8. See her letter in 1617 (Edwards, ii, 411–12), which it is painful to read.
9. S. R. Gardiner, *History of England,* 1603–1642, ii, 47.
10. Carew Ralegh to Long Parliament, 1648.

entreaty," and the timid King gave way. Kerr was bought off with £20,000 (or possibly, £25,000), which was what James reckoned Sherborne to be worth except when he was compensating the Raleghs. Henry held it, intending to return it to the family when his friend had been pardoned, and his possessions therefore made safe from the lawyers.

The bitterness of the loss was deepened by the fact that Ralegh continually saw hopes of release drawing very close. In 1606 James's brother-in-law, the King of Denmark, visited England. He wanted Ralegh to be his own admiral, and interceded for him. In the day of his final ruin, Ralegh—who had every argument on his side except that of power—asked if it had ever been known before that a king's wife, a king's son and a king's brother had all pleaded for a traitor. As his letter to Kerr shows, and as everything shows, he confidently asserted that the whole world knew his condemnation had been nonsensical. No one ever contradicted him.

Ralegh's steady patronage of literature never shone more conspicuously than when he managed to send from his imprisonment £50 toward the establishment of the Bodleian Library. His own studies had been formerly prosecuted mainly at sea, where he "had nothing to divert him," but only "a trunk of books."[11]

His sleeping hours he reduced (like John Wesley) to five.[12] Of his literary work much has been lost. We no longer have a *Treatise of the West Indies* and a *Description of the River of the Amazons;* nor a study of Queen Elizabeth, "of which," Jonson told Drummond, there were "copies extant." But enough remains to have filled up a long life that had no other interests.

Instructions to his Son and to Posterity is in its hard fashion almost as hateful as Lord Burghley's advice to his son. Bitter generalizations about servants and dependents we can justify. And some leaning to the side of caution, even of what looks like cynicism, is understandable when we remember the character of young Walter. About him, as about his father, a crop of stories gathered; and of those which have been preserved one or two show that he had a reputation for filthy horseplay. But his misdeeds are no defense for the meanness of his

11. Aubrey, ii, 182.   12. D. Lloyd, *State Worthies*, p. 671.

father's remarks about women, and the sordidness of his comments on marriage. They square neither with his actions nor his experience. If ever any women endured a heart-breaking lot with magnanimity, it was Lady Ralegh. And his own letters to her are the most beautiful testimonies that any husband ever paid to a wife's qualities. We can suppose only that the *Instructions* were written in some "black night of the soul," when his sick mind and body fell back on acceptance of the smug narrow doctrine of men comfortable and padded in their lives. That his own experience had liberated him, in this as in other matters, and set him far ahead of his age, he shows elsewhere, in *A Treatise of the Soul* with quiet contempt setting right a renowned doctor of the Early Church:

Cyril affirmeth, "That the souls of women are very womanish; hard, and slow to understand hard things." But, by his leave, some women, even in this, have been able to match the greatest men.[13]

The man who had served Elizabeth Tudor and loved Elizabeth Throckmorton could have thought nothing else.

We have seen how, encouraged by Prince Henry, Ralegh put forth from his imprisonment political arguments. For the same admirable prince he toiled at his stupendous *History of the World*. This, like Dr. Johnson's *Dictionary,* is one of the books which, though superseded since, impressed the author's own contemporaries as having added to the conception of what was possible to human effort. Its vast stores of knowledge seemed to some then, as to one or two critics subsequently, beyond the range of one author. The elder Disraeli went so far as to regard the book as a compilation made for its nominal writer, to which he put only the cover of his name and renown. This theory has no justification except the statement haphazardly set down to Ben Jonson by Drummond:[14] "That Sir W. Raughley esteemed more of fame than conscience. The best wits of England were employed for making his *History*. Ben himself had written a piece for him on the Punick war, which he altered and set in his book." That statement, deducting what is due to Jonson's inflated conceit of himself, may be accepted in what it actually says (but nothing more). Of necessity, a man in captivity must have used friends to forage out materials, which then he "al-

13. *Works*, viii, 573.   14. *Conversations*.

tered," sign-marking them with his own brooding and profoundly melancholy mind, "and set in his book." Sir Charles Firth, who has closely examined the *History,* is of opinion that "the piece on the Punick war" makes an awkward and clumsy wedge in the narrative.[15]

Jonson was not the only helper. Assistance came by means of the same tyranny that had ruined him. In 1606 his acquaintance Henry Percy, Earl of Northumberland, was tried before the Star Chamber on charges connected with the previous year's Gunpowder Plot, and after the usual passionate and irrelevant harangues by Coke (who mentioned, "as he had done in Raleigh's case, all manner of plots with which he was unable to prove that the prisoner had ever been connected"[16]), for misprision of treason[17] was sentenced to imprisonment during the King's pleasure and a fine of £30,000. The fine was reduced to £11,000; but the King's pleasure kept him in the Tower until 1621. Allowed wide latitude under restraint, he "converted that abode of misery into a temple of the Muses."[18] "The favorer of all good learning and Maecenas of learned men,"[19] he had living with him his "three Magi," "to converse with, singly or together." Ralegh certainly sometimes sat with this convocation; for Hariot was one of the Magi, and his first patron relied on him for chronology, mathematics and geography. As he got the *History* written, Ralegh showed it to his friends, as Ben Jonson's testimony indicates.

In writing of this mighty work we must be careful not to exaggerate. This historian can but lay down his life's labors as foundation in a mire, where they must be pressed deeper and deeper down. Even so, Sir Charles Firth points out, "critics incline to undervalue" the book "as history":

They judge it from too modern a standpoint; they allow the growth of a different conception of the aim of History and the demand for the scientific treatment of evidence to obscure their vision.[20]

15. See *Proceedings of British Academy*, 1917–1918, p. 429.

16. Gardiner, *History of England*, 1603–1642, i, 283.

17. He had admitted to attendance on the King a Catholic kinsman whom he had excused from taking the oath of supremacy: "a weakness—for undoubtedly it was no more than a weakness" (Gardiner).

18. Lingard, *History of England*, ix, 225.   19. Aubrey, i, 287.

20. *B.A. Proceedings*, etc., p. 427.

They have poured scorn on its "Rabbinical learning." Yet even they (for example, Hume), when they have gone further into it, away from the Wars of Jehovah, have found it a haunted book, the home of what Stow (like Ralegh, an Elizabethan) calls "the searching and unsatisfied spirits of the English." For something of this quality we have to thank Prince Henry, who persuaded Ralegh that he need not overweight his narrative with sops to orthodoxy (even though orthodoxy was occupying the throne), and who asked for a larger account of Greeks, Romans and Persians, a task which Ralegh undertook eagerly and performed superbly. He performed it so well that it was a great while before men's knowledge overtook and surpassed his work. Oliver Cromwell told his son Richard (April 2, 1650) to "recreate" himself by reading this "Body of History," which "will add much more to your understanding than fragments of story." Together with much that has perished, the *History* must have been among the 3452 sheets of Ralegh's writings which Hampden was at the trouble of having transcribed, "a little before the wars," as a witness relates, in "his closet chamber," with a fire and candle, and an attendant to hand him the originals and take his copies as fast as he could write them.[21] Many saw in the book a compensation for the imprisonment which had made anything so noble possible. Bishop Hall in his *Consolations* expresses this view: "the Tower reformed the courtier in him." This "most God-fearing and God-seeing history known of among human writings"[22] "swept away"—and finally—"the old calumny"[23] of his atheism. Not only Puritans delighted in it, in the stormy years that followed; it built up also the reckless chivalry of Montrose.[24] It accompanied the King's daughter, Princess Elizabeth,[25] in her vicissitudes and was captured with her baggage when she fled from her kingdom. Milton and Bunyan studied it.

It is as a series of personal studies that it is still valuable. What historian can more vividly make a pageant or a once-mighty figure live before us again? If you avoid the passages which are mere rewritings of Scripture (where he was fettered, and could not allow his recon-

21. Lloyd, *State Worthies*, p. 675.   22. Charles Kingsley.
23. Stebbing, p. 279.   24. Napier, *Life of Montrose*, pp. 21, 28.
25. Brushfield, *Bibliography of Ralegh*, p. 20.

structing power freedom),[26] and launch yourself on those great scenes, Greek for choice, where his mind was most at home, you will read on and on, however well you know the story he is telling. How sympathetically he has studied Xenophon, that gallant amateur, his retelling of the March of the Ten Thousand shows. Artaxerxes, routed at Cunaxa, thinks to awe these strangers, "by showing a manly look half a mile off." But mark the sequel, says this historian who had played a part himself in the pricking of other glittering bubbles:

On the top of this Hill therefore he advanced his standard, a golden Eagle displayed on the top of a Spear. This Ensign might have encouraged his People, had not some of the Greeks espied it, who not meaning that he should abide so near them, with all their Power marched towards him.

Artaxerxes flees; and as if by contrast the shadow of their betrayed and desolate lot falls on the valiant handful. "It was now about the setting of the Sun, and they bringing home dark Night with them, found their Camp spoiled."

Pope, according to Spence, found Ralegh's style "too affected" to serve as one of the foundations of an English dictionary. But the truth is, no Elizabethan is less affected, none freer from intolerable divagations and toilsome "Asiatic" circumlocutions, from thought tied up in loops and expressed with conceits, from an irrelevant and weak fancy pretending itself as imagination. His final judgment on Epaminondas is unsurpassed for conciseness, epigrammatic without being false, packed without being obscure. Of a different style of excellence is the description of Jezebel hoping to browbeat her rebellious servant: of her forlorn courage he remarks that her taunts were "in mere human valuation stoutly spoken." Pyrrhus, Hannibal, Alexander, Demetrius, an endless line of captains and conquerors, pass before us, in this narrative so restrained and in the true sense "magnanimous," with all that is petty or personal purged away from its commentary. Indeed, the reader saddens to reflect how little of this deep sanity Ralegh had been able to put into his own deeds. "Impetuous and rash" in action, "he surveyed life in his writings with wisdom and insight, and recorded his observations with dignity and judicial calmness."[27] His outcry to "elo-

26. Yet many of these, even, are fine.   27. *D.N.B.*, article "Ralegh."

quent, just and mighty Death"—who draws together "all the far-stretched greatness, all the pride, cruelty and ambition of man," and covers it "with these two narrow words, *Hic jacet*"—has carried this quality, a little flamboyantly perhaps, into the anthologies and commonplace books.

The book made its immediate appeal, not least because of a personal illumination we can find in hardly any historian. The narrative is always apt to be lit up by some tersely vivid citation from experience. This is what I saw done in the French wars. This is the true doctrine of defense, whether by land or sea; and I can illustrate it by what I saw in "eighty-eight," the great Armada year, and by my own taking of Fayal. He breaks off his discussion of the wars between Rome and Macedon to compare English and Roman soldiers in valor. He takes occasion, when telling of the Amazons of classical legend, to glance at an old sneer against himself, who had also brought back a rumor of Amazons.

But when all is said, it was by its style, so laden with music and solemn reflection, that the book won such acceptance, and most of all from the few who have been Ralegh's peers. His influence on Milton's style has never been considered;[28] it is greater, I believe, than that of any other English prose writer. If you ask for literal proof, there are particularities which reappear in *Paradise Lost,* such as the warfare waged between Griffins and Arimaspi, for the former's hoarded gold. But the real proof lies in the cadence, the mingling of imagination and of personal pathos. Keats has observed that in Milton there is a pathos found in no other writer, of an allusive and almost muttered kind, passed off in parenthesis, where none but another poet would note it:

> rocks and stones had ears
> To rapture, till the savage clamour drowned
> Both voice and song (nor could the Muse defend
> Her son). . . .

Every student of Milton's work knows how this utterance in an undertone, as if to himself, will startle in some prose passage of a very different kind. I know no other writer who has it, of this precise quality, except Ralegh. In the Preface to the *History* are sentences which, quoted

28. Except by Sir Charles Firth, in his too brief comments (*B.A. Proceedings*).

to a sensitive ear without indication of their context, might be guessed immediately and wrongly as the work of Milton. He apologizes for beginning such a work so late:

For had it been begotten then, with my first dawn of day, when the light of common knowledge began to open itself to my younger years, and before any wound received, either from Fortune or Time, I might yet well have doubted that the darkness of Age and Death would have covered over both It and Me, long before the performance. . . . I confess that it had better sorted with my disability, the better part of whose times are run out in other travels, to have set together as I could the unjointed and scattered frame of our English affairs, than of the universal—in whom, had there been no other defect (who am all defect) than the time of the day, it were enough—the day of a tempestuous life, drawn on to the very evening ere I began.

With "the desire to satisfy those few friends, which I have tried by the fire of adversity," these pages "to the world I present them, to which I am nothing indebted; neither have others that were (Fortune changing) sped much better in any age."

The book's appearance was twice delayed. First, after its entry in Stationers' Register, April 15, 1611, it was held back to satisfy Prince Henry's demand for a far fuller secular narrative. Next, though published in 1614 (March), its circulation was impeded by the Government. On December 22 the Archbishop of Canterbury wrote ordering Stationers' Company to call in and suppress all copies, by the King's direction. The reason for this is known from several sources. Chamberlain says (January 5, 1615):

Sir Walter Ralegh's book is called in by the King's commandment, for divers exceptions, but specially for being too saucy in censuring princes. I hear he takes it much to heart, for he thought he had won his spurs, and pleased the King extraordinarily.

Osborne says, "after much scorn cast upon Ralegh's *History,* the King, being modestly demanded what fault he found, answered, as one surprised, that Ralegh had spoken irreverently of King Henry the Eighth"—against whom, the narrator adds, "none ever exclaimed more than usually himself." This objection suggests that the critic did not get beyond the Preface, for it is there that Ralegh, unsuspecting of the offense he was to give in every paragraph, calmly and judicially goes over the record of a number of kings, among them such English ones as Richard III, whom he calls "cruel," Henry VII (praised for a canniness which leaves the reader unenthusiastic, and doubtful of the author's enthusiasm), and Henry VIII, who is dealt with faithfully, even adequately:

if all the Pictures and Patterns of a merciless Prince were lost in the World, they might all again be painted to the life, out of the Story of this King. . . . To how many . . . gave he abundant Flowers, from whence to gather Honey, and in the end of Harvest burnt them in the Hive?

The writer of the *Observations on Sanderson's History*[29] says: "It is well known King James forbade the book for some passages in it which offended the Spaniards, and for being too plain with the faults of princes in his preface." Interesting confirmation (which no one seems to have noticed) lies in the King's long letter of affectionate reproof to Kerr, where he glances at "Sir Walter Ralegh's description of the kings that he hates, of whom he speaketh but evil."[30]

Contemporaries asserted that James, whose mind moved with irritable nervousness whenever it approached Ralegh, and who showed a remarkable readiness to think that any cap the latter held up with ridicule was meant to fit him, resented the description of the effeminate monarch Ninias. What made it seem personal to his uneasy conscience was the vigorous contrast painted with Ninias's predecessor Semiramis, of whom Ralegh wrote with an admiration that has emotion in it, making it plain that in memory moved still his fealty to "the Lady whom time surprised." The certainty that he was thinking of Elizabeth —by scandal, equally with Semiramis, accused of licentiousness—adds interest to his championing the latter: "for her vicious life I ascribe the report thereof to the envious and lying Grecians. For delicacy and ease do more often accompany licentiousness in men and women, than labour and hazard do." *That* (as I believe) by suggestion defends Elizabeth (equally with Semiramis troubled with incessant toil and peril). And James felt that Elizabeth's successor came uncomfortably close to delineation here: "But her son having changed nature and condition

29. See Bibliography, under "Heylin, Peter"; also under "Ralegh, Carew."
30. For the whole letter see Charles Williams, *James I* (1934), pp. 218 ff.

with his mother proved no less feminine than she was masculine." He thought it tactless to stress the fact that Jehoram's slaughter took place in Naboth's vineyard, "that field, which, purchased with the blood of the rightful owner, was to be watered with blood of the unjust possessor." It was unnecessary to strew the biblical story with reminders of Sherborne!

Suppression, however, was not carried through. Delight was too instantaneous.[31] The book catered to every taste, with its closely knit narrative that glanced over the whole expanse of human endeavor; its skilful selections from pagan classical poets, set in it like candles flinging a shadowed light; its solemn reflections, and its note of doom and judgment, its resolute justification of God's ways; its passages from those mighty events of which no other great captain now remained alive; its bits of curious information about places the reader would never see but must always be "thrilled" by thought of, such as the spreading Pyramid from whose summit no arrow could be shot so as not to fall on some one of its own steps, never reaching the earth. After Ralegh's day, others abridged and paraphrased the *History*. But it remained unapproached in magnificence of design and nobility of spirit. Blake should have illustrated it.

One change, however, the King insisted on. Ralegh had had "the impudence to show that he was very much alive, not only by writing a great book, which might have been winked at, but by putting his name, and even his portrait, on the title-page."[32] The title-page was therefore removed.

Men told stories to explain why no further part was issued, and the narrative left where it had reached, not half-way through the Romans. Ralegh was believed to have written a second volume, but to have destroyed it, saying, "If I am not considered worthy to be of the world, the world is not worthy of my works."[33] This seems more probable than the better-known story that he asked the printer, a few days before

31. For the only notable dissentient (apart from King James) see MSS. Tanner, 299, fol. 32, where a problem by Donne is preserved, asking and answering the question "Why was Sir Walter Raleigh thought the fittest Man to write the History of these Times?" Donne's son found the squib too bitter to print. It is, as a matter of fact, harmful only to its writer, being of an almost imbecile feebleness. Ralegh was in a cage, and caged birds sing, etc. But Donne was a courtier, and had been a partisan of Essex.

32. Firth, *B.A. Proceedings*, p. 442.   33. Aubrey, *Brief Lives*, ii, 191.

his execution, how the book had sold, and on receiving the answer that it had sold so badly as to have undone him, said, "Ah, my friend, hath the first part undone thee? The second volume shall undo no man; this ungrateful world is unworthy of it"; and took out the manuscript and held it in the fire with his foot till it was all consumed. For there is no doubt that Ralegh, with the sanguineness of genius, expected the book to appeal to the King and to establish even there his reputation for piety. The piety was deep and genuine, the scholarship was unequalled; but the royal reader was a fool. The world continued to be a place of which Ralegh was held not worthy.

The book's conclusion speaks of its title as "implying a second and third volume, which I also intended, and have hewn out." He collected materials; and somewhere these, as well as other lost work of his, may be lying unsuspected. But the materials were never used—*why* is plain from the note of discouragement with which the published portion ends. For Prince Henry he had written so much, besides this: a *Discourse of the Invention of Ships, Anchors, Compass, &c.,*[34] a *Letter to Prince Henry on the Model of a Ship, Observations concerning the Royal Navy and Sea-Service.*[35] These on every page witness to his catholic interests, as alert in the section "Of beer-casks"[36] as when they treat of construction to withstand weather and human foes. He had half written a treatise

of the Art of War by Sea . . . for the Lord Henry, Prince of Wales, a subject, to my knowledge, never handled by any man, ancient or modern. But God hath spared me the labour of finishing it, by his loss; by the eclipse of that brave Prince; of which, like an Eclipse of the Sun, we shall find the effects hereafter. Impossible it is to equal words and sorrows; I will therefore leave him in the hands of God that hath him.

The *History* ends, therefore, with the definite statement (made with a somberness that carries conviction) that the work had closed because, "besides many other discouragements, persuading my silence, it hath pleased God to take that glorious Prince," to whom Ralegh's labors were "directed," "out of the world." "Othello's occupation was gone."

Prince Henry's death took place, November, 1612. His friendship

34. *Works*, viii, 317 ff. 35. *Ibid.*, p. 338.
36. *Ibid.*, p. 345.

had brought the dream of restitution very near. Sherborne was in his hands, and he had obtained from his father a promise to release Ralegh at Christmas. On October 20, 1608, the keel had been laid of the first three-decker ever built for the English navy. Ralegh's plans had been followed in its construction, when, nearly four years later, *The Prince Royal* was ready for launching. The launching failed temporarily, through no fault in the ship, which played a distinguished part in after years. Then the young man, whose practice was to exercise immoderately and to swim in the Thames at Richmond after a full supper consisting of fruit, caught a fever, which developed into what is now known to have been typhoid. His mother pressed for Ralegh's cordial, but neither the physicians nor the Privy Council would permit help from so suspected and irregular a source, until their prolonged discussions had made his case hopeless. Only on the twelfth day of illness was the cordial brought, and forced between the dying man's lips; it revived him enough to speak, but failed to save him.

James and Henry were as widely severed in sympathies as any two men could be. A belief spread that the Prince had been poisoned.[37] The Overbury scandal presently strengthened it. The Queen held it always, for Ralegh, "with the dash of empirical confidence always observable in him,"[38] had unfortunately "assured her that his cordial was sovereign against everything but poison. This assurance and the poison rumor did nothing to draw the King nearer to his prisoner. Christmas passed, and release was indefinitely postponed. Sherborne, lapsing to the Crown with Prince Henry's death, became the property of Kerr, who was now Viscount Rochester.

In May, 1612, had been another death, one which caused Ralegh no sorrow. The Earl of Salisbury, old and broken down at the age of forty-eight, had outlived his reputation and the King's esteem; had he lived a brief while longer, it seems certain that he would have fallen from favor. Hurrying to London, to "countermine his underminers," he died suddenly in an inn at Marlborough; and his friend Richard

37. Incidentally, by his extensive medical practice Ralegh showed a temerity in keeping with his general recklessness. Chamberlain told Carleton (Aug. 11, 1611) that the Countess of Rutland, Sir Philip Sidney's daughter, was said to have died of Ralegh's "pills" (*Calendar of State Papers, Domestic,* 1611–1618, p. 143).

38. Edwards, i, 512.

Sackville, Earl of Dorset, neatly expressed the general satisfaction: "His death hath wiped away the memory of other men's misdeeds." "Quietly and calmly the last of the Elizabethan statesmen went to his rest."[39]

His death was reported as due to venereal disease; and when this was heard, a howl of savage delight went up:

> The divel now hath fetcht the Ape
> Of crooked manners, crooked shape.
> Great were his infirmities,
> But greater his enormities.
> Oppression, lechery, blood and pride
> He lived in; and like Herod died. . . .

> Not Robin goodfellow, nor Robin Hood,
> But Robin the devil, that never did good. . . .

> Here lieth Robin Crookback, unjustly reckoned
> A Richard the Third, he was Judas the Second. . . .

These are perhaps the only quotable lines of a collection preserved in Sancroft's handwriting,[40] examples of the hobbies of an archbishop. Among them is an epigram ascribed to Ralegh. It was said to have been repeated to the King, who exclaimed, "I hope the writer of those lines will die before I do!" (a hope whose fulfilment he himself saw to). James's exclamation may have been savage wrath; or chuckling pleasure (for he had come to detest Cecil), with the proviso that he himself had no wish to come under the same sharpness. The epigram, "coarse and truculent,"[41] "does no honour to Ralegh's memory."[42] Its bitterness, however, was supremely well earned. The main argument against Ralegh's authorship is the piece's crude and poor quality. It gives us the measure of contemporary hatred of Cecil, that such a clumsy trifle should have been eagerly repeated and treasured.

39. Gardiner, *History*, ii, 143.
40. Tanner MSS. (Bodleian Library, Oxford).
41. Stebbing, p. 258.   42. Edwards, i, 508.

CHAPTER XXI

Release

Sir Walter Raleghe is enlarged out of the Tower, and is to go his journey to Guiana, but remains unpardoned until his return. He left his mansion in the Tower, the 19th day of this month. LORD CAREW to Sir Thomas Roe, March, 1617.

RALEGH had opened up Virginia, a region "by God's providence reserved for England." In 1606 James issued a charter to a London Company which included friends of the prisoner, such as Richard Hakluyt, and a kinsman and one-time opponent, Sir Ferdinando Gorges. In 1609 Cecil, Suffolk and others took out a fresh charter. England, as we presently see from Shakespeare's *Tempest,* began to grow excited about Virginia. With what anguish Ralegh heard of what was happening, we know from a letter to his patroness the Queen:

. . . I long since presumed to offer your Majesty my service in Virginia, with a short repetition of the commodity, honour and safety which the King's Majesty might reap by that plantation, if it were followed to effect. I do still humbly beseech your Majesty that I may rather die in serving the King and my country, than to perish here.

Enemies were objecting that, if liberated, he would sail, not to Virginia, but off on some piracy or privateering such as the King was bent on putting down. He offers to forfeit life and his last possessions, if he does not sail by a fixed date: to leave his wife and two sons hostages, the former willing to "yield herself to death, if I perform not my duty to the King." If this is not enough, let his own captains and sailors be authorized, "if I offer to sail elsewhere," to cast him into the sea. He makes the final appeal to that which no critic has proved that he ever betrayed, his loyalty to his friends:

But, were there nothing else, let your Majesty, I beseech you, be resolved that it shall never be said of me that the Queen of England gave her word for this man: that the Queen took him out of the hands of Death: that he, like a villain and perjured slave, hath betrayed so worthy a princess, and hath broken his faith . . . there is neither death nor life that can allure me or fear me from the performance of my duty to so worthy and charitable a Lady.

The Earl of Salisbury, if he wishes, can free him; he holds the keys. He begs her "please to engage your word for me" to him, "if your Majesty think me worthy of life, or that I have any blood of gentleman in me." Salisbury, however, was determined not to free him; the tale which contains the romantic grace of Pocahontas does not contain the greater name of Ralegh.

Harassed by the King's desperate financial troubles, in 1611 Salisbury had remembered that His Majesty was honor's fountain, a stream of which many were athirst to drink and would pay for being allowed to drink. The title of baronet was invented, and offered in exchange for £1080 paid in three annual instalments, "to all persons of good repute, being knights or esquires possessed of lands worth £1000 a year." The Crown gained only £90,000 in three years, so peerages were also flung on the market. Their price was sometimes shared between the King and some favorite; and sometimes went as a straight gift to persons who were allowed to "make a peer" (or several peers), at rates fixed between them and the purchaser. James's embarrassments did not cease; his "pension list grew longer," his "jewels more costly," his "robes more gorgeous than those with which Elizabeth had been content."[1] He would promise repentance, and when the state of his affairs was brought to his notice would be deeply shocked, "sensible" (he wrote to Cecil, October 18, 1605)

of that needless profusion of expenses, whereof you wrote me in your last. My only hope that upholds me is my good servants, that will sweat and labour for my relief. Otherwise I could rather have wished, with Job, never to have been than that the glorious sunshine of my first entry here should be so soon overcast with the dark clouds of irreparable misery.

But he remained incorrigible. And his Queen in spending proved an adequate helpmeet; her main contribution to public life was incessant entertainments, elaborate festivities, progresses and processions.

1. Gardiner, *History*, etc., i, 296.

This appalling extravagance at last won attention for Ralegh's project of occupying Guiana. His acceptance of its tribes' fealty in Elizabeth's name was an advantage which the King in his most pro-Spanish moods steadfastly refused to relinquish, though he could never bring himself to decide to act strongly on it. Yet, even if England stood aside, Spain no longer had any chance of getting a monopoly of the country unchallenged. Ralegh's explorations and writings had awakened Dutch and French interest; Guiana's threefold division to-day has no other man as its founder. Two ships from Holland had followed swiftly on his graphic exposition of the land's wealth and beauty.[2] They reached the coast, February 15, 1598, and found that Ralegh's greatness lived on, in the field where he was finally ruined. A canoe glided out from a river-mouth; and its occupants, once they had ascertained that the newcomers were not Spaniards, cried out joyfully, "Anglees! Anglees!" The Dutch encouraged them by assenting, explaining later that they were "Hollandees." In June two more Dutch ships arrived, and in late July an expedition ascended the Orinoco, to examine "all those places where Sir Walther Halley had been, and where he was said to have got his minerals." They heard a report that an Indian chief, when the Spaniards were about to hang him, said he had spoken with the spirit Wattopa, "and the latter had prophesied to him" his people's liberation by the Dutch and the English. "I should like," observes the Dutch captain, "to aid in doing the same, if it might be done with the profit and interest of the country, and succeed."

The Dutch established trading posts, which they vainly trusted the Spaniards would leave alone. Nor did the English forsake Guiana. All through his imprisonment Ralegh sent every second year a ship of some kind or other, to keep him in touch with the Indians. Dutch vessels, in March, 1598, found an English trading ship off the river Cuyuni, which was probably his; and on October 6 of the same year they spoke with "the galley of Sir Walther Halley, of London," a pinnace of 25 tons, which they met near St. Lucia. In 1602 Ralegh's friend Charles Leigh voyaged to Guiana to select a site for a colony; and on his return he and his brothers, Sir Oliph and Sir John, the latter known to us for his courageous kindness to Ralegh when he was finally ruined, raised funds for another journey, which Charles Leigh made in

2. See *British Guiana Boundary Arbitration, British Case*, App., Vol. I, pp. 18–22.

1604. He widely explored both the rivers and the land, seeking for gold deposits; and reported to the Privy Council that Guiana promised well for cotton, sugar, flax. If a hundred agricultural workers were sent, adequately armed, it would "in a few years yield you satisfaction beyond your expectations." Prince Henry was interested, and entered enthusiastically into Ralegh's vision. He persuaded the King in 1609 to sanction an attempt by Robert Harcourt to establish a colony in Guiana. The tribes received Harcourt with enthusiasm, but were disappointed not to see Ralegh. "I excused his not returning according to his promise, by reason of other employments of great importance imposed on him by the late Queen." As to the reason for his not coming now, Harcourt was silent. But he bragged to them of England's new ruler, and he told them he intended to "make search for convenient places, where such of our Nation, as shall hereafter come to defend them, may be seated to dwell amongst them"; and "took possession of the Land, by turf and twig, in behalf of our Sovereign Lord, King James . . . lying betwixt the Rivers of Amazons and Orenoque, not being actually possessed, and inhabited by, any other Christian Prince or State." Harcourt's brother Michael did the same in another district.

Ralegh desperately seconded these efforts, so far as he could. To James he made the only appeal which could have any effect, that Guiana would bring in far more revenue than could be wrung out of a Parliament growing increasingly resentful of doctrines of Divine Right and Divine Taxation. He offered "a most easy way of being enriched, both despite of your malicious enemies abroad" (by which, now as always blind to James's infatuation, he meant the Spaniards, and assumed that every right-thinking man must mean the same) "and of your grunting subjects at home." Never were letters written which give so vivid a picture of wings beating against bars. Against the argument that it would be "a great levity of state" to trust a man situated as he was, Ralegh urges:

it had been indeed well said, if I had desired the trust of any great sum of money, of any great army, or any great fleet, or of anything else whereby your Majesty might have received prejudice. But where nothing else had been put in hazard with me, but mine own shame and infamy, where I was to be trusted in nothing, but to make myself a Ridiculous Liar, and a Beggar, and to leave that mark upon my children and posterity. . . . Why should so notable a service for your Majesty be balanced with the Liberty of one man, whose fortune, when it was at greatest, never overshadowed anything but itself?

He wrote to Cecil, even more urgently, reminding him that others had originally persuaded him, four years earlier, in 1607, to put up his Guiana proposals, by the consideration of the difficulty with which "such sums are raised in England, as may serve his Majesty's occasions, and answer the great Liberality and goodness of his heart." Consideration of that Liberality and goodness brings him up against a sharp sorrow of his own. Cecil in 1607 had promised to intercede for his freedom and forfeited estates, if he really brought back enormous wealth. Those negotiations had been broken off, and Sherborne had since gone; "if the same trial be again required, the Bargain is now Twenty Thousand pound worse for me than the former, my Land being now disposed." Notwithstanding, let the trial be made, and himself sent with Kemys. It is sixteen years since they both saw Guiana, and the country is a tropical jungle—as he reminds the Privy Council in another letter, it is

a difficult matter—of exceeding difficulty—for any man to find the same acre of ground in a country desolate and overgrown which he hath seen but once, and that sixteen years since (which were hard enough to do upon Salisbury Plain).

He "dare not trust mine own memory, and mine own marks for the finding it." "Two guides are better than one." If Kemys goes alone, and dies or is wrecked and lost (very common happenings), Ralegh's expense is wasted, and the effort also. If Kemys goes alone, the King will get nothing from the mine for two years or more, whereas with two men, one being himself (in his own driving power, like everyone else, he had boundless faith), the business can be accomplished in nine months.

He was finally brought to the scaffold for having deceived his King, by concealing the fact that there were already Spaniards in Guiana—a sharp practice for which historians have freely censured him. Note, then, his absolute frankness on this matter:

If the mine be once opened and discovered, those Spaniards which dwell upon the same river, and which since my being there have tormented an hundred of the natural people to death to find the place, will work it to the last pound weight. . . . The neighbouring Spaniards will easily work it out in a short time, ere Kemys can return, and a new fleet be prepared here . . . and when it shall arrive the next year, what can we otherwise look for, but to be laughed at by our enemies, for having discovered for them, at our charge, a mine of gold which themselves, having inhabited upon the same river twenty year, neither by tormenting others, nor by their own travail, could ever find? . . . this treasure may be had upon the first opening of the mine, without breach of peace, because the Spaniard hath neither knowledge nor possession of the place where it is. It cannot be gotten by a second voyage, without public force. It may now be brought away by two ships, the next year hardly with twenty. And better it were (so far as my weak judgment can discern) that the Spaniards should give cause of quarrel to us, than we to them.

How could statements be more explicit? The King is to take no risk, to be at no charges; all is to depend on "this hazard of a reed," this "adventuring of an old and sorrow-worn man." Let not the King do as Henry VII did, when he put by Columbus' offer to discover new lands for him! Let not the Spaniards, "who endangered all the States of Europe" because of the wealth they gained by that deplorable lack of foresight, find the Guianan treasure also!

He is able to remind the Privy Council that they had once gone so far as to

offer to be at the charge to transport Kemys into Guiana with such a proportion of men in two ships as should be able to defend him against the Spaniards inhabiting upon Orenoque, if they offered to assail him (not that it is meant to offend the Spaniards there, or to begin any quarrel with them, except themselves shall begin the war).

He refers them to Captain Moate, "who came from Orenoque this last spring, and was oftentimes ashore at St. Thomé, where the Spaniards inhabit," for information as to the number of men Kemys will need to go unmolested to the mine. The Privy Council had gone back on their proposal, and made a new one—if Kemys did not bring back half a ton of "that slate gold ore whereof I gave a sample to my Lord Knevett," then Ralegh should pay the whole costs of the voyage. Even this shameful meanness he is willing to close with—to risk all on

Kemys' memory and luck, asking only that if the half ton *is* brought he shall have his liberty and his free pardon, under the great seal, the latter to be kept in the King's hands until Kemys' return. When Ralegh finally came to grief, it was because he trusted men incapable of elementary honesty,[3] and went accepting a verbal promise, instead of his pardon made out provisionally under the great seal.

From now until his death, Ralegh's life was used as a pawn, first on the board of English politics, then in the constantly transshifting game of European statecraft. Or rather, not as a mere pawn, but as the piece of greatest value. The Government were quite ready to lose him, but they wanted first to exact his full potency and value. The idea of getting inexhaustible riches, with pickings for his Majesty's Councillors as well as his pretty young men, was attractive. If Ralegh succeeded, Parliament could then be dismissed forever (James told the Spanish Ambassador that he was astonished his ancestors had ever been so foolish as to allow such an institution to be established). If Ralegh failed, he was of course ruined.

His old friend would not mind that. But would he fail? There was only one Ralegh. Cecil could not ignore the chance that he might pull off practically anything, whatever the odds against him—as he had pulled off the schoolboyishly reckless assault on Cadiz, in years that were fast dimming into legend. With that vitality which even close imprisonment could not sap, that energy as of someone exempt from physical limitations, Ralegh, returning with the wealth of a new and richer Peru, might again be a dangerous rival. Cecil, therefore, would read Ralegh's letters—would call at the Tower and in the laboratory where he was working—would ask about the assayers' tests of the ore that had been brought back by him and Kemys, long ago—would play with the captive's miserable fears and wild longings—would hold out hopes and speak kindly, and then withdraw into "an *arrière boutique*,"[4] and lie there unassailable and unapproachable. This was being a statesman. If ever man had cause to hate and despise another, Ralegh

3. I see no justification whatever for the assumptions which mar Mr. Harlow's *Ralegh's Last Voyage*, e.g., "The central figure of the tragedy was an irrepressible genius, who combined passionate sincerity with an incurable habit of prevarication" (p. 98). Which one of his enemies was truthful?

4. Ralegh's phrase.

had it with Robert Cecil. It is strange that anyone has demanded that he should have felt a decent regret when his enemy died.

Cecil and James finally sent, not Ralegh and not Kemys, but Sir Thomas Roe, afterwards England's first Ambassador in India, at the Mogul Court. He had been esquire of the body to Queen Elizabeth, and must have known Ralegh well. It is certain that he regarded him with kindness, for he was a friend of George Carew and a close friend of Princess Elizabeth, to whom he was her "fat honest Thom." A man honest in any age, and in that age almost out of the course of nature, Roe lights up the mind upon every remembrance of him.

The projected voyage was spoken of as one to "Virginia," for Spain was growing worse than restive about proposals which the King could not, or would not, keep secret. Ralegh and Lord Southampton (Essex's friend—so far had James's reign reshuffled the old alignments) provided £600 and £800, Roe and his partners another £1100; and two ships sailed from Dartmouth, February 24, 1610. The expedition, fully (but secretly) authorized by Lord Salisbury, proceeded to explore the region between the Amazon and Orinoco more thoroughly than any previous expedition had done; and Roe settled a colony of twenty men in Guiana. These feeble settlements were destined to die out, from disease, Spanish hostility, or simple desertion back to England. But Roe was able to claim that he had seen "more of this coast, rivers, and inland from the Great River of the Amazons under the line to Orenoque in 8 degrees, than any Englishman now alive." He wrote home to Cecil a letter which throbs with indignation equal to Ralegh's own, at the way Englishmen were expected to keep a peace which Spain made no bones about breaking. It reveals also what no one has any right to overlook, the Government's entire collusion with its seamen, in events which it righteously washed its hands of responsibility for, when a scapegoat was wanted:

The Spaniards here are equally proud, insolent, yet needy and weak: their force is reputation, and their safety opinion: yet dare they use us, whose hands are bound, with any contumely and treachery. For me, I will resist and prevent both these, and for that end do rather stay with some English, than for any trade; I hope your noble disposition will not take it ill that we defend ourselves and the Honour of our Nation. . . . I will not exceed the honourable caution your Lordship gave me, nor stoop to so

wretched an enemy (for so he is here), nor sink under the injuries I am
able to repulse . . . our countrymen . . . they used worse than Moors. All
seamen here bless your Lordship, and wish that the state would not be offended if they made themselves recompense. If the example were sure, we
could second it, but we dare not handle fire, nor cannot take fast-hold of air.

Roe had talked with discontented Spaniards who were lurking inland
as outlaws and, if safeguarded against betrayal, would show the English all the land and water passages, and undiscovered gold mines.
Spain's handful of settlers had no power to enforce the monopoly they
claimed. The river was regularly used by English and Dutch merchants. In consequence, in 1615, the Madrid authorities commanded
their Governor of Trinidad and Guiana to "extirpate utterly" these
visitors and their colonies. "It was precisely into this area of international friction that the English Government with full knowledge
allowed Ralegh to penetrate with a powerful armament in 1616."[5]
    Roe reported that El Dorado and Manoa were myths; henceforward
they drop out of discussion. This discovery lessened Cecil's interest.
Any gold that was in Guiana plainly did not lie about in logs, in front
of a barbaric potentate's palace; it would have to be painfully searched
out, dug up and smelted. The project was therefore postponed.
Ralegh's prison-doors, which had stood ajar, clanged to again.
    Guiana was never for one moment abandoned by him, however.
And events were on his side; the bars that held him in the Tower began one by one to give way of themselves. Cecil, and then Howard,
died. Kerr's influence was waning. The King resented his domineering
ways; his physical perfection was yielding to the effects of time and soft
living. And presently, King and favorite together, by a succession of
crimes and follies so revolting as to stagger belief, strengthened the
hands of the patriotic anti-Spain party, which desired not a marriage
with the Infanta but war with her country. The leaders of this party
were George Abbot, Archbishop of Canterbury, and Sir Ralph Winwood, the Secretary of State. A brief recital of the events which threw
temporary power into their hands and resulted in Ralegh's release is
now necessary.
    In July, 1613, Diego Sarmiento de Acuña, better known by his later

5. Harlow, *Ralegh's Last Voyage*, p. 15.

title of Count Gondomar, the strongest Ambassador Spain ever sent to
London, arrived in England. He was soon deep in intrigues with Kerr
(now Viscount Rochester). These intrigues had the King's support,
though with characteristic laziness he neglected to keep himself thoroughly cognizant of them all. In 1614, Sir John Digby went to Madrid
to negotiate the marriage of Charles and the Infanta, and brought back
Spain's terms, at last formally written down. All children of the marriage should be baptized as Catholics; their wet-nurses and servants
should be Catholics, and their education in their mother's charge; they
should be free, when they came of age, to choose their religion, without
their right in the succession being affected; there should be in London
a Catholic chapel open to everybody, and served by priests who were
free to go abroad in their robes; the laws against Catholics were to be
abrogated. These terms illustrate how utterly unable to understand the
English situation the Spanish authorities, their Ambassador included,
were; they could never imagine anything other than that the national
religion and laws could be changed by the King's mere will. Though
they had not frightened Rochester, the terms frightened James. Their
revelation came at a time when his timidity had become excessive. He
was sleeping inside a barricade of beds; and drove by day as fast as the
streets permitted, with a flock of footmen running about his chariot.
He grew suspicious of "Baby Charles," aged fourteen; and saw him
dethroning his poor old father, and shutting him in a dungeon until
death. In his dread of the outcry if the Spanish demands became
known, he weakened, and gave the anti-Spanish party more scope than
he wanted to give them. Nevertheless, after awhile he told Gondomar
that he would accept the terms if modified; he stuck only at the demand
that the penal laws against Catholics should go. That could wait until
the marriage negotiations had gone through.

In August, 1614, George Villiers, a young Buckinghamshire gentleman, was presented at Court. He was as impressively beautiful, men
agreed, as the unforgotten Earl of Essex; and patriots immediately saw
in him what had long been sought, an English candidate for the King's
caresses. Kerr's friendship with the Spanish Ambassador being notorious, the Archbishop of Canterbury pushed forward this golden youth
as the antidote, begging the Queen to ask James to appoint him a
gentleman of his bedchamber. King and Queen lived separately; but

COUNT GONDOMAR

SPANISH AMBASSADOR IN THE
REIGN OF JAMES I

AFTER THE PAINTING BY VELASQUEZ

the King had established a convention that all requests of a personal kind must come through her. This was in order that afterwards, if she complained of the person appointed, he could say, "You asked me to appoint him." The convention was well enough understood. If he disliked the person she recommended, he could be stiff in the extreme, as the case of Ralegh proved during many years. He now wanted Villiers, and wanted his Queen to ask him to take Villiers. This the Archbishop begged her to do. For long she refused, warning Abbot that Villiers would not prove the complaisant instrument he expected. She only yielded the indispensable formality of her intervention at last, on England's national day—April 23, 1615—whose evening was spent by the country's rulers in a remarkable manner. Inside the King's bedroom was the Queen, beseeching him to appoint Mr. George Villiers Gentleman of his Bedchamber. Outside, at one door, was Kerr, sending in messages imploring James not to do this, or, if he must have the young man near him, to make him only Groom (not Gentleman)—and, at the other door, was the Archbishop, exhorting the Queen to persevere. As was only right, the Queen and the Archbishop won. Villiers was made Gentleman of the Bedchamber, knighted, and given a pension of £1000 a year. Once his foot was inside the royal sleeping-room, his advance was rapid. His master was struck by the resemblance of his face to that of the martyr Stephen, when his murderers saw it "as the face of an angel." Villiers became "Steenie," therefore. As the King's knowledge of him grew still more intimate, other Scriptural resemblances emerged. His Privy Council, once venturing to cross Steenie, were told they must never again do anything so impious. For "God does not love all men alike; and as Christ had his John, so have I my Steenie."

Kerr (who had become Earl of Somerset in November, 1613) was provoked by jealousy to incessant bad temper, which drove the King to long angry answers:

I have been needlessly troubled this day with your desperate letters; you may take the right way, if you list, and neither grieve me nor yourself . . . if you do but the half your duty unto me, you may be with me in the old manner, only by expressing that love to my person and respect to your master that God and man crave of you, with a hearty and feeling penitence of your bypast errors. God move your heart to take the right course.

Then, not too tactfully, James sent his new minion to ask Somerset to be his patron. "I will none of your service," was the answer, "and you shall none of my favour. I will, if I can, break your neck, and of that be confident."[6]

James had enough kindness left to wish to make his discarded favorite safe against those who hated him; the shadow of reprisals was already falling over one whose day was so obviously going. The King therefore had a pardon drawn up for Somerset in advance, to cover as many offenses as could be committed. This document its beneficiary completed, by adding some crimes that had been overlooked, among them that of being accessory to a murder before it was done. Lord Ellesmere, the Lord Chancellor, found the pardon too comprehensive, and declined to affix the Great Seal to it. The King summoned a Privy Council, and stormed at them, and at Ellesmere in particular. But the latter, though kneeling (as Speaker Lenthall was to kneel to James's successor) in protestation of his loyalty, refused to accept what would permit Somerset (he pointed out) to loot the Crown jewels if he became so minded.

The provision which asked pardon in advance for being accessory to murder was about to prove unlucky for Somerset. We have to go back, and notice some of the ways in which "his set" had been distinguishing themselves. After his accession, James had been anxious to knit together in marriage the old families, with whom mutual hostility was such a tradition. He had not forgotten his hero, the executed Earl of Essex; and for his son, a boy of fourteen, he arranged an alliance so fine as (he hoped) to obliterate memories of his father's fate. On January 5, 1606, the young Earl took to wife Lady Frances Howard, aged thirteen. The child grew into a great beauty; her husband, when, after a period of living apart, he joined her four years later, found her far more attractive than she found him. She had been brought up by the Howards, in a court incredibly loose-living and cynical, and was startled by the somber apparition of a husband—and such a husband. This was the Earl of Essex whose concise judgment on the proper treatment of the Earl of Strafford, "Stone dead hath no fellow," has become proverbial. An eye-witness has preserved a picture of him receiving the Parliament's representatives at the outbreak of the Civil War, in which he

6. Welldon, i, 407.

was their Commander-in-Chief; he did it as he did all things, gravely —removing his hat a moment as he took his pipe from his mouth, and standing in silence. All his father's puritanism survived in him, and nothing of his impetuousness or his irresistible way with women. His experience was to leave with him only contempt and resentment of courts and their ethics.

He was not puritanical toward the lovely girl whom her parents compelled, after bitter refusal, to live with him. She complained angrily that he wanted to consummate the marriage. She saw to it that he failed; and they spent three terrible years, in what must have seemed to her a savage wilderness, in the depths of Staffordshire. Between her marriage and her husband's coming to claim her, she had won the admiration of Robert Kerr, Lord Rochester. Her lover she meant to have; and for this end, if the superior Powers would not help her, she was prepared to move Acheron. James's reign resembled Saul's; he had put out of the world all those who were accused of dealings with familiar spirits; helpless men and women died miserably. But the really devilish practitioners remained, and had exalted encouragement. There was a Dr. Forman, who provided love and hatred philters, and dealt in astrology and quack remedies, his clientèle being largely Court ladies. With him worked a beautiful young woman, who may have been his daughter, Mrs. Ann Turner. These two provided the Countess with drugs that half-poisoned her husband, and enabled her to preserve her person from his advances. She may have tried to help him altogether out of this world, but the evidence does not make this absolutely certain. However, having preserved her virginity (so far as her husband was concerned) for three years, she consulted her father and her uncle, Henry Howard, Earl of Northampton, about getting a divorce on the ground that the Earl of Essex was physically impotent. They eagerly supported the idea, as it would unite their family with the King's favorite. They were then on unsatisfactory terms with Lord Rochester, and the ship of the Howard fortunes was laboring in heavy seas, and making no headway. The King was easily won over; anything that completed the happiness of his Robbie was to be encouraged.

All that was needed was that Essex himself should be helpful. But this he refused to be. He had had so much unhappiness that he was willing enough to be rid of his wife; but he flatly declined to be pub-

licly certified as impotent, for he intended to remarry. His selfishness
put his wife to immense vexation. It become clear that the Church's
assistance was needed. So, on May 16, 1613, a Commission on which
were three Bishops was appointed, under the Archbishop of Canterbury.

Church and State at this time were working together so amicably
that James did not anticipate what trouble Abbot was about to give
over so simple an affair. King and Archbishop in alliance had recently
burnt the last two persons executed in this horrible fashion for doc-
trinal unorthodoxy. One wretched man James had driven out of his
presence, after hearing his admission that for six years he had not
prayed to Christ; and Abbot had sent instructions that both heretics
should be sent before judges who had first of all been ascertained to
entertain no doubts as to the legality of burning heretics under the
Common Law (the special *de haeretico comburendo* statute of Henry
IV having been repealed).[7] Sexual arrangements, however, were a different matter. Abbot refused to put through a divorce. The question
dragged on, with the imbecility which is as striking as the inquity of
James's reign. Lady Essex offered the most repulsively obscene evidence ever offered in even a divorce court; and her lawyers argued
that her husband, though not impotent toward her sex as a whole, had
been bewitched, so that he had a special and peculiar impotence toward
her. The argument struck the King as very forceful. But Abbot also
was an authority on witchcraft; and he was firm that the Earl's disability could not really have been Satan's doing. This was not the way
that Satan worked. The Commissioners became equally divided; there
was evidently going to be no divorce. Abbot, frightened of annoying
the King, begged to withdraw. James found a better way, by appoint-
ing two more Bishops, on whom he could rely to turn the scale when it
came to a vote. The more energetic of these was Bilson, Bishop of
Winchester, whom we have met before, as Ralegh's spiritual comforter
when he was expecting death. This notable man, "as revered and
learned a prelate as England ever afforded," had gone from praise to
praise, until "at length he was found to be no longer a soldier but a
commander-in-chief of the spiritual warfare," and "carried prelature in

7. *Egerton Papers*, pp. 447 ff.

his very aspect."[8] As these reinforcements took the field against him, Abbot made a last effort, addressing to James a long letter which ignored everything that mattered—the wretched evidence that Lady Essex had put forward and the unprecedented horror excited by the whole business, which

formed the general topic of conversation wherever men met together in public or in private. The effrontery of the Countess, the shameless meddling of the King and of his courtiers, the truckling subserviency . . . were discussed with a remarkable unanimity of abhorrence in every corner of the land. The sober stood aghast at James's disregard for the decencies of life, whilst the light-hearted laughed at the easy credulity with which he took for granted all the tales of a profligate woman.[9] It may be doubted whether his rupture with the House of Commons contributed so much to widen the breach between himself and his subjects as his conduct on this occasion.[10]

Abbot argued that the Bible said nothing apposite to Lady Essex's case; and that, where the Gospel Light was so overwhelmingly luminous as it was near King James, Satan could not possibly be powerful. In the old bad days of Popery, such things might have been, perhaps. But surely, not now! Had Lord and Lady Essex tried prayer and fasting (combined with medical advice)? He strengthened his thesis with a string of idiotic quotations from leading Protestant divines. James, however, felt himself competent to handle such reasoning, and he triumphantly reminded the Archbishop of his own theological prowess. He knew all there was to know of Satan and his devices; and urged Abbot to own himself vanquished and to "rest his faith for the future upon the unerring judgment" of his sovereign.

On September 25, the Commissioners voted. Seven, including four "reverend bawdy Bishops,"[11] voted for Essex's impotence and his lady's

8. Anthony à Wood, *Athenae Oxonienses*, i, 404.

9. She became popularly known as Lord Somerset's "*Articulate* Lady, called so for articling against the frigidity and impotence of her former Lord" (*Epistolae Ho-Elianae*, p. 20).

10. Gardiner, *History*, ii, 174. A breach was made between the nation and the Church also. It was now that the seeds of the Civil War were sown, the ecclesiastical no less than the political seeds. Church and King shattered the general respect for established religion and the monarchy at one and the same time.

11. Welldon, p. 80. Among these four, it is deeply perplexing to remember, was Lancelot Andrewes.

divorce; five, including the Archbishop and one Bishop, voted against it. Church and State set the Countess free for Robert Kerr. As the French peasant remarked when the English subaltern explained that he wanted *œuf, jambon, lapin, "pour la messe"*—*"Mon Dieu! quelle religion!"* A "Jury of grave Matrons, fearing God and mothers of children," assisted by five midwives, next examined Lady Essex and reported her *virgo intacta,* a finding received by the world as a miracle (and with the scoffing unbelief usually afforded to one). Her modesty carefully consulted, she had undergone her examination veiled, a delicacy which led the lewder sort to speculate that a lady of less energetic history had deputized for her. The King, slobbering over their cheeks, congratulated the lovers, and they were married with great rejoicings, December 26, 1613. The bride suffered no dereliction of rank, even temporarily, Kerr having become Earl of Somerset seven weeks earlier. Bilson became a national character, as "Sir Nullity Bilson"; his son obtained a knighthood (gracefully transferred by the popular voice to the father whose services had earned it), and he himself the prize for which Ralegh had worked in vain, a Privy Councillorship.

The affair was to sink lower yet, to the meanest depths to which any King or his creatures ever descended. Somerset had a friend, Sir Thomas Overbury, deep in his secrets and influential with him. The divorce, however, proved too much for Overbury; he called Lady Essex a strumpet and her family bawds.[12] She was not a person to overlook such language, nor to have near her husband a man acquainted with Somerset's past and exercising authority over his weak mind. The King was accordingly told that people said Somerset ruled him, and Overbury ruled Somerset. In consequence, he directed the Archbishop to write to Overbury, and, as if speaking personally in an advisory capacity, suggest that he go abroad as an ambassador. Overbury refused, whereupon the King made him a formal offer; he declined it, and was sent to the Tower for insolence (April 21, 1613). The Privy Council, dutifully supporting this spirited reprisal, rated the offender and committed him for contempt of his sovereign's commands. The sequel is well known. Lady Essex and her uncle, Lord Northampton, determined to have Overbury poisoned. Sir William Waad was dismissed from the Tower lieutenancy and Sir Gervase Helwys appointed and

12. Welldon, p. 67.

ordered to give their messengers free access to his prisoner. He was made to appoint as a keeper, and put in special charge of Overbury, one Richard Weston, who had long acted as the Countess's go-between with Mrs. Turner and with her lover, Lord Somerset. Mrs. Turner instructed Weston to wait on Lady Essex, and Lady Essex gave him a bottle to mix with Overbury's food, warning him not to touch it himself. Weston, supposing Sir Gervase Helwys in the plot, told him of this. Helwys was shocked, and persuaded him to pour the stuff away. But Helwys dreaded Lady Essex so much that he kept quiet; and presently, when Weston said that he would have to administer the poison sooner or later, he only asked that he should be kept out of the business.

Lady Essex came to suspect that Weston was fooling her with his stories of having given the poison, and of its effects. So she herself mixed poison with tarts, jellies, wine, which her lover sent to his old friend. Overbury died (September 14, 1613), ten days before she obtained her divorce. Nine months later, her closest accomplice, Lord Northampton, died, universally loathed but undetected in his latest villainy. A year passed; then men began to whisper that Overbury had been murdered. Sir Ralph Winwood heard the rumor, and told the King. James had long wearied of Lord Somerset, but he took no special notice as yet. Helwys heard of Winwood's suspicions, and in terror went to him and confessed that there had been an attempt to poison Overbury, which he had prevented. He thought Winwood betrayed a confidence by passing on this disclosure to the King, who ordered Helwys to write down all he knew. Coke was charged to investigate the mystery, a task he undertook with intense glee. But, finding himself on the track of greater culprits than he dared to handle alone, he asked to have some persons of higher rank associated with him. James appointed the Chancellor and two other peers. Lord Somerset, who was with him at Royston, where the King was hunting, took fright, and hurried up to London, to clear himself at once. James hung on his neck, vowing he would neither eat nor sleep until his friend was back again. "For God's sake, tell me I shall see thee again!" The moment he was gone, he said with a smile of relief, "I shall never see him more."

The astrologer Dr. Forman had had the good luck to die some years previously (1611). His books were examined, and an embarrassing list of his clients was found, with information enough to justify the divorce of half the court. Arrests and trials followed, and the lesser culprits were hanged, beginning with the beautiful Mrs. Turner. Sentenced to death "in very pious and religious terms,"[13] she died with a composure and charm that touched beholders. One of her fellow-sufferers, when condemned, expressed a hope that, while the lesser flies perished, "the great flies" would not be allowed to escape. His judges solemnly reassured him on this point. But the only fly of any magnitude that was executed was Sir Gervase Helwys, hanged on his own Tower green. Coke thoroughly enjoyed himself, dragging in a cloud of irrelevances, one being a hint that "a most sweet Prince" (Henry, Prince of Wales) had also been cut off by poison. Unexpected information elicited by his researches was Northampton's share in the murder, and the fact that a number of English statesmen, including the late Lord Salisbury, had been Spain's pensioners.[14]

Lady Somerset had her trial postponed, because of her only childbirth. When she came to trial, May 24, 1616, her beauty and her notoriety crowded the court with spectators of rank. She was terrified and humbled. With no choice but to plead guilty, she was sentenced to death. Next day her husband also was convicted, after a ruthless handling by Bacon of the case against him. He may, nevertheless, have been innocent of the actual murder. They did not suffer long. On July 13 the Countess was pardoned, as was inevitable with a criminal of such loveliness and powerful friends. Gusts of scornful ribaldry accompanied the affair to its conclusion. She and her husband, people jested, with a glance at the notorious filching of the Sherborne lease from Ralegh, had "got a Lease of 90 years" of prison from their royal patron. She had been "afraid that Coke, the Lord Chief Justice . . . would have made white *Broth*" of them, like the broth she had sent in to Overbury. But "the *Prerogative* kept them from the *Pot*."[15] Somerset, the less guilty, was not pardoned; and a queer parody of what had happened after Ralegh's conviction took place. James spared his life, and offered pardon on terms—which apparently included that he would consent to ask it through the good offices of young Villiers, and

13. *Epistolae Ho-Elianae*, p. 20.
14. The King had known it since 1614, when Digby discovered it in Madrid.
15. *Epistolae Ho-Elianae*, p. 20.

would surrender Sherborne to the latter. But Somerset maintained his innocence, as Ralegh had done. He was therefore not pardoned until 1625. He and the Countess remained in the Tower until 1622.

Without the background of these ghastly doings we cannot understand the confidence which accompanied Ralegh's renewed clamor for release. It was obviously during the period when the King was "rattled" by the discovery of the Overbury murder, when the lesser flies were being killed off and the greater caught every day closer in the web, that he wrote to Winwood—in late 1615. Friends had advised him that his Guiana project "would be better understood now, than when it was first propounded." The letter is a desperate appeal for freedom, addressed to one of whose goodwill he is assured:

Our late worthy Prince of Wales was extreme curious in searching out the nature of my offences: the Queen's Majesty hath informed herself from the beginning: the King of Denmark, at both times of his being here, was throughly satisfied of my innocency. They would otherwise never have moved his Majesty on my behalf.

The wife, the brother, and the son of a King do not use to sue for men suspect. . . . It is true, Sir, that his Majesty hath sometimes answered, that his Council knew me better than he did—meaning, some two or three of them—and it was indeed my infelicity! For, had his Majesty known me, I had never been here where I now am; or had I known his Majesty, they had never been so long there where they now are. His Majesty not knowing of me hath been my ruin; and his Majesty misknowing of them hath been the ruin of a goodly part of his estate. But they are all of them now—some living and some dying—come to his Majesty's knowledge. . . . To die for the King, and not by the King, is all the ambition I have in the world.

And freedom came, at last. Ralegh paid £750 apiece to Sir Edward Villiers and Sir William St. John, the favorite's brother and half-brother. Then Villiers himself had a talk with the King; and on March 19, 1616, the Lieutenant of the Tower received a warrant to release Ralegh to sail for Guiana:

His Majesty, out of his gracious inclination towards you, being pleased to release you out of your imprisonment in the Tower, to go abroad with a keeper, to make your provisions for your intended voyage, we think it good to admonish you—though we do not prejudice your own discretion so much as to think you would attempt it without leave—that you should not presume to resort either to his Majesty's Court, the Queen's, or Prince's; nor go into any public assemblies whatsoever, without especial licence obtained from his Majesty for your warrant. But only that you use the benefit of his Majesty's grace to follow the business which you are to undertake, and for which, upon your humble request, his Majesty hath been graciously pleased to grant you that freedom.[16]

It was not until January 30, 1617, that the King "fully and wholly enlarged him." But the Tower lost its prisoner nearly a year earlier—one month before William Shakespeare died.

Ralegh emerged as into a kind of posthumous fame. All eyes were curiously on him, and people noted with kindly amusement that his first action was to stretch his long legs, poor walker though he always admitted he was, in walking all over this new London on which Inigo Jones was working. The discoverer of strange worlds was staring on one still stranger to him.

In this brief period he and Pocahontas *may* have met. "The Virginian woman" reached London in June, as Mrs. John Rolfe, wife of an Englishman. Her hero, Captain John Smith, introduced her to the Queen, who took her straightway into fairyland; she was at the Court Mask for Twelfth Night, 1617. The King ordered her to return to Virginia, "sore against her will";[17] and, drooping under the strain of new scenes and wild excitements, rebellious and unhappy, she died in March. It is tempting to believe that Ralegh saw the Indian lady who was the capital's latest sensation. But it is unlikely; for, as we have seen, he was strictly forbidden to approach the exalted regions where she moved.

Luckily, when he was released the Court was absent from Westminster, so his sight-seeing, at any rate, was not circumscribed. He would be particularly interested in a new canopy and effigy in the Abbey, and an inscription commemorating two sisters who, "sharers of kingdom and tomb, sleep here, Elizabeth and Mary, in hope of the Resurrection" (*"Regno consortes et urna, hic obdormimus Elizabetha et Maria sorores, in spe Resurrectionis"*). He would be interested hardly less in the fine "New Exchange" that Robert Cecil, Earl of Salisbury, had erected

16. Minute of Instructions from the Privy Council, March 19, 1616.
17. Chamberlain to Carleton (*Calendar of State Papers, Domestic,* 1611–1618, p. 428).

on part of the grounds of that Durham House which had been his own home.

But for the necessity of finding room in the Tower for Lord and Lady Somerset, he would almost certainly have remained there much longer. Eight days after he went, Lady Somerset arrived, March 27, 1616. Hearing she was to occupy the room in which Overbury had died, she showed one of her rare lapses into feeling, and screamed, "Not that! not that!" She was accordingly allowed to have Ralegh's old chambers, which were probably not quite ready. Lord Carew, watching over his kinsman's interests and recording his movements minutely, in letters to their common friend, Sir Thomas Roe—now England's first ambassador at the Great Mogul's court, in Lahore (where the word "Guiana" must have come like a trumpet's sound)—wrote:

The Countess of Somerset hath a pardon, but she remaineth in the Tower in Sir Walter Raleghe his lodging.[18]

The Earl of Somerset hath the liberty of the Tower, which he useth very sparingly. His wife and he lodge together, he lies in the Bloody Tower, Sir Walter Ralegh's ancient lodging, and she in Sir Walter's new buildings. All doors are open between them.[19]

Legend synchronized Ralegh's departure from his den of so many years with Somerset's actual entry, and made him observe as they passed each other, "That his whole History had not the like Precedent, of a King's chief Prisoner to purchase freedom, and his bosom Favourite to have the halter, but in Scripture, Mordecai and Haman." His sharp tongue, and his refusal to check it, were as notorious as his ability. His temerity shocked men now, "the common world wondering at this man's wit, who had a way to break Jests, though to hazard his head again."[20] James glowered when he heard, and sent back the menace, "That he might die in this deceit"—"which he did, and Somerset saved." Determination to rob Ralegh of his vengeance may have been a factor in the King's clemency to the latter. But report went astray in placing Ralegh's remark[21] in the doorway of his cell, for he had already left the Tower—unless we suppose a return to fetch away the last of his belongings.

18. July 1616 (Carew, Letters to Roe, p. 39).
19. Ibid., p. 44 (August).   20. Sanderson, p. 459.
21. Stebbing rejects it, unnecessarily (I think).

CHAPTER XXII

An Admiral at Last

Sir Walter Raleghe hath built a goodly ship of 500 tons; in this month she was launched; and is called the *Destiny*. God grant her to be no less fortunate unto her owner than is wished by me! In February next he purposes to set sail towards his golden mine, whereof he is extremely confident. The alarm of his journey is flown into Spain, and, as he tells me, sea forces are prepared to lie for him, but he is nothing appalled with the report, for he will be a good fleet and well manned. . . . I am sure he will be able to land 500 men, which is a competent army to perform any exploit upon the Continent of America, the Spaniards (and especially about Orenoque) being so poorly planted as they are. LORD CAREW to Sir Thomas Roe, December, 1617.

The only man of note left alive that had helped to beat them in the year 1588. FRANCIS OSBORNE.

THANKS to Devon support, the Raleghs raised a joint stock of £30,000. They called in £3000 (part of the Sherborne compensation), which had been lent to the Countess of Bedford. Lady Ralegh sold for £2500 her estate at Mitcham. The Crown provided £175, the bounty paid to encourage shipbuilding. Ralegh began building in the Thames.

When he had entered the Tower, Spain had been long suing for peace, and her threats were taken for the empty bluster that they were. Now, however, England was the suppliant. This change was due largely to the character of Spain's Ambassador, Count Gondomar;[1] and those who longed to see a restoration of national prestige and independence turned in despair from the Court to Elizabeth's old Admiral.

Ralegh's last two years of life "may be said with all the sobriety of truth, to have been simply a protracted death-struggle between him and Gondomar."[2] We must look carefully at his antagonist. Count

1. He did not receive this title till after his success in bringing Ralegh to the scaffold. But he is so well known by this name that it is commonly used by English writers.
2. Edwards, i, 568.

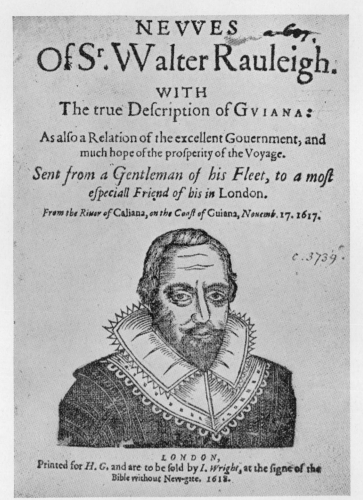

NEVVES
Of Sr. Walter Rauleigh.

WITH
The true Description of GVIANA:

As also a Relation of the excellent Gouernment, and
much hope of the prosperity of the Voyage.

Sent from a Gentleman of his Fleet, to a most
especiall Friend of his in London.

From the Riuer of Caliana, on the Coast of Guiana, Nouemb. 17. 1617.

c. 3739.

LONDON,
Printed for H. G. and are to be sold by I. Wright, at the signe of the
Bible without New-gate. 1618.

By courtesy of The Walpole Society and the Oxford University Press.

RALEGH

AFTER RELEASE FROM THE TOWER

FROM A WOODCUT ON A CONTEMPORARY BROADSHEET

Gondomar had been in arms against the English at an early age; and when he reached Portsmouth as Ambassador, in July, 1613, he came charged with belligerence. The naval authorities, preserving West Country traditions, demanded from his ship the customary recognition of the English flag; but he "had the time of day perfectly in mind. And, in exact accordance with the chronology,"[3] he refused the respect that was claimed, as something vanished with the vanished Elizabethan Age; and, immediately he reached the Court, laid his complaint with James. James reprimanded the Lord Admiral and the Portsmouth Governor, and commended the Ambassador, who became a watched man at once; in the correspondence of the period, stories of him "are as abundant as are apple blossoms in our orchards at the end of April."

The Ambassador was very unlike the polished Castilian, the traditional Spaniard of those days. He was "of a tall meagre stature," "with short, thin, black hair, a longish visage, and a close austere aspect, which made his open and jocose humour so much more taking"[4]—"one of those crafty Gallegos whose assumed clownishness of speech and boorishness of manner are often made to mask intense earnestness of purpose and boldness of action."[5] The clownishness was useful; he could play the buffoon with the royal buffoon, and "pipe James asleep with facetious words and gestures,"[6] broad enough to appeal to the lowest mental organisms. Under his ordinary rôle of the good bluff fellow, an Englishman with Englishmen, was couched "a threatening savagery that frightened James, and a pride that humiliated him";[7] but he could easily put this out of sight behind a grave courtliness. He had great conversational powers, and could indulge the King's passion for chattering at large on all sorts of matters; could flatter adroitly, as when he let James detect him (or think he detected him) in a mispronunciation and accepted royal correction with the apology that he, poor fellow, spoke Latin "like a King," whereas the King spoke it "like a Master of Arts."[8] He could be dignified, hurt or indignant—so wounded and outraged as to storm threateningly—and he was imperturbably firm, a fact which awed and comforted the vacillating silly creature whom he

3. Edwards, i, 571. 4. Oldys, *Ralegh* (Ralegh's *Works*, i, 514).
5. Hume, p. 311.
6. Oldys (quoted from *Vox Populi, or News from Spain*), i, 515.
7. Hume, p. 311. 8. Goodman, *Court of King James*, i, 29.

courted. James admitted his right to know everything that happened in his Government's discussions—a favor for which he expressed his gratitude, as he well might, in a letter written from Madrid, September 19, 1622:[9] "that a Spaniard has been and should be counsellor, not only of your Council of State, but also of the Privy Council,[10] that surpasses not only all the deserts, but also all the services that I have been able to render." His influence with the King he did not selfishly keep to himself; at one time or another he sold the honor of being mistress of the robes to six different ladies.[11] With women, as with men, he used bribery, frugally and wisely; and his "correspondence shows his high appreciation"[12] of the beauty and kindness of the former at James's Court. It is a pity that he has not left an itemized account of all his complex financial transactions.

Few foreign visitors have ever found us more intriguing a problem, and it would be ungrateful not to acknowledge this. He was a student of English literature, a connoisseur in English gold-work and tapestry. James recognized his taste by presenting him with 2000 ounces of gold plate, at a time when he was finding money exceptionally hard to come by; and in various ways (not excluding purchase) Gondomar collected twenty chests of needlework and tapestries and forty chests of books, part of the enormous baggage he took into Spain three weeks before Ralegh's execution. He was a student of men also, commenting blandly on the Englishmen he met, and on the King in particular, telling his own master that the latter's vanity was so colossal that the art of beguiling him was simply to suggest that you were his pupil, learning the game of politics from him. These qualities Ralegh could have recognized—probably in part did recognize, when he found himself fallen a victim to them; and along with them he would recognize that "invincible constancy" which he admired in his Spanish adversaries. Nor would he have resented their use, as he resented the treachery of Cecil and Howard. After all, Gondomar was an enemy, with a long list of defeats to avenge, and was merely serving his country in bringing English diplomacy into derision.

Gondomar hated Ralegh, honestly regarding him as "Public Enemy

9. Goodman, *Court of King James,* i, 234 ff.
10. *"Non seulement de votre Conseil d'état, mais du Cabinet intérieur."*
11. Oldys, p. 517.   12. Edwards, i, 573.

Number One"—a pirate, pestilential even for a Protestant. He took alarm on his release, writing to the King of Spain (April 27, 1616) that he wanted leave to visit Madrid, to see the latter personally about English maritime schemes,

especially the formation of another company for Guiana and the river Orinoco . . . the prime promoter and originator of which is Sir Walter Ralegh, a great seaman, who took many prizes in the time of Queen Elizabeth, and who first colonised Virginia. . . . He has already been in the country, and assures people here that he knows of a mine that will swell all England with gold.

He urged that the Spanish Navy be strengthened, and no ship allowed to sail without a convoy; and said he was doing all he could to stop Ralegh. He wrote again, a month later (May 20), that he had settled the Courts of Admiralty, who were not behaving as he wished; he had seen King James, who had at once set things right, "not a single pirate daring either openly or secretly to come to England." It must be remembered that to Gondomar "pirate" meant anyone who trespassed in that vast region of the world which Spain claimed. The Judge of the Admiralty not "acting properly," the Ambassador had been allowed to nominate two judges to sit with him. When the Admiralty judge refused to allow them to take their seats, "at my instance the King and the Lord Admiral compelled him to do so. This has caused great annoyance to those who go to Brazil for wood. But I have prosecuted them criminally as disturbers of the peace." "I am trying to do the same with Ralegh . . . but, after all, the sure and necessary thing is for us to increase our naval force, as I recommended before."

In the jargon of the World War, Ralegh's was a "hush-hush" expedition. Europe (not Spain only) was busy guessing what James was after in freeing his renowned corsair. James enjoyed the uncertainty and resultant fear. Ralegh was like one of the lions for which the Tower was famous. He was being unchained, to be loosed upon—what prey? There were times when it looked as if it would not be Guiana. The first of many earnest inquirers who found their way to James's counsellors, and then to Ralegh himself, was the Ambassador of Savoy, the Count of Scarnafissi.

A few years previously, Ralegh had opposed a Savoyard alliance, because Savoy was a dependency of Spain. Since then, however, Savoy had been at war with Spain; had obtained a truce; and in 1616 was at war again. Spanish troops were being embarked at the nominally neutral port of Genoa; Genoese bankers were providing the funds without which Spain could not wage a war. Hence what has been called Ralegh's "piratical attempt to seize the city of Genoa." Gardiner coolly states,[13] "Raleigh sent a message to Scarnafissi, suggesting that it would be well, if the consent of James could be obtained, to make preparations to strike a blow at Genoa." Mr. Harlow follows Gardiner: "Ralegh accordingly suggested to Scarnafissi" that his fleet, if the King would consent, should be joined with French and Dutch ships to surprise Genoa.[14] Scarnafissi, however, made the proposal first—to Winwood, James's Secretary of State: Winwood then introduced Ralegh to him, and Scarnafissi's proposal was discussed. The King, who was feeling humiliated by the procrastinating reception of his wishes for a Spanish marriage, was quite willing to use the dreaded "Gualteral" as a threat. He was in the negotiations throughout, and on January 12, 1617, ordered Winwood and Edmondes, members of his Privy Council, to go into the suggestion thoroughly with Scarnafissi. His only demurrer was a fear lest the expedition might not get for him the money he must have; the Savoy troops, as being on the spot, would keep the loot, or Ralegh's financial backers might prove "sticky" about their own full share of it. In the end, James refused to allow Ralegh to be deflected from Guiana. But the "piracy" of the proposal is a responsibility that falls on other heads than Ralegh's.

Scarnafissi reported to the Duke of Savoy that in his talks he found Ralegh "eager to fall upon the Spaniard wherever he could, and to spare neither his coasts, his lands, nor his vessels, nor anything else that depended on Spain, or where he could hope for gain." *That* no one doubted; this most consistent of the Elizabethans, from start to finish, risked all for the fulfilment of one dream, the displacing of the Spanish Empire by an English one. He was old—by our forefathers' standards, very old. But, as Stebbing points out, the astonishing thing is that no one, in England or abroad, thought of him as old. It was as if his own cordial had worked in him as an elixir. And in this evening of his

13. *History*, iii, 51.   14. *Ralegh's Last Voyage*, p. 28.

life he stood fast to his traditions and aims. "The old man of sixty-six[15] maintained the traditions of his youth."[16]

The Savoyard Ambassador next proposed to James an alliance of States that disliked the Spanish hegemony, and that Ralegh's fleet and English Royal ships should be joined with Dutch and Venetian vessels. These negotiations were watched by Venice with particular closeness, as was natural, and she was certainly a party to them.[17] The Venetian Ambassador was another of the people who respectfully asked the old lion if he would consider putting his strength at his master's disposal; he reported that *Sir Vate Ralo,* "who is destined to go to the West Indies to discover the country of Guiana, has let me know that if he could obtain permission from his King he would willingly go to serve your Serenity."[18] The writer had previously reported[19] the King of Denmark's last request of his brother-in-law (in August, 1614), not to let his great Admiral's abilities waste into the grave, but to let him use them. Venice took a deep interest in Ralegh.

So did France. He had kept up relations with friends there, ever since his youthful campaigning. As his fleet was now being got together, the French Government experienced a spasm of alarm lest it should after all not sail for Guiana, but swoop down on one of their own ports, to help Ralegh's old acquaintances the Huguenots. He had built a fine ship, the *Destiny,* and equipped it with his traditional magnificence. It became "a fashionable lounge" to inspect it as it lay in the Thames. The Queen herself wanted to see it, but James forbade her. Among those who dropped in on the white-haired admiral was the French Ambassador, M. des Marêts, March 15, 1617. He found Ralegh busy but courteous, desiring further talk "at a time and place less inconvenient than the present," for he was making his last preparations to leave the river. Sherborne, taken from the disgraced Earl of Somerset, had just been granted to Sir John Digby; des Marêts, who had heard (as he told Richelieu) that Ralegh was feeling particularly resentful, told him he felt the deepest sympathy with him "in the sufferings in-

15. He was a little less at this time.   16. Williams, *James I,* p. 273.
17. See Venetian Archives, *Consiglio X, Communicationi, vii,* 1615–1617, quoted in Edwards, i, 579 ff.
18. *Calendar of State Papers, Venetian,* 1615–1617, p. 210.
19. *Ibid.,* 1613–1615, p. 180.

flicted on him by his long and unjust imprisonment, and by the confiscation of his property." Ralegh seems to have kept himself bottled up for once. But, a fortnight later, he sent a message that he would now like a further talk. He did not get it until April, after he had left London. He then knew more of the dishonesty with which he was being treated, and was in a mood to be drawn by kindness, of which so little had come his way. He was never a cautious person. But, for that matter, few of us, if in the depths of humiliation and helplessness under cruel wrong, would fail to respond to an assurance that our case was understood. According to the Ambassador, Ralegh said "he had a great and signal enterprise in hand, from which he hoped for great advantage." It would bring "both honour and profit to the Sovereign who shall reap the fruit of my labours. Seeing myself so evilly and tyrannically treated by my own King, I have made up my mind—if God shall send me good success—to leave my country, and to make to the King, your Master, the first offer of what shall fall under my power."[20] This was what des Marêts "was able to extract," and "I did my best to strengthen him in this good purpose," though des Marêts did "not anticipate that his voyage will have much fruit." Neither he nor Ralegh took the interview very seriously; it was an exchange of compliments, probably in French and English mixed, and even hostile critics recognize that it is very unlikely that Ralegh expressed himself as indiscreetly and categorically as the Ambassador reported. Both talked rather above their real meaning, and both understood this. The Frenchman went away satisfied that *his* country, at any rate, was in no danger; and Richelieu, who thought Ralegh "a great seaman but a poor commander" (*grand marinier et mauvais capitaine*), was relieved. But he remained interested. Ralegh was offered a commission by the French Admiral, de Montmorency, authorizing him to take into French ports any prizes he captured.

This offer Ralegh presently decided to take up. Sanguine as he always was, he began to see that he was in a trap; and though confident that his proved valor and the luck that was surely overdue would together enable him to break out of it, he could not afford to neglect any possible chances of escape if the doors should close on him.

20. *MSS. du fond Dupuis,* p. 420, tom. ii. (Imperial Library, Paris), quoted, Edwards, i, 595–596.

The time came for the fleet to collect at Plymouth. On March 15 the
Admiralty took an official "view and survey of such ships as were in
the river of Thames, ready to go to sea, under the command of Sir
Walter Rauleigh, Knight":

The *Destiny* . . . of the burthen of 440 tons, whereof Sir Walter
Rauleigh goeth General, Walter Rauleigh the younger, Captain . . . 200
men, whereof 100 sailors, 20 watermen, 80 Gentlemen, the rest Servants
and Labourers; 36 pieces of Ordnance.

The *Starre,* alias the *Jason,* of the burthen of 240 tons. . . . 80 men, one
Gentleman and no more; 25 pieces of Ordnance.

The *Encounter* . . . 160 tons. . . . 17 pieces of Ordnance.

The *John and Francis,* alias the *Thunder* . . . 150 tons: Sir William
Sentleiger, Knight, Captain. . . . 60 soldiers, 10 land-men, 6 Gentlemen, 20
pieces of Ordnance.

The *Flying Joan* . . . 120 tons. . . . 25 men, 14 pieces of Ordnance.

The *Husband,* alias the *Southampton* . . . 80 tons. . . . 25 mariners, 2
Gentlemen, 6 pieces of Ordnance.

A pinnace called the *Page,* 25 tons. . . . 8 sailors, 3 Robinets of brass.[21]

The total came to 1215 tons, 431 men, 121 pieces of ordnance; the *Encounter* had not yet picked her crew, and had only captain and master.
Assayers, refiners, miners and their implements Ralegh was going to
take in at Plymouth. Thither, on March 28, the fleet "fell down the
river into the Downs,"[22] the Admiral going overland to join the *Destiny* at Dover. "God grant," wrote Carew, "he may return deep laden
with Guianan gold ore."

From Dover to Plymouth, Ralegh was accompanied by a Frenchman, Captain Faige. They talked freely of possible developments, and
in May Ralegh sent Faige with a letter to M. de Bisseaux, a French
Councillor of State, and asked for the commission he had been promised. Unfortunately Faige was accompanied by one Antoine Belle, one
of the many worthless people who beguiled Ralegh into confidences
which they betrayed. Belle and Faige neglected to do what they had
promised; and instead journeyed to Genoa, of all places, where the latter fell sick, and was also imprisoned for debt. Trouble is a great awak-
ener of conscience, and Belle became remorseful for having thought of

---

21. Schomburgk edition of Ralegh's *Discoverie of Guiana,* pp. 171–172.
22. Lord Carew to Sir Thomas Roe (*Letters,* etc., p. 97).

carrying letters to Huguenots. He went to Rome, and confessed to a Jesuit father, who told him he ought at once to let the Spanish Government know what was being planned. He therefore went on to Madrid, where he left Ralegh's letter, along with a map of Guiana and other papers.

When the whole enterprise had failed, and the King and his party had to find some colorable pretext for sending him to the scaffold, these French negotiations were one of the counts most pressed against Ralegh. They have been pressed ever since. Gardiner remarks that he was not only being tempted by wicked Frenchmen (Huguenots, that is), but that there were not wanting "voices at home to urge him along the evil path on which he was too willing to be guided."[23] Will it be believed that one of these voices was King James's? On October 4, 1618, Sir Thomas Wilson, who had been fastened on to Ralegh as a spy to break him down into admissions that might be used to murder him legally, reported that his prisoner had answered his badgerings with the statement

that his first dealing with Captain Faige was well known to your Majesty, for what cause it was; and his last, at Plymouth, about bringing French ships and men to him to displant the Spaniards at St. Thomé, that the English might after pass to the mine without offence.

To this allegation James made no reply, for the simple reason that it was true. Ralegh had sent the French Government a request, which Faige seems to have omitted to deliver, to let Faige bring ships to points in the West Indies on which he and Ralegh had agreed in their discussions while dropping down the Channel. What ships were these, that the French Government were to send? The answer is a very unexpected one.

This is *part* of what had been happening. The Spanish Ambassador had been one of those who had a look at the *Destiny* while she was in the Thames. Angry and alarmed, he told James that his own master possessed all America (for the moment conveniently forgetting Virginia, where English occupation was at last becoming effective). James could not admit this, having himself sanctioned previous expeditions which had been authorized to plant colonies; and the statement that

23. Gardiner, *History,* iii, 53.

Ralegh had deceived him into thinking there were no Spaniards on the Orinoco is nonsense, though nonsense often repeated. Every English captain who had visited Guiana knew there was a Spanish settlement there, and this information had been put before the Privy Council by everyone concerned, including Ralegh. And, since there were Spaniards near Ralegh's gold mine, and the Spaniards made no secret of their intention to murder every foreigner who ventured into Guiana, and had a long list of such murders to their credit already, there was no question that to let Ralegh go up the river was to ask for armed resistance. A powerful section of the Privy Council faced such a situation joyfully; the Archbishop, Winwood, Carew and others, the first two most of all, *wanted* war with Spain, and a breaking off, once for all, of these negotiations for a Spanish marriage. James in his normal moods did *not* want war. But he did want the Guiana gold, and must have it. He therefore sanctioned Ralegh's taking an armed force that would enable him to defend himself if attacked. But he thought it would be a fine stroke if a French force went along with him, to do any necessary fighting. Ralegh and his men could then say, "This fighting between Christian men is deplorable. But it is no concern of ours. It is a matter between France and Spain"; and could push on to the mine, beyond San Thomé. If Spain were thoroughly frightened, so much the better. It might yield its Infanta, lest the terrible Gualteral should repeat the day of Cadiz! Ralegh, with Winwood's authority and the King's connivance,

was suffered to concert measures with one foreign ally of England against another. . . . The King was informed of the intrigue, and knew as much as his indolence permitted of its various steps. He was never obliged to know so much, or to betray such signs of knowing anything, as not to be in a position on an exigency to disavow the whole. This was his idea of statecraft.[24]

Ralegh, left in a half-light, saw the King's idea, but he did not see—yet—that *his* life and fortunes were the only things that were being risked by anyone. The game was becoming so exactly like the Elizabethan one which he had been trained to play, that he thought it exceedingly probable that something would happen—a collision with

24. Stebbing, p. 309.

Spain—which the King would deplore publicly while privately pleased. He might have to make a temporary sojourn in French territory, to save James's face, while the trouble blew over. That is why he wanted —and thought he had obtained, except that his agent had never returned—sanction to use French ports in an emergency. And that is the truth of these terrible intrigues with France.

Meanwhile James was harassed almost to madness by Gondomar. Gondomar, who had access to anything he wanted, brought forward Ralegh's own suggestion to the Privy Council, long before, to take two ships only. Two ships should go with a safe-conduct; they should have guidance to the mine, and assistance to work it! Only, they must go unarmed. The King of Spain was quite willing to fling a rich handful of his abounding riches to his impecunious brother of England! It looked a generous proposal. But acceptance involved the abandonment of England's claim that Guiana had been ceded to her by its natural lords, the Indian chieftains. Also, Ralegh, sadly suspicious and mistrustful after his long imprisonment, rejected the open-hearted offer. He said he knew the Spaniards would "fall upon him, wherever they found him." They had recently given a notable proof of their amicable intentions by tying back to back twenty-six men of his and Mr. Hall's, and cutting their throats—"men who had traded with them the whole month" and went ashore by invitation, without a sword among them. Ralegh subsequently referred to this incident so frequently that it is to be feared that he genuinely resented it.

His commission was made out in correct form, to "Our trusty and well beloved," and was to be under the Great Seal. But James could not stand out against Gondomar's rage at his loosing corsairs, "and that old pirate in especial, bred under the English virago, and by her fleshed in Spanish blood and ruin." The fact that Ralegh was still under sentence of death was seen to supply a method of satisfying Gondomar without stopping the voyage. James no more than anyone else believed that Ralegh had ever been guilty of treason. But he frankly regarded his conviction as the master-card which Providence had placed in his hand; he held the Admiral's life as a hostage. This is the small part of the whole truth, which can be pleaded in the King's exculpation. James therefore erased "trusty and well beloved," and sent Ralegh as still unpardoned, with a commission under the Privy Seal only. Under orders, Ralegh handed over a list of his ships, their burden and armament, places of call, and dates when he expected to reach them. This, "on the hand and word of a King," James promised to keep secret . . . and passed on to the Spanish Ambassador. James gave the latter a second solemn promise (which he meant to observe), that if Ralegh so much as dared to look on anything that belonged to the King of Spain, he would send him to be hanged in chains in the Plaza at Madrid. Two friendly nobles, the Earls of Pembroke and Arundel, had to stand as sureties for Ralegh's return. He was being sent out with permission to try to effect an impossibility, on terms that his life should pay for failure. No legend of fairy, of the princess's suitors condemned to weave straw into gold, demanded anything unfairer; and no pitying spirit came to him in the darkness, to offer to spin his stubble for him. "All hands were loose, but mine bound," he said with strict truth afterwards.

His captains could only be a scratch lot, after fourteen years of King James's naval administration; and when it became generally known that the Admiral was sailing under the King's displeasure, officers of good quality hung back. Among the few who came in, practically everyone turned against him in his hour of failure—which gives us both the measure of their characters and of the kind of support that they gave him. They included Sir William St. Leger, under whose father he himself had served in Ireland, nearly forty years ago; Roger North, Lord North's brother; several dissipated cadets of noble families; as well as Ralegh's nephew, George Ralegh, and his son Walter. They included an element already known as definitely dangerous, whose record was such as to make the King's fears of piracy not altogether baseless: such men as Sir John Ferne, a distinguished nuisance who had tried to privateer in Eastern waters, under cover of a commission from the French King. The East India Company, precariously clinging to the rim of the Indian sea-board, had appealed to the Privy Council against him, and he had fled to France. On May 30, 1617, when Ferne was embarrassing Ralegh with his assistance (which later did much toward bringing him to the scaffold), Sir Thomas Roe, still nervous about him, had written home from Lahore:

I much fear some ill news from the Red Sea that will bring us all in trouble by the fugitive Fearn. . . . If he touch any of this country's goods, the Prince will prosecute revenge and satisfaction with all malice.[25]

Ralegh's kinsmen and friends who went made it a condition that they should serve directly under him. His rank and file he characterized as "a mere rabble of men," "the very scum of the world, Drunkards, Blasphemers, and such like."[26] They "left their country for their country's good," and with the entire consent of their families, who "thought it an exceeding gain to be discharged" of them, "with the hazard of some thirty, forty, or fifty pounds, knowing they could not live one whole year so good cheap at home." They began their warfare at Gravesend, with "a sharp contest for masterdom" with the townsmen, who in the end "prevailed and drove many of Sir Walter's men into the mud of the river." Hardly anyone, in England or abroad, for one minute believed that their leader would be such a fool as to return; he would sadly gainsay his reputation for skill and daring if he did not use this force to turn into a super-pirate! People indulged their wit at his expense; if his fleet drowned it would save the King much expense, of halters to hang them.

But Ralegh's worst embarrassment was to come by his son. Wat, inheriting all his father's handsome boldness, had grown up without his father's advice and restraint, very much spoiled by his admiring mother. With a father under sentence of death, his opportunities for making an impression must have been limited—one presumes he had to keep away from Court. He had nevertheless made an impression. He was quarrelsome and addicted to unsavory practical jests. The least censurable has come down to us on the unassailable authority of its victim, Ben Jonson (who growled it out to Drummond). Wat's education had been chequered; after matriculating at Corpus Christi College, Oxford, in 1607, he failed to commend himself to his teachers— for which his father, after careful inquiry, blamed him, but his mother did not, applauding his conduct as high-spirited. So in 1613 his father sent him to France, with Jonson as tutor. Those who remember Ben's reputation for conviviality (which has kept green through three centuries) may think this was a measure of desperation. But Ralegh,

25. See Sir William Foster, *First Letter Book of the East India Company*, p. 463; and *The Embassy of Sir Thomas Roe to India*, p. 384.
26. Ralegh's *Apology*.

singular in many respects, was singular also in his contempt for insobriety; his son, apparently, was equally safe from it, for we never hear of it among his sins. Wat's tutor, however, was not going to change the habits of a lifetime, merely because he happened to be in Paris; and his pupil, "being knavishly inclined, among other pastimes"

caused him to be drunken, and dead drunk, so that he knew not where he was, thereafter laid him on a car, which he made to be drawen by pioneers through the streets, at every corner showing his governor stretched out, and telling them that was a more lively image of the Crucifix than any they had: at which sport young Raughlie's mother delighted much (saying, his father young was so inclined), though his father abhorred it.[27]

It is to be hoped that Drummond, as he heard this sad recital, was properly sympathetic. Another tradition in this same Wat Ralegh cycle says that he and his tutor had an angry parting.[28] It seems not improbable.

Wat visited the Continent again, without Ben Jonson. In April, 1615, having wounded a servant of the Lord Treasurer, he fled to the Low Countries, "where he is entertained by the Prince Maurice."[29] Sir Henry Wotton, then representing England in Holland, took an interest in him. He wrote to Sir Ralph Winwood (May 21, 1615)[30] that Wat had dangerously wounded "one Jaye" (a different name from that given by Carew) in a private chamber; Jaye had recovered, and both belligerents were so far from being cooled that they had gone abroad expressly to finish the fight. "Rawley . . . (as it is thought) . . . hath only gotten leave to travel for this purpose"; he and Jaye had eaten together in outward amity, in Leyden, "to cover their intent." Wotton had sent for Wat, and had talked to him, but was not hopeful of success; interference, "I think, will rather defer than prevent this evil, for the difference between them is irreconcilable." No one took the scattering of wild oats of this brave kind seriously, and it is clear that there must have been something very taking about the younger Walter. His father's pride in him was great. But he was plainly not fitted for a quiet

27. Conversations with Drummond of Hawthornden.
28. Aubrey, Letters, etc. Believed to be on Izaak Walton's authority.
29. Lord Carew, Letters to Sir Thomas Roe, p. 10.
30. Logan Pearsall Smith, The Life and Letters of Sir Henry Wotton, ii, 79.

voyage to the Spanish main. If an enemy ever stood before him, with no father to restrain him, the King's peace would go.

There were people who felt distress at the sight of the dauntless old man going out to obvious destruction. A friend of Kemys, Sylvanus Scory, sent a remonstrance in verse:

> Raleigh, in this thyself thyself transcends,
>   When, hourly tasting of a bitter chalice,
> Scanning the sad faces of thy friends,
>   Thou smil'st at Fortune's menaces and malice!
>
> Hold thee firm *here:* cast anchor in this port!
>   Here art thou safe till Death enfranchise thee.
> Here neither harm, nor fears of harm, resort;
>   Here—though enchained—thou liv'st in liberty. . . .

Sir William St. John offered to get him a pardon for another £1500.[31] He and Edward Villiers had already collected that sum for procuring Ralegh's release. Another story is that they were prepared to crown their kindness by winning the pardon for only £700, with a clause added, granting him leave to drop the Guiana enterprise if he wished.[32] Why did he not accept one of these offers? The answer lies partly in his poverty; partly in his sanguine temperament, that believed devoutly in Guiana and thought that with luck he could "bring the goods home." He could not both pay and sail; and he was playing for far higher stakes than mere safety—for the chance to bring himself and his abilities back into the main stream of national life.

Also, he was misled. Bacon, one of the two contemporaries who might claim intellectual equality with him, is believed to have been in friendly intercourse, and occasional coöperation, while *The History of the World* was being written. They were seeing something of one another now; on one occasion, Bacon records that he "continued . . . still walking in Gray's Inn walks with Sir Walter Ralegh a good while." It may have been then that Ralegh asked whether he had not better get a pardon, and was told not to squander his pinched resources.

Money is the knee-timber of your voyage. Spare your money in this par-

31. Carew Ralegh, *Observations* (on Sanderson's *Lives and Reigns*, etc.).
32. *Ibid.*

ticular; for, upon my life, you have a sufficient pardon for all that is past already, the King having under his Great Seal made you Admiral, and given you power of martial law.

His commission was certainly wide and ample. It gave "full power and authority to the said Sir Walter Ralegh, in cases of rebellion or mutiny by sea or land, to use and exercise martial law . . . in as large and ample manner as our lieutenant-general by sea or land, or lieutenants in our counties." "Your commission," Bacon assured him, "is as good a pardon for all former offences as the law of England can afford you." That seemed good enough, from such an authority—"Lord Chancellor Verulam, who was no fool, nor no ill lawyer."[33]

As another anecdote shows, Ralegh's carelessness still beset him. Not even *his* experience had taught him to be guarded with men who were themselves always guarded—who stored up playful sallies, and then, when "the cruelty of the law of England" was demanding the speaker's life, produced them and ruined him with them. Bacon had asked, either laughingly or in natural curiosity, "What will you do, if after all this expenditure, you miss of the gold mine?" "We will look after the Plate Fleet, to be sure," was the playful reply—the Mexican Plate Fleet which in 1618 carried treasure amounting to over two and a half millions sterling. "But then you will be pirates!" "Oh, no! who ever heard of men being pirates for millions?" And of course, Ralegh was right. If he *had* brought back such undreamt-of bullion to James, whose exchequer was empty and whose annual revenues scarcely amounted to a fifth of such a sum, the bearer of such a gift would never have been treated as a pirate! The Court would have seen to that. But to talk so to Bacon, old friend though he apparently was, was suicidal. It is to Bacon's credit, however, that the story has come down to us from another source—it seems, from Ralegh himself, who was later on alleged by Sir Thomas Wilson (the spy set to entrap him into damning evidence against himself), to have related it to him—proof sufficient that the conversation was a jesting one.

Before he left the Thames, one of his sureties, Lord Arundel, visited him at the last moment, and asked for his promise that, good voyage or bad, he would come back to England. That promise he gave; and the

33. *Ibid.*

answer to all those who call him pirate and build vast superstructures
of alleged disloyalty on his negotiations with Frenchmen and others,
is *that he came back,* when he need not have done so.

His own West rejoiced to have him in its midst again. Plymouth "by
a general consent" entertained the adventurers at public expense, and
paid a drummer to call them to the feast. We may let our eyes rest a
moment on this picture, and imagine Lady Ralegh for once free of
anxiety, as she saw her husband among his friends, and heard the
speeches of welcome and reply. They did not know that Gondomar's
express messenger had carried to Madrid all that needed to be known,
and that instructions had been sent out to all the Governors of the
Indies, to extirpate the English when they arrived.

Lady Ralegh's rest and happiness were of brief duration. Captain
Pennington could not sail because he could not pay his grocers. She
entered into a bond for the money. Captain Whitney, of the *Encounter,*
also had difficulties with victuallers; the Raleghs sold their plate. Sir
John Ferne, of the *Flying Hart,* needed money; £200 was borrowed
from friends. At last, in one way and another, the ships were pulled
together, and Ralegh made a gallant attempt to make the ragged expedition look like a navy.

He published his *Orders,* May 3, "a model of godly, severe, and martial government." Divine Service was to be read twice daily, and God
to be praised with a Psalm when the watch was set. Blasphemers were
to be admonished, and then fined; and, if still obdurate, reported to the
Admiral, for the Scriptures state that *"The Curse shall not depart from
the house of the Swearer,* much less from the Ship of the Swearer."
Search was to be made every night for fires carelessly left burning, "for
there is no danger so inevitable as the Ship's firing, which may also as
well happen by taking of Tobacco between the Decks"—a wise pre-
caution that will come particularly home to us to-day. Landsmen were
to learn the technicalities, so that they could do their full share of work.
Firearms were to be kept clean. The fleet was not to scatter in chase of
ships seen, nor was any ship belonging to a friendly Power to be mo-
lested. There was to be no "feasting or drinking between meals," nor
any drinking of healths at the ship's cost. Anyone who showed cowardice would be disarmed, and made a laborer to fetch and carry for his
comrades. No woman was to be forced, whether Christian or heathen,

on pain of death. "You shall take especial care, when God shall suffer us to land in the Indies, not to eat any fruits unknown; such fruits as you do not find eaten by birds on the tree or beasts under the tree you shall avoid." There was to be no sleeping on the ground, no eating of new flesh until it had been salted, nor of "over-fat hogs or turkeys." There was to be "a great care" not to swim in any river but where Indians were seen swimming, for the rivers were all full of alligators (his negro servant had been taken in his sight by one, on his former voyage). Nothing was to be taken from any Indian by force, or "from thenceforth we shall never be relieved." All Indians were to be treated with courtesy. Every prohibition is followed by a reason for it. Ralegh never demanded obedience without understanding, or issued ferocious menaces against disobedience. His sailors were encouraged to be sentient beings.

On June 12, 1617, seven warships and three pinnaces at last left Plymouth, and were joined by another three ships outside the harbor. Gondomar notified his master, June 26, that "Gualtero Rale" was "indifferently equipped both as regards men and provisions, but with very good guns and munitions of war." Madrid thereupon consulted that renegade, "Count Shirley," as to the best way "to put an end to this enterprise as well as the lives of all who go with Don Gualtero Rauli."[34] He thought the recommendations already given should be simplified, by absolute discretion being given to all Governors to take any steps they thought fit. If this were done, "within two or three years neither Virginia nor the Bermudas nor any rebels or trace of them would be left in the Indies." He was prepared to stake his life on this, and offered to help in person, asking plaintively why his Majesty should give him "such an ample salary," if unwilling to use him to extirpate his fellow-countrymen.

Shirley's letter is dated August 9—the year, with perhaps pardonable confusion in a gentleman who for so many years had cut himself free from ties of time and space, being given as 1613. Ralegh was then still in British waters. The seas had buffeted his ships back into Plymouth; and, when they sailed once more, into Falmouth. At the third attempt

34. Translated and printed by Harlow, *Ralegh's Last Voyage*, p. 141. See also Sir Denison Ross, *Sir Anthony Sherley*, pp. 82 ff. Sir Denison Ross thinks that this "Count Shirley" is Anthony Shirley, not Robert, but his reasoning is not convincing.

a pinnace was sunk off Scilly; the rest of the fleet reached Kinsale harbor, August 3, to stay for recovery and refitting.

Lord Boyle, who had bought Ralegh's Irish estates, gave the Admiral a good time, including falconry, his favorite sport in the days when Ranger of Gillingham Forest. At Ralegh's old home, Lismore, they talked business. All the purchase money for the Irish lands had not been paid when Ralegh was condemned (it was paid later), and Boyle was being troubled by one of Ralegh's former partners, Pyne, whose claims had perhaps been somewhat overlooked at the time of the transfer. Boyle found Ralegh's visit opportune, and Ralegh rather hastily concurred in his view of the dispute. Memory of this recurred to him later, and troubled him; his last official act, before execution, was to ask that he be considered neutral, as witness for neither Boyle nor Pyne.

Boyle gave him a hundred oxen, and many other stores, including beer and a thirty-two gallon cask of whisky, some iron, biscuit and £350 in money. On August 19 the fleet set out again. Off Cape St. Vincent Captain Bailey stopped four French ships, which he wished to seize as belonging to pirates (as was afterwards found to be the case). Ralegh offended him by giving full market value for what was taken—three pipes of oil and a seven-ton pinnace—saying that they had no right to molest such ships.

We have Ralegh's *Journal,* twenty-three large sheets written closely in tiny script—a faded document, most moving to any imaginative reader. It has the absorption of a man talking to himself in deep loneliness. The sharpness of its pictures of natural phenomena—the tempests encountered, the rainbows and the moonlight—is very striking. We see with what freshness they came to the man who from roaming the earth had passed to the long imprisonment of the Tower, driven into candle-dimness after each day's curfew, as year followed year. The record begins on August 29, and ends abruptly, February 13, 1618—a fact which has been considered (no doubt rightly) to date the arrival of Kemys' letter telling that Wat Ralegh had been killed.

Lanzarote, one of the Canary Islands, was reached, September 7. Its people lived in terror of Moorish incursions, and when some of the English landed to stretch their legs they sent down armed men with a flag of truce. Ralegh saw the Governor, who promised to sell him fresh provisions, but was merely playing for time. The Spaniards removed all their goods into the interior, and then defied Ralegh to do his worst, which his captains clamored to be allowed to do. He restrained them, for there was an English trading vessel in the harbor, and "I knew" that reprisals "would offend his Majesty, and the poor English merchant whose goods were in their hands would have been ruined." Having wasted several days, and had three men murdered, Ralegh satisfied himself by merely sending the Governor word that, if he had not been careful not to offend his own King, he would have pulled him and his people out of the town by their ears. It is satisfactory to know that next year the Barbary pirates did this job at Lanzarote.

Bailey considered he now had the excuse for which he had been watching, and sailed back to England with the news that Ralegh had turned pirate, as everyone had known he would. Yet he did not dare actually to allege this, but only that he feared he was going to: "he doth not charge him with any fact committed."[35] George Carew predicted that he would presently be ashamed of this, but "in the meantime there is a doubtful opinion held of Sir Walter, and those that malice him boldly affirm him to be a pirate, which for my part I will never believe."

There was nothing doubtful in the opinion held by the Spanish Ambassador and Ralegh's King. Gondomar wrote,[36] October 22, to Philip III, triumphantly telling that he was asking people "what right they have to complain of pirates, since they let this man sail, who has no other intention." Whatever measures King Philip cared to take "will be fully justified, and many honourable Englishmen will be very glad of it." One of these was Sir John Digby, the possessor of Sherborne and a Privy Councillor; another was Sir Thomas Lake, also a Privy Councillor, but more famous with contemporaries because his wife was known to thrash him (no doubt for good reason). Lake called to express officially "the great sorrow of all good people, at what Ralegh has done. The King promises that he will do whatever we like to remedy and redress . . . so atrocious a wickedness as this." Gondomar repeats that he had over and over again warned King James, and "also Secretary Winwood, who really was Ralegh's supporter," that this kind of thing was bound to happen; he had told them that they would

35. Carew, *Letters to Roe,* p. 129 (October, 1617).
36. Translated and quoted in full in Hume, pp. 329 ff.

force the King of Spain to attach the goods and persons of all English-men resident in his dominions. Bailey had testified that Ralegh was landing and fortifying himself in the Canaries, to lie in wait for the plate fleet. Gondomar urged that the Seville authorities, as if of their own volition, should draw up a formal statement that an English fleet, commissioned by its own King, had raided the Canaries, and that in reprisals they had seized all English property. This would humble James immediately; "but he will be very insolent if it be not done." A fleet should also be sent to capture Ralegh's; the latter was so small that this would be an easy job. Every prisoner should be put to death, except the Admiral and his officers, and these should be brought to Seville for public execution there. England would never properly punish Ralegh, for there were many who thought the silver fleet would be better "in Ralegh's hands than in those of Your Majesty. . . . The King should now be made to feel his responsibility. It is certain that the King does not wish for war." Finally, the Spanish Ambassador inclosed a letter written to him by Sir Thomas Lake, who told him that Viscount Fenton (Ralegh's supplanter as Captain of the Guard) had just written that

His Majesty is very disposed and determined against Ralegh, and will join the King of Spain in ruining him, but he wishes this resolution to be kept secret for some little while, in order that . . . he may keep an eye on the disposition of some of the people here.

Lake humbly begged leave to wait on his Excellency next day.

Ralegh's friends were still powerful enough to manage to get Bailey's crew questioned by James himself, who had to tell the Ambassador that their evidence was contradictory, some saying Ralegh had done nothing amiss, while others affirmed he was a shocking pirate. He added wistfully that he wished there were some reliable news from Spain, "because he was anxious to proclaim Ralegh at once as a traitor, and proceed against his sureties, and against all those who took part in the voyage."

Ralegh meanwhile had gone on to Gomera, the last of the Canaries. Pestilence was ravaging the English, and they must get some good water. At the only landing-place shots greeted them, so he sent back a few demi-culverin balls, as evidence that he could gleek himself upon occasion; and followed them up with a message that he merely wanted water, and promised, "on the faith of a Christian," not to land above thirty mariners, and these without weapons. This was allowed; and he kept rigid order, while holding ten vessels broadside on the town, to blow it to pieces if there were treachery. But there was only mutual kindness. The Governor's lady was half-English; her mother had been a Stafford. It is clear that she was stirred by the visit of her celebrated countryman; and he sent her six pairs of gloves, and half a dozen fine kerchiefs, to which she returned

four great loaves of sugar, a basket of lemons, which I much desired to comfort and refresh our sick men, a basket of oranges, a basket of most delicate grapes, another of pomegranates and figs, which trifles were better welcome to me than 1000 crowns would have been.[37]

Not to be outdone, he replied with "ambergris, an ounce of delicate extract of amber, a great glass of rosewater in high estimation here, a very excellent picture of Mary Magdalen, and a cutwork ruff." At sailing he received more fruit, a basket of fine white bread, two dozen fat hens, and all the water they needed. "And we departed without any offence given or received to the value of a farthing," the Governor giving Ralegh a letter addressed "to Don Diego de Sarmiento, Ambassador in England, witnessing how nobly we had behaved ourselves, and how justly we had dealt with the inhabitants of the island."

It was awkward when news of these doings filtered through to London. Captain John Bailey "had given the cue prematurely."[38] Captain Reeks, for whose sake Ralegh had forborne to answer the outrages he indured at Lanzarote, reached England in December, and told how patient Ralegh had been under provocation, and how thoughtful for others. The Lord Admiral had Bailey summoned before the Privy Council, where his demeanor was unsatisfactory; "he blancheth and deals not ingenuously in his Answer."[39] He was committed to Westminster Gatehouse, and on January 11, 1618, the Council told him he had been undutiful and contemptuous. He spent the next seven weeks in prison, and then apologized abjectly.[40]

37. *Journal.*   38. Edwards, i, 606.
39. *Acts of the Privy Council, Colonial Series,* 1613–1680, p. 16.
40. *Ibid.,* p. 26.

After Gomera the fleet reeled to and fro in tempests, while fever consumed them. Forty-two men died on the *Destiny* alone. When the storms dropped, they came into a nightmare region like that of *The Ancient Mariner*. The seas were burnished copper, as still and as deadly breathless as the Persian Gulf in August; overcrowded and stifled with terrible heat, men continued to die. Thick darkness encompassed them for two whole days, and they steered by light of candles. On October 31 a hurricane swept up. Ralegh rushed on deck, and caught a chill which passed into a burning fever, so that for four weeks he could take no solid food. But for the gift of fruit from the gracious lady he had found at Gomera, "I could not have lived."[41] Yet somehow or other he managed, though thought to be dying, to keep control of everything. At last, on November 11, the South American mainland was sighted; and three days later they sailed into the mouth of the River Caliana (Cayenne). The same day he wrote home to his wife:

SWEETHEART,

I can yet write unto you but with a weak hand, for I have suffered the most violent calenture, for fifteen days, that ever man did, and lived: but God, that gave me a strong heart in all my adversities, hath also now strengthened it in the hell-fire of heat. . . .

We are yet two hundred men;[42] and the rest of our fleet are reasonably strong—strong enough, I hope, to perform what we have undertaken, if the diligent care at London to make our strength known to the Spanish king by his ambassadors have not taught the Spanish king to fortify all the entrances against us. Howsoever, we must make the adventure; and if we perish, it shall be no honour for England, nor gain for his Majesty, to lose, among many other, one hundred as valiant gentlemen as England hath in it.

Of Captain Bailey's base coming from us at the Canaries, see a letter of Kemish's to Mr. Scory; and of the unnatural weather, storms, and rains, and winds, he hath, in the same letter, given a touch. Of the way that hath ever been sailed in fourteen days, now hardly performed in forty days, God, I trust, will give us comfort in that which is to come. . . .

Your son had never so good health, having no distemper, in all the heat under the Line. My servants have escaped, but Crab and my cook; yet all

41. Letter to Lady Ralegh, Nov. 14.   42. That is, on board the *Destiny*.

have had the sickness. Crofts, and March, and the rest are all well. Remember my service to my Lord Carew and Mr. Secretary Winwood.

I wrote not to them, for I can write of nought but miseries yet. Of men of sort, we have lost our Sergeant-major, Captain Pigott; and his lieutenant, Captain Edward Hastings—who would have died at home, for both his liver, spleen and brains were rotten. . . .

And so the sorrowful catalogue continues (listed for one who knew his followers as he did, and mourned with him in "mine inestimable grief"). In it occurs "Kemish of London," no doubt a near relative of that Kemish (Kemys) of Somerset who was his right hand. "By the next, I trust, you shall hear better of us; in God's hands we are, and in Him we trust." Commendations to various friends follow, and "my most devoted and humble service to Her Majesty." Then this pardonable pleasure at finding his name, after all these years, so remembered. "To tell you that I might be here King of the Indians were a vanity; but my name hath still lived among them. Here they feed me with fresh meat, and all that the country affords; all offer to obey me." It must have seemed miraculous to the Indians, to see the great leader again after so many years.

This is our last glimpse of his mind at peace, happy under all its remembrance of sorrows hardly past. He has reached the coasts of Guiana, and has faithful comrades still, and a welcoming simple folk along its rivers. Harry, an Indian chief who had lived two years with him in the Tower, sent provisions, and followed in person with "great plenty of roasted mullets (which were very good meat), great store of plantains and pineapples, with pistachios (or ground-nuts), and divers other sorts of fruits." The pineapples in especial "tempted me exceedingly." But he was too ill to eat them, and kept to his Gomera lemons, which he had preserved in sand. Out of the foul ship, fetid with its many sick, he was carried ashore and placed in a tent, and began to recover. "I began to eat of the pine, which greatly refresht me, and after that I fed on the pork of the country[43] and of the Armadillios, and began to gather a little strength."[44]

Captain Alley was sent home with one ship, to bear the news that Guiana had been reached. The rest of the adventurers landed and

43. Peccaries.   44. *Journal*, November 17, 1617.

shook off their sea miseries, and began the work of overhauling their vessels. Alley reached Portsmouth in February. The Spanish Ambassador avidly collected up his tidings and sent them post-haste to Madrid, exulting in Ralegh's difficulties: his losses by disease, his shortage of food, the currents which made his position one of constant peril. These troubles were grim enough, and were soon widely known. Ralegh's letters, Sir Edward Conway told Carleton, "come charged with misfortunes and tears, and his wife is in great affliction."[45]

Alley and his men talked despondently. But only those who are sure that Ralegh's enemies always kept a rigid path of unhesitating truthfulness will accept Gondomar's farrago of scandal:

Most of the men on board are desperate, and some of them gave letters for their friends in England to the captain who has come hither. But Ralegh took the letters, and, amongst others complaining of his proceedings, he opened one from a gentleman, saying in what misery they were, and that, if things did not improve, they had resolved to throw Ralegh overboard, and return to England. Ralegh attempted to arrest this gentleman, and showed him his own letter; but the rest of them would not allow it. All those who have come hither agree that nothing but entire failure can be expected from Ralegh's voyage, and they think that those who remain with him will either be lost, or, if they are able to get out, will turn pirates.[46]

In the Spanish correspondence flying between the mother-country and the Indies, or from one colonial governor to another, "Gualtero Rale" is never called anything but "pirate." Gondomar had seen to it that this was the accepted color put on his proceedings.

Gondomar's report was not all invention. Ralegh's fleet was full of croakers and traitors, and its discipline was strained continually. He had to keep an eye (like modern commanders) on the stories that imaginative pessimists were sending home. From Indians and from intercepted letters, the English had immediately discovered with what alarm and hatred the Spanish were buzzing. An "armada" was being gathered to block the Orinoco's exit, and they would be choked to death, like wasps in a hole. Officers and men alike clamored that they would go up to the mine, only if the Admiral gave his word that, what-

45. *Calendar of State Papers, Domestic,* 1611–1618, p. 53.
46. Quoted, Hume, p. 343.

ever happened, they would find him waiting when they returned. They
would trust no one else, for valor or wisdom or loyalty. It was a magnificent tribute. Even Gardiner is moved to admiration. "His followers
were ready enough to grumble at him; but when the time of trial
came, they knew well enough what his value was."[47] He promised.
"You shall find me at Puncto Gallo, dead or alive. And if you find not
my ships there, you shall find their ashes. For I will fire with the galleons, if it come to extremity; run will I never." But indeed, he was still
too sick for the terrible journey up Orinoco.

It was settled that the five vessels of shallow enough draught should
sail by the most direct route for the mine, taking 150 sailors and 250
soldiers. Many of the best officers were dead; and St. Leger, the second-
in-command, was as sick as Ralegh himself. Kemys was therefore given
the general oversight, and George Ralegh was "sergeant-major" over
the land forces. Wat Ralegh was a captain. "The crisis of his fortunes
had come," and the Admiral "had to stand aside while the stake upon
which his life and his honour were set was being played for by rough
sailors and beardless boys."[48] The rough sailor was Kemys, ex-Fellow
of Balliol, writer of Latin verse and of a donnishly pedantic English
prose, brocaded with erudite classical quotations. But the description
will pass. His instructions were to justify his and Ralegh's report of the
mine. If the ore proved disappointing,

then you shall bring but a basket or two, to satisfy His Majesty that my
design was not imaginary, but true, though not answerable to His Majesty's
expectations.

If, as rumor said, the river was guarded by enemy reinforcements,
Kemys was to be careful how he landed, lest he let down his country's
well-justified fame. "For I know, a few gentlemen excepted, what a
scum of men you have. And I would not, for all the world, receive a
blow from the Spaniards, to the dishonour of our nation."

After Ralegh's execution the King's Government alleged that at a
preliminary Council of War Ralegh said that San Thomé must be captured before the mine was sought. When an officer objected that this
would be breaking the peace, he replied "audaciously"[49] that he had

47. *History*, iii, 118.   48. *Ibid.*, iii, 121.
49. *Ibid.*, iii, 119.

verbal orders to take the town. He *may* have said something of the sort, with qualifications that his enemies omitted: highly placed people, the King's principal Secretary of State among them, had urged him to oust the Spaniards and "damn the consequences" (which they would look after). Nevertheless he definitely forbade offensive action. If the mine proved worth working, soldiers were to cover the workers; only "if the Spaniards begin to war upon you, you, George Ralegh, are to repel them, and to drive them as far as you can." He had reached Guiana after such pains to keep the peace as no Elizabethan had ever taken before him, and was under no illusions as to the flimsy character of the instrument with which he was blindly thrusting upstream. He knew Kemys' limitations, and how little he could expect from inexperienced youths like his son and nephew. Sending inland every man who by any construction of the words could fairly be termed physically fit (yet, even so, many must have hardly come within the category of "C3" men), he was risking his whole safety on a journey whose perils and privations he vividly remembered. With or without an armed collision, considerable loss was certain; a river like the Orinoco was not going to let invaders by without toll of life and health. Meanwhile he and a handful of sick and convalescent men would wait for their return—all that stood between them and Spain's naval and military resources.

CHAPTER XXIII

The Fight at San Thomé

Whatever else may have been in Ralegh's mind, there was no thought of paying the slightest attention to his promise to the King. S. R. GARDINER.

His object was not colonisation, or trade, or even the discovery of Manoa, but simply to stir up war with Spain. J. A. WILLIAMSON, *English Colonies in Guiana.*

They alone will treat Ralegh's assertions as "evidence of his unblushing effrontery," to whom his accounts are necessarily mendacious, and those of the Court, King James's Court, necessarily honest. W. STEBBING.

KEMYS and his party went forward, December 10, taking a month's provisions. The river ran fiercely, through infinite intricacies and primeval forest that was worse than a fortress armed; and accidents further slowed up their progress.

Ralegh went to the place of agreed rendezvous, Puncto Gallo, on the southwest of Trinidad. Presently, on January 19, 1618, he tried to open up friendly trading with the Spaniards of the island. They received him with musketry, and attacked him intermittently thereafter; their hostility cost him a sailor and a boy. He treated it with contemptuous indifference, while he hunted for medicinal plants and rarities, and generally conducted himself characteristically. There is something sublime in his nonchalance, for he had merely skeleton crews on his ships. Because of the currents, he cruised watchfully, to the north of Trinidad and back again; the *Declaration* after his death, raking up all the mud it could, used this trivial and sensible shifting of position within narrow limits as proof that he did not mind if his forces starved, from returning and not finding him where he promised! Then suddenly, from a canoe of Indians passing by him, he heard a rumor that must have made his heart stand still with wretchedness: the English had stormed a Spanish town, and two of their captains had fallen. He dispatched parties daily for news, and his distress deepened; his *Journal,* telling how closely he questioned any natives he could find, mirrors his agony.

And certainty fell, like a benumbing blow, in Kemys' letter, dated January 8. It reached him February 14. San Thomé had been taken, and Wat Ralegh was dead.

James had assumed that Spain would ultimately concur in his thesis that only effective occupation counted, and that the English might legitimately seek for gold, if they kept away from San Thomé. Kemys did not keep away from San Thomé (why, we shall consider presently), and the inevitable had happened. The King's peace had been broken.

Not by Ralegh, however, nor by Ralegh's men.[1] The ruthless harassing of his tortured mind and body afterwards never shook his testimony on this point. He wrote to Winwood, March 21, 1618. After a brief narration of the horrors of the outward voyage, he proceeds:

Myself having been in the hands of Death, without hope, some six weeks (and not yet able otherwise to move, than as I was carried in a chair), gave order to five small ships to sail for Orenoke, having Captain Kemish for their conductor towards the mine; and in those five ships five companies of fifty, under the command of Captain Parker and Captain North, brothers to the Lord Mounteagle and the Lord North, valiant gentlemen, and of infinite patience for the labour, hunger, and heat which they have endured. My son had the third company; Captain Thornix of Kent the fourth; Captain Chidley, by his lieutenant, the fifth. But, as my Sergeant-major, Captain Pigott, of the Low Countries, died in the former miserable passage, so my lieutenant, Sir Warham St. Leger, lay sick, without hope of life; and the charge conferred on my nephew, George Ralegh, who had also served long with singular commendations in the Low Countries, but by reason of my absence and of Sir Warham's was not so well obeyed as the enterprise required.

As they passed up the river, the Spaniards began the war, and shot at us, both with their ordnance and muskets; whereupon the companies were first to charge them, and soon after beat them out of their town. In the assault whereof, my son (having more desire of honour than of safety) was slain, and with whom, to say the truth, all respect of the world hath taken end in me. And although these five captains had as weak companies as ever followed valiant leaders, yet were there amongst them some 20 or 30 very adventurous gentlemen, and of singular courage; as, of my son's company, Mr. Knevet, Mr. Hamon, Mr. Langworth, Mr. John Plessington, his officers; Sir

1. For Spanish evidence see Hume, *Ralegh*, p. 358.

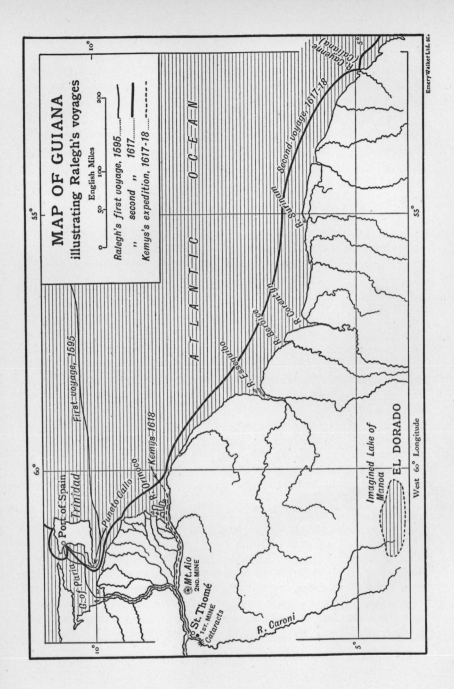

MAP OF GUIANA
illustrating Ralegh's voyages

English Miles

Ralegh's first voyage, 1595
  "   second   "   1617
Kemys's expedition, 1617-18

ATLANTIC OCEAN

First voyage, 1695

Second voyage, 1617-18

R. Surinam

R. Corentin

R. Berbice

R. Essequibo

Kemys-1618

R. Orinoco

Puncto Gallo

Trinidad

Port of Spain

G. of Paria

Mt. Aio
2ND. MINE

St. Thomé
1ST. MINE
Cataracts

R. Caroni

Imagined Lake of
Manoa
EL DORADO

West 60° Longitude

Cayenne
(Oajiana)

EmeryWalker Ltd. sc.

John Hampden, Mr. Simon Leak (corporal of the field); Mr. Hamon's elder brother; Mr. Nicholas, of Buckingham; Mr. Roberts, of Kent; Mr. Perin; Mr. Tresham; Mr. Mullinax; Mr. Winter, and his brother; Mr. Way; Mr. Miles Herbert; Mr. William Herbert; Mr. Bradshaw; Captain Hall, and others.

Sir, I set down the names of these gentlemen, to the end that if his Majesty shall have cause to use their service, it may please you to take knowledge of them for very sufficient men.

This letter has been often taken to be that of an unscrupulous buccaneer, who knows he has broken the law of nations and must fly if he is to escape the gallows. On this interpretation, his commendation of those who have done notable service must be taken as a list of men that he thinks should be hanged at Execution Dock. Another interpretation, however, seems to me possible. It may be the dispatch of a responsible naval and military commander, writing to his immediate civilian chief, both understanding the situation perfectly.

The letter goes on to tell Winwood what he himself did, while waiting for the expedition to return from the mine:

The other five ships stayed at Trinidado, having no other port capable of them near Guiana. The second ship was commanded by my vice-admiral, Captain John Pennington, of whom (to do him right) I must confess that he is one of the sufficientest men for the sea that England hath. The third, by Sir Warham St. Leger, an exceeding valiant and worthy gentleman. The fourth, by Sir John Ferne; and the fifth, by Captain Chidley of Devon. With these five ships I daily attended the Armada of Spain, which, had they set upon us, our force divided—the one half in Orenoque, a hundred and fifty miles from us—we had not only been torn in pieces, but all those in the river had also perished, being of no defence at all for a sea-fight; for we had resolved to have burnt by their sides, and to have died there, had the Armada arrived. But, belike, they stay for us at Marguerita, by which they know we must pass towards the Indies.

For it pleased his Majesty to value us at so little, as to command me, upon my allegiance, to set down under my hand the country, and the very river[2] by which I was to enter it; to set down the number of my men, and burden of my ships; with what ordnance every ship carried; which, being made known to the Spanish ambassador, and by him, in post, sent to the King of Spain, a despatch was made by him and his letters sent from

2. i.e., the branch of the Orinoco estuary.

Madril,[3] before my departure out of the Thames; for his first letter, sent by a bark of advice, was dated the 19th of March, at Madril, which letter I have here enclosed sent your Honour. . . .

Carew Ralegh afterwards said that the English found in San Thomé Ralegh's inventory of his fleet in his own handwriting; that he brought it back, and showed it to the Lords of the Council. The list, at any rate, was found, and with it a copy of Gondomar's report. It is a poor-spirited reader who will not share the indignation and contempt in Ralegh's account. Unfortunately Winwood, under whose orders he was acting, had died in the previous October; the letter fell into the hands of his successor, Sir Robert Naunton, whose career began as a creature of the Earl of Essex and had degenerated into that of a subservient follower of Villiers[4]—into Naunton's hands and the King's. Its sharp scornful sentences must have seemed the worst of treason. Yet it is impossible not to feel pleasure that James read them, and learnt that his baseness was known.

The letter added that Ralegh was reserving other highly interesting documents found in San Thomé, lest they be intercepted. They included a letter, dated May 17, sent by the King of Spain to the "Governor of Guiana, El Dorado [the Spaniards, at any rate, believed in it] and Trinidado": a second letter, from the Bishop of Porto Rico to the same Governor, which had reached the addressee, July 15: and a third letter of the same period, from the head of the Spanish commercial organization in the Indies. The Bishop's letter said that he was sending three hundred soldiers and ten guns to defend Guiana. (According to Carew Ralegh, these three hundred men made all the resistance that was made at San Thomé, a statement probably true.) "Now, sir," Ralegh concludes, "if all that have traded to the Indies since His Majesty's time" (with its enforcement of the rule of no defense against the arrogance which reserved a whole half-globe to one nation)

know it that the Spaniards have flayed alive those poor men which they have taken, being but merchantmen, what death and torment shall we expect, if they conquer us? Certainly, they have hitherto failed grossly, being set out unto them as we were, and discovered, both for our numbers, time, and place!

3. Madrid.
4. He had also married the daughter of Ralegh's old antagonist, Sir Thomas Perrot.

Lastly, to make an apology for not working the mine,—although I know not (his Majesty excepted) whom I am to satisfy so much as myself, having lost my son and my estate in the enterprise—yet it is true that the Spaniards took more care to defend the passages leading unto it than they did their town, which (say the King's instructions) they might easily do, the country being *"aspera et fragosa."*

But to quote the rest of the letter merely anticipates our narrative, to which we must return.

We have seen how firmly Ralegh held his expedition together, and vetoed any return in kind to Spanish hostility, in the voyage out. When his hand was lifted, that sense of responsibility lifted also. Kemys, besides being an irresolute leader (for the habit of a lifetime had been to follow Ralegh), was an incorrigible Elizabethan. Though Spain had begun the fighting, yet he had put himself in the wrong, by going near San Thomé at all. Ralegh, when he returned, upbraided him for his "obstinacy"; and to the end insisted that he had shown himself "a wilful man," a phrase which seems infelicitously astray from the irresolution and nervousness which make up the last act of Kemys' life. That word *wilful* has evaded a host of skilful biographers of Ralegh; I believe we can at last appreciate it. Intrusted with a task which called for almost superhuman delicacy in the performing, Kemys scrapped his plain orders from his chief *and substituted another plan*—which he further bungled by his utter lack of firmness.

The key to the problem of what happened is the question of where Ralegh's (or rather, Kemys') "mine" lay. Queerly enough, no one seems to have seen this until Gardiner saw it, and he saw it, only to force the lock with a wrong key. To some, of course, no problem has ever existed. The "mine" was a mere invention, to get out of the Tower:

If James was dishonest, so was Ralegh; the former accepted a lie, and the latter told it, and the weaker party became the scapegoat of the inevitable exposure.

Ralegh's practical admission of the lie is proved, for

he made no effort to exploit it[5] during the years 1598–1603, a period when

5. i.e., the mine.

he was principally occupied with court and political business, from which he could certainly have freed himself for the necessary few months.[6]

He himself, when he was soon to die, looking back on this period, told Lord Carew that he was then "mad with intricate affairs and want of means." The Queen was slowly dying: Cadiz and the Islands voyage, the Essex rebellion, entertainment of foreign ambassadors and visitors, unofficial attendance at the Privy Council, duties naval and administrative, occupied him: his resources had been strained by five Virginian and four Guianan expeditions, and the last of the Virginian ones *had instructions,* after relieving the neglected settlers in North America, to endeavor to visit Guiana also. As if anticipating his twentieth-century critics, Ralegh told Carew:

That Orenoque itself had, long ere this, 5000 English in it, I assure myself—had not my employment at Cales, the next year after my return from Guiana, and after that our journey to the Islands, hindered me for those two years; after which Tyrone's rebellion made her Majesty unwilling that any great number of ships or men should be taken out of England till that rebellion were ended. And, lastly, her Majesty's death, and my long imprisonment, gave time to the Spaniards to set up a town of stakes, covered with leaves of trees, upon the banks of Orenoque, which they called "St. Thomé."

But all this, no doubt, was only his notorious exaggeration! Had he really tried, "he could certainly have freed himself for the necessary few months" in which to set on a sound political and commercial basis the exploitation of a treasury of precious metals suspected to lie buried behind what he called Orinoco's unexampled "labyrinth of waters" and "confluence of streams and branches"—a chaos dimly visible through the mists of aboriginal obscurity now beginning to lift from a corner of it!

The "lie" explanation has been considered, by the school of thinkers who hold it, to be established beyond controversy by King James's own testimony (and what need can there be of any further witness?) after Ralegh's execution. "His Majesty, in his own princely judgment, gave no belief" to the mine, because, if there had been a mine (and here the *Declaration* flings up the streak of laziness which underlies its sturdy

6. James A. Williamson, *English Colonies in Guiana*, pp. 77–78.

studied mendacity), "the Spaniards, who were so industrious in the chase of treasure, would not have neglected it so long."[7] But popular clamor that England be given an opportunity of expansion and a luckless man one last chance overpersuaded this best and wisest of kings into trusting "Sir Walter Ralegh, invested with such circumstances both of his disposition and fortune." He who "had so enchanted the world" enchanted James also—with stories of a mythical mine and an Orinoco region free from Spaniards!

This explanation, however, has been seen to be grotesque by everyone, whether friendly or unfriendly to Ralegh, who has read the evidence. And all these have assumed that the trouble happened because Kemys came upon San Thomé where he never thought to find it, lower down the river. Roe in his report (1612) mentioned that such a removal was expected; and Gardiner surmised that it was effected about 1611. This left a choice, between supposing that Ralegh knew of the change, but concealed it from James; and supposing that he did not know, and that Kemys was startled when he came on San Thomé, and thrown out of his plans. The former supposition did not take into consideration that Ralegh (so long imprisoned) and Kemys had no more means of knowing of a removal subsequent to Roe's journey than James had—indeed, not anything like as much, for neither of them enjoyed the advantage of continual interviews with the voluble and infuriated Ambassador, whose near kinsman was Governor of Guiana and Trinidad. And the latter supposition, favored by Ralegh's biographers hitherto, has in its support a passage in his *Apology:*

It seems that the Serjeant-Major, Kemys, and the rest were by accident forced to change their first resolution, and that, finding a Spanish town, or, rather, a village, set up twenty miles distance from the place where Antonio Berreo the first Governor taken by me in my first discovery had attempted to plant, viz., some two leagues to the westward of the Mine, they agreed to land and encamp between the mine and the town, which they did not suspect to be so near them as it was. And, meaning to rest themselves on the River side till the next day, they were in the night set upon and charged by the Spaniards.

This implies that Ralegh did not know where San Thomé now was and that the fact (after the sacking) came to him as a shock.

7. King James's *Declaration.*

This passage, however, Mr. Harlow characterizes as a deliberate falsification. And, though he has missed one or two minor pieces which make the puzzle fit together, and has heightened the degree of Ralegh's offense, his discussion has disposed of every explanation held hitherto. Gardiner was the first to see that Ralegh and Kemys had in mind not one mine but *two*. But Mr. Harlow changed the whole problem by showing that San Thomé had *not* been moved (unless by a mile or two), but in 1618 was substantially where Kemys found it in 1596. Moreover, he has brought out the importance of the disaffection among the Spaniards at San Thomé, and of the disaffection among the Indians, of which Ralegh wrote to Lord Carew, saying that the invaders

have not reconciled nor conquered any of the Caciques or natural lords of the country, which Caciques are still in arms against them, as by the Governor's letter to the King of Spain may appear.

The reader will remember that, before San Thomé was founded,[8] Ralegh and Kemys picked up stones a little inland from its site later, and these stones were pronounced auriferous by London assayers. They were therefore convinced that a mine lay here—which I shall refer to hereafter as "the first mine." But Kemys next year (1596) found the beginnings of San Thomé blocking the approaches to it, so he and Ralegh began to take more note of "the second mine"—the one *which neither had visited,* near Mt. Aio. Ralegh had seen the hill from a distance; Kemys had been assured that it was very rich, both by a guide (in 1595) and by his pilot when he came to Guiana without Ralegh. The gold-bearing "specimens" which Ralegh showed in England were necessarily from "the first mine." But it seems unduly severe to frown on this as quibbling or prevarication; the two mines were not more than at most a score of miles apart, and specimens from either would seem similar. All that Ralegh wanted to prove was that Guiana contained gold. He and Kemys firmly believed that their "second mine" was as rich as the first, if not richer; Indian testimony impressed them—reasonably, since their generation was close to the one which had seen Peru's astounding wealth unveiled. But they lived on into a sceptical unexploring age. Ralegh, when he returned from Guiana in 1595, found

8. At the end of 1595. Some think there was a very feeble colony established in 1591 or 1592, and extirpated by Ralegh in 1594.

his mines a theme for Court witticisms, and hostile laughter grew louder still when James became King. He and Kemys concentrated on one mine only, the second mine, being unwilling to make themselves look bigger fools than was necessary, by appearing to suggest that Guiana spawned gold-mines! *One* mine James's Councillors were prepared, grudgingly, to accept as possible, even likely. But to talk of a plurality of mines was to risk having the whole enterprise shut down peremptorily as a fairy tale. As it was, it took many years of persistence, and finally the King's financial desperation, to win permission to go out again. Ralegh and Kemys therefore dropped all mention of the first mine; the second mine—unlocated except vaguely as under Mt. Aio— with the easy sanguineness of men at a distance and willing to endure boundless toil and peril, they were sure they could find. And this second mine explains why Ralegh accepted the impossible terms imposed on him. Since it was twenty miles down the river from San Thomé, he believed that he could open it without going near the Spanish settlement. There would doubtless be hostile acts from prowling Spaniards. But nothing that could be called a breaking of the peace which the King chose to pretend existed. This, I believe, was the secret understanding between Ralegh and James which Mr. Harlow has detected. James sanctioned the opening of a mine *at a distance from San Thomé,* and allowed a force sufficient to repel aggression from San Thomé. Ralegh never anticipated that when the trial came he himself would be far away, incapacitated by deadly sickness.

We must now consider the disaffection among the Spaniards. The Conquistadores were at war among themselves continually. In Guiana, Berreo's own countrymen had tried to eject him by force from San Thomé in 1595, the very year of its founding. Roe in 1611 discovered that the bonds of patriotism had worn so thin that there were Spaniards who wanted to bring in the English—which is another reason why a man of Ralegh's fervent patriotism did not take too seriously the swash-bucklers who had entered Guiana since his annexation of it. They were out for their own hand, not their country's. Occasionally seeking gold in desultory fashion, but too terrified of the Indians to venture far from San Thomé, they made their main business the raising, by forced labor, of tobacco, which they sold to Dutch and English traders, buying European stores in return. Ralegh's Berreo had died in 1597, and his son succeeded him. The illicit traffic which he permitted became known in Spain; and after repeated warnings that he must stop it, he was officially visited in 1612 by the Governor of Venezuela, who found no less than eighteen Dutch and English ships in Orinoco, into which Spanish traders rarely came. San Thomé's forty inhabitants were supplying all this shipping, and both parties were growing wealthy. The visitor absolutely forbade tobacco-growing or tobacco-selling; and Berreo was sent home.

When Ralegh arrived in 1618, the Governor of the Orinoco region was Diego Palomeque de Acuña, a near relation of the Spanish Ambassador in London.[9] He tried to enforce the trading prohibition, with little success, Orinoco's network of waters lying between San Thomé and his headquarters at Trinidad. He went to San Thomé in person, expressly to organize the attack on the English expedition of which King James had provided particulars; and his savage temper and harshness, and his interference with their methods of livelihood, brought the settlers into a mind like that of the New Englanders when their Revolution broke out. Mr. Harlow shows that, if the English had not sacked San Thomé, there would have been one more of the innumerable Spanish revolts. An official inquiry afterwards discovered that there had been a plot to murder the Governor; and he was one of the few Spanish casualties, having been deserted by his own men, if not actually killed by them (as some testified) in the San Thomé fight.

Ralegh, more sober and sensible than either his friends or his enemies, did not expect to get a great store of gold on this first prospecting trip. Kemys' orders, as we have seen, were to throw out a screen against possible attacks, open the mine, and bring enough ore to place their good faith beyond all doubt. Mr. Harlow thinks that he disembarked near San Thomé, instead of lower down—where the way to the "second mine" had been indicated to Kemys, in 1595 and 1596—by Ralegh's orders. I do not think so. A screen of men would have been ineffective, unless close to the actual mine. Nor would Kemys have aroused Ralegh's unforgiving fury, by "obstinacy" and "wilfulness," if he had been carrying out orders, however clumsily. No; Kemys was ordered, I believe, to give San Thomé a wide berth—to land twenty miles short of it, and march the fifteen miles inland to Mt. Aio. I believe

9. On the authority of Captain King (Oldys, p. 514).

that he had instructions to go on to San Thomé, but only *after* he had found the mine, to buy up the tobacco which the settlers persisted in growing. This secondary purpose was very important to Ralegh, who was anxious to repair his broken fortunes, as well as convince the King. He of course knew all about the tobacco traffic, and in his too expansive talking on the way out, told some of his captains that he knew where they could get a store of tobacco that would enrich them. Tobacco was practically all that Kemys got by his wretched folly in sacking San Thomé.

We can now reconstruct Kemys' actions. As he went upstream, when his squadron were moored for the night canoes would come through the darkness, bringing Indians with letters from Spaniards, telling of their unwelcome Governor's presence, and offering to open San Thomé. The narratives make it clear that Kemys' men resented the surprise attack on them later, as if it were a breach of some kind of "gentlemen's agreement." Mr. Harlow may be right also in suggesting that Kemys and Ralegh expected a general Indian rising; it may have entered increasingly into Kemys' calculations, as he began to lose grip on his orders and plans. We can see him, as he neared the mine of which he knew only by native report, pondering the chances of a blood-less surrender of San Thomé itself. He was moving through disquiet-ing proofs of unsuspected Spanish strength (the three hundred auxil-iaries sent by Porto Rico). Captain Alley, when he reached England in February, spread news of the dismay which had resulted from prelimi-nary reconnaissances by Ralegh at the very outset, when he had appar-ently looked into the delta, and "to his greater wonder, found the Span-iards all alongst the river."[10] Thanks to King James's thoughtfulness in providing Madrid with an inventory of Ralegh's fleet, and information of their course, it was no longer possible (Kemys thought) to sail quietly to where they were to disembark, and then march fifteen miles through Guianan forest to find "the second mine." The English may even have been harassed by occasional snipers. A scheme which in Lon-don looked feasible now looked crazed. Had Ralegh been present, his prestige with the tribes would doubtless have found a way. But Kemys (humbly conscious that he was not Ralegh) "funked" the search for the second mine, and remembered that the other mine, the "first mine,"

10. Lovelace to Carleton, February 10, 1618.

that near San Thomé, was a certainty—he had himself handled its auriferous stones, he knew roughly where it lay (or thought he knew). And when emissaries from San Thomé itself (which, so far as he knew, was merely a small cluster of huts—of its growth in size and solidity he was genuinely ignorant) offered to acknowledge English suzerainty and invited him to enter, he saw a way whereby the mine could be worked in perfect security, leaving the authorities in London and Madrid to settle Guiana's political future. He therefore went past the place where he should have disembarked, and on to three miles below San Thomé; and landed (January 2, 1618), having taken more than three weeks to ascend less than two hundred miles of river. The ships went a little higher, and anchored opposite the town, whose garrison opened fire on them from two mortars. The English could have blown the settlement to bits, but did not return the fire.

Kemys now hesitated. He knew that some kind of settlement lay between him and the "first mine," which he was now going to seek. This might involve some fighting. But did it matter so much if it did? When the King sanctioned Ralegh's trying to obtain French auxiliaries to do any fighting that might prove necessary, had he not quite indifferently visualized the possibility, so long as he were left able to clear himself? He would be cleared now, if San Thomé yielded voluntarily. While the English on land debated what to do—whether to assault San Thomé, or wait for its friendly surrender, or try to brush by without hostilities (which the map will show was almost impossible)—the Spaniards settled the question once for all. A clash took place, about one o'clock in the morning. A Spanish patrol of less than a dozen men attacked in the darkness, shouting *"Perros Engleses"* ("English dogs"). "Our men, ready to repose themselves for the night, were assaulted . . . from the skirts of a wood."[11] The surprise caused a brief panic:

the common sort, as weak sort as ever followed valiant leaders, were so amazed as, had not the captains and some other valiant gentlemen made a head and encouraged the rest, they had all been broken and cut to pieces.

There was a recovery, in which Wat Ralegh specially distinguished himself, and it brought the English "to the town almost before themselves knew of it." Here they found the Governor, with thirty-six regu-

11. The Rev. Samuel Jones's narrative (in Spedding's *Letters and Life of Bacon*).

lars (the Porto Ricans) drawn up in defense. A momentary hesitation was ended (according to the *Declaration,* which here we need not doubt)[12] by Captain Ralegh, crying "Come on, my hearts! This is the mine that you must expect! they that look for any other are fools!" Then he attacked practically single-handed, leaving his company of pikes. He fell mortally wounded, and his precipitate gallantry was remembered afterwards, not with gratitude but with resentment. Captain Parker, one of the fiercest of Sir Walter's critics when the expedition was back in England, says angrily: "we lost Captain Ralegh and Captain Cosmor, but Captain Ralegh lost himself with his unadvised daringness . . . which gave him no time to call for mercy to our heavenly father for his sinful life he had led."[13] The young man sent his men on; his last words ("with constant vigour of mind, being in the hands of death") were[14] "Go on! Lord have mercy upon me, and prosper your enterprise!" The garrison, such as it was, decamped, except for the Governor and two captains, who "bravely died" (by English or Spanish hands). The San Thomé inhabitants by dawn were collected on Seiba, a fortified island in the Orinoco, opposite its confluence with the Caroni. Such was the "storming" of San Thomé (so often represented as a ruthless invasion)—an action accomplished accidentally, and costing the victors and the vanquished five dead each, all officers. Kemys buried his slain in the church (probably to prevent desecration), Cosmor and Wat Ralegh before the high altar, with muffled drums beating, pikes trailing, and banners borne before them, to signify that they were captains.[15] Then he waited, perplexed and miserable.

It was almost a week before he dared write to Ralegh. He softened the blow all he could, stressing Wat's valor and making his recklessness their salvation in the confusion caused by the enemy's assault (instead of the cruel embarrassment it actually was).[16] "Had not his extraordinary valour and forwardness . . . led them on, when some began to

12. Though we need not accept its triumphant conclusion that this boyish outcry *proved* that his father was nothing but a filibuster, for "young Mr. Ralegh was likest to know his father's secret."

13. Printed in Schomburgk's *Discoverie of Guiana.*

14. Kemys to Ralegh.

15. Schomburgk, *Discoverie of Guiana,* p. 213.

16. Mr. Harlow detects a hint of this, as frank as was consistent with generous affection, in the words I have italicized.

pause and recoil shamefully, *this action had neither been attempted as it was,* nor performed as it is, with this surviving honour." This tribute to the dead boy is considered by Gardiner[17] (as is almost everything else) very heavy testimony against Sir Walter. Kemys' language "is hardly the language of a man to whom 'this action' was a mere accident." Kemys and George Ralegh, questioned by Ralegh later, as to "why they followed not my last directions for the trial of the mine before the taking of the town," answered that they had meant to do so, although they hardly dared march past San Thomé, "having a garrison of Spaniards between them and their boats." But a dubious phrase in one of Ralegh's distracted letters is twisted into an admission that the English had landed *above* the town; and Ralegh's whole testimony is then shown to be deliberately untruthful, by the report of a Spanish friar[18] ("evidently founded upon the report of an eye-witness"—Ralegh's, apparently, was not). "It must be remembered that Ralegh had every motive to falsify the narrative, so as to make it appear that his men were not the aggressors" (a Spanish friar, of course, could have no motives to write anything but disinterested truth). Ralegh's story "is improbable in itself. It is most unlikely that Kemys should not have discovered where the town was" (Kemys stated very plainly that he *did* know where the town was, and that the English were very unhappy at the prospect of having their communications cut by its inhabitants). However, the argument thoughtfully concludes, "no doubt . . . the English were preparing to attack, but the Spaniards actually struck the first blow." So that is that.[19]

The storming, even if intended (which it was not) was premature,

17. *History,* iii, 123.

18. Printed 1626, from information gathered in 1622.

19. Not altogether, however. Mr. Harlow has printed in full Gardiner's authority, Fray Simon's narrative, and it is now manifest as a piece of fiction. The English attack at nine o'clock at night; whereas not Ralegh but his hostile captains all testify that it was four hours later. One Englishman marches ahead "singing 'Victory'"; and a Spanish leader gives him "such a sword-thrust on the left side of his gullet that he sent the heretic to re-echo his song in Hell." The Spaniards maintain a severe struggle for hours, with a mortar as well as musketry, and chase the enemy all over the town next morning, inflicting terrific losses, mowing their massed attacks down (as our own journalists used to mow the Germans down, in their advance through Belgium). The Governor gets accidentally separated from the rest of his troops, and so killed. San Thomé is deliberately burnt on the morning of its capture, and the tobacco stores with the houses. And so on.

for two of Kemys' five ships had been held up in the difficult channels, and arrived only on the day of the funeral. No man deliberately brings on war with a handful, and out of so small a force as Kemys controlled at best. He now completely lost his head. One night he slipped out secretly with a few men, and brought back some stones which he showed with cheerful triumph. But a refiner tested them, and said they were nothing. He had little standing with his officers, who angrily demanded to be shown the mine immediately, and styled his "delays" "mere illusions" and "himself a mere machiavel."[20] He soon discovered how infinitely more dangerous a Spanish garrison ambushed in the wilderness was, than one boxed up in San Thomé. After a wasted week he went up the Orinoco with two launches, intending to turn into the Caroni and find his mine that way. A sudden volley from the bank killed or wounded eight of the nine men in one of the launches, and their officer with them. Kemys turned back for more soldiers. In San Thomé he found evidence of three mines in the neighborhood, two gold and one silver, which the Spaniards had worked intermittently, when the Indians permitted and they could get negroes. Sometimes he wavered toward trying to work these, keeping his own mine secret until England possessed Guiana politically. His uncertainty as to where his mine was provided great sport in King James's *Declaration* afterwards. The heart of a Guianan jungle, where Kemys had been twice only (over twenty years previously) of course was something as plainly mapped as the streets round Whitehall!

At this juncture George Ralegh showed more resolution. He took boats up the Orinoco for over three hundred miles further (according to Spanish accounts). After his cousin, who was dead, he might be presumed to be likeliest to know his uncle's mind; and he undertook this gallant task, not because he was bothering about gold, but because the country supremely interested him, and because he was thinking of colonization of it. Possibly also, because he was anxious to find out if there were any chance of an Indian rising. But snipers steadily picked the English off, and those in San Thomé were in a state of siege day and night, and subject to constant attacks. The terror of the wilderness, the distance from their base, and—most of all—the papers they found in San Thomé, telling only too clearly how their own King willed their

20. Captain Parker's phrases.

destruction and had done all he could to facilitate it, broke morale down. Whatever happened, James was going to see that the Spaniards had the mine! In his last inexpressibly unhappy interview with his chief, Kemys told him[21]

four reasons which moved him not to open the mine—the one, the death of my son: the second, the weakness of the English, and their impossibilities to work and to be victualled: a third, that it were a folly to discover it for the Spaniards; and the last, both my weakness and my being unpardoned.

They had left the Admiral apparently certain to die, and this correspondence between their King and his brother of Spain emphasized startlingly what they had almost forgotten, that their leader was a man whose neck was in a noose. To reach the mine, their depleted forces, already almost starving and far from all succor, would have to pass through "thick woods," where all eyes were with their enemies.

George Ralegh returned from exploration, and Kemys was forced to go back; he must have gone, as Ralegh to England later, "more like a prisoner than commander."[22] He had lost 250 of his 400 men; he had hung out white flags, inviting the Spaniards to come to a parley, but they preferred to continue their highly successful guerilla warfare. So San Thomé, which the English had held for twenty-nine days, was evacuated and burnt.

As the demoralized remnant dropped down stream, the Indians were aghast at the prospect of abandonment to Spain. A cacique implored them to stay, and swore he could show them an abundant gold mine. Kemys himself, as they went by where he should have landed, instead of near San Thomé, told his captains he could bring them to a mine from there, in two hours' march. The statement was merely a gesture of despair, dying out with itself. Spirits had dropped too far for recovery; the wretched journey continued.

Kemys returned to an appalling interview with his desperate master. It did not come at once. One of the basest of the many basenesses with which the King's *Declaration* after Ralegh's execution is crowded is that it makes special complaint that he received Kemys affectionately and kindly, and supped and dined with him. Kemys the suicide being

21. Ralegh, letter to Lady Ralegh, March 22, 1618.
22. Sanderson, p. 461.

then accepted as a man who knew himself guilty of great bad faith toward the King (else why did he kill himself?), Ralegh was plainly in the plot with him! But there came a time when Ralegh had to question his follower closely about all details. He must have asked him then, "But what were you doing so near San Thomé at all? You did not have to go so close to it, to guard a mine that was twenty miles south of it." And then the whole terrible story of Kemys' "wilfulness" came out—of the lack of self-confidence which had led to the change of plans, and the nervelessness afterwards. We can understand now why Ralegh went out of his mind, and

told him that he had undone me, and wounded my credit with the King past recovery . . . that, seeing my son was lost, I cared not if he had lost an hundred more in opening the mine, so my credit had been saved.

His mind turning over and over upon itself in its agony, Ralegh told him he might answer for himself to the King and State, as to why he had shrunk back when so near to the mine. He utterly rejected a letter Kemys had composed, addressed to Lord Arundel; he would have nothing to do with it, and would give it no sanction. Kemys said he would "wait on me presently, and give me better satisfaction": and went out. Ralegh heard a pistol go off above his head, and sent up to ask who fired it. Kemys himself called out that he had merely been firing his pistol off to clean it. He was later found with a knife through his heart. The pistol had glanced off a rib, so he had taken that surer way out of life.

To those who love Ralegh, his hardness to Kemys, "the one instance in his career of harshness to a follower," is deeply painful. Even more painful is the settled "coldness, which only gnawing despair can explain, not excuse,"[23] with which he refers to him after his death. Yet the story, as I have told it, does (I think) partly excuse it. He had lost his most important witness for the defense—the only witness likely to be any use. It is true that that witness, if Ralegh had really abandoned him to speak for himself, might have ended on the gallows. But, whatever he might say in the agony of Kemys' disclosures, Ralegh would never have really left him to face the consequences of his disobedience alone. As it was, Kemys' suicide must have seemed the most appalling

23. Stebbing, p. 325.

completion of his offense, and, instead of softening his leader's heart, hardened it. If Ralegh moved San Thomé down stream, as Mr. Harlow has shown that he did,[24] it was a lie. But what lie was ever told under more awful pressure? What chance had he of being believed if he told the truth, that Kemys had not looked for the proper mine at all? As it was, the King and Bacon and the rest had great fun over the mine's movable properties. The more you look at Ralegh's situation, the less you will wonder that he preferred to tell just this one falsehood to men who were incapable of listening to the truth except with derision. He had evidence now from San Thomé that the King was more than ready to hang him if he could find the least excuse; for the first time he realized how closely fitted with a halter he had been allowed to sail. If he once said that Kemys had deliberately gone up to San Thomé, instead of where he had been ordered to go, Government would have answered, "So you let your close friend and second-in-command do what you told the King you were not going to do, and what you dared not do yourself! No doubt that was why you stayed behind at Orinoco's mouth, shamming sickness!"

I owe too much to Mr. Harlow's invaluable study, in helping me to reconstruct what I believe is the real story, to want to criticize his criticisms of Ralegh. But I trust he will forgive a protest against building on such lapses as this one an accusation of "an incurable habit of prevarication." Ralegh was not *superstitiose verax*. But what Elizabethan was? How many supremely imaginative men have been? Even so, from a study of his life and writings I am left with the conviction that he was at least as honest as any contemporary, except for such a very occasional phoenix as Sir Thomas Roe. He is crystal clear beside the Cecils and Howards.

In his letter to Winwood, relating these miserable events, Ralegh glanced at the possibility of his getting foreign employment, if his own King utterly disowned him. "What shall become of me now, I know not. I am unpardoned in England, and my poor estate consumed; and

24. Why should it not have been Kemys who originally told Ralegh that San Thomé was not where he had expected to find it? That would explain why Ralegh at first received him so generously; and explain also his fury when the inevitable closer questioning came, and the truth was dragged out. There seems to have been no officer with Kemys who had been up the Orinoco previously.

whether any other Prince or State will give me bread, I know not." Yet he was still far from throwing up the sponge: he had "found many things of importance for discovering the estate and weakness of the Indies, which, if I live, I shall hereafter impart unto your Honour." Even now he did not consider his usefulness as finished. But he dared not write to "my poor wife . . . for renewing the sorrow for her son." He begged Winwood to comfort her, and to give a copy of his letter and inclosures to Lord Carew. Next day (March 22, 1618) he steeled himself to the inevitable, and wrote Lady Ralegh this astonishingly beautiful letter:

I was loth to write, because I knew not how to comfort you: and, God knows, I never knew what sorrow meant till now. All that I can say to you is, that you must obey the will and providence of God; and remember, that the Queen's Majesty bare the loss of Prince Henry with a magnanimous heart, and the Lady Harrington of her only son. Comfort your heart (dearest Bess), I shall sorrow for us both. I shall sorrow the less, because I have not long to sorrow, because not long to live. I refer you to Mr. Secretary Winwood's letter, who will give you a copy of it, if you send for it. Therein you shall know what hath passed. I have written but that letter, for my brains are broken, and it is a torment for me to write, and especially of misery. I have desired Mr. Secretary to give my Lord Carew a copy of his letter. I have cleansed my ship of sick men, and sent them home. I hope God will send us somewhat ere we return. Commend me to all at Lothbury. You shall hear from me, if I live, from the Newfoundland, where I mean to make clean my ships and revictual: for I have tobacco enough to pay for it. The Lord bless and comfort you, that you may bear patiently the death of your valiant son.

That is all the letter, as he intended to write it. But his passion, so long suppressed, breaks out uncontrollably in a *Postscript* more than four times as long, which tells her the whole wretched story.

I protest before the majesty of God, that as Sir Francis Drake and Sir John Hawkins died heartbroken when they failed of their enterprise, I could willingly do the like, did I not contend against sorrow for your sake, in hope to provide somewhat for you, and to comfort and relieve you. If I live to return, resolve yourself, that it is the care for you that hath strengthened my heart. It is true, that Kemish might have gone directly to the mine and meant it. But after my son's death he made them to believe he knew not the way, and excused himself upon the want of water in the river, and, counterfeiting many impediments, left it unfound. When he came back, I told him that he had undone me, and that my credit was lost for ever. . . .

For the rest, there was never poor man so exposed to the slaughter as I was; for, being commanded upon my allegiance to set down, not only the country, but the very river by which I was to enter it, to name my ships, number my men, and my artillery—this was sent by the Spanish ambassador to his master, the King of Spain. The King wrote his letters to all parts of the Indies, especially to the governor Polomeque of Guiana, El Dorado, and Trinidado; on which the first letter bare date the 19th of March, 1617, at Madrid, when I had not yet left the Thames. . . .

He runs over the mass of evidence of treachery which he possesses. Finally,

I live yet, and I have told you why. Whitney, for whom I sold my plate at Plymouth, and to whom I gave more credit and countenance than all the captains of my fleet, ran from me at the Grenadas, and Woolaston with him; so as I am now but five ships, and one of those I have sent home—my flyboat—and in her a pack of idle rascals, which I know will not spare to wound me; but I care not. I am sure there is never a base slave in all the fleet hath taken the pains and care that I have, hath slept so little and travailed so much. My friends will not believe them; and for the rest I care not. God in heaven bless you and strengthen your heart.

Yours

W. Ralegh.

CHAPTER XXIV

The Return

It seems that that golden mine is proved a mere chimera, an imaginary airy mine; and indeed his Majesty had never any other concept of it. But what will not one in captivity (as Sir Walter was) promise to regain his freedom? who would not promise not only mines, but mountains of gold, for liberty? . . . the *Destiny* . . . is like to prove a fatal destiny to him. JAMES HOWELL to Sir James Crofts, June 21, 1618.

You give me an unanswerable reason, the plundering of St. Thomas was an act done beyond the equator, where the articles of peace 'twixt the two kingdoms does not extend. JAMES HOWELL to Carew Ralegh, in 1645.

Ralegh can have had but little hope. He must have known well that his case would not bear the light. S. R. GARDINER.

Why did the Lords of the Council then . . . examine him at the Tower every week, to pick out what they could to condemn him? CAREW RALEGH.

It is an insult to our intelligence to try to persuade us that Ralegh staked his life and fortune, only to take a poor, half-savage town of 130 palm-leaf huts. MARTIN HUME.

AFTER Kemys' suicide despair broke into a mad clamor. Ralegh said he would go back and find the mine, or lay his bones beside his son's. He clung to the hope, almost up to the scaffold itself, that if he could achieve what Kemys had neglected to do, bring even one hundredweight of ore which the assayers could testify as gold-bearing, then his countrymen would send him out again, to occupy Guiana effectively. But no one would go with him. In San Thomé, his men had learnt that every day fresh reinforcements were expected by the Spaniards on the Orinoco.

It was now that to everyone (though to him, with his incorrigibly sanguine temperament, less than any) the implications of his having sailed unpardoned began to loom in their black likelihood. Their King (after finding those letters in San Thomé, they were beginning to know him) would receive them as pirates, whether they were pirates or no. Wilson, the spy set to torment Ralegh, in the Tower later, into some confession on which he could be decently hanged, told James that the prisoner reported that

when we found so ill success at St. Thomé we fell to counsel for taking the Plate fleet or the Mexico fleet, at which said some, "What shall we be better? for, when we come home, the King will have what we have gotten, and we shall be hanged." Then quoth Rawley, "You shall not need to fear that, for I have a French commission, by which it is lawful to take any beyond the Canaries." "And I have another," quoth Sir John Ferne, "and by that we may go lie under Brest or Belle Isle, and with one part thereof satisfy France, and with another part procure our peace with England."

It must be remembered that when Wilson was with Ralegh the latter pretty well understood what was happening, and that he was pouring water into a greedy sponge which his enemies meant to squeeze dry afterwards. Badgered all the time with "Confess, confess, confess—and trust his Majesty's unparalleled clemency!" he was sometimes short and tart, as when he said that "he knew that the more he confessed the sooner he should be hanged," or when he remarked that the King knew all about his dealings with France and that French commissions were all on official record—the expenditure of "a crown" would get the information. As Edwards wrote, as far back as 1868, if his persecutors had cared to follow up this pithy observation, "it would certainly have abridged" the correspondence of James's friends and agents. "Possibly, it might also have abridged some of the epithets—'Liar,' 'Traitor,' and the like—which have been indulged in more recently"[1] (of which there has been a second spate since Edwards' day).

At other times, to Wilson, Ralegh was recklessly cynical, as a man who knows there is no hope for him and feels he may at least have the intellectual pleasure of seeing how far his enemies can be led on into baseness. Thus, he told the King's spy of his talk with Bacon before sailing, and of his asking, "Did you ever know of any that were pirates for millions? They that *risk* for small things are pirates! I could have given £10,000 to this man, £10,000 to such an one, and £600,000 to

1. *Ralegh,* ii, 367.

the King, and several *more* besides." We can still feel the contempt behind that estimate, and see the gestures accompanying it, as Ralegh shovels a fortune to this imaginary recipient and then to that, with colossal wealth to the most grasping of all. That Ralegh would have thought it no sin to seize the Plate Fleet is certain. He differed by a chasm from the Court and Government, assessing Spain's power as what he knew by proof it was, something English seamen need not fear: and he agreed with the English nation outside Court circles, in believing what was the fact, that there was "no peace beyond the Line." It would be strange if the possibility of seizing the treasure fleet had never been discussed; and he admitted quite freely that it was. He so little took the discussion seriously that he never bothered to hide it. Sir John Ferne and Captain Pennington, both of whom deserted him in the last stages of the return, testified of the proposal to the Privy Council. Ralegh merely observed, in answer, that it had been "but discourse at large"—a plan propounded to keep together a fleet threatening to disband in mutiny and misery.

Nor was it more. He had given his word, this man whose word is so freely rejected by men who accept every word of people like James and Villiers and Wilson—had given it to Arundel before sailing, and to his men before they went up the Orinoco—and he had kept it. His actions were steadfast and unshakably loyal, though a host of traitors were round him. Against his actions his critics prefer "discourse at large," which even James and his creatures had to see was no basis for a condemnation:

The entire pile of charges against him, proved, unproved, or disproved, was talk. All began and ended in talk—unless that Bayley captured French boats, and Ralegh redeemed them; that the Lancerota islanders murdered English sailors, and he did not retaliate; that the San Giuseppe Spaniards were aggressors, and he bore it; and that the garrison of San Thomé laid an ambush for his men, to hinder their access to a district which his Sovereign had commissioned him to enter, and were soundly beaten for their hostility.[2]

At a Council of War off Orinoco's mouth, Ralegh's wish to lead a second expedition was overruled. It was decided to go home by way of

2. Stebbing, p. 357.

Newfoundland, partly because he longed to see Virginia. Carew Ralegh says his father meant to winter there, revictual and refurbish, and have another shot at the mine next spring.

Two captains, Whitney and Wollaston, promptly deserted. They had warned the Admiral of death awaiting him in England, and their proposal (which they proceeded to carry into effect) was to capture Spanish ships bound for Europe. When he refused to join them, they simply went (March 6). According to the Rev. Samuel Jones, chaplain of the *Flying Chudleigh*—an office he had undertaken because of "my want of employment at that time in the Church (under which misery I still suffer)"—Ralegh gave his captains permission to go wherever each chose. The bitterness of Ralegh's reference to Whitney's betrayal rules this out as mistaken. Mr. Jones's letter is a butler-like and bewildered effusion ("My pen hath not been used to so high employment, but my prayers shall never cease to mount the throne of Grace, that God will be pleased to make you all glorious in Heaven whom he hath made so gracious and honourable on earth," he tells the Privy Council). It brings together a lot of tittle-tattle and reports of what this and that captain said. But it is entirely honest, and its testimony is not all against his unfortunate Admiral. He describes a mutiny off Newfoundland, when some clamored to get home at once and others, whose normal profession was piracy, "would stay at sea till they had gotten something."

Sir Walter to appease this tumult came up from his cabin, read his Majesty's commission to them, and lastly put it to their own choice by most voices what they should do; giving, as I hear, his own voice at that time very confidently for England.

That ever he slighted the King's Majesty, or his authority, by any words of his, or suffered it to be done, or that it ever was done by anyone in the fleet, I never yet heard.

It is doubtful (I think) if the Rev. Samuel Jones ever got any preferment for his letter of dubious effectiveness toward the anti-Ralegh case.

Meanwhile, long before England received any word of how things had gone, King James had gladdened the Spanish Ambassador (March, 1618) with renewed assurance that Ralegh should be handed over if guilty of the least hostility. King Philip's secretary congratulated Gondomar (April 19, 1618):

Your Excellency's account of the conference you had with the King, about Ralegh's affair, pleased our people here so much, that they found it almost too sweet. It really seemed too much that Ralegh should be sent hither, but with the choice your Excellency has left open to have the punishment inflicted there, they say there never was such an Ambassador before!

On May 3 Madrid had the news of San Thomé. It reached London ten days later. Gondomar forced an interview on James; being told the King was occupied, he said he wished to say one word only. He was allowed to burst in and say it, three times—*"Piratas! piratas! piratas!"*[3] Then he went out as dramatically as he had entered, leaving the King terrified.

Gondomar's instructions were, "Exaggerate as much as you can Ralegh's guilt, and try to get the King to make a great demonstration." "Make him understand," wrote Philip, "that if a proper remedy be not forthcoming at once, we shall make reprisals and seize English property in Spain." He saw James constantly, and spoke "high language." On May 23 Captain Roger North, sent ahead by Ralegh with the letter for Winwood, reached England. He came full of rage against Kemys, and against Ralegh. After the latter had in public

seemed to expostulate with Kemys in sharp and round fashion, within few days Kemys was private with him in his cabin as he had wont to be before, and did eat and drink with Sir W. Ralegh without any words of expostulation.

Asked whether he thought Ralegh knew Guiana was inhabited by Spaniards, he said, certainly he did, for he had heard him say before they left London, that he knew "where they might make a saving voyage in tobacco." Also, on the voyage Ralegh (that too free speaker!), cheerfully canvassing possibilities, had said that "if they could surprise the Town in the river Orenoque, they might be sure of forty thousand pounds weight or worth" (North did not seem certain which, and indeed, his whole evidence is a mass of incoherently jumbled memory, of

3. James Howell, *Epistolae Ho-Elianae*, p. 23.

which his suggestion that a long period elapsed between Kemys' return and his suicide is but one example) "of tobacco." It has not been noticed how every detail of Ralegh's failure seemed intended by an evil fate to exasperate James; even the fact that the only spoil of importance was—tobacco. He had sent Ralegh, the arch-devil who introduced and popularized that detestable vice of smoking, to fetch gold; instead, he brought a vast quantity of the drug which the King detested.

North's stories were the spark that made the flare. On June 9, James drew up, and on June 11 issued, a Proclamation, brief and violent. It got in two affectionate references to "our dear Brother the King of Spain"; and "by a common fame" condemned Ralegh for having "maliciously broken and infringed the peace," and expressed utter detestation of "insolence and excesses" and "scandalous and enormous outrages."

The words "by a common fame" left a loophole of escape. But that loophole was closed by the King's private actions. Gondomar by letters and interviews drove him to a pitch of cowardice which could not have been justified if London were in the hands of a Spanish army. He reiterated his pledge "on his faith, his hand, and his word," to hand Ralegh over for punishment, as soon as the formality of a judicial examination was over. Digby and Villiers were sent to assure the Ambassador that "Ralegh's friends and all England shall not save him from the gallows." Gondomar replied with letters in which he assumed, as known and proved, that Ralegh had sacked promiscuously in the Canaries and devastated Guiana, burning more churches and cites than had ever existed there.

The Ambassador was about to revisit Madrid on leave, and James was anxious to have his good offices to complete the marriage negotiations. The two had repeated farewell interviews. At one, James lamented that his subjects were not as generous to him as the Spaniards were to Philip III. Then he checked himself, and said, six times over, "Of course I know that, so far as greatness is concerned, the King of Spain is greater than all the rest of us Christian kings put together." Alternately soothing and hectoring, Gondomar "applied the medicines I thought necessary. To persons who do not know the constitution of the patient, they may seem violent." The treatment was entirely successful. To Carew, who knelt pleading that Ralegh be given a fair show, James admitted that his pledges forbade this. "As good hang him as deliver him to the King of Spain; and one of these two I must, if the case be as Gondomar has represented."

To make all sure, Gondomar postponed his going, telling Villiers (now Marquis of Buckingham) that he wished to see the Privy Council. Villiers ordered the Council, in the King's name, to wait on His Excellency at whatever time he fixed. His Excellency fixed five o'clock on June 29. The Council were all present, and came out humbly to meet him, the Archbishop of Canterbury "saying that they had suspended all their business, and willingly attended my orders." Gondomar talked at large about Ralegh's "murders, sackings, pillage and burnings, such as never were seen even in time of war"; reminded them of their King's promise to surrender him and his captains to be publicly hanged in Spain; emphasized his own King's forbearance in not chastising them himself when they first sailed; and threatened them with what would happen in future. Finally, "I took off my hat, calmly said that I had stated my case, and then re-covered myself." The Councillors whispered together, after which Bacon expressed regret for what had happened and drew attention to the steps King James had already taken. Ralegh (who had reached Plymouth) had been arrested. He trusted that "these little accidents" would not upset the friendship of Spain and England. Possibly the Archbishop felt that Bacon had gone a little too far in suavity, for he followed with a few remarks which Gondomar dealt with very firmly:

Doffing his bonnet and bowing his head low, he very artfully said that Ralegh's proceedings certainly deserved exemplary punishment, and he did not know what answer Ralegh would make, thus trying to indicate that it would be necessary to hear him. I stopped him at once, and said that it was no part of my business to act as Ralegh's prosecutor, and this was not a case for tribunals at all. . . . I made the most of San Thomé and Guiana, as many people here think that it is licit to make captures and conquests south of the line, and that San Thomé belonged to England.[4]

Two days later, James held a special Council on Sunday. Ralegh's friends were in a minority, but managed to make a protest against having been treated by Gondomar as no King or Council had ever been

4. Translated and quoted by Hume, p. 371.

treated by an Ambassador. They confronted James with his promise to hand Ralegh over to Spain, as if England were a dependent country. James was uncomfortable, until Villiers defended him, saying that Gondomar had been in the right all along, and "was very courteous and kind not to be more violent than he was." James then recovered himself, and shambled about, asking questions which he answered himself. Was he to stick up for such a scoundrel as Ralegh? What would the world think if he did that? He was going to show his courage, not in warring against Spain, but in warring against traitors who promised him gold and so persuaded him to allow the Guiana voyage. He was renowned for being a man of his word, and that word had been passed, and should be kept. All he wanted to know was, Did his Council think Ralegh should be punished or not? Browbeaten, most of them said he should, Carew and Ralegh's other friends keeping silent. James then remarked that they were unanimous; so, if he ever heard of any of them, publicly or privately, speaking for Ralegh, he should consider them traitors.

Next day James promised Gondomar that the Council should meet on Wednesday to settle Ralegh's condemnation; and on Thursday the Ambassador should say his good-byes. Gondomar made the King of England deliriously happy by promising him an autograph letter of thanks from the greatest King in Christendom; and went off to write the most exultant of all his exultant letters. Amenities were not finished, however; a messenger with a basket of cherries from the King overtook him. Gondomar was eating them as he strode along, when gusts of laughter came from a window. He looked up—to see His Majesty—who had staged this jolly piece of humor and must have been unusually active to get to the place where he could bring it off—overcome with amusement. "Whaur's your Spanish gravity now? An Ambassador! eating cherries oot of a basket!"

On July 4 the Council met, as James promised. But the enormity of the proposal to send Ralegh and his companions to be hanged in Madrid shocked all except Villiers. Carew led the opposition; and even Bacon, though agreeing that Spain must be given every satisfaction, maintained that the talk of sending an Englishman to public execution in a foreign country was talk—as Ralegh would have put it, "discourse at large"—and that no one could expect it to be taken literally. James insisted that he had no choice, and burst away in anger.

Next day saw the farewell meeting of the two friends. The Ambassador, in sham complaisance, said he would act as a mere "secretary," and write to his own master just what James dictated. This was the kind of nursery game that the King enjoyed, and he entered into it with eagerness. But his letter, deeply humble though it was, Gondomar rejected, and demanded one yet more abject. He must explicitly say he was sending Ralegh, his ships and captains, to Spain. "It was not much to ask him, surely, to send ten or a dozen of the worst of them to be executed in Spain." James hesitated, but gave way before Gondomar's threats, and promised to send Ralegh and others, in the *Destiny,* to Spain. He called in Digby and Villiers, both of them pensioners of Spain, and in their presence made the promise required. Gondomar said he must have the promise in writing. James instructed Villiers to write a letter, which even to-day makes an English heart sink with shame. It promised that, after a summary legal process, "which cannot be altogether avoided," Ralegh should be sent to Spain, unless the King of Spain himself decided otherwise. This letter Gondomar took with him to Madrid.

Meanwhile, what of Ralegh? His men were frightened; and some of them had pasts which were still valid reason to dread the law. He was unable to refit in Virginia, because he learnt that over a hundred, including some of the gentlemen, intended to join the colony there. He kept the seas therefore, and, probably about June 21, reached Plymouth. Three of his ships, all he had left, had stayed in Kinsale harbor; their crews felt safer in Ireland. Rumor alleged that on reaching Plymouth he was given a message from Lord Carew, "Get you gone." This Ralegh afterwards denied. The advice nevertheless would have been sound. Most people marvelled that he did not quietly slip over to France until the peril had blown over—if necessary, until the death of King James. His critics blame him severely for *thinking* of flight; at the time, men jeered because he was such a fool as *not* to fly. "The world wonders extremely that so great a wise man as Sir Walter Ralegh would return to cast himself upon so inevitable a Rock, as I fear he will; and much more, that such choice Men, and so great a power of ships, should all come home and do nothing."[5] That is, why on earth had they come back meekly to destruction, instead of wasting Spanish commerce? Everyone knew there was always war between Spain and England in the Indies!

Ill and bewildered, Ralegh when he reached England did not at first take the sacking of San Thomé very seriously. He knew there would be unpleasantness over it. But he was armed with letters which showed how long beforehand the Spaniards had prepared to assail the English, invariably (as he pointed out) referring to the latter succinctly as "the enemy." His men were not the first to break the peace, nor had he himself been present. His own mind was perfectly clear, that any Spaniards in Guiana were interlopers in a country whose natural possessors had deliberately come under English protection and whose position as subjects entitled to protection had been accepted by his own Government consistently. The Spaniards had not lost half a dozen men, though they had inflicted very heavy casualties on the English. All this was quite apart from the larger consideration, that the Spaniards without hesitation attacked any Englishman they found in the Indies, and killed any they could, by battle or by execution afterwards. As he wrote to Lord Carew,

> That by landing in Guiana there can be any breach of peace, I think it, under favour, impossible. To break peace where there is no peace, it cannot be.

He goes on to cite proofs of the kind of peace Spain kept with Englishmen, beginning with the letters found in San Thomé, that ordered the Governor to put to death any Spaniards or Indians who traded *"con los Engleses enemigos."* He was in a strong position here. Facts and public opinion were with him: *"no peace beyond the line* was a belief so riveted in the opinion of all, as he could not have been indicted anew."[6]

I have quoted Gardiner's opinion that Ralegh "must have known well that his case would not bear the light." Few cases, however, have ever borne more light. In the end, the King's (not Ralegh's) case was abandoned, and Ralegh died on a judgment which had practically faded out of men's minds. Out of the whole surprising tissue of com-

5. James Howell to Sir James Crofts, June 21, 1618 (*Epistolae Ho-Elianae*, p. 25).
6. Osborne, *Traditional Memoirs*, p. 18.

ments by Gardiner, this one must be held to bear the bell for obtuse irrelevance.

Lady Ralegh met her husband, and he heard of the King's proclamation. His one faithful captain, King, in a *Narrative* which he wrote after the execution, says that Ralegh decided to surrender and face the music. On June 12 the Lord Admiral had ordered Sir Lewis Stukeley, Vice-Admiral of Devon, to arrest him. But Stukeley was in no hurry. Ralegh had at least a fortnight in which he could have escaped, and friends were urging him to do so. In the *Declaration* it is stated that when he arrived "it was easy to discern with what good will he came thither, by his immediate attempt to escape from thence . . . he had a purpose to fly, and escape from his first arrival into England." It is a deliberate lie. He might have pleaded that he had fulfilled his pledges to Pembroke and Arundel; and might have now gone to France. He did nothing of the sort. He waited, and quietly put his case (June 21) in Lord Carew's hands, as a Privy Councillor:[7]

I am sure your Lordship will have received a copy of my letter sent by Captain North to Secretary Winwood, of whose death I learnt with great sorrow in Ireland. By that letter your Lordship will have learnt the reasons given by Kemys for not discovering the mine, which could have been done, notwithstanding his obstinacy, by means of a cacique of the country, an old acquaintance of mine, if the companies had remained in the river two days longer; inasmuch as the cacique offered pledges to do it. The servant of the Governor, moreover, who is now with me, could have led them to two gold mines, not two leagues distant from the town, as well as to a silver mine at not more than three harquebus shots distant; and I will make this truth manifest, when my health allows me to go to London. As for the rest, if Whitney and Wollaston had not gone from me at the Granadas, and the rest had not abandoned me in distress at Meny, as if they had some great enterprise in hand, I would have returned from Newfoundland to Guiana, and would have died there or fulfilled my undertaking. When I saw that they had deserted me, I resolved to steer for Newfoundland to take in water and clean the ship, which resolution we had all adopted six days before they left me. But when I was approaching the land I was informed that a hundred of my men had determined to go ashore and join the English settlement, or at all events to do so when the ship was hauled up on the beach for cleaning.

7. Gondomar obtained a copy of this, and sent it in Spanish to his King. Major Hume discovered it at Seville, retranslated it, and prints it in his *Ralegh,* pp. 383 ff.

Their intention was to board the best ship of the English flotilla at night, and plunder all the friends of England and the Portuguese in these ports, knowing that I should not be able to get the other ship in order under ten or twelve days, and that I had no men to navigate the ship I had left. I thereupon called all the company together, and told them that I had no wish to accuse any of them, but as I had been told by some of the masters of the violence they intended to commit, I had decided to return without taking in any fresh provisions, rather than enter the Newfoundland ports to the great prejudice of my countrymen and of the fishermen of other nations therein. I then ordered the master to set sail for England; and the conspirators at once discovered themselves, resisting and shouting that they would rather die than return to England. They were the greater number, and some of the best men I had, some of them being gentlemen. All the harquebuses and swords were in the magazine with the armour for cleaning, and the mutineers had taken possession of them, refusing me admission into the magazine. Finding myself in this peril, I gave way to the mutiny for a time, and during that night I set my course again for Newfoundland, treating in the meanwhile with some of the leaders to abandon the mutiny. With great difficulty I persuaded them to do so, on condition that I would not return to England until I had obtained their pardon for some past piracies; and they demanded my oath. At last we all agreed to sail for Ireland, and they chose the port of Killibeg in the north, a miserable place frequented by desperate corsairs. If I had not consented to this, they would have murdered me and those who stood by me, or else I should have killed most of them, in which case, as the mutineers were the best of my men, I should have been unable to bring the ship into port. It is true that when they had calmed down, they said that if I returned home poor I should be despised, and I answered that even if I were a beggar I would not be a robber, or do anything base, nor would I abuse the confidence and commission of the King. Before doing that, I would choose, not poverty alone, but death itself. I am well aware that with my ship (than which in the world there is no better) I could have enriched myself by £100,000 in the space of three months, and could have collected a company which would have impeded the traffic of Europe. But those who have told the King that I had feigned the mine, and really intended to turn corsair, are now mistaken in their malice, for, after failing in the discovery of the mine (by the fault of another), and after having lost my estate and my son and being without pardon for myself or security for my life, I have held it all as nought, and offer myself to His Majesty to do with me as he will, without making any terms. As for the mutineers, the greater number of them fled from me in Ireland, and some have been persuaded to surrender themselves to His Majesty's mercy. Since my arrival in Ireland I have been alarmed not a little, and have been told that I have fallen into the grave displeasure of His Majesty for having taken a town in Guiana which was in the possession of Spaniards. When they heard this, my men were so afraid of being hanged that they were on the point of making me sail away again by force. With regard to taking the town, although I gave no authority for it to be done, it was impossible to avoid, because, when the English were landed at night to ensure Kemys's passage, the Spaniards attacked them with the intention of destroying them, killing several and wounding many. Our companies thereupon pursued them, and found themselves inside the town before they knew it. It was at the entrance of the town that my son was killed, and when the men saw him dead they became so enraged that, if the King of Spain himself had been there in person, they would have shown him but little respect. With regard to the burning of the houses near the Plaza, they were obliged to do it, because the people had made loopholes in the walls, and kept up so hot a fire through them, that in a quarter of an hour they would have killed them all.

And, my Lord: that Guiana be Spanish territory can never be acknowledged, for I myself took possession of it for the Queen of England, by virtue of a cession of all the native chiefs of the country. His Majesty knows this to be true, as is proved by the concession granted by him under the great seal of England to Harcourt. Henri IV also, considering it a country not justly in possession of any Christian prince, gave it to Montbariot, whose lieutenant held it until, for want of support, he was captured and taken prisoner to Lisbon. Your Lordship has a copy of the patent that Count Maurice and the States gave to some Flemings, who held part of the country for ten years, until by reason of negligence they were surprised and defeated by the Spaniards. They are now again beginning to settle there. It will thus be seen that His Majesty, in any case, has a better right and title than anyone. I heard in Ireland that my enemies have declared that my intention was to turn corsair and fly; but, at the manifest peril of my life, I have brought myself and my ship to England. I have suffered as many miseries as it was possible for me to suffer, which I could not have endured if God had not given me strength. If His Majesty wishes that I should suffer even more, let God's will be done; for even death itself shall not make me turn thief or vagabond, nor will I ever betray the noble courtesy of the several gentlemen who gave sureties for me.

Your poor kinsman,

W. RALEGH.

Postscript. I beg you will excuse me to my lords for not writing to them, because want of sleep for fear of being surprised in my cabin at night has almost deprived me of my sight, and some return of the pleurisy which I had in the Tower has so weakened my hand that I cannot hold the pen.

This letter makes his attitude clear. I have printed it in full because, without its context of close unexcited narrative, his scorn for the suggestion that he would let down his sureties might seem rhetoric. It cannot seem rhetoric to anyone who reads it in its place. The letter shows how little he expected the trivial affray at San Thomé to be taken as a capital matter. Mr. Harlow thinks, I believe rightly, that the sentence expressing his surprised alarm at hearing of the King's anger "is one of several pieces of evidence that support the view that there was an understanding between Ralegh and his Sovereign."[8] For the rest, the letter shows that amid unexampled difficulties Ralegh had carried himself tactfully and bravely; and his justified pride in the ship he had built, and confidence in the prowess it could have shown in action, is very attractive.

With this letter he inclosed a second, written hurriedly because he had just got hold of the charges his absconding captains were making against him. The two letters together must have seemed to him to make his defense lawyer-proof, even under James; and to the end they did make it lawyer-proof. If his view-point about Guiana was mistaken, the King should have overruled it. Instead, he had sanctioned it, because gold was what he needed most.

And gold was to be the reason why he sacrificed Ralegh. Guiana was one string of his financial bow: a second, parliamentary grants from his people, he was determined not to use: the third was a matrimonial string. While Ralegh was sailing to the Orinoco, Digby was sent to Madrid (September, 1617), to finish off the royal romance with a marriage contract. His instructions were admirably explicit:

As marriage-portion you are to demand two millions of crowns, and you are not to descend lower than so many crowns as may make the sum of £500,000, besides the jewels.

He was back, May, 1618; and, since Guiana had failed to replenish the

8. *Ralegh's Last Voyage,* p. 248. What that understanding exactly was, I have discussed in the preceding chapter.

treasury, the thrifty King determined to use Ralegh's head as an asset, and sell it to make sure of that "£500,000, besides the jewels."

Stukeley arrested Ralegh at last, when he and his wife and Captain King had already started for London. He had no formal warrant, but Ralegh did not dispute his authority, observing pleasantly that he himself "had saved" Stukeley "the labour, and done it to his hands."[9] They all turned back to Plymouth, where Stukeley, still in no hurry, settled down to sell the *Destiny's* stores and cargo, mainly tobacco. As when Ralegh was arrested, fifteen years earlier, it had been assumed that he was already condemned; and the first pounce was made on his goods.

Stukeley was a nephew of Sir Richard Grenville, and had received kindness from Ralegh. Ralegh might therefore suppose him friendly disposed, a supposition borne out by the little attention Stukeley gave to securing him. If he had fled to France, as he was given every chance of doing, he would have relieved the Government of a heavy embarrassment. They could have blackened his name before the nation, and have been cleared of the King's dastardly promise to send him to Spain for execution. He had been given clear warning that he was going to be prosecuted in London, and he had the San Thomé letters telling him (if his memory of his trial, fifteen years ago, did not tell him) exactly what kind of justice he was going to get. Captain King and Lady Ralegh after long pleading persuaded him to run; and King arranged with two French captains to come close inshore. Then, one night, he and Ralegh rowed out. But when they had practically reached the ship, Ralegh insisted on returning. Once more he was persuaded to row out, and once more returned.[10] He did not believe the case was black against him; in fact, he did not believe there was any case at all. There would be bluster and brutality; and after that, release. What was it he could be accused of? The King had sent him to Guiana.

While Ralegh was resisting his wife's entreaties to escape, the King's Government stiffened, and ordered that he be brought up to London:

We command you, upon your allegiance, that, all delays set apart, you do safely and speedily bring hither the person of Sir Walter Ralegh, to answer

9. i.e., had arrested himself before Stukeley came. Captain King's *Narrative*, quoted in Oldys, *Life of Ralegh* (Ralegh's *Works*, i, 519).

10. Captain King observes that he had four nights in which he might have escaped.

before us such matters as shall be objected against him in his Majesty's behalf.[11]

Stukeley closed his tobacco sales, and the party set off, July 25. A French doctor of sorts, called Manourie, who had settled in Devon, brought the regular warrant of arrest; and Stukeley, remembering Ralegh's inveterate interest in scientists and science, used him as a spy. Manourie talked chemistry assiduously, and won the prisoner's easy confidence. He reported that the news of the order to repair to London wrung out of Ralegh the exclamation: "God's wounds! Is it possible that my fortune should thus return upon me again?" And that, as they rode by Sherborne, he said "All this was mine, and it was taken from me unjustly!" "I wish we were all safe in Paris!" sighed Captain King, his mind busy on thoughts of escape. He often expressed his sorrow that Ralegh had not carried through his half-formed resolution at Plymouth; and Ralegh admitted that he had only himself to thank that he had not escaped. In all this Manourie joined with a sly mendacity that he greatly enjoyed while practicing it. He trusted King's (and Ralegh's) forebodings of what would happen in London would prove mistaken. He was very sympathetic, very anxious to be serviceable.

As they were going from Sherborne to Salisbury, downhill, Ralegh dismounted, and he and Manourie walked together. Ralegh asked if he could make up some vomits and purgatives, partly because he wanted to get poisons ("bad humours") out of his system, but mainly because he wanted an excuse for sufficient delay to write a formal defense. If he did not do it now, as soon as he reached London he would be rushed to the scaffold, and his friends would have neither time nor material to do anything effective for him. When they reached Salisbury, he counterfeited dizziness; as Stukeley was helping him to his bedroom, he struck his head against a post and staggered. Next day, after sending Lady Ralegh and Captain King and most of his own servants ahead to London, he rolled about naked on the rushes in his room, as if in pain and demented. Stukeley sent Manourie to him, and Ralegh demanded the vomit he had asked for. It was given, and he swallowed it, and with its help he got his body into contractions and convulsions. Stukeley and others in alarm chafed and rubbed him; and, according to Manourie

11. *Acts of the Privy Council, Colonial Series*, 1613–1680, pp. 19–30.

(whose account need not be rejected *in toto,* though it needs a big handful of the salt of scepticism and selection), Ralegh afterwards laughed about their energy, saying "that he had well exercised Sir Lewis Stukeley, and taught him to be a physician."[12] It was not enough for Ralegh's purpose, however. He got Manourie to smear him with a skin-irritant that made him come out in blotches. Terror of contagion took hold on Stukeley. Hardly daring on his own responsibility to detain the prisoner at Salisbury, and afraid to bring a leper before the Lords of the Privy Council (who were not anxious to leave the world sooner than they could help), he went to Lancelot Andrewes, Bishop of Winchester. Andrewes sent two doctors, who called in a third, "a bachelor in physic." Ralegh's malady completely baffled them, but they signed a bulletin that it was extremely serious and the patient must not be moved. So far Manourie kept Ralegh's secret, "seeing Sir Walter Ralegh had not yet told him that he meant to fly out of England, but that it was only to gain time to satisfy His Majesty." He signed the report with his fellow-Thebans, and assisted Ralegh to some still more revolting proofs of his terrible condition. If we may trust the *Declaration,* Ralegh found the alarm of his physicians and keeper very amusing. He "was very jocund and merry with Manourie."

The trick when found out did Ralegh's case no good, and we may allow it as some mitigation of Stukeley's black treachery to a kinsman, that he felt that kinsman had made an uncommon ass of him. The trick also, not unnaturally, prejudices readers of to-day against Ralegh. He himself, however, never saw any reason for the least shame about it. He justified it by the example of heroes of Holy Writ, notably David, who had pretended to be ill or mad when they wanted to gain time. His own knowledge of his position was that it was desperate; if he was going to be squeamish, he would be at the gallows before he had time to speak. His only chance was to get his defense written before he reached London. Manourie therefore smuggled in "a leg of mutton and three loaves" from the White Hart Inn at Salisbury; and Ralegh, eating ravenously, wrote savagely all night, toiling more "terribly" than ever before in even his hard-driven life. The result was his "Apology," which bears witness in every line of the furious pressure under which it was composed. It is superb in rushing indignation and strength, from

12. King James's *Declaration.*

the very first sentences, which take the field like a man with sword unsheathed and brandished:

> If the ill success of this enterprise of mine had been without example, I should have needed a large discourse, and many arguments for my justification. But if the vain attempts of the greatest Princes of Europe . . . have miscarried, then it is not so strange that myself, being but a private man, and drawing after me the chains and fetters wherewith I had been thirteen years tied in the Tower, being unpardoned and in disgrace with my Sovereign King, have by other men's errors failed in the attempt I undertook.

He proceeds to swift citation of instance after instance of failure in enterprises undertaken with every advantage, yet failure condoned:

> For if that Charles the Fifth returned with unexampled losses (I will not say dishonour) from Algier in Africa, If King Sebastian. . . . If the invincible fleet and force of Spain in '88. . . . If Sir Francis Drake, Sir John Hawkins . . . men for their experience and valour as eminent as England had any. . . . If afterwards they were repulsed with 59 Negroes. . . . If Sir John Norris . . .

if all these men had encountered disaster, what wonder that he, with volunteers who had very few of them seen either sea-service or fighting, and ("some forty gentlemen excepted") "the very scum of the world,"

> I say, what wonder is it that I have failed, where I could neither be present myself, nor had any of the Commanders whom I might trust living, or in state to supply my place?

The rest traverses ground that by now must be familiar to the reader, and supports Ralegh's argument with documentary evidence and exultant conviction. He will not for one minute bate England's claim to Guiana, or his own claim that Guiana is magnificently worth having, not for gold only but for its wealth of other commodities, and its agricultural potentialities. Nor is his continual assertion that Guiana was England's, because its "natural lords" had ceded it, the absurdity we are tempted to think it. It is true that no civilized country has ever bothered about "rights" possessed or granted by a land's aboriginal inhabitants. But Ralegh thought it important that these aboriginals wanted English rule and had continued in an agony of revolt (revolt, moreover, that had been uniquely successful) against Spanish rule. He had ejected Spain from Guiana's borders when Spain and England were regularly at war; and the whole question of the Indies, as too controversial, had been tacitly omitted when Spain and England made peace in 1604. Guiana was England's by conquest, voluntary cession, and England's acceptance; and his honor was involved in keeping his promise, made so long ago, and renewed during his imprisonment, with such power and opportunity as had been granted him.

Mr. Milton Waldman seems to be the only biographer who has remarked on the extraordinary fact that Ralegh's own Government, long after his death, vindicated him in every particular. The long-standing controversy as to boundaries, between Great Britain and Venezuela (a State which came into existence, 1814, almost exactly two centuries after Kemys led his disastrous expedition up the Orinoco), was forced to a settlement when the United States demanded its submission to their arbitrament. The territories that were in dispute were mainly these which Ralegh had claimed, described by the Marquis of Salisbury as "large tracts . . . which from their auriferous nature are known to be of almost untold value."[13] It is perhaps poetic justice that the country which had repudiated Ralegh lost the Orinoco (and much else besides). But it was at least established that he "was not even trespassing."[14] The San Thomé garrison had been from the beginning in a state of siege. The Spaniards gave the vast region of Guiana a wide berth, and Ralegh's claim that it was an uninhabited region was literally true, so far as Europeans were concerned, and was indorsed after exhaustive examination:

It seemeth to me that this empire is reserved for Her Majesty and the English nation, by reason of the hard success which all these and other Spaniards found in attempting the same.[15]

There is no perfect evidence of the existence before 1648 of any other Spanish settlement than San Thomé in the region between the Orinoco and the Essequibo, or of any other than a temporary occupation of any position in that region.[16]

13. November 26, 1895 (U.S.A. Commission on Boundary, etc., *Report,* vii, 434).
14. Waldman, *Ralegh,* p. 224.   15. Ralegh, *Discoverie of Guiana.*
16. U.S.A. Commission, *Report,* i, 45.

Ralegh had sought an empty country for colonization, and had found it. It remained empty, except for San Thomé; and the Orinoco was almost entirely a Dutch and English river.

Ralegh's defense, in conclusion, strides forward until it has set him face to face with his real antagonist, Gondomar:

> But in truth the Spanish Ambassador hath complained against me to no other end than to prevent any Complaint against the Spaniards. . . . My men . . . were invaded and slain before any violence was offered to any of the Spaniards; and I hope the Ambassador does not esteem us for so wretched and miserable a people, as to offer our throats to their swords without any manner of resistance. Howsoever, I have said it already, and I will say it again, that if Guiana be not our sovereign's, the working of a mine there and the taking of a Town there had been equally perilous to me. For by doing the one I had robbed the King of Spain and been a thief, and by the other a disturber and breaker of the Peace.

James, who was on a "progress," arrived in Salisbury while Ralegh was there. Ralegh probably hoped to see him. But the King angrily ordered Stukeley to delay no longer. On August 1, accordingly, the journey was resumed. All the way, Manourie afterwards testified, the prisoner was speaking unlovingly of His Gracious Majesty. This Ralegh denied in a testamentary note written the night before execution, adding, "If I had not loved and honoured the King truly, and trusted in his goodness somewhat too much, I had not suffered death." We may accept that, for the reason that Ralegh, so reckless in many things, was consistently careful in his speaking of King James. This was not merely watchful wisdom. He regarded the King as God's Anointed.

The *Declaration*, which incorporates this charge of disaffected speech concerning His Majesty, says also that Ralegh tried to bribe Manourie and Stukeley to help him to escape. He may have done so, although Manourie afterwards accused Stukeley of bribing *him*, to take advantage of Ralegh's confidence not only to entrap Ralegh but to invent plausible speeches and proposals by Ralegh, which would prove useful to the prosecution. These are the speeches and proposals which Bacon worked into the *Declaration*, touching them up with all his skill.

While Ralegh was at Brentford, before he reached London, he was surprised by a visit from La Chesnée, the interpreter attached to the

French Embassy in London. La Chesnée told him that his master, the Resident[17] Le Clerc, wished to see him. The Government discovered this visit, and laid a snare, hoping that Ralegh might be beguiled into something that might be called treason. In the end they failed, for Bacon had to admit to the King (October 18), "In what concerns the French, Sir Walter Ralegh was rather passive than active." Captain King had already made arrangements[18] for Ralegh's escape by boat from London. Ralegh, therefore, was not at first anxious to accept French help.

In London Ralegh was allowed to live in his own house, not in prison, with a deceptive appearance of freedom. When he arrived, August 7, Lady Ralegh had everything ready. Stukeley, as responsible for him, was present also, but so were his friends and personal servants. The French offers now became definite. They were believed at the time to have been made at the Queen's instance; she wanted her son to marry a French princess, and the French Government wanted to prevent an Anglo-Spanish alliance. Something may also be put down, perhaps, to Ralegh's friends in France. It is not very easy to see what he could do for French interests. On the other hand, one interest, not always forgotten as unimportant, is the preservation of honor, and the French had been originally approached about helping him when he went to Guiana. Not Ralegh only, the King also had thought of an Anglo-French expedition; and Ralegh to the scaffold maintained that his French plottings had had official sanction. French help had not materialized, his agents had betrayed him; but chivalrous minds do not dismiss responsibility easily, and there may have been people in the French Government, though not in King James's Court, who were troubled about a man brought low, in part because he had been led to trust them. No one seems to have considered this possibility, or to have thought of connecting up the French offer of asylum now with the former negotiations. However this may be, the fact remains that Ralegh was offered means of escape and an honorable reception when he had escaped. Le Clerc and Chesnée called together on the evening of August 9, and talked openly in a room full of Ralegh's friends. Ralegh thanked them, and was very grateful for their kindness, but said he

17. Or what to-day we call an Ambassador (the title I have used for Gondomar).
18. They had been immediately betrayed, so were useless, as we shall see.

preferred to escape in an English boat. After they had gone, he consulted Stukeley, who had special orders from James to sham affection toward his kinsman and did it successfully. Stukeley warmly entered into his plans, and said he himself would fly with him.

That night Ralegh disguised himself with a false beard, and with King, Stukeley, and two others, entered a boat on the Thames. They were followed by Sir William St. John (Buckingham's half-brother) and William Herbert, a connection of Stukeley, in another boat. Stukeley, in high spirits, asked triumphantly "whether thus far he had not distinguished himself an honest man." Captain King, more observant than Ralegh, significantly "hoped he would continue so."[19] The second boat's movements presently excited Ralegh's suspicions, whereupon Stukeley swore at him, and at himself for a fool in risking everything with such a timorous colleague. Ralegh idiotically asked the boatmen if they would continue to row on, even if commanded to stop in the King's name; he gave them a flimsy story of a quarrel with the Spanish Ambassador. They not unnaturally grew alarmed, and for a time ceased to row, and lost the tide. There was no longer any chance of reaching Gravesend before morning. Ralegh, now convinced he had been betrayed, ordered them to row back; they were still being shadowed by the other, more powerful boat. They returned, and landed at Greenwich, where Ralegh, still trusting Stukeley, gave him from his pocket some things of value, and Stukeley embraced him lovingly. Then, as Sir William St. John's crew landed silently, and came up, "Sir Judas" (as he was ever after called) arrested King and Ralegh, and handed them over. At last understanding, Ralegh said merely, "Sir Lewis, these actions will not turn out to your credit." He had more to say to King, whom he begged to accept the rôle of an accomplice in Stukeley's plot. King refused. They were parted at the Tower gates, where Ralegh tried to comfort his friend. "You need be in fear of no danger. It is I only that am the mark shot at." Dawn saw him once more entering the Tower as a prisoner, while King was wretched at being held back. "I was forced to take my leave of him. I left him to His tuition, with whom, I doubt not, his soul resteth."

At the Tower they stripped Ralegh of his personal possessions. They included: £50 in gold; a Guiana idol of gold and copper; a jacinth

19. Captain King's *Narrative* (Oldys, Ralegh's *Works*, i, 434).

seal, set in gold, with a Neptune cut in it, and Guiana ore tied to it; a lodestone, in a scarlet purse; a silver ancient seal of his own arms; a Symson stone, set in gold; a wedge of 22 carats gold, and a "stobb" of coarser gold; a chain of gold, with diamond sparks; a diamond ring of nine sparks; a naval officer's gold whistle, set with small diamonds; sixty-three gold buttons, with diamond sparks; an ounce of ambergris; a diamond ring, given him by the late Queen; a sprig jewel, set with soft stones "and a made ruby" in the midst; a gold-cased miniature set with diamonds; charts of Guiana and Nova Regnia, and of the river Orinoco and of Panama; a description of the Orinoco; a sample of Guiana ore, with a description of it; five silver-mine samples. It reads like the contents of the pockets of some super-schoolboy.

"Even in our ashes live our wonted fires"; and Ralegh, ruined and wasted, was Ralegh still, with his passion for jewels and bright things. The ambergris and spleen stone (as of supposed medicinal value) were left with him. The miniature he insisted on leaving with the friendly Tower Lieutenant, Sir Allen Apsley, and refused to give it into Sir Lewis Stukeley's hands. We can guess whose picture it held.

CHAPTER XXV

The Lords of the Council

To sacrifice to a concealed enemy of England the life of the only man in the nation who had a high reputation for valour and military experience was regarded as meanness and indiscretion. DAVID HUME, *History of England.*

His sins had brought with them their own punishment, a punishment which did not tarry because he was so utterly unconscious of them. S. R. GARDINER, *History of England,* 1603–1642.

Justice was indeed blind, blindly executing one and the same person upon one and the same condemnation, for things contradictory; for Sir W. R. was condemned for being a friend to the Spaniard, and lost his life for being their utter enemy. CAREW RALEGH.

RALEGH'S attempt to escape, like his shamming sickness at Salisbury, gave his enemies a handle. He was conscious of great guilt, it was argued, seeking to evade the King's notorious clemency. As to the attempt to escape, even Stebbing finds it deplorable:

It was a foolish business. Nothing, except success, could have been more woful than all its features and its failure. If the attempt be blamed as rebellion against the law, the correctness of the condemnation cannot be disputed. Ralegh derived no right to fly from the injustice of his treatment.[1]

Perhaps not.

King James, that valiant swashbuckler, thought Ralegh blamable on other grounds. He was "wont to say that he was a coward to be so taken and conveyed, for else he might easily have made his escape from so slight a guard."[2] We may take that opinion in many ways, and find it always illuminating: as showing the ethical level of King James's thinking; as indicating how little seriously he took Ralegh's alleged treason and that, even at this late hour, he would not have been sorry

1. *Ralegh,* p. 340.   2. Aubrey, *Brief Lives,* ii, 188.

if he had escaped, and if the Spanish Ambassador's demands could have vanished in a dust and smoke of fury about the fugitive's "breach of faith and loyalty"; as illustrating the extraordinary fashion in which Ralegh has been censured, *whatever he did*—for indignity because he thought of escape and for cowardice because he did not carry it through.

Ralegh himself, to Sir Thomas Wilson in the Tower afterwards, said that he had tried to escape, because residence in France might have given him a chance to do service against Spain. Everyone who had followed intelligently the imbecile protracted business of intrigue for a marriage with the Infanta—which had become the main part of what passed with James for statesmanship—knew that Madrid by now had the latter's measure absolutely and was playing with him. The negotiations were bound to fail, as Spain intended they should, when they had served their purpose. A spell of anti-Spanish resentment would succeed; and Ralegh, who, like everyone else, never doubted his abilities, was sure he would then be wanted.

He meant to sojourn in France, he said, only until "the Queen should have made means for his pardon and recalling."[3] Those who criticize him for his last-minute thoughts of flight forget what pressure was put on him, and not merely by his wife and Captain King. The Queen told Lady Carew that "she had rather have the match with Madam Chrestienne than the Spanish lady with all her gold."

Pity was stirring for him everywhere, except in the King and his friends. Before James Montagu, Bishop of Winchester, died, July, 1618, he tried to draw on the merit he had acquired by editing and translating the King's Latin works, by a deathbed request:

when the King came to visit him, a little before his death, he told the King that he never looked to see His Majesty more, and therefore said he would beg but one thing of him, and that was the life of an old gentleman that had incurred His Majesty's grievous indignation, yet because he had been so dearly respected of that noble Queen his predecessor and many other respects, that he would save his life and let him die in peace and not come to untimely death. By this he meant Sir W. R.

3. Cf. Captain King's testimony: "he sought to absent himself till the Spanish fury was over. Yet, as he always said, No misery should make him disloyal to his King or country" (Oldys, p. 521).

Men remembered this prayer of a dying man; and they were remembering other things, which presently were never to be out of their minds.

The Queen remained staunch as ever. Even the French Government's anxiety to prevent an Anglo-Spanish alliance would hardly have made them willing to help Ralegh to escape, had she not instigated the attempt. He made no secret of what was notorious—her efforts on his behalf. Lady Ralegh was "great with her," and Wilson, when Ralegh hinted that he had friends, wrote disrespectfully to Secretary Naunton: "I perceived he meant that great lady *de qua non fas est verba facere.*" That great lady, however, was herself dying, her mind disordered[4] and miserable; her husband had long since abandoned all pretense of caring for her, and rarely (and never willingly) saw her. Nevertheless, she responded, when Ralegh in touching verses approached her:

> O had Truth power, the guiltless could not fall,
>   Malice win glory, or Revenge triùmph.
> But Truth, alone, cannot encounter all!
>
> Mercy is fled to God, which Mercy made;
>   Compassion dead; Faith turned to Policy.
> Friends know not those who sit in Sorrow's shade.
>
> For what we sometimes were, we are no more;
>   Fortune hath changed our shape, and Destiny
> Defaced the very form we had before.
>
> All love, and all desert of former times,
>   Malice hath covered from my Sovereign's eyes,
> And largely laid abroad supposèd crimes. . . .
>
> If I have sold my duty, sold my faith,
>   To strangers—which was only due to one—
> Nothing I should esteem so dear as death.
>
> But if both God and Time shall make you know
>   That I, your humblest vassal, am opprest,
> Then cast your eyes on undeservèd woe!

4. Cf. the Rev. Robert Tounson's cheery information, at the conclusion to his letter about Ralegh's death: "The King and Prince, thanks be to God, are very well. The Queen is still at Hampton Court, and crazy, they say."

> That I and mine may never mourn the miss
> Of Her we had, but praise our living Queen
> Who brings us equal, if not greater bliss.

The sick woman had pleaded repeatedly the good she had obtained in her long illness from Ralegh's "recipes."[5] But she knew that her husband despised her appeals; she humiliated herself therefore to write to Villiers the note "which survives to show at once her own generous impulsiveness of heart, and the foul state of things at Whitehall":[6]

MY KIND DOGGE,

If I have any power or creditt with you, I pray you let me have a trial of it at this time in dealing sincerely and earnestly with the King that Sir Valter Raleigh's life may not be called in question. . . .[7]

King and minion, however, were both alike pledged to find a way to present Ralegh's head on a charger to Spain.

The story of the moral rack on which Ralegh was stretched before death is indescribably loathsome. Naunton set over him as keeper one of Robert Cecil's basest spies—Sir Thomas Wilson. But Ralegh, though "at all times a free speaker, whose words could seldom be regarded as an infallible key to his settled purposes,"[8] was at last awake to the treachery with which he was surrounded. Wilson's report to his employer, and to the King who had been "pleased to confront the cunning of this arch-imposter with my simplicity and plainness," show that contempt for his persecutors had put iron into Ralegh's conversation. He spoke recklessly enough on occasion, but it was a recklessness born of perception of the impossibility of his being convicted. Wilson complains that he can wring nothing deadly out of him, though he plies him continually with panegyrics of the King's mercy to those who trust him, and with Scriptural examples. Some of the latter were unfortunate, as when he compared James and King David, and extolled the latter for refusing to execute Shimei and other great offenders. Yes, said

5. Chamberlain to Carleton, Oct. 31 (*Calendar of State Papers, Domestic,* 1611–1618, p. 588).

6. Edwards, i, 687.   7. Cayley, *Life of Raleigh,* ii, 164.

8. Gardiner, *History,* iii, 142. The remark is meant to convict Ralegh of being baser than the men who slew him: "in the inquiry for truth" (which, it seems, was what they were prosecuting) "they got no assistance from Raleigh."

Ralegh drily; he merely left strict orders to his son to settle with them. If Ralegh seemed in a communicative mood, Wilson proudly told Naunton, he himself would specially stay and sup with him, would give him affection and sympathy, and try to cheer him with reminder of Bible worthies who had passed through a cloud and been brought to peace and happiness at last. He wrote of him in a manner calculated to commend himself to the pious King:

Since my last letter yesterday morning I have been wholly busied in removing this man to a safer and higher lodging, which though it seems nearer heaven, yet is there no means of escape from thence for him to any place but Hell. . . . The things he seems to make most recking of are his chemical stuffs, amongst which there are so many spirits of things, that I think there is none wanting that ever I heard of, unless it be the spirit of God . . .

Here hath your Majesty something more ex farragine istius veteratoris, but what it is I know not. I only told him that your Majesty said that what he had before written was something, but that you looked for more and knew he could say more.

In talking with "this Arch-hypocrite," Wilson promised mercy in exchange for frankness, so regularly and explicitly that at last he brought down on himself a sharp rebuke from Naunton that he was not to pledge the King *in definite words*. If at this late time of day Ralegh had been fooled by this kind of double-dealing, he would have deserved to be fooled by it. But he was not. He was merely weary of it.

It is strange that men, even in what they knew was strictly confidential correspondence, should so have written down their utter baseness as Wilson and Naunton and James did. They "were engaged in a common conspiracy that the first, without directly pledging the royal word to a grant of grace, should coax from Ralegh a confession by allowing him to fancy a pledge had been given."[9] Forget them a moment, for a very different picture. From the underkeeper, Edward Wilson, Ralegh received kindness, which he acknowledges in a note of introduction of him to his wife:

I am sick and weak. This honest gentleman, Mr. Edward Wilson, is my

9. Stebbing, p. 349.

keeper, and takes much pain with me. My swollen side keeps me in perpetual pain and unrest. God comfort us!

Yours
W. R.

Lady Ralegh's answer has survived upon the same sheet of paper:

I am sorry to hear amongst many discomforts that your health is so ill. 'Tis merely sorrow and grief that with wind hath gathered into your side. I hope your health and comforts will mend and mend us for God. I am glad to hear you have the company and comfort of so good a keeper. I was something dismayed, at the first, that you had no servant of your own left you, but I hear this Knight's[10] servants are very necessary. God requite his courtesies; and God, in mercy, look on us.

Yours
E. RALEGH.

When Ralegh had been near Sherborne, Sir John Digby, his successor there, had called to assure him that, though he was not to be caught (evidently) by the common law, they were going to get him under the civil law and the admiralty laws (those sanctioning summary treatment of pirates). These hopes, however, slowly vanished from his enemies. Only over the San Thomé incident had they even colorable pretext for the "piracy" line of prosecution. This, to historians, has seemed a satisfactory pretext. It did not seem one to James and his lawyers. There was never any suggestion of prosecuting any of the men or officers actually engaged in the taking of San Thomé. Why? And, though the piracy charge was pressed against Ralegh, and some of his captains gave the kind of evidence that the Government wanted, it amounted to nothing much. Common sense, as well as a growing common opinion, told the Court they could not execute one man only for San Thomé, and that man one who had been deadly sick at a great distance.

Wilson's knavery found out little. Nor was anything obtained from the interception of the Raleghs' letters to each other, or the imprisonment of Lady Ralegh[11] from August 20 to October 15. James could not be bothered even to read her letters when they were brought to him, as was admitted by Naunton, when he excused himself for not sending on

10. Sir Allen Apsley, Lieutenant of the Tower.   11. In her own house in London.

to James an unusually loquacious effusion from Wilson: "I forbear to send your long letter to the King, who would not read over the Lady's, being glutted and cloyed with business."

So, in early September, the Government in desperation decided to take up another line of attack—Ralegh's attempt to escape by French assistance. The inquiry proved disappointing. La Chesnée was arrested, and rigorously and often examined. Then the Ambassador himself, Le Clerc, was told to attend the Privy Council. Neither he nor La Chesnée would admit anything whatsoever. The Council therefore suspended Le Clerc from his duties, because

it now most manifestly appeared—howsoever he denied the same—that he had held secret intelligence and conference, to the notable disservice of His Majesty and the Estate, with one of His Majesty's subjects attainted of High Treason and since detected of other heinous crimes.

France received this action with indignation mingled with derision. In reprisal, the English Ambassador in France was also suspended from diplomatic functions, and sent racing about for audience, which when he got it was audience flung contemptuously at him. "I did not know whether they held me as a free man or as a prisoner." France, standing by its representatives, asserted that Ralegh was in captivity "rather to content the Spaniards, than for any interest of His Majesty," and had been "so much at liberty that he could be visited in his own house." "Our Agent is not even so much as accused to have had any intention to do His Majesty any disservice—but only to draw service for him, against the Spaniard. This is no such great matter, but might well have been dissembled in a Public Minister." Nor was this unsatisfactory result much supplemented by what Lady Carew reported. The Privy Council made her, as the wife of Ralegh's trusted kinsman, investigate the French business, questioning the accused and also Le Clerc. She asked the latter, "But what would Sir Walter have *done,* if he had escaped to France?" "Why, he would have eaten and drunk and had a good time" (*"Il mangera, il boyera, if fera bien"*). She must have enjoyed passing on this valuable information.

The net result of this intensive search, which included close and constant questioning of Ralegh's captains and others, was a "medley"[12]

12. Stebbing, p. 352.

which Gardiner "marshalled" in a notorious essay.[13] It satisfied him; but it profoundly disappointed King James. Bacon frankly advised that the French charges be dropped; they amounted to nothing, and in any case Ralegh was little to blame in them. (The real offender, so far as there was an offense, was the Queen, as I have said.)

Then, on September 24, Ralegh, unable to stand his badgerings any longer, exploded in a letter to the King, which it is good, even now, to remember that that monarch received. It must have burst in on the pestilential praises by which he was surrounded, like a bomb from treason's pit, and have shocked him suitably:

May it please YOUR MOST EXCELLENT MAJESTY,

If in my journey outward bound I had of my men murthered at the Islands, and spared to take revenge; if I did discharge some Spanish barks taken, without spoil; if I forbare all parts of the Spanish Indies, wherein I might have taken twenty of their towns on the sea-coast, and did only follow the enterprise which I undertook, for Guiana—where without any direction from me, a Spanish village was burnt, which was newly set up within three miles of the mine—by Your Majesty's favour I find no reason why the Spanish Ambassador should complain of me. If it were lawful for the Spanish to murther 26 Englishmen, tying them back to back, and then to cut their throats, when they had traded with them a whole month and came to them on the land without so much as one sword amongst them all —and that it may not be lawful for Your Majesty's subjects, being forced by them, to repel force by force—we may justly say, "O miserable English!"

If Parker and Mutam took Campeach and other places in the Honduraes, seated in the heart of the Spanish Indies; burnt towns, killed the Spaniards; and had nothing said to them at their return—and that my self forbore to look into the Indies, because I would not offend I may as justly say, "O miserable Sir Walter Ralegh!"

If I had[14] spent my poor estate, lost my son, suffered, by sickness and otherwise, a world of miseries; if I had resisted with the manifest hazard of my life the rebels and spoils which my companies would have made; if when I was poor I could have made myself rich; if when I had gotten my liberty, which all men and Nature itself doth so much prize, I voluntarily lost it; if when I was master of my life I rendered it again; if, though I

13. "The Case against Sir Walter Ralegh," *Fortnightly Review,* Vol. vii; new series, Vol. i.

14. The letter bears marks of its writer's confusion of mind, in its confusion of tenses.

might elsewhere have sold my ships and goods, and put five or six thousand pounds in my purse, I have brought her into England—I beseech Your Majesty to believe that all this I have done because it should not be said to Your Majesty that Your Majesty had given liberty and trust to a man whose end was but the recovery of his liberty, and who had betrayed Your Majesty's trust.

My mutineers told me that if I returned for England I should be undone. But I believed more in Your Majesty's goodness than in their arguments. Sure I am, that I am the first who, being free and able to enrich myself, hath embraced poverty. And as sure I am that my example shall make me the last. But Your Majesty's wisdom and goodness I have made my judges, who have ever been, and shall ever remain,

Your Majesty's most humble vassal,

W. RAULEIGH.

There was not much to help the Government here! Balked in its prosecution, "floundering about in futile efforts," it

imputed its embarrassment to his cunning. He had no intention to deceive, or even to abstain from promoting a revelation of the truth, which he did not fear. Simply he and it were radically at cross purposes. They were mutually unintelligible. The sincerity of his ardour for the attainment of a footing in Guiana is unquestionable. . . . Guiana was the means he had finally and deliberately chosen to inflame the English people and Crown with an inextinguishable ambition for the creation of an American empire. He did not much mind how the national imagination was kindled, provided that it caught fire.[15]

On August 11, the day after he reëntered the Tower, his real condemnation had taken place—not in London but in Madrid, where Philip III's Council of State formally decided it would be better to have him executed in England. The Spanish Legation received this decision, October 15, and passed their master's orders on to James. The execution was to be at once. That settled the matter. Ralegh had endured the torment of repeated interrogation, and stuck to his opinions: Guiana was English; the King had so recognized it; the King had sent him there; and the Spaniards kept no sort of peace in the Indies. Carleton was told, October 3, that the King wished to "hang Ralegh, but it

15. Stebbing, p. 356.

cannot handsomely be done, and he is likely to live out his days."
Handsomely or otherwise, it had definitely got to be done now, however.

So, on October 18, Sir Edward Coke drew up the Commissioners'
recommendations to the King[16] as to "what form and manner of proceeding against Sir Walter Ralegh might best stand with Your Majesty's justice and honour," "according to your commandment given
unto us." This document suggested a choice of two courses. Both rested
on the fact that Ralegh was "civilly dead," having been "attainted of
high treason (which is the highest and last work of law)." One proposed that, together with the warrant for his execution, should be issued a printed narrative of his "late crimes and offences." The narrative was humbly recommended ("albeit Your Majesty is not bound to
give an account of your actions in these cases to any but only to God
alone"), because of "the great effluxion of time since his attainder" and
"his employment by Your Majesty's commission" and because "his late
crimes and offences are not yet publicly known." The other course suggested was an informal hearing (not a trial) before the Privy Council
and principal judges, with a selected sprinkling of nobility and gentry
to listen. Ralegh should first be reminded that he had no legal existence, and then should be denounced by His Majesty's Learned Counsel
(Sir Edward Coke and others) for his numerous recent sins; after his
answer had been heard, he was to be sent back to prison and death.
The whole transaction should be dignified by "a solemn act of Council," "with a memorial of the whole presence."

The King unhesitatingly rejected the latter course. "We think it not
fit, because it would make him too popular, as was found by experi-
ment at the arraignment at Winchester, where by his wit he turned the
hatred of men into compassion for him. Also, it were too great honour
to him to have that course to be taken against one of his state, which
we have observed never to have been used not toward persons of great
quality, as namely the Countess of Shrewsbury and some such." James
had "therefore thought of a middle course." Ralegh should be brought
before the group who had hitherto examined him; should be confronted with the witnesses against him and told of his crimes; and,
after he had answered, be told he must die. James approved, however,

16. It is generally considered to have been mainly Bacon's work.

the suggestion of a printed *Declaration* afterwards, and he ordered that an execution warrant be "sent down for us to sign."

On October 22 Ralegh was accordingly brought before his judges, and first the Attorney-General, Sir Henry Yelverton, ran over his "faults before his going this last voyage," "faults committed in his voyage," "faults committed since," observing wittily that all these had been "committed against him who hath saved his life by his grace." Never had "subject been so obliged to his sovereign," as this man had been, who, "not weary of his fault but of his restraint of liberty," had promised to produce a gold mine. The rest of the charges were afterwards worked up by Bacon in the *Declaration,* and have all at one time or another come before us. For example, "he abandoned and put in danger all his company" (because he had temporarily shifted his quarters in the currents at Orinoco's mouth); he carried no miners or mining instruments; all he wanted was a piece of ore "to blear the King's eyes." With this went all the unproved talk of what Sir Walter had said at this time and what someone reported he had said at another time. It was an intolerable deal of sack and hardly a pennyworth of bread.

The Solicitor-General, Sir Thomas Coventry, followed with what was more to the purpose as regards Ralegh's behavior, but very little toward the legal purpose of convicting him of a capital crime. He concentrated on his pitiful efforts or half-efforts at flight, his alleged speeches against the King, his pseudo-illness at Salisbury, his (alleged) attempts to corrupt those incorruptible persons, Manourie and Sir Lewis Stukeley. Ralegh had said that his trust in the King had undone him. This, at any rate, he had said, and it was true. He never denied this statement, and the reader will have found something uncommonly like it in his letter to the King himself. It is the only "disloyal" speech against his "dread Sovereign" that has ever been proved against Ralegh.[17]

Ralegh's answer, if this had been a genuine trial, was very much to the point. He confidently claimed (what I have never found that anyone denied) that the King himself never believed him guilty of the original treason of 1603. (Had he believed him guilty, it certainly was

17. "I must protest till my last hour that in all the years I followed him, I never heard him name His Majesty but with reverence. I am sorry the assertions of that man" (Manourie) "should prevail so much against the dead" (Captain King [Oldys, p. 521]).

an astounding action to let him go out to Guiana with a powerful armament. Even if that liberty were merely a device to show him up as a
traitor, for success it depended on his having loyalty or stupidity sufficient to bring him back to England.) Ralegh said what he had said before, "that he verily thinketh that His Majesty doth in his conscience
clear him" of that old condemnation, and he repeated James's remark
about being tried by a Middlesex jury and Justice Gaudy's death-bed
remark about English justice being "never so depraved and injured" as
in his condemnation.

Coming to the particulars of his Guiana voyage, his answer to the
Attorney-General was brief, and we can still judge of the contempt
which went with it. He denied all four charges, and for the last two
did not even bother to add circumstance beyond denial. The Solicitor-
General's charges he met by pointing out that he made no attempt to
escape until after his arrest by Sir Lewis Stukeley (this fact the *Declaration* mendaciously ignores, as we have seen), by citing David's pretending to be ill (or, rather, demented), and by confessing he had said
"his confidence in the King" had been "deceived." Also, confronted by
Captains St. Leger and Pennington, he admitted that he "proposed the
taking of the Mexico fleet if the mine failed." This is the one real piece
of evidence that was extracted against him. Its effective value is limited
by the fact that he did *not* attempt to take the fleet when the mine
failed, and that he said it (he always asserted—and it seems an obvious
explanation) to keep together a disheartened and mutinous following.
Bacon closed the proceedings with a heavy rebuke for the mischief he
had done to Spanish possessions, and told him he was to die.

The law officers met next day to settle the form to be observed. They
decided that a mere warrant of execution on the condemnation of 1603
was not enough. Ralegh might plead that a pardon had since been
granted, or that he was not the same person. Accordingly he was
brought before the Council, October 24, and told his life was to be
taken on his old sentence. The Council accepted his request that he be
beheaded, and promised to be responsible for its being granted.

Yet one more formality had to be endured. He was waked early,
October 28, and taken to the King's Bench. Ever since he had reached
London he had been ill; a fever was on him now, and he did not
trouble to dress his white curling hair. This uncharacteristic casualness

was becoming a habit; he had once repulsed Sir Thomas Wilson's suggestion of a hairdresser, by saying he would first know who was to have his locks, and if it was the hangman he was not going to bother about them. An old servant now wanted to set the omission right, but he answered, "Let them kem it that have it"; and then, smiling, added, "Peter, dost thou know of any plaster to set a man's head on again when it is off?"

The long wrangling and bullying finished, decency descends on the story at last. After the writ of *habeas corpus* had been read, the Attorney-General drew attention to the fact that for high treason the prisoner at the bar had formerly been sentenced to death. His Majesty "of his abundant grace" had "been pleased to show mercy upon him till now," when "justice calls unto him for execution." Something of their victim's splendor fell on his judges, gazing at this man whose far-off greatness and mighty actions had become legendary; Yelverton spoke of him as lawyers have rarely spoken of a man whose blood they were demanding:

Sir Walter Ralegh hath been a statesman, and a man who in regard of his parts and quality is to be pitied. He hath been a star at which the world hath gazed. But stars may fall, nay, they must fall when they trouble the sphere wherein they abide.

He asked for execution.

The Clerk of the Crown read the record of the former conviction and judgment, and Ralegh was required to hold up his hand. He was asked if he had anything to say as to why execution should not be granted. His voice had always been a noticeably weak and small one, and he apologized for it now, on account of his sickness and the ague that was on him. The Lord Chief Justice told him it was "audible enough." He began to speak of his clash with Spain, when he was interrupted and told "that it was not for any offence committed in his Voyage" that he was in question, "but for his first fact"[18] (of condemnation in 1603). So he pleaded that "the judgment which I received to die was so long since, I hope it cannot now be strained to take away my life." The King had commissioned him for "a voyage beyond the seas," with power "on the life and death of others." Thereby he presumed,

18. Tanner MSS., 299, fol. 29.

"under favour," he had been "discharged of" the old judgment. The Lord Chief Justice interrupted, and told him this was irrelevant; treason must be pardoned, "by words of a special nature, and not implicitly." There were no such words in his commission; so, unless he could say something to the purpose, execution must be granted. Ralegh bowed to this opinion, demurring only that, "As concerning that judgment which is so long past, I think here are some could witness—nay, His Majesty was of opinion—that I had hard measure therein."

This was coming too close to what was matter of notorious fact. The Lord Chief Justice rebuked him, and told him it would be more becoming ("you had an honourable trial, and so were justly convicted") to submit himself and confess he deserved what was then pronounced against him. He had been a dead man in law for fifteen years past, "and might at any minute have been cut off." The speaker admitted it might seem hard measure to call him to death now, if it were not that new offenses had reminded his Majesty "to revive what the law hath formerly cast upon you." Then the ancient atheism charge reared its head for the last time. The Lord Chief Justice, passing sentence, could not help remembering how unique was this prisoner before him—no mere ordinary victim, but one whose words and opinions were discussed throughout the land. "Your Faith hath heretofore been questioned." However, "I am resolved you are a good Christian, for *The History of the World,* which is an admirable work, doth testify as much." He spoke respectfully still, advising Ralegh to sorrow for his sins, and recommending him to "do as that valiant captain did, who perceived himself in danger" and said defiantly, "Death, thou expectest me. But maugre thy spite I expect thee!" "Fear not death too much, nor fear death too little; not too much, lest you fail in your hopes; not too little, lest you die presumptuously." According to one account, he repeated the Attorney-General's striking phrase: "You have lived like a star; and like a star you must fall when the firmament is shaked." He concluded by the usual prayer that God would have mercy on the condemned man's soul; and granted execution.

All efforts were now hopeless, and had failed: the Queen's, and Lord Carew's. Nor was any attention paid to the appeal which young Carew Ralegh, aged thirteen, put up for the life "of my poor father, sometime honoured with many great places of command by the most worthy

Queen Elizabeth, the possessor whereof she left him at her death, as a token of her good will to his loyalty." The reminders of what had been unjustly taken from Ralegh did not add to the petition's strength. But of course James never supposed it had been written by the child, and would not have cared if it had been. He was busy hunting, and composing *Meditations on the Lord's Prayer*—dully pedantic, and commonplace except for their illustration by examples drawn from the Christian and Apostolic pastime of the Chase. They were dedicated to Villiers. The warrant for Ralegh's execution had been prepared, Naunton told Carleton, and was ready for signature, but "it had better not be talked about, as it is *de futuro contingente.*"

James suddenly decided to sign it, and directed that Ralegh be hurried out of the world, early next morning, October 29.[19] The warrant's phrasing bears marks of a huddled mind, precipitating tragedy. "Our pleasure is, to have the head only of the said Sir Walter Ralegh cut-off, at or within our palace of Westminster, in or upon some fit and convenient place or scaffold to be provided in that behalf, and that in such sort and order as in such cases have been heretofore done; the said judgment to be drawn, hanged, and quartered, or any law, or other thing or matter whatsoever to the contrary notwithstanding."

Ralegh was taken to spend his last night in the gatehouse of St. Peter's monastery, Westminster, at the western entrance of what is now Tothill Street. As he crossed the palace yard he met an old friend, Sir Hugh Beeston, of Cheshire, and asked him if he would be present at the scaffold next morning. Beeston said he hoped so. Then Ralegh smiled, foreseeing that the crowd on such occasions was likely to be even greater than usual. "I do not know what you may do for a place. For my own part, I am sure of one. You must make what shift you can."[20]

To some time that evening, or in the night that followed, tradition ascribes the couplet:

> Cowards may fear to die. But courage stout,
> Rather than live in snuff, will be put out.

19. Old Style. November 10, Lord Mayor's Day.
20. Birch, *Court and Times of King James,* ii, 97.

CHAPTER XXVI

The Scaffold

His death was by him managed with so high and Religious a resolution, as if a Roman had acted a Christian, or rather a Christian a Roman; so as amongst the number that contributed to the destruction of the Earl of Essex, none but he died pitied. OSBORNE, *Traditional Memoirs.*

> Great Heart! who taught thee so to die?
> Death yielding thee the Victory!
> Where took'st thou leave of Life? If here,
> How could'st thou be so far from Fear?
> But sure thou died'st, and quit'd'st the state
> Of Flesh and Blood, before that Fate!
> Else what a Miracle were wrought,
> To triumph both in Flesh and Thought!
> I saw in every Stander-by
> Pale Death, Life only in thy Eye.
> Farewell! Truth shall this Story say,
> We died, Thou only lived'st that Day.
>
> Contemporary Verses.

He was the most fearless of death that ever was known, and the most resolute and confident, yet with reverence and conscience. THE REV. ROBERT TOUNSON.

His happiest hours were those of his arraignment and execution. SIR DUDLEY CARLETON to John Chamberlain, Nov. 14, 1618.

NOW that all uncertainty was finished, Ralegh's triumph began. He had suffered enough, drawn up to death and then released from dying—not once, but repeatedly. Chance and caprice had ended. His spirit fell back into lines of strength and repose.

All that evening, friends came to bid him good-bye. They came to comfort him; and found him lifted above the need of comfort, to an exaltation of courage which seemed improper. His kinsman Francis Thynne advised him, "Do not carry it with too much bravery. Your enemies will take exception, if you do." But Ralegh had been put by his enemies where he no longer need consider them and their opinions. "It is my last mirth in this world," he answered. "Do not grudge it to me. When I come to the sad parting, you will see me grave enough." He reminded visitors that "the world is itself but a larger prison, out of which some are daily selected for execution."

The same rebuke was given him later in the night, by the official comforter, the Rev. Robert Tounson, Dean of Westminster—a successful young ecclesiastic,[1] a royal chaplain, on every count entitled to his conviction that he stood well with God and man. His letter to Sir John Isham after the execution is written with professional briskness; no doubt he had consoled many unfortunates. He could take even the execution of a Walter Ralegh as all in the day's work:

The last week was a busy week with me; and the week afore that, was more. I would gladly have been with you, but could find no time; yet I hope you had the relation of Sir Walter Rawleigh's death; for so I gave order, that it should be brought unto you.[2] I was commanded by the Lords of the Council to be with him, both in prison and at his death, and so set down the manner of his death, as near as I can. There be other reports of it, but that which you have from me is true; one Crawford, who was sometime Mr. Rodeknight's pupil, hath penned it prettily, and meaneth to put it to the press, and came to me about it, but I hear not that it is come forth.

Tounson began automatically to tell the condemned to cheer up; dying was no such great matter for a Christian who had properly confessed. But he found, with some chagrin, that here was a convict with very little sense of anything to get off his conscience:

he told me that he was charged to have broken the peace of Spain, but he put that, he said, out of the count of his offences, saying that he heard the King was displeased at it; for how could he break peace with him, who within these 4 years, as he said, took divers of his men, and bound them back to back and drowned them?

That was the killing of "Mr. Hall's and my men," so often cited by Ralegh.[3] Tounson's memory evidently telescoped this incident with

1. He was forty-three.   2. This letter has been lost.
3. The incident has not been traced, but probably occurred about 1609, the year in which Harcourt tells us he met Hall at Trinidad.

others that Ralegh cited. Ralegh stood by his guns to the last, as concerned San Thomé:

And for burning the town, he said it stood upon the King's own ground, and therefore he did no wrong in that.

Nor did the condemned seem much in awe of death. The visitor's consolation seemed humiliatingly superfluous:

When I began to encourage him against the fear of death, he seemed to make so light of it that I wondered at him; and when I told him that the dear servants of God, in better causes than his, had shrunk back and trembled a little, he denied not, but yet gave God thanks, he never feared death . . . it was but an opinion and imagination; and the manner of death though to others might seem grievous, yet he had rather die so than of a burning fever, with much more to that purpose, with such confidence and cheerfulness, that I was fain to divert my speech another way, and wished him not to flatter himself, for this extraordinary boldness, I was afraid, came from some false ground. If it sprung from the assurance he had of the love and favour of God, of the hope of his Salvation by Christ, and his own innocency, as he pleaded, I said he was an happy man. But if it were out of an humour of vain glory or carelessness or contempt of death, or senselessness of his own estate, he were much to be lamented, &c.,

says Dr. Tounson, very fittingly rolling his own talk up into the ball of an "&c." Before he finished with the white-haired old Admiral, he had to speak to him with some severity. That, however, was toward the end of the night. Now, Ralegh managed temporarily to assuage his professional doubts and urgencies:

For I told him that Heathen Men had set as little by their lives as he could do, and seemed to die as bravely.[4] He answered that he was persuaded that no man, that knew God and feared Him, could die with cheerfulness and courage, except he were assured of the love and favour of God unto him: that other men might make shows outwardly, but they felt no joy within: with much more to that effect, very Christianly, so that he satisfied me then, as I think he did all his spectators at his death.

Tounson seems to have withdrawn for awhile to return before daybreak.

4. As if Ralegh needed to be told how bravely "heathen men" could die!

Lady Ralegh came; and he kept her mind off next morning's scene by talking of the necessity for clearing his name, which ill-luck and enemies had left so wounded. If the King, as he dreaded, forbade any speech on the scaffold, he would go hence unheard and unvindicated. He told her what he wanted said, and placed his papers in her hands; and they talked of the education of their son Carew. Then she broke down, so that he hardly caught what she was saying. This was that the Lords of the Council had refused to intercede for a pardon, but had granted her the favor of disposing of his body. "It is well, dear Bess," he replied, "that you should have the disposal of that dead, which living was so often denied to you!" It struck midnight; and she had to leave "the tumultuous adventurer who had been her life."[5] The Carews were waiting, and took her to their home.

Some time in that night Ralegh drew up two testamentary notes. The first dealt merely with certain business matters. They show the cold astonishing clearness of his mind, an atmosphere in which every air had dropped still and left only vision and dazzling memory. They show also his lifelong care for dependents. He withdraws a testimony hastily given under the spell of Boyle's generous hospitality when he set out for Guiana, against a lease claimed by his old colleague Henry Pyne, and asks that he be considered neutral in that dispute; he asks his wife, "according to her ability" (he knew how small that would now be), to have consideration of two widows of men who had given him faithful service. One had lost her only son also, and, if Lady Ralegh could not help her, "I fear me, will otherwise perish." Only in the last brief paragraph is a note of sternness. It is about Sir Lewis Stukeley, who had sold all the tobacco brought back from San Thomé, and had cozened Ralegh out of ten gold pieces the day that he trapped him on the river with the sham escape. The tobacco, at any rate, he should not get away with, if his victim could help it. "I desire that he may give his account for the tobacco."

The second testamentary note categorically, in short sentences, denies nine statements made against his conduct of the Guiana expedition and afterwards. It would be tedious to remind the reader of them again. Ralegh concludes, after denying that he had abused the King to Manourie:

5. Harlow, *Ralegh's Last Voyage*, p. 93.

No; if I had not loved and honoured the King truly, and trusted in his goodness somewhat too much, I had not suffered death.

These things are true, as there is a God, and as I am now to appear before His tribunal-seat, where I renounce all mercy and salvation if this be not a truth.

> At my death,
>
> W. RALEGH.

Some time in this night also, he must have written the verses found in his Bible afterwards:

> Even such is Time! who takes in trust
> Our youth, our joys, and all we have,
> And pays us but with earth and dust:
> Who in the dark and silent grave,
> When we have wandered all our ways,
> Shuts up the story of our days.
> But from that earth, that grave, that dust,
> The Lord shall raise me up, I trust.

Those verses have moved men ever since. But A. H. Bullen showed their pathos as even deeper than was guessed. The first six lines, except for a slight change in the opening line,

> Oh cruel Time, which takes in trust,

are the conclusion of a love-poem[6] which Ralegh wrote many years previously. Even his light songs, which contemporaries in Elizabeth's reign found "lofty, insolent, and passionate," were so laden with his own individual and imaginative melancholy, that with a slight twist they could serve for the hour of his death! The lines had been written when he was reckless of what enmity might do to him, and secure in his Queen's esteem and his own strength. But what had been expressive of a passing mood, not too deeply felt, the years had proved true. Now he added his postscript of faith.

As the night passed, we may be sure that its hours came crowded with memories. No man that ever passed from our English stage had more or more varied ones. It is natural, but it is mistaken, to suppose that his superb carriage in death's antechamber and then in death's

6. Printed by Bullen, 1902, from Harley MSS.

very presence was the posing of a man who dramatized himself and his deeds. He was the last representative of an age whose lesson to posterity is that the mind is alive only when imagination flames intensely, making us spirit and not mere body. The relief and almost zest with which Ralegh played out his last part were spontaneous. "He must have seen that it was a good time for him to die."[7]

> The generation of thy peers are fled,
> And thou thyself must go!

As his *daemon* whispered to Achilles, "Die soon, O faerie's sonne!" The Elizabethan epoch belonged to the ages: Marlowe, Gilbert, Sidney, Essex, Spenser, Shakespeare, Drake. If the dead have sense and memory, we can believe that they were watching in that gatehouse prison. And if Ralegh's thoughts, as he sat there smoking and writing, turned momentarily to Gondomar, the strong enemy who had won for Spain this poor revenge for a generation of harrying her navies and her shipping, for the Armada's repulse, for Cadiz, for Fayal, there was nothing here either for tears, or to wail or knock the breast:

> If you have writ your annals true, 'tis there!
> That, like an eagle in a dovecot, I
> Fluttered your Volscians in Corioli!

Toward dawn the Rev. Robert Tounson returned, troubled in conscience at having let the culprit "get away with" his unseemly serenity. That serenity continued unabated. Ralegh received the Sacrament, and "was very cheerful and merry." He talked of persuading the world, in his dying speech,

that he died an innocent man, as he said. Thereat I told him that he should do well to advise what he said. Men in these days did not die in that sort innocent, and his pleading innocency was an oblique taxing of the Justice of the Realm upon him.

Ralegh, courteous and becomingly submissive as ever where the King was concerned,

confessed Justice had been done, and by course of Law he must die. But yet,

7. M. Waldman, *Ralegh*, p. 233.

I should give him leave, he said, to stand upon his innocency in the fact; and he thought, both the King, and all that heard his answers, thought verily he was innocent for that matter.

It was getting too puzzling for Dr. Tounson. So he fell back on the favorite gag of those days, that misfortune was catching you justly— if not for some sin that people could see, or thought they could see, then for some other sin that you had cunningly managed to keep dark. There was his treatment of Lord Essex—that controversy raised its head for the last time; and incidentally reminded Ralegh of something it would be as well to get said on the scaffold. And, seeing the kind of officious and official ass he had before him, a man who this evening would be going round the town, preening himself on exclusive knowledge and saying, "This is what I told Ralegh" and "This is what Ralegh said," he gave him a bit of special inside information:

I then pressed him to call to mind what he had done formerly; and though perhaps in that particular, for which he was condemned, he was clear, yet for some other matter, it might be, he was guilty, and now the hand of God had found him out, and therefore he should acknowledge the Justice of God in it, though at the hands of men he had but hard measure. And here I put him in mind of the death of my Lord of Essex, how it was generally reported that he was a great instrument of his death, which if his heart did charge him of, he should heartily repent and ask God forgiveness. To which he made answer, as is in the former relation, and said moreover, that my Lord of Essex was fetcht off by a trick, which he privately told me of.

What that trick was Tounson unfortunately omitted to set down; you can see him bored in his letter, with having to repeat what he had said to Isham already, and doubtless to many others; he is plainly trying to hurry to a finish. Ralegh perhaps told him the story that Essex died because Lady Nottingham kept back from Elizabeth the ring which the Queen had given him with the promise that she would grant any request he made, if he sent this reminder. This story was not printed till nearly a century later.[8] But it comes then in a context of obviously intimate knowledge contemporary with the events of which it treats;

8. *The Secret History of the Most Renowned Queen Elizabeth and the Earl of Essex, by a Person of Quality* (1708).

and it falls in with Elizabeth's statement to Biron that she let Essex die because he was too proud to ask for his life, and with her hysterical unhappiness whenever she recalled him.

Lord Mayor's Day had been chosen for the execution, in order that "the pageants and fine shows might draw away the people from beholding the tragedy of one of the gallantest worthies that ever England bred."[9] His death was to be got over early, before the crowds were stirring. Breakfast was brought in; "very cheerful," Ralegh ate it heartily, and enjoyed a pipe afterwards, perhaps none the less because he knew how defiantly callous it would seem to the King when he heard. He "made no more of his death, than if it had been to take a journey"; and went out between the Sheriffs, with Dr. Tounson still accompanying and upholding him, to a crowd overwhelmingly friendly and pitiful and admiring. It included many noblemen on horseback, and ladies of rank at windows. According to John Eliot, who was present, and whose life was to be changed by this day's spectacle, it included enemies as well as friends. But all were to be swept by one overmastering wave of sorrow and affection.

They offered him a cup of sack, which he drank. Asked if it were to his liking, he replied smiling, "I will answer you as did the fellow who drank of St. Giles's bowl as he went to Tyburn: 'It is good drink, if a man might but tarry by it.'" About the scaffold was such a host that he and his company got out of breath pushing through it. Noticing a very old man with bald head, he asked him why he had come out on such a raw morning, and if there was anything he wanted. "Nothing," said the man, "but to see you, and to pray God to have mercy on your soul." Ralegh thanked him and, as the only return he could make for such good-will, gave him his lace night-cap, "for thou hast more need of it now than I."[10]

This was Ralegh's first appearance before the general world, since days of whose traditional grandeur he had so long been a part. It saw him erect and tall, white-haired and marked with his recent passion; attired gravely and decently, in hair-colored satin doublet, with black-wrought waistcoat under it, black taffeta breeches, a ruff band, ash-

9. Aubrey, *Letters*, ii, 520.
10. Thomas Lorkin to Sir Thomas Puckering, Nov. 3, 1618 (Birch, *Court and Times of King James*, ii, 100). Ralegh obviously recalls Sir Philip Sidney's dying action.

colored silk stockings, and a wrought black velvet gown.[11] The day was sharp, and the Sheriffs invited him to descend from the scaffold, and warm himself at a fire at its foot.[12] He declined, lest his ague, which had temporarily left him, should return, and teeth chattering with cold should be set down to fear.

Taking off his hat, he saluted the company, and in especial the many friends who were present; and apologized for anything cast down in his appearance and his voice. Taken from bed only yesterday, in a raging sickness, he desired "to be borne withal, because this is the third day of my fever. And if I show any weakness, I beseech you to attribute it to my malady, for this is the hour I look for it." He had to pause to gather strength; then, addressing himself directly to a balcony in Sir Randolph Carew's house, where Arundel (who had stood surety for him in his last voyage), Doncaster (James Hay, the Scot whose attitude toward Ralegh had been changed once for all by witnessing his first trial at Winchester) and other friends were, he said loudly, "I thank God of his Infinite Goodness, that he hath sent me to die in the sight of so honourable an assembly, and not in darkness." But his words not reaching those whom he wished to reach, he added, "I will strain myself, for I would willingly have your Honours hear me." Lord Arundel called back, "We will come upon the scaffold." The proceedings halted while they came, and one by one shook hands with the man about to die.

Then Ralegh resumed, and repeated, "I thank my God heartily that he hath brought me into the light to die, and hath not suffered me to die in the dark prison of the Tower, where I have suffered a great deal of adversity and a long sickness. And I thank God that my fever hath not taken me at this time, as I prayed God it might not."

Those who feared that he would take advantage of the tumultuous emotion of the occasion to stir up prejudice against the King did not know their man. His respect for the Crown was as genuine as that of any British military or naval officer of our day; and he was not out for any personal conquest in a war which he recognized was over, and about whose result he did not trouble himself. That he had to bring in

11. Tanner MSS. (Bodleian Library, Oxford), 299, fol. 29.

12. *Calendar of State Papers, Domestic,* 1611–1618, p. 588: John Pory to Carleton, Oct. 31.

the King at all, he apologized, with all but imperceptible shrug of dismissal of James to his proper importance. "But what have I to do with kings, who am about to go before the King of kings?" He had no intention

> To call the Gods, with vulgar spite,
> To vindicate his helpless right.

He meant to clear himself, though; and it has been taken amiss by some that he should have wanted to clear himself, even from accusations which his enemies tried to prove, but failed to prove. He went on to "two main Points of Suspicion, that his Majesty hath conceived against me, and wherein his Majesty cannot be satisfied, which I desire to clear and resolve you of." The first was his "practices" with the French, both before he sailed and after his return.

> But this I say, for a man to call God to witness to a falsehood at any time is a grievous sin, and what shall he hope for at the Tribunal Day of Judgment? But to call God to witness to a falsehood at the time of Death is far more grievous and impious, and there is no hope for such an one. And what should I expect that am now going to render an Account of my Faith? I do therefore call the Lord to witness, as I hope to be saved, and as I hope to see Him in his Kingdom, which I hope will be within this quarter of this hour: I never had any Commission from the King of France, nor any Treaty with the French Agent, nor with any from the French King; neither knew I that there was an Agent, or what he was, till I met him in my Gallery at my Lodging unlooked for.[13] If I speak not true, O Lord, let me never come into Thy Kingdom.

So the denial runs in the report preserved in Archbishop Sancroft's handwriting.[14] There is a fuller and more categorical denial preserved among the State Papers in the Public Record Office. As Stebbing remarks, it obviously needs, and there can be no doubt that Ralegh gave it, the qualification plainly set down in his testamentary note—"unknowing to the King." He had to get said in a very few minutes all

13. Another eyewitness (Thomas Lorkin) says that what Ralegh said was that he saw the French agent at Whitehall once, "before he undertook his voyage" (Cayley, *Life of Ralegh*, ii, Appendix, pp. 78–82). We evidently have not a trustworthy verbatim report.

14. Tanner MSS. (Bodleian Library, Oxford).

that he would ever want to have said; and on the French negotiations, the little that he could say at such an hour and to so general a public must necessarily be a statement exceedingly complicated, compressed and comprehensive. Nevertheless, of this statement Gardiner remarks that it "is a marvel of ingenuity. Not a word of it is untrue, but the general impression is completely false."[15] If that is so, it is because Ralegh could not say in his last words what Gardiner completely ignores, that James and Winwood (with James's sanction) had started the suggestion of using a French contingent for any fighting that might prove necessary to get at the mine; that the talk about a French commission had never proceeded further than mere talk—a general assurance that so distinguished an admiral, an old friend of many in France, might be sure of a welcome in France; that French commissions are presumably on record, as our own commissions are, and that (as Ralegh had said) anyone could find out the facts if he cared to expend a crown; and finally, that his examiners had tried to establish a "French plot" and had thrown the effort up. Ralegh would have been strictly and fully truthful if he had said, "The King himself started negotiations for French help, a fact which he cannot possibly afford to have made public, least of all to Spain (and hardly even to France), and those negotiations he suddenly dropped." Had there been any real handle in the talk of Ralegh's "plot with France," it would have been used ruthlessly and not flung down in disgust.

And here we may notice what surely makes this execution unique. It was remarked at the time that Ralegh made not the most fleeting reference to the "treasons" for which he was dying, on the 1603 condemnation. Neither he nor (he was sure, and he was right) his hearers thought that pretense worth wasting a word on. Nevertheless, as a matter of plain *legal* fact, he was dying for having practiced *with* Spain to dethrone James.

He mentioned the charge that he tried to escape to Rochelle instead of coming to Plymouth; but did not trouble to answer it. He went on to the charge that he had spoken disloyally of the King. It rested on the testimony of a Frenchman of no character; and he merely denied it.

15. *History*, iii, 150. "His speech had been carefully prepared. Every word he spoke was, as far as we can judge, literally true; but it was not the whole truth, and it was calculated in many points to produce a false impression on his hearers."

His undignified malingering at Salisbury he confessed, but did not give his real reason, that he wanted a chance to write out his defense. That explanation would have seemed hard on the King, implying that the King was intending to rush him out of life. In courtesy Ralegh suppressed it, saying, "I did it to prolong time till his Majesty came, hoping for some commiseration from him"—which was part reason, at any rate.

He dealt with a brief selection from Sir Lewis Stukeley's lies. One was that he had told "Sir Lewis Stukeley, my Kinsman and Keeper," that Lord Carew and Lord Doncaster were privy to his intended escape. "It was not likely that I should acquaint two Privy Councillors of my pretended escape." (Doncaster, as we have seen, was standing beside him on the scaffold.) Nor was there any need to have told them; for Stukeley, after effecting a nominal arrest, "left me 6, 7, 8, 9, or 10 days to go where I listed, while he rode about the country." A second lie was that he had told Stukeley that these two Privy Councillors had planned to meet him in France, throwing up their careers. A third was that he had offered Stukeley £10,000 for help to escape. "But cast my soul into everlasting fire, if I ever made him offer of £10,000 or £1000." All he had done was to offer him, a man of broken fortunes, a written promise to get his debts paid after they had both fled overseas. "Neither had I £1000, for if I had had so much," said Ralegh, contemptuously blurting out notorious truth, "I could have done better with it, and made my Peace otherwise." A fourth denial was given to a story which reflected on a trusted friend's hospitality. And so Ralegh, in whose references to Stukeley alone there still lives strong feeling, dismissed his betrayer: "I desire God to forgive him, as I hope to be forgiven."

"Then he looked over his Note of Remembrance. 'Well, faith be, thus far have I gone. Now a little more, and I will have done bye-and-bye.'" So he handled the charges of disloyalty and treachery to his followers in the Guiana voyage; and I do not know that anyone would be so hardy as to challenge either tone or phrase as containing any *suggestio falsi* here.

And then he turned to my Lord of Arundel, and said: "Being in the Gallery in my ship at my departure, your Honour took me by the hand, and said you would request me one thing, that was, That whether I made a good voyage or bad, yet I should return again unto England, when I made a promise and gave you my faith that I would."

"And so you did!" cried Lord Arundel. "It is true. They were the last words I spake unto you."

With a courteous glance toward the Sheriff ("I will speak but a word or two more, because I will not trouble Mr. Sheriff too long"), he mentioned the old story that he had rejoiced when the Earl of Essex was dying, and had been at a window in full view, puffing out tobacco "in disdain of him." But all through the execution he had been in the Armory, where Essex could not see him and he could only just see Essex. He had often regretted this, "for I heard he had a desire to see me, and be reconciled to me." "I confess I was of a contrary faction. But I knew that my Lord of Essex was a noble gentleman, and that it would be worse with me when he was gone. For those that set me up against him did afterwards set themselves against me."

"In all the time he was upon the scaffold, nor before, there appeared not the least alteration in him, either in his voice or countenance; but he seemed as free from all manner of apprehension, as if he had come hither rather to be a spectator than a sufferer. Nay, the beholders seemed much more sensible than did he."[16] Having cleared his name, as he hoped, he begged the spectators to

all join with me in prayer to that great God of Heaven whom I have grievously offended, being a man full of all vanity, who has lived a sinful life in such callings as have been most inducing to it. Of a long time, my course was a course of vanity. I have been a seafaring man, a soldier, and a courtier, and in the temptations of the least of these there is enough to overthrow a good mind and a good man—

apologizing, says Sir Charles Firth, "for his lapses from strict rectitude; and he might also have claimed the indulgence accorded to poets."[17] He died "in the faith professed by the Church of England," and hoped for salvation through our Savior Christ. "So I take my leave of you all,

16. Thomas Lorkin to Sir Thomas Puckering, Nov. 5.
17. *Sir Walter Ralegh's "History of the World"* (*British Academy Proceedings*, 1917–1918), p. 428.

making my peace with God. I have a long journey to take, and must bid the company farewell."

We can hardly imagine the emotional release which our ancestors got from such a scene. The sufferer fully shared in it. The passionate pity and sense of fineness wantonly flung down—this spectacle of the greatest living Englishman sacrificed because the Spanish Ambassador ordered it—were something the Stuart house would have been wise to have never evoked. There was no event which so shocked James's subjects as an unparalleled exercise of tyrannical power. After such a conviction as men now knew that old Winchester one had been, and the cruelty of those years in the Tower, to behead a man so great and so greatly and terribly unfortunate, was an error such as even judicial murders have rarely been. Had the execution taken place in 1603, at any rate it would have followed upon the discovery of a plot or plots (whether Ralegh were in them or not), and while Ralegh was hated. Now there was not even any talk of a plot anywhere. When indignation spread out over the country, and reached the seamen, it was not going to be a passing mood. Among those present before the scaffold was a future Vice-Admiral of Devon,[18] Sir John Eliot, a follower of Villiers, Lord Buckingham. This day was to change his attitude, as it changed that of many others. "Our Ralegh," he wrote in a tumult of admiration,[19] gave an example of fortitude such as history could scarcely parallel:

All preparations that are terrible were presented to his eye. Guards and officers were about him, the scaffold and the executioner, the axe, and the more cruel expectation of his enemies. And what did all this work on the resolution of our Ralegh? Made it an impression of weak fear, to distract his reason? Nothing so little did that great soul suffer. His mind became the clearer, as if already it had been freed from the cloud and oppression of the body. Such was his unmoved courage and placid temper that, while it changed the affection of the enemies who had come to witness it, and turned their joy to sorrow, it filled all men else with emotion and admiration, leaving with them only this doubt—whether death were more acceptable to him or he more welcome unto death.

The writer of those words was himself to do naval service in Ralegh's

18. He succeeded Sir Lewis Stukeley, 1619.
19. *Monarchy of Man,* Harleian MSS., 2228 (British Museum). See J. Forster, *Life of Eliot,* i, 34.

own county, and to die in the darkness of the Tower which Ralegh had dreaded as destined to see his own passing.

Ralegh took off his gown and doublet, and called the headsman to show him the axe. The man hesitating, he said, "I pray thee, let me see it. Dost thou think that I am afraid of it?" He handled it, and felt along the edge, and smilingly remarked to the Sheriff, with a glance back at his own cordials and "balsam of Guiana," "This is a sharp medicine, but it is a physician for all diseases." "Then going to and fro upon the Scaffold, on every side he prayed the Company to pray to God to assist him and strengthen him." The executioner had flung down his own cloak for Ralegh (thereby saving his gown) to kneel on. He now knelt himself, and begged forgiveness. Ralegh placed both hands on his shoulders, and comforted him. "When I stretch forth my hands, despatch me."

He lay down for the blow. Someone asked him, would he not prefer to lie with his face to the East of Our Lord's arising. He replied, "So the heart be right, it is no matter which way the head lieth." After praying a few moments, he stretched out his hands. But the headsman was unnerved, and would not strike, even after Ralegh had stretched them out again. At last the tension seemed as if it could be borne no longer, but must snap. "Strike, man! strike!" he cried, and the man struck, two blows, Ralegh's body "never shrinking nor moving." The head was held up to the multitude, but the time-honored formula that it was the head of a traitor was omitted. A voice from the crowd supplied a better one: "We have not another such head to be cut off!" We are told there was a universal groan when the axe fell.

His head was put in a red velvet bag, and with his body taken away in a black mourning coach. That day Lady Ralegh wrote to Sir Nicholas Carew, at Beddington, Surrey:

I desiar, good brother, that you will be plessed to let me berri the worthi boddi of my nobell hosban, Sur Walter Ralegh, in your chorche at Beddington, wher I desiar to be berred. The Lordes have geven me his ded boddi, though they denied me his life. This nit hee shall be brought you with two or three of my men. Let me here presently. God hold me in my wites.[20]

20. Manning and Bray, *History of Surrey,* ii, 495.

CHAPTER XXVII

Afterwards

King James, after the manner of weak and ill-consulted princes, set forth a Declaration, which, according to the ordinary success of such apologies, rendered the condition of that proceeding worse in the world's opinion. FRANCIS OSBORNE.

The ghost of Ralegh pursued the House of Stuart to the scaffold. G. M. TREVELYAN, *History of England.*

GONDOMAR was still in Spain when news of his victory arrived. He persuaded Sir Francis Cottington not to wait for a formal notification, but to take the tidings at once to Court. "I told the King of Spain," Cottington wrote to Buckingham, "of the justice which the King my master had commanded to be done, and expressed, in the best terms I could, the great demonstration his Majesty had therein made." Philip III showed his "contentment." His Council decided that "His Spanish Majesty should, in a letter to the King my master, take notice of the obligation he hath unto him." The King of England had earned his autograph letter.

The Spanish marriage, as everyone knows, continued a greater jest and mockery than ever. Four years later, Buckingham and Prince Charles, clownish knight-errants, made their gesture of a personal trip to Madrid, to win the Infanta by direct attack. They made fools of themselves and their country; Buckingham quarrelled with his hosts, and on his return called loudly for war. He got it, and managed to squander national resources and prestige on expeditions against both France and Spain. Those against Rochelle were of almost unexampled ineptitude and shame; but the attempt on Cadiz (1625) was the climax of a series of disasters that covered British arms with infamy. That the men who did Ralegh to death should have displayed their worst of foolishness at Cadiz, of all places, is one of many things that make the years that followed his death seem like events arranged by a dramatist, rather than the natural folly of men.

How well it was understood that James's sacrifice of Ralegh was a personal action, with nothing of principle behind it, was shown when the East India Company in 1620, without any shadow of justification, allowed their forces to assist the Shah of Persia to eject Spain and Portugal from Ormuz and the Gulf. James and Buckingham were assailed with protests. But there was no thought of placating Madrid with another English head. Buckingham merely demanded, as Lord Admiral, a tenth of a mythical £100,000 loot. The Company had no choice but to pay, whereupon the royal mendicant extended his palm also. "What! did I deliver you from the complaint of the Spaniard, and am I to get nothing?" He took a second £10,000, and the incident was closed.[1]

Gondomar returned to London, March, 1619, and in conjunction with Buckingham continued to misgovern England. He won Buckingham over from support of the Protestant cause, that of King James's daughter Elizabeth, the one-year Queen of Bohemia; and he defeated English desires to save her from expulsion and ruin. In 1620 he bullied James into abandoning the English colonists on the Amazon. But at Easter, 1622, he accidentally achieved something toward bringing England and Scotland together in friendliness. William Lithgow, a Scots traveller who had been in the hands of the Inquisition, made representations which Gondomar treated contemptuously. Thereupon Lithgow cuffed his head soundly and repeatedly, before a concourse of delighted beholders, an exploit which cost him nine weeks in the Marshalsea but made him a national hero and greatly softened English hearts toward Scotland.

Ralegh's death had an effect which many had foreseen. A Spanish Dominican, in London on a political mission, had tried to save him, predicting that his sacrifice "would much alienate the hearts of Englishmen."[2] The Earl of Northumberland, still a Tower prisoner, had remarked that if the Spanish match went forward, Spain had better have given £100,000 than have him killed; and if it did not go forward, England (which would need him in the ensuing Anglo-Spanish War) had better have given £100,000 than have killed him.[3] John Pym, who

1. See Thompson and Garratt, *Rise and Fulfilment of British Rule in India*, p. 14.
2. Chamberlain to Carleton, Oct. 31 (Birch, *Court and Times of King James*, ii, 98).
3. John Pory to Carleton (*Calendar of State Papers, Domestic*, 1611–1618), p. 591.

was probably a spectator, wrote in his notebook of *Memorable Accidents:* "Sir Walter Ralegh had the favour to be beheaded at Westminster, where he died with great applause of the beholders, most constantly, most Christianly, most religiously." Sir Edward Harwood wrote to Sir Dudley Carleton, October 30, that the town was "full of the worthy end of Sir Walter Ralegh," whose "Christian and truthful manner made all believe that he was neither guilty of former treasons nor of unjustly injuring the King of Spain."[4] The Sheriffs got into trouble for their courtesy to him: "they had no thanks, that suffered him to talk so long on the scaffold."[5] His enemies had "shown versatility as well as virulence,"[6] using his condemnation as a friend of Spain to execute him as an enemy of Spain; and their success was that they revived the dying flames of enmity to Spain, and made his martyrdom a source of lasting grief to his countrymen. The news that Bacon was preparing a justification was greeted with derision. It "will not be believed," Chamberlain wrote to Carleton, November 21, "unless it be well proved." Thomas Fuller, in a "pleasant passage,"[7] tells how one M. Wiemark, a wealthy citizen, a "great novilant and constant Paul's walker," hearing on Lord Mayor's Day of the deed which had marked its beginning, observed that "his head would do very well on the shoulders of Sir Robert Naunton, Secretary of State." Naunton was in no mood to endure criticism, and, when the remark was reported to him, summoned Wiemark, who tried to ride off on the plea that he had meant no disrespect, but was merely referring to the proverb that "two heads are better than one." Naunton bided his time. As a fervent Churchman he was presently collecting money to repair St. Paul's. Wiemark put himself down for £100, and was grimly advised that "two £100 are better than one," and "betwixt fear and charity" he had to double his benevolence.

James ordered Cottington, in Madrid, to stress the service he had rendered the Spanish court. He had

caused Sir Walter Ralegh to be put to death, chiefly for the giving them satisfaction . . . in many actions of late His Majesty had strained upon the

4. *Calendar of State Papers, Domestic,* 1611–1618, p. 588.
5. Chamberlain to Carleton, Nov. 7 (Birch, ii, 104).
6. Stebbing, p. 383.
7. See also Osborne, *Traditional Memoirs,* p. 19.

affections of his people, and especially in this last concerning Sir Walter Ralegh, who died with a great deal of courage and constancy. To give them content, he had not spared a man able to have done His Majesty much service, when by preserving him he might have given great satisfaction to his subjects, and have had at command upon all occasions as useful a man as served any prince in Christendom.[8]

When, two years later, his daughter Elizabeth, Queen of Bohemia, was dethroned by Austria with Spanish help,[9] it was alleged that James angrily cried out that he would insist on having the Spanish general's head. Would Philip prove as complaisant as *he* had proved in the matter of Ralegh, asked someone. "Then I would that Ralegh's head were again on his shoulders," said James.

Dr. Tounson, in his dismissal of the duty of official consolation in which he had been occupied, told his correspondent that Ralegh's last words

left a great impression in the minds of those that beheld him, inasmuch that Sir Lewis Stukely and the Frenchman grow very odious. This was the news a week since. But now it is blown over, and he almost forgotten.

The news which I hear is, that the promoter of Kowel hath gotten his charges of Sir Thomas Brookes, and Sir Thomas much cheated, and hath entered into a bond of £100 to the promoter, never to molest or trouble him again, and the promoter is as crank, and triumpheth in his victory very much; and Sir Thomas glad he hath escaped so. I once saw Henry Tremill, and that is all. What is become of Robin Dallison, I cannot tell. But he was here in great expectation of a place, which I think now he has fallen from, for all officers here are much younger than himself. The business of the Treasurer sleepeth; and that of my Lord of Exeter and Sir Thomas Lake will not be called upon this term. There be, as I hear, 17,000 sheets of paper in that Book, which upon ordinary account cometh to eight hundred and fifty pounds.

I have cited beyond the reference to Ralegh, for the letter's own sake. Not even Shakespeare, in Master Shallow, has given such a portrayal of vacuous officialism. But the Dean, thus deftly differentiating between the news that has all blown over and the real news that matters, was

8. John Rushworth, *Historical Collection of Private Passages of State*, i, 9.

9. Her copy of Ralegh's *History of the World*, probably a presentation copy, was captured in her baggage by the Spaniards.

mistaken. Ralegh's execution did not blow over that quickly. Two years after the execution, the Court was still in a fever of touchiness about it. Naunton and Villiers wrathfully exerted themselves to suppress a thin satire by Captain Thomas Gainsford, *Vox Spiritus, or Sir Walter Ralegh's Ghost,* which was being passed from hand to hand in manuscript.

In November Manourie, "a French physician, lately sent for from Plymouth," was paid £20.[10] On December 29 the Exchequer passed a warrant to pay Sir Lewis Stukeley, "for performance of his service and expenses in bringing up out of Devonshire the person of Sir Walter Ralegh, £965 6s. 3d." The payment seems heavy, but its recipient found it inadequate, so crushing was the load of hatred that accompanied it. He was "Sir Judas Stukeley" to the end of his days, which were to be few. Ever since his conduct at Ralegh's re-arrest on the river, he had been shunned;[11] after the tragedy was consummated, "every man" declined his company "as treacherous." Desperately he offered the King to take the Sacrament upon his evidence's truth, which Ralegh had denied in his dying words.[12] A bystander suggested an emendation, to make the offer more convincing: it was a good notion, if only the King would order his execution, and he would take the oath in exactly the same circumstances as Ralegh. Men might then perhaps believe him! The King dismissed his complaint. "I have done amiss. Ralegh's blood be upon thy head!"[13] As Vice-Admiral of Devon, he had to visit the Lord Admiral on official business. Nottingham at last remembered that he had once been Ralegh's comrade, and turned on him in fury. "What, thou base fellow! *Thou,* who art reputed the scorn and contempt of men, how darest thou offer thyself into my presence? Were it not in my own house, I would cudgel thee with my staff, for presuming to be so saucy!"[14] He tried James again, and told him that men were reviling him. James seemed to think it very likely.[15] "What wouldst thou have me do?" he asked, appealing to Stukeley to take a reasonable view of the matter. Did he want the King to hang people who spoke evil of him? "On my soul, if I should hang all that

10. Nov. 9 (*Pells Order Book,* 1618).　　11. Chamberlain to Carleton, Aug. 20.
12. Lorkin to Puckering, Nov. 3 (Harleian MSS., 7002, fol. 420).
13. John Pory to Carleton, Nov. 7.
14. Goodman, *Court of King James,* ii, 173.
15. Lorkin to Puckering, Jan. 5, 1619 (Goodman, *Court of King James,* ii, 173).

speak ill of thee, all the trees in my kingdom would not suffice." He sought the help of a royal chaplain, Dr. Leonel Sharpe, to draw up a *Humble Petition and Information of Sir Lewis Stukeley, touching his own behaviour in the charge committed to him for the bringing up of Sir Walter Ralegh, and the scandalous aspersions cast upon him for the same.* Few literary works have met with such instantaneous and unanimous rejection.

The warrant for his payment was dated, as we have seen, December 29. Almost simultaneously the nation was thrilled with news that seemed too good to be true. Manourie had been arrested at Plymouth, trying (like Ralegh) to fly the country, and for excellent reason; he had been caught clipping coin, and accused Stukeley as accomplice.[16] It transpired that they had for years eked out their earnings in other ways, by clipping and sweating money. The age was a deeply religious one, and men readily and at once believed that Providence, a dramatist always, had arranged that Sir Lewis' detection should occur when he was actually tampering with the blood-money received for his recent services. He was sent to Ralegh's last prison at the Gatehouse, and then to the Tower; and in due course convicted and sentenced to death. James, however, added to his own growing unpopularity by pardoning him.[17] Stukeley returned to Devon, its Vice-Admiral no longer. He found Devon no place for the betrayer of Ralegh, so fled to Lundy, where he died a raving madman within two years of his kinsman's execution.[18]

Sir Thomas Wilson "had failed to spy out treason in Ralegh's talk . . . or in the correspondence with Lady Ralegh," but thought payment due to him "for his good intentions of treachery."[19] His exchequer being empty, James took some time to consider. He decided, January, 1619, that the headship of a Cambridge College was the right post for this type of man, and drew up a letter commanding the Fellows of Caius College to elect him to their vacant Mastership, certifying Wilson to be a man of learning and sufficiency, and adding that he would "take no denial." The letter, however, was never sent. Possibly the

16. Chamberlain to Carleton, Jan. 9; Lorkin to Puckering, Jan. 12, and February.
17. Feb. 18, 1619.
18. Howell to Carew Ralegh, May 5, 1645.
19. Stebbing, p. 383.

King began to wonder if the faithful service which it stressed had been useful service, after all.

Lady Ralegh, for some unknown reason, did not bury her husband at Beddington, but in front of the Communion table of St. Margaret's Church, Westminster. In 1845 a brass plate was put up drawing attention to the grave, and concluding with the advice: "Reader, should you reflect on his errors, remember his many virtues, and that he was a Mortal." I hope my own readers will not feel that they need confine their reflections to such limits. The head was embalmed and remained with Lady Ralegh till her death; and with her son Carew until it was buried with him. Bishop Godfrey Goodman, who managed to be at once King James's and Ralegh's admirer, testified: "No man doth honour the memory of Sir Walter Ralegh and his excellent parts more than myself; and in token thereof I know where his skull is kept to this day, and I have kissed it."[20]

Lady Ralegh received kindness and help from the Carews, beginning with Lady Carew's intercession to Sir Thomas Wilson

to surcease the pursuit of my husband's books or library, they being all the land and living which he left his poor child, hoping that he would inherit him in those only,[21] and that he would apply himself to learning to be fit for them, which request I hope I shall fulfil as far as in me lieth.[22]

Wilson was Keeper of Records, and had persuaded the King to seize Ralegh's library, globes, maps, and mathematical instruments. One of the last, Lady Ralegh said, had cost £100. In November a royal warrant took all, on the grounds that they could be "small use to Sir Walter's surviving wife." She fought passionately for the books, willing enough to let His Majesty have them if they had been "rare, and not to be had elsewhere. But they tell me that Byll, the book-binder or stationer, hath the very same." She secured a promise of them, how or when we do not know (just as she long ago had secured a promise of

20. *Court of King James*, i, 69. Goodman died, 1655.
21. Here we obviously have a quotation from their last talk together before the execution.
22. Nov. 8, *Calendar of State Papers, Domestic*, 1611–1618, p. 592.

Sherborne). But Wilson did not release them, so she had again to beg
Lady Carew to

be a mean unto Sir Thomas that I may be troubled no more in this matter
concerning the books, having had so many unspeakable losses and troubles,
as none of worth will seek to molest me, but rather give me comfort and
help.

We do not know if she ever got back Ralegh's books, or if she recovered his manuscript *Treatise on the Art of War* and his description
of all the world's seaports. The Government, which had confiscated
Ralegh's *Destiny* and all its contents, gave her for it £2250,[23] possibly
because this was practically the sum she herself had put into the ship,
by sale of her estate at Mitcham. She died in 1647, aged eighty-two.

Carew Ralegh, in 1621, at the age of sixteen, entered Wadham College, Oxford, as a gentleman commoner. The same year, the House of
Lords passed a bill restoring him in blood, which both Houses accepted in 1624. James refused his assent. About the same time, his
father's friend Lord Pembroke, whose hand we may see in the early
action taken by the House of Lords, introduced him at Court. But the
King complained that he was like "the ghost of his father," so Pembroke advised him not to trouble the royal conscience longer, but to
travel, "which he did until the death of King James, which happened
about a year after." Charles, the new king, had been hostile to Sir Walter, but Carew Ralegh's restoration in blood continued to be pressed on
him. It was resubmitted in 1626; Charles held out until 1628, and then
accepted it, on condition that Carew resigned all claim to Sherborne.
This he was most reluctant to do. But the King sent for him, and spoke
kindly but firmly, pointing out that Lord Digby had given him when
Prince of Wales £10,000 to keep him safe in the estate. Carew Ralegh
went away, still sullenly prepared to fight. But friends argued with him
on the folly of such a course, all the power being with the King. He
acquiesced, therefore. The stigma of treason was taken off his name,
and he served as a gentleman of the Privy Chamber, 1635–1639, a career
varied once by a week in Fleet prison for drawing his sword on a fel-

23. See *Acts of the Privy Council, Colonial Series*, 1613–1680, ed. W. L. Grant and
James Munro, Vol. i, Acts 52 and 203.

low-courtier. He was granted the reversion of the £400 a year paid to
his mother for Sherborne, which was to have gone to his elder brother
Wat, had he lived. Carew Ralegh was an attendant on King Charles
in his imprisonment at Hampton Court. Incidentally, his cousin the
Rev. Walter Ralegh, son of Sir Carew Ralegh, was also distinguished
for his loyalty, and was greatly persecuted as a malignant.

Lord Bristol (formerly Lord Digby) fled to the Continent after the
capitulation of Exeter, 1646, and his estates were supposed to be forfeited. Carew Ralegh was therefore pertinacious in his attempts to recover Sherborne between 1648 and 1660; and the Committee for the
sale of the estates of malignants recommended him to the House of
Commons as "a fit object" of its mercy. Lord Bristol, however, though
in exile was not powerless, and the matter stayed in abeyance. Carew
Ralegh was M.P. for Haslemere, 1648–1653, and Cromwell put him
in the Tower for a week, in May, 1650. He served when the Rump of
the Long Parliament returned for a few months in 1659. He worked
for Charles II's restoration, and when the King enjoyed his own again
was appointed to what had been his father's last official post, the Governorship of Jersey (1660); it is doubtful if he ever took it up. Charles
also offered him the honor of knighthood; he declined it, and it was
given as a special favor to his son. He wrote verses, some of which
were set to music by Milton's friend, Harry Lawes. Sir Henry Wotton
thought him "a gentleman of dexterous abilities,"[24] tactful and careful,
an opinion which Anthony à Wood quotes but qualifies by the statement that he was "far, God wot, from his father's parts, either as to the
sword or pen." He may have been (and doubtless was), and yet could
have been far above the average. He is kindly referred to in Evelyn's
Diary, August 10, 1658. He was respected; and he was unfalteringly
loyal to his father's memory.

Ralegh's faults were shown on a stage as public as can be imagined.
He was accused of overbearing pride and of base truckling. Both
charges were sometimes true; and letters survive of a humility that
pains us the more because addressed to such mean ministers of power
and punishment. Yet even these letters, closely examined with full
awareness of their context, rarely fail to reveal some stiffness of self-

24. Logan Pearsall Smith, *The Life and Letters of Sir Henry Wotton*, ii, 400.

respect suddenly breaking through a phraseology which may seem to us more abject than it really was, so much have fashions changed. We to-day can be sycophantic enough, God knows; but we no longer ascribe divinity to our rulers. Nor is there any word written by Ralegh under stress of utter anguish and helplessness which cannot be more than matched by words spoken by men who lived serenely above the need to beg for their lives. Howard of Effingham himself, the victor of 1588, though he pillaged Ralegh when he fell, while Ralegh was dear to the Queen could stoop low to him:

Old John Long, who then waited on Sir W. Long, being one time in the privy garden with his master, saw the Earl of Nottingham wipe the dust from Sir Walter Ralegh's shoes with his cloak, in compliment—[25]

presumably as near as a Howard could come to Ralegh's gesture when he flung his cloak beneath his Queen's tread.

It is horrible to remember Ralegh in Ireland; it is horrible to remember *any* Elizabethan in Ireland. And of course, by that high and noble tradition of truthfulness which distinguishes the Anglo-Saxon race (not in our own idealization of ourselves only, but in the general judgment of the outside world), he falls short. But that tradition has been "British" for a very brief period. It was not Elizabethan; still less, infinitely less, was it Jacobean. Yet even by this test Ralegh falls less than most contemporaries, though he was exposed to the temptations which beset the poet and the man whose mind stirs fiercely and always. When the worst has been said against him, he belongs to a different world from that of the Cecils and Bacons; and mankind will less and less be in any peril of confounding him with them.

Reckless, casual, often irresponsible, sometimes utterly undignified,

no figure, no life gathers up in itself more completely the whole spirit of an epoch; none more firmly enchains admiration for invincible individuality or ends by winning a more personal tenderness and affection.[26]

Every minute of his life he lived dangerously. To remember Walter Ralegh is to remember valor, imagination, magnanimity. Fashion in heroes changes. But some names keep their brightness—like gold coins when the kingdom that minted them has long been dust and legend.

25. Aubrey.   26. Stebbing, p. 400.

Appendix A

THE SPELLING OF RALEGH'S NAME

THE following contemporary variants have been collected by Mr. Stebbing: Raleigh, Rawly, Rawley, Raweley, Raulie, Rawlegh, Rawleigh, Rawleighe, Raughleigh, Raleghe, Rawlye, Rawleie, Rawligh, Raileigh, Raughlie, Rauleigh, Raleighe, Raylie, Raghley, Rawliegh, Raligh, Rawely, Wrawly, Raghlie, Rawleygh, Ralighe, Raule, Rawlee, Rauley, Rawleye, Raulyghe, Rawlyghe, Ralleigh, Rawlighe, Rawleighe, Rauleighe, Raughlie, Rallegh, Rawlei, Rauly, Raughley, Raughly, Raylye, Rolye, Ralle, Raughleigh, Raleikk, Rale, Real, Reali, Ralego, Rhalegh, Raley, Raleye, Raleagh, Raleygh, Raleyghe, Ralli, Raughleye, Rauleghe, Raulghe, Raweleigh, Raylygh, Reigley, Rhaleigh, Rhaly, Wrawley, Rauley. To these we could add other spellings: the Gualtero, Guatteral, Gualteral, of Gondomar and other Spaniards; the Dutch Sir Walter Halley; the French Raleich; the Venetian Ralo and Rallé: the Latin Raulaeus and Raleghus.

He himself signs himself once, in 1578, as Rawleyghe; then, until 1583, he usually signs Rauley. "From June 9, 1584, he used till his death no other signature than Ralegh. It appears in his books when the name is mentioned. Of the 169 letters collected by Mr. Edward Edwards, 135 are thus signed. . . . The spelling Raleigh, which posterity has preferred, happens to be the one he is not known to have ever employed."[1]

A deed signed by his father has Ralegh; and his brother Carew Ralegh signed himself Rawlygh.

1. Stebbing, *Life of Ralegh*, p. 31.

Appendix B

THE "POOR DAUGHTER" LETTER

THIS letter was printed in 1839, by the Rev. J. S. Brewer,[1] from a MS. copy in All Souls College Library: "by Sir Walter Ralegh to his Wife, after he had hurt himself in the Tower," i.e., after his attempt to kill himself:

Receive from thy unfortunate husband these his last lines; these the last words that ever thou shalt receive from him. That I can live never to see thee and my child more!—I cannot! I have desired God and disputed with my reason, but nature and compassion hath the victory. That I can live to think how you are both left a spoil to my enemies, and that my name shall be a dishonour to my child—I cannot! I cannot endure the memory thereof! Unfortunate woman, unfortunate child, comfort yourselves; trust God, and be contented with your poor estate! I would have bettered it, if I had enjoyed it a few years.

Thou art a young woman, and forbear not to marry again. It is now nothing to me; thou art no more mine; nor I thine. To witness that thou didst love me once, take care that thou marry not to please sense, but to avoid poverty and to preserve thy child. That thou didst also love me living, witness it to others—to my poor daughter, to whom I have given nothing; for his sake, who will be cruel to himself to preserve thee! Be charitable to her, and teach thy son to love her for his father's sake.

For myself, I am left of all men, that have done good to many. All my good turns forgotten; all my errors revived and expounded to all extremity of ill. All my services, hazards, and expenses for my country—plantings, discoveries, fights, councils, and whatsoever else—malice hath now covered over. I am now made an enemy and traitor by the word of an unworthy man. He hath proclaimed me to be a partaker of his vain imaginations, notwithstanding the whole course of my life hath approved the contrary, as my death shall approve it. Woe, woe, woe be unto him, by whose falsehood we are lost! He hath separated us asunder! He hath slain my honour; my fortune! He hath robbed thee of thy husband, and me of you both! O God! thou dost know my wrongs! . . .

There is a great deal more of this, in a similar strain. It has been much admired. Gardiner, for example, though he found Ralegh's *Pilgrimage* disappointing, thought this letter "one of the most touching compositions in the English language," and quoted it at length. It is, as a matter of fact, one of the most nauseating compositions in the English language, and biographers have been loth to accept it, since we can test its genuineness by Ralegh's unquestioned letter of farewell to his wife. "Hard as it may be to distinguish rhetoric and passion in the death-bed phrases of men who have lived

1. As an Appendix to Goodman, *Court of King James*, ii, 93.

before the world, the contrast here with the natural pathos of the other . . .
is too irreconcilably vivid. Then there is the extraordinary apparition of an
otherwise invisible daughter."[2]

Of that daughter we have not a word anywhere else; and, since plainly
she must have been an illegitimate daughter, with a man so hated and vili-
fied as Ralegh some enemy or other (one thinks) would have put her existence on record. The argument from "internal evidence," which is generally
worth so little, in this case seems almost convincing. The letter's style is not
Ralegh's, nor are its vague generalities; he delighted too much (one argues)
in the concrete instance to have suppressed it and have written of his services as "hazards, and expenses for my country." The "poor daughter" *looks*
like a myth, and the letter like an invention; for this reason I ignored them
in my narrative.

The publication of this book in England, however, brought me a great
many letters, and revealed the tenacity with which family history and tradition are cherished in the western counties. I heard not only from direct descendants of Ralegh himself, but from the family of Laurence Kemys, with
additional proof that the latter was a man of quite exceptional scholarship
and far from "the rough sailor" of his and his master's critics. And among
my letters is one that possibly concerns Ralegh's "poor daughter." A lady,
Miss Lucy Selina French, has sent me a copy of a paper she found in an
old dressing case, many years ago. "The writing was like a very old person's
and the illegible words most aggravating." The paper stated: "Sir Walter
Raleigh's daughter married his friend Sir John Kempthorne" (here came
some illegible words) "who married a man named Whitcombé, who built
Whitcombe Street and who lent Prince Rupert £30,000 which he never re-
paid and so ruined Whitcombe. Whitcombe's daughter Lydia married John
Lapp (a Dutchman) of Waterford" (Ireland). From John Lapp the family
line runs down in eight generations to my informant, Miss French herself.
Miss French tells me that her family tried to trace Lady Kempthorne in
the Herald's Office, but that the reply was that since she was illegitimate
this was impossible.

The incident is one more proof of what is now recognized, the wealth of
historical material buried in family records and traditions all over England.
(I do not despair of Ralegh's *Life of Queen Elizabeth,* which Ben Jonson
said was "extant," one day coming to light.) This "poor daughter," then,
calls for further investigation; and she may, after all, prove to have existed,
an illegitimate child of Ralegh but not of Lady Ralegh. In that case, the

2. Stebbing, 197–198.

letter, so often and convincingly rejected, will have to be accepted—with this excuse, that Ralegh, like all men who are capable of "wallowing" in imagination and in mental wretchedness, could write very poorly and falsely sometimes.

Bibliography

Aikin, Lucy, *Memoirs of the Court of King James the First,* 2 vols. (1822).

Anthony, Irvin, *Ralegh* (1934).

Arber, Edward, English Reprints.

Archaeologica, vols. 34 and 35.

Ashmolean MSS. DCCLXXXVI, fol. 101, Bodleian Library, Oxford.

Aubrey, John, *Brief Lives,* ed. A. Clark (1898), 2 vols.

Aulicus Coquinariae, or a Vindication in Answer to a Pamphlet entitled the Court and Character of King James (1650), *Pretended to be penned by Sir A. W., and published since his death* (1650).

Azores, Papers Relating to Expedition to, Brit. Mus. Additional MSS. 5752.

Bacon, Anthony, Correspondence. MSS. Tenison, Lambeth, and Catalogue, Lambeth Palace MSS.

Bacon, Francis, Lord Verulam, *Letters and Life,* James Spedding.

——*Apophthegms.*

Bagwell, Richard, *Ireland under the Tudors.*

Bancroft, Edward, *Essay on the Natural History of Guiana* (1769).

Bayley, John, *History and Antiquities of the Tower of London* (1821).

Beard, Charles A. and Mary R., *The Rise of American Civilization* (1930).

Beaumont, Christopher de Harlay de, *Lettres à Henri IV.*

Birch, Thomas, *Life of Sir Walter Ralegh* (in vol. i of 1829 edition of Ralegh's *Works*).

——*Memoirs of the Reign of Queen Elizabeth,* 2 vols. (1754).

——*Life of Henry, Prince of Wales, Son of James the First* (1760).

——*The Court and Times of James the First,* 2 vols. (1848).

Boas, F. S., *Marlowe and his Circle.*

Bruce, John, *Correspondence of King James VI of Scotland with Sir Robert Cecil and Others in England* (Camden Society, 1861).

Brushfield, T. N., *Raleghana* (Devon Association *Transactions,* vols. xxi, xxviii).

——*Western Antiquary,* iv.

——*Bibliography of Sir Walter Ralegh* (reprinted from *Western Antiquary*).

——*Tobacco and Potatoes* (Devon Association *Transactions,* xxx).

Buchan, John, *Walter Ralegh* (Stanhope Historical Prize Essay, University of Oxford, 1897).

Bullen, A. H., *England's Helicon* and F. Davison's *Poetical Rhapsody.*

Burghley, Lord. *See* Murdin, W.

Byrne, M. St. Clare, *Elizabethan Life in Town and Country* (1925).

Calendar, Carew MSS. (6 vols.) 1515–1624, ed. S. S. Brewer and W. Bullen.

Calendar of State Papers, Colonial.

——*Domestic,* Elizabeth, 1558–1603. James I, 1603–1618.

——*Ireland,* Elizabeth.

——*Spanish,* 1587–1603 (Simancas Papers, ed. Martin Hume).

——*Venetian,* Elizabeth and James I.

Camden Miscellany, vol. 5, ed. S. R. Gardiner. *Documents Relating to Raleigh's Last Voyage.*

Camden, William, *Annales, etc., regnante Elizabetha,* ed. Thomas Hearne (1717).

——*Annales Regni Jacobi: Epistolae,* ed. T. Smith (1691).

Carew, George, Lord, *Letters from, to Sir Thomas Roe,* 1615–1617, ed. John Maclean (Camden Society, 1860).

Carew, Richard, Survey of Cornwall (1602), ed. Lord de Dunstanville (1811).

Cary, Robert, *Memoirs of Robert Cary, Earl of Monmouth* (1808 ed.).

Cayley, A., *Life of Sir Walter Raleigh,* 2 vols. (1806).

Cecil, Algernon, *Life of Robert Cecil, First Earl of Salisbury* (1915).

Cecil MSS., Historical MSS. Commission, vols. 4, 6, 7.

Chamberlain, John, *Letters by . . . during the Reign of Elizabeth* (Camden Society, 1861). *See also* Statham, E. P.

Chamberlin, F., *The Private Character of Queen Elizabeth* (1922).

Chapman, George, *Poetical Works,* with Introduction by Algernon C. Swinburne (1875), 3 vols.

Clarendon, Edward Hyde, Earl of, *The Difference and Disparity between the Estates and Conditions of George, Duke of Buckingham and Robert, Earl of Essex (Reliq. Wotton.,* 1685).

Cobbett. *See* Howell, T. B.

Collier, J. Payne, *Archaeologia,* 1852–1853.

——*Egerton Papers.*

——*Notes and Queries,* 3rd series, vol. 5.

Collins, Arthur, *Letters and Memorials of State in the Reigns of Queen Mary, Queen Elizabeth, King James* (1726).

Corbett, Sir J. S., *The Successors of Drake.*

Corney, Bolton, *Curiosities of Literature* (by I. D'Israeli). *Illustrated by B. C.*

Costello, Louisa Stuart, *Memoirs of Eminent Englishwomen.*
Cotton Library MSS., Brit. Mus., Galba.
Creighton, Mandell, *Elizabeth.*
Cromwell, Oliver, *Letters and Speeches,* ed. Thomas Carlyle.
——*Memoirs of the Protector Oliver Cromwell and of his Sons Richard and Henry,* by Oliver Cromwell (1820).
Cust, Lionel, *Portraits of Sir Walter Raleigh* (Walpole Society, vol. 8).

Dalton, Henry E. *The History of British Guiana* (1855).
Declaration of the Demeanour and Carriage of Sir W. Raleigh, as well in his Voyage, as in and since his Return: printed by the King's Printers, 1618, reprinted, *Harleian Miscellany* (1809), and in Harlow's *Ralegh's Last Voyage* (1932).
Dee, Dr. John, *Private Diary,* ed. J. P. Halliwell (Camden Society, 1842).
Devereux, Walter B., *Lives and Letters of the Earls of Essex.*
Devonshire Association for the Advancement of Science, Literature and Art, *Transactions* of the. *See also* Brushfield.
D'Ewes, Sir Simonds, *Journals of all the Parliaments during the Reign of Queen Elizabeth,* ed. Paul Bowes (1682).
Dictionary of National Biography.
D'Israeli, Isaac, *Curiosities of Literature.*
——*Amenities of Literature* (*Psychological History of Rawleigh*).
Dixon, W. H., *Her Majesty's Tower.*
Drexelius, Jeremiah, *Trismegistus Christianus* (Antwerp, 1643).
Drummond, William, of Hawthornden, *Conversations with Ben Jonson.* *See* Jonson.

Edwards, Edward, *The Life of Sir Walter Ralegh,* 2 vols. (1868).
Egerton Papers, ed. J. P. Collier.
Eliot, Sir John, *The Monarchy of Man,* Harleian MSS.
Ellis-Fermor, V. M., *Christopher Marlowe* (1927).
Encyclopaedia Britannica.
Evelyn, John, *Diary and Correspondence.*

Febre, Nicholas de, *Discours sur le Grand Cordial de Sir W. R.* (1664).
Firth, Sir Charles, *Sir W. Raleigh's History of the World* (*Proceedings,* British Academy, 1917–1918).
Flying Chudleigh, narrative of the Chaplain of the, MSS. Corpus Christi, Oxford: printed *Notes and Queries,* Jan. 5, 1861, also in J. Spedding, *Letters and Life of Francis Bacon,* vol. vi, and in E. Harlow, *Ralegh's Last Voyage.*

Foley, Henry, S. J., *Records of the English Province of the Society of Jesus* (1878).

Forster, John, *Life of Sir John Eliot* (1864).

Fortescue Papers, collected by John Packer, Secretary to G. Villiers, Duke of Buckingham, ed. S. R. Gardiner.

Fortnightly Review, vol. vii (1867); *The Case against Sir Walter Ralegh* by S. R. Gardiner.

Foss, Edward, *Judges of England.*

Foster, Sir Michael, *Trial of the Rebels in 1746 and other Crown Cases.*

Foster, Sir William, *First Letter-Book of the East India Company.*

——*The Embassy of Sir Thomas Roe to India.*

Foxe, John, *Acts and Monuments,* etc. ("Book of Martyrs"; 1684 ed.).

Froude, J. A., *English Seamen of the Sixteenth Century.*

——*History of England, Elizabeth* (references usually to "Everyman's" ed.).

Fugger News-Letters, 1st and 2nd Series.

Fuller, Thomas, *Worthies of England.*

Gainsford, Thomas, *Vox Spiritus, or Sir Walter Rawleigh's Ghost* (1620). Printed Utrecht, 1626: Harleian Miscellany, v. (1745).

Gardiner, S. R., *History of England,* 1603–1642, 3 vols.

——*Prince Charles and the Spanish Marriage,* 1617–1623, 2 vols.

——*The Case against Sir Walter Raleigh* (*Fortnightly Review,* vol. vii, new series, vol. i).

Gascoigne, George, *The Glasse of Gouernment,* ed. W. C. Hazlitt.

——*The Steele Glas.* See Gilbert, Sir Humphrey.

Gayley, Charles Mills, *Shakespeare and the Founders of Liberty in America* (Macmillan Company, New York, 1918; University of California semi-centennial publication).

Geographical Journal, August, 1914.

Gerard, John, *Herbal* (1597; with dedication to Sir Walter Ralegh).

Gibbon, Edward, *Life and Works,* ed. John, Lord Sheffield (1814).

Gibson MSS., Lambeth Palace Library, viii, fol. 21.

Gifford, William, Ben Jonson's *Works.*

Gilbert, Sir Humphrey, *A Discourse to Prove a Passage by the North-West to Cathaia* (1576). Published by Gascoigne.

Goodman, Godfrey, Bishop, *The Court of King James the First,* ed. J. S. Brewer, 2 vols.

Gorges, Sir Arthur, *A Large Relation of the said Island Voyage* (in *Purchas his Pilgrimes*).

Gosse, Edmund, *Ralegh* (1886). Also in *Athenaeum,* Jan. 2 and 9, 1886, *Sir W. Raleigh's "Cynthia."*

Gutch, J., *Collectanea Curiosa* (1781). *See also* Wood, Anthony à.

Hailes, Lord, *Secret Correspondence of Sir Robert Cecil with James VI* (1766).

Hakluyt, Richard, *Voyages,* etc. The best edition is the elaborate one published by Maclehose; but I have usually cited the "Everyman's" one.

Hall, Bishop Joseph, *Balm of Gilead* (1660).

Hallam, Henry, *Constitutional History of England.*

——*Introduction to the Literature of Europe.*

Hannah, John, *Courtly Poets, from Ralegh to Montrose.*

Harington, Sir John, *Nugae Antiquae* (1804).

——*A Brief State of the Church of England.*

——*Letters.*

Hariot, Thomas, *A Brief and True Report of the new found Land of Virginia* (reprinted, Hakluyt's *Voyages*).

Harleian MSS., Brit. Mus.

Harleian Miscellany, ed. W. Oldys and Thomas Park.

Harlow, Edward, *The Discoverie of Guiana,* ed. Argonaut Press (1928).

——*Ralegh's Last Voyage* (1932).

Harrison, G. B., *An Elizabethan Journal.*

——*A Second Elizabethan Journal.*

——*A Last Elizabethan Journal.*

Hatfield Papers. *See* Murdin, W.

Hearne, Thomas, Appendix to Preface to *Chronic. Walteri Hemingford, Edward I, II, & III.*

Heylin, Peter, "Observations upon some particular persons and passages in a Book intituled *A Compleat History of the Lives and Reigns of Queen Mary and King James.* By a Lover of the Truth," 1656. (This pamphlet is often ascribed to Carew Ralegh as the real author, and in any case is accepted as having been inspired by him.)

Historical Account of Sir Walter Raleigh's Voyages and Adventures (1719).

Holinshed, Raphael, *Chronicles of England, Scotland, and Ireland* (1807).

Hooker, John (alias Vowell), *Epistle Dedicatory* to translation of *The Irish Histories of Giraldus Cambrensis.*

——*Continuation* of Holinshed's *Chronicles of Ireland.*

Howell, James, *Epistolae Ho-Elianae,* ed. Joseph Jacobs (1890).

Howell, T. B., edition of Cobbett's *Complete Collection of State Trials.*

Humboldt, F. H. Alexander von, *Personal Narrative of Travels,* 2 vols.

Hume, David, *History of England*.
Hume, Martin, *Sir Walter Ralegh*.
——*Simancas Papers*.
Hutchinson, Lucy, *Life of Colonel Hutchinson*.

Irish Correspondence, Elizabeth. Record Office.
Issues of the Exchequer during the Reign of James I.

James VI of Scotland. *See* Bruce, John.
——*Works* of.
Jonson, Ben, *Works,* ed. William Gifford and Cunningham (1910). Also, edition of Percy Simpson (Oxford University Press).

Kemys, Laurence, *The Second Voyage of Guiana performed and written in the year 1596* (Hakluyt).
King, Captain Samuel, *Narrative of Sir Walter Ralegh's Motives and Opportunities for conveying himself out of the Kingdom, with the Manner in which he was betrayed* (cited by William Oldys—otherwise not known).
Kingsley, Rev. Charles, *Miscellanies* (1859).
Kirkpatrick, F. A., *The Spanish Conquistadores* (1934).

Lansdowne MSS., Brit. Mus.
Latham, Agnes, *The Poems of Sir Walter Ralegh* (1929).
Lee, Sir Sidney, *Great Englishmen of the Sixteenth Century*.
Lingard, Rev. John, *History of England*.
Linschoten, Jan Huyghen van, *Itinerario,* 1596 (English translation, 1598).
Lismore Papers. Notes and Diaries of Sir Richard Boyle, first Earl of Cork, ed. Alexander B. Grosart.
Lloyd, David, *State Worthies* (1670).
Lodge, Edmund, *Portraits of Illustrious Personages*.
Loseley MSS., Henry VIII–James I, ed. A. J. Kempe.
Lyon, F. H., *El Conde de Gondomar* (1910).

McFee, W., *Sir Martin Frobisher*.
Marêtz, Comte des, *Despatches,* MSS. 1616–1617 (Bibliothèque Nationale, Paris).
Markham, Sir Clements, *Expeditions into the Valley of the Amazons* (1859).
Masham, Thomas, *The Third Voyage set forth by Sir Walter Ralegh to Guiana . . . in the year 1596* (Hakluyt).

Matthew, Sir Toby, *Collection of Letters.*

Monson, Sir William, *Narrative of the Principal Naval Expeditions of English Fleets,* 1588–1603. MSS. Cotton; also in Churchill's *Collection of Voyages and Travels,* and in *Naval Tracts,* ed. M. Oppenheim, 5 vols. (Navy Records Society).

Murdin, W., *State Papers, etc.* (Lord Burghley's Papers), 2 vols.

Napier, Macvey, *Lord Bacon and Sir Walter Raleigh.*

Naunton, Sir Robert, *Fragmenta Regalia.*

Navy Records Society (Slingsby's *Voyage to Cadiz*).

Neale, J. E., *Queen Elizabeth.*

Newes of Sir Walter Rauleigh from the River of Caliana (1618).

Nicolas, Sir Nicholas Harris, *Life and Times of Sir Christopher Hatton.*

Notes and Queries. See also Collier, J. P.

Observations upon a Book, etc. *See* Heylin, Peter.

Oldys, William, *Life of Sir Walter Ralegh* (in vol. i of 1829 edition of Ralegh's *Works*).

Orders to be Observed in the Fleet under Raleigh (Navy Records Society, vol. 29; see *Newes of Sir Walter Rauleigh;* reprinted by Harlow, *Ralegh's Last Voyage*).

Osborne, Francis, *Traditional Memoirs,* etc.

Overbury, Sir Thomas, *Trial of Sir Walter Ralegh.* MSS. Cotton. Titus, C7, Brit. Mus.

Oxford, Register of the University of, ed. Andrew Clark.

Parsons, Robert (alias R. Doleman the Jesuit), *Per D. Andraeam Philopatrum ad idem* (i.e., *Elizabethae Reginae Edictum,* Nov. 29, 1592) *Responsio* (Lyons, 1592).

——*Leicester's Commonwealth* (IV, *Harleian Miscellany*). (Query, falsely attributed to Parsons.)

Pope-Hennessy, Sir John, *Ralegh in Ireland* (1883).

Prince, John, *The Worthies of Devon.*

Privy Councils, Acts of, from 1580 onwards.

Privy Council Registers, Elizabeth and James I.

Purchas, Samuel, *Purchas his Pilgrimes* (best edition, Maclehose's).

Puttenham, George, *The Art of English Poesie.*

Ralegh, Carew. *See* Heylin, Peter; also vol. viii of Sir Walter Ralegh's *Works;* and *Harleian Miscellany* (1745), iv.

Ralegh, Sir Walter, *Works* (Oxford University Press, 1829).

——Selections from his Prose, ed. G. E. Hadow (Oxford University Press, 1917).

——*Apology* for his Voyage to Guiana (reprinted in Harlow, *Ralegh's Last Voyage*).

——*The Discoverie of Guiana* (reprinted and edited by Schomburgk, and Harlow; also in "Everyman's" edition of Hakluyt's *Voyages,* etc.).

——*A Discourse of War in General.*

——*A Discourse Touching a War with Spain.*

——*Instructions to his Son and to Posterity.*

——*A Discourse Touching a Marriage between Prince Henry of England and a Daughter of Savoy.*

——*A Discourse, etc. Touching a Match between the Lady Elizabeth and the Prince of Piedmont.*

——*Maxims of State.*

——*The History of the World.*

——*Orders to Commanders,* etc. (voyage to Guiana, 1617).

——*Poems (see* Hannah, and Latham).

——*The Prerogative of Parliaments.*

——*A Relation of the Action at Cadiz.*

——*A Report of the Truth of the Fight about the Isle of Azores* (not in collected edition of *Works,* but see Hakluyt's *Voyages*).

Read, Conyers, *Mr. Secretary Walsingham and the Policy of Queen Elizabeth,* 3 vols.

Record Office MSS.

Rodd, Rennell, *Sir W. Ralegh.*

Rodway, James, *Guiana* (1912).

Ros, Lt.-General Lord de, *Memorials of the Tower of London.*

Ross, Sir Denison, *Sir Arthur Sherley* ("Broadway Travellers," 1933).

Rushworth, John, *Historical Collections of Private Papers of State.*

St. John, J. A., *Life of Sir W. Ralegh.*

Sanderson, Sir William, *The Lives and Reigns of Mary Queen of Scotland and James the Sixth, King of Scotland* (1656).

Schomburgk, R. H., edition of Ralegh's *Discoverie of Guiana.*

Shirley, John (or Benjamin, or James), *Life of the Valiant and Learned Sir Walter Ralegh, Kt.* (1677).

Smith, Logan Pearsall, *The Life and Letters of Sir Henry Wotton* (1907).

Somers, Lord, Collection of Tracts, ed. Walter Scott (1809). Petition of Carew Ralegh, "only son of Sir Walter Ralegh, late deceased."

Spedding, James, edition of Bacon's *Works.*

Spence, Rev. Joseph, *Observations, Anecdotes and Characters of Men,* ed.
   G. Malone.
Spenser, Edmund, *Works* (Globe ed.).
Statham, E. P., *A Jacobean Letter-Writer* (*see* Chamberlain, John).
Stebbing, W., *Sir Walter Ralegh* (1891 and 1899).
Stephen, Sir H. L., *State Trials,* 2 vols.
——*The Trial of Raleigh* (Royal Historical Society, *Transactions,* 1919).
——*History of the Criminal Law of England.*
Stowe, J., *A Survey of London and Westminster.*
——*Annals.*
Strachey, J. Lytton, *Elizabeth and Essex.*
Strype, J., *Annals of the Reformation,* etc.
Stukeley, Sir Lewis, *Apology,* etc. (vol. viii, Ralegh's *Works*).
Sully, Maximilien de Bethune, Duc de, *Mémoires* (Paris, 1768).
Sydney, Sir Henry, *Letters and Memorials of State* (Queen Mary to Oliver
   Cromwell).

Tanner MSS., Bodleian Library, Oxford (Archbishop Sancroft's collection).
Tenison MSS. Catalogue, Lambeth Palace Library.
Townshend, Heywood, *The Four Last Parliaments of Queen Elizabeth*
   (1680).
Trevelyan, G. M., *History of England.*
Trial of Sir Walter Ralegh, Harleian MSS. vol. 39.
Tytler, Patrick Fraser, *Life of Sir Walter Raleigh.*

U.S.A. Commission of Boundary between Venezuela and British Guiana:
   Report (Washington, 1897).

Venezuela-British Guiana Boundary Dispute, Bluebooks issued by Foreign
   Office, 1897–1899, 17 vols.
Vere, Sir Francis, *Commentaries,* ed. William Dillingham (1657), reprinted
   Edward Arber in vii, *English Garner* (1883).

Waldman, Milton, *Sir Walter Ralegh.*
——*Queen Elizabeth.*
Walton, Sir Izaak, *The Compleat Angler.*
Welldon, Sir Anthony, *The Court and Character of King James* (1650).
Wharton MSS., Bodleian Library, Oxford.
Williams, Charles, *James I* (1934).
Williamson, James A., *English Colonies in Guiana* (1923).
——*Sir John Hawkins.*

Willoughby, Henry, *His Avisa,* ed. G. B. Harrison (1926).

Winstanley, W., *English Worthies.*

Winwood, Sir Ralph, *Memorials of Affairs of State in the Reigns of Queen Elizabeth and King James I,* ed. E. Sawyer (1725).

Wood, Anthony à, *Athenae Oxonienses.*

Wotton, Sir Henry, *Reliquiae Wottonianae* (4th ed., 1685).

Index

Abbot, George (Archbishop of Canterbury), 75, 257, 271 ff., 276 ff., 293, 337
Acton, Lord, 246
Acuña, Diego Palomeque de, 320, 330
—— Diego Sarmiento de. *See* Gondomar
Aio, Mt., 114, 319, 320
Allen, Cardinal, 39
—— Sir Francis, 66
Alley, Captain, 307, 321
All Souls College, Oxford, 28, 395
Anderson, Sir Edmund, 203
Andrewes, Lancelot, 277, 347
Anglicanism, 14 ff., 74 ff.
Anne, Queen, 56, 192, 220, 237 ff., 245, 261, 263 ff., 272 ff., 281, 289, 351, 355 ff., 367
Anthropophagi, 103
Antonio, Don, 29, 52, 62, 65
Apology, Ralegh's, 317
Apsley, Sir Allen, 353, 359
Arenberg, Count d', 193 ff., 197 ff., 217 ff.
Ark Ralegh, 40, 61
Armada, Invincible, 40, 58 ff., 64 ff., 86, 256
Armadillo, 108
Artaxerxes, 255
Arundel, Lord, 295, 299, 333, 341, 377, 380 ff.
Ashley, Sir Anthony, 120
Ashton, Roger, 213
Atabalipa, 115
Atheism, 74 ff.
Aubrey, John, 7, 23, 75, 187
Azores, 44, 49, 84 ff., 96, 136 ff.
Aztecs, 110

Babington, Anthony, 31 ff., 39, 52 ff.
Bacon, Anthony, 90, 120
—— Francis, 7, 32, 170, 280, 298, 328, 337
Bahamas, 48
Bailey, Captain, 302, 304
Balsam of Guiana, 236, 238, 261
Bark Ralegh, 40, 42

Baronetcies, sale of, 264
Basing, 167
Bath, 116, 144, 231
—— Earl of, 60, 97
Beaumont, Comte de, 200, 220 ff., 227
—— Comtesse de, 236
Bedford, Countess of, 250, 284
Beeston, Sir Hugh, 368
Belle, Antoine, 291
Berkley, Mary, 16
Bermudas, 49
Berreo, Antonio de, 105 ff., 111, 319
Bible, Authorized Version of, 180, 185
Bilbao, 48
Bilson, Bishop, 223, 276, 278
Biron, Duke of, 166
Blackwater, battle of the, 148
Blount, Sir Christopher, 140, 151, 160 ff.
Bodleian Library, 130, 251
Bonner, Bishop, 39, 75
Bothwell, Francis, Earl of, 154, 157
Boyle, Robert, 169, 302
Brewer, J. S., 395
Bridges, Robert, 77
Bristol, 4, 21
Brittany, 119
Broadcloth, 30, 37
Brooke, George, 194, 196, 223
Brownists, 82
Buckingham, Duke of. *See* Villiers, George
Budleigh Salterton, 1
Bullen, A. H., 373
Bunyan, John, 115, 213, 254
Burghley, Lord, 4, 16, 22 ff., 25 ff., 52, 70 ff., 91 ff., 97 ff., 112, 130, 148, 207, 217
Burrough, Sir John, 96
Burton, William, 76
Butlers (Irish family of), 24
Bye Plot, 196 ff.

Cadiz, 59, 112, 119 ff., 132, 232, 269, 293, 316, 374
Caesar, Sir Julius, 97, 238

Caliana River, 306
Caliban, 114
Cambridge University, 30, 76, 389
Camden, William, 63, 89
Campion, Edmund, 203, 210
Canary Islands, 302 ff.
Carew, George, 3, 19, 62, 67, 94, 120, 124, 134, 149, 159, 165, 169, 174, 183, 186 ff., 238, 239, 263, 270, 283, 284, 293, 303, 316, 318, 329, 338 ff., 367, 372, 380, 390
—— Lady, 355 ff., 360, 372, 390 ff.
—— Sir Nicholas, 189, 383
—— Sir Peter (elder), 15
—— Sir Peter (younger), 3, 18
—— Sir Randolph, 377
Carleton, Sir Dudley, 209, 221, 223, 227, 249, 308, 362, 368, 386
Caroni River, 109, 113, 323
Cartagena, 49, 58
Cary, Sir R., 185
Catholicism, 2 ff., 14 ff., 39, 40, 41, 59, 74, 83, 119, 195 ff.
Cayley, Arthur, 216
Cecil, Lady, 131
—— Robert, Earl of Salisbury, 32, 89, 91 ff., 95, 101, 112, 119, 132 ff., 145 ff., 152 ff., 163, 164, 174 ff., 186 ff., 195 ff., 213 ff., 220, 223, 229, 230 ff., 237, 241, 244, 247 ff., 261 ff., 263 ff., 269 ff., 280, 357
—— William. See Burghley, Lord
—— William, Earl of Salisbury, 132, 154, 168
Cedars, 146
Chamberlain, John, 148, 151, 209, 261, 369, 386
Champernoun, Sir Arthur, 3
—— Gawain, 8. See also Ralegh, Katharine
Chapman, George, 116, 117
Charles I, 204, 384, 391
—— II, 392
Child, Thomas, 7
Cinque Ports, 173
Clerke (Jesuit), 195 ff., 223
Clifford, Sir Conyers, 120
Clyst St. Mary, battle of, 2
Cobham, Lord, 146, 152, 159, 161 ff., 167,

172, 173, 176 ff., 181 ff., 191 ff., 196 ff., 206 ff., 210 ff., 231, 234, 238, 244. See also Howard, Katharine
—— Thomas, 5
Coke, Sir Edward, 204 ff., 247, 253, 279, 363
Condé, Prince of, 6, 8
Copley, Anthony, 196
Cordial, Ralegh's. See Balsam of Guiana
Cork, 14, 18
Cornelius, Father, 83
Cornwall, 5, 32, 60, 68, 83, 111, 116, 142, 144, 146, 187, 202, 211
Cottington, Lord, 384, 386
Coventry, Sir Thomas, 364
Crockern Tor, 32
Cromwell, Oliver, 254
—— Richard, 254
Cuba, 47
Cuff, Henry, 162
Cumberland, Earl of, 96, 98
"Cynthia," Ralegh's poem to, 70 ff.

Darnley, Lord, 35
Dartmoor, 1, 32
Dartmouth, 12, 96 ff., 270
Davies, John, 45
Declaration, King James's, 311, 316 ff., 323, 341, 347, 350
Dee, Dr. John, 75, 83
Denmark, 62, 211
—— King of, 251, 289
Desmond, Countess of, 169
—— Earl of, 18, 22
Destiny, 289 ff., 306, 339, 345
Devereux. See Essex, Earl of
Devon, 1, 3, 15, 18, 32, 35, 51, 60, 86, 97, 116, 149, 346, 382, 388
Devonshire, Earl of, 197, 203, 218
Digby, Sir John, 272, 280, 303, 336 ff., 344, 359, 391
—— Sir Kenelm, 238
Discoverie of Guiana, 107 ff., 114 ff.
D'Israeli, Isaac, 252
Doncaster, Lord. See Hay, James
Donne, John, 259
Dorset, Earl of, 218, 262
Doughty, Thomas, 139
Drake, Richard, 61

—— Sir Francis, 6, 29, 37, 51, 58 ff., 65 ff., 68, 112, 119, 136, 139, 329, 348, 374

Drexelius, 30

Drummond, Mrs., 218

—— of Hawthornden, 35, 296

Dudley, Edmund, 34, 177. *See also* Leicester, Earl of

Durham House, 76, 100, 160, 163, 167 ff., 174 ff., 177, 182, 190, 283

Dutch. *See* Low Countries

East India Company, 295, 385

Edmondes, Sir Thomas, 288

Edward VI, 2

Edwards, Edward, v–vi, 36, 394

Effingham, Lady, 236

—— Lord. *See* Howard, Charles

Egerton, Lord, 101, 149

El Dorado, 68, 104 ff., 111, 271, 314, 330

Eliot, Sir John, 382

Elizabeth, Princess, 241, 254, 270, 387

—— Queen, 4, 11, 16 ff., 22 ff., 27 ff., 32 ff., 37 ff., 46 ff., 51 ff., 58 ff., 64 ff., 75 ff., 84, 87 ff., 94 ff., 105 ff., 112 ff., 119 ff., 129 ff., 131 ff., 135 ff., 142 ff., 145, 148 ff., 162 ff., 164 ff., 171 ff., 177 ff., 180, 184, 207 ff., 212, 243 ff., 258, 266, 270, 282, 294, 316, 343, 355

Ellesmere, Lord, 274

Ellis-Fermor, Miss, 78

Empson, Sir Richard, 1, 177

Erskine, Sir Thomas, 189, 304

Essex, Lady (Howard, Frances), 87, 274 ff., 283

—— Robert Devereux, Second Earl of, 29, 64, 72, 81, 87, 90, 94, 119 ff., 131 ff., 143, 147 ff., 164 ff., 170 ff., 177, 182, 185, 189, 192, 205, 274, 375, 381

—— Robert Devereux, Third Earl of, 274 ff.

Evelyn, John, 392

Exeter, 2, 34, 60, 97, 120

Faerie Queene, The, 70 ff.

Faige, Captain, 292

Faint, Nicholas, 101

Falmouth, 45

Falstaff, Sir John, 10

Farnese, Alexander. *See* Parma, Prince of

Fayal, capture of, 138, 256

Fenton, Lord. *See* Erskine, Sir Thomas

Ferne, Sir John, 295, 300, 332 ff.

Field, Dr. Richard, 227

Firth, Sir Charles, vi, 253, 381

Fitton, Mary, 92

Fitzgerald, Sir James, 18. *See also* Desmond, Earl of

Fitzwilliams, Sir William, 20, 66 ff.

Fleet Prison, 234

Flemings, 25, 68, 343

Flores, 136

Florida, 40

Forman, Dr., 275, 279

Forster, E. M., 41 ff.

France and the French, 8 ff., 59, 119, 153, 165 ff., 174, 200, 221, 229, 242, 256, 265, 289, 291 ff., 295, 302, 350 ff., 360 ff., 379

Frobisher, Sir Martin, 25, 37, 88, 96, 112

Fuller, Thomas, 23, 27, 386

Gainsford, 388

Galicia, 13

Gama, Vasco da, 57

Gardiner, S. R., 215, 226, 277, 288, 292, 311, 317 ff., 324, 331, 340 ff., 354, 361, 379, 395

Garnet, Henry, 195

Gascoigne, George, 10 ff.

Gaudy, Justice, 204, 215, 365

Genoa, 288, 291

Gibb, John, 226

Gilbert, Adrian, 3, 45, 61, 169

—— Sir Humphrey, 3, 11 ff., 15 ff., 22, 38 ff., 88, 112

—— Sir John (the elder), 3, 12, 45, 60 ff., 98, 126

—— Sir John (the younger), 146, 170, 183

—— Otho, 3

—— Ralph, 56

Gillingham Forest, 233, 302

Godolphin, Sir Francis, 202

Gold, 100, 102, 110, 114, 117

Golden Hind, 43

Gomera, 304

Gondomar, Count, 52, 272, 284 ff., 294, 335 ff., 385

Gorges, Sir Arthur, 94, 134

Gorges, Sir Ferdinando, 160, 263

Gosse, Sir Edmund, 60, 89

Gravelines, battle of, 61

Gravesend, 119

Greeks, 254 ff.

Grenville, Sir Richard, 6, 11, 39, 47 ff., 56, 60, 84 ff., 141, 345

Grey, Lord (the elder), 20 ff., 69

Grey, Lord (the younger), 196, 199, 224, 227 ff., 231, 234, 244

Guard, Captaincy of the Queen's, 32

Guiana, 48, 100 ff., 146, 211, 232, 236, 239, 263 ff., 283, 287, 292 ff., 338, 352 ff., 380

Gunpowder Plot, 195, 236 ff., 253

Hakluyt, Richard, 37, 46, 56, 263

Hall, Bishop, 254

—— Captain, 294, 360, 370

Hallam, Henry, 215 ff.

Halley's Comet, 50

Hampden, John, 254

Hampton Court, 248

Harcourt, R., 266, 344, 370

Harington, Sir John, 84, 136, 158, 164, 185, 203

Hariot, Thomas, 50, 80 ff., 117, 214, 225, 253

Harlow, V. T., 78, 114, 226, 269, 288, 292, 301, 318 ff., 328, 332, 344, 370

Harry (Indian Chief), 307

Harvey, Sir George, 200, 235

Hastings, Edward, 307

—— Warren, vi

Hatton, Sir Christopher, 18, 27 ff., 35, 64, 99, 154 ff.

Hawkins, Sir John, 29, 38, 51, 54, 96 ff., 112, 119, 329, 348

—— William, 29

Hay, James (Lord Doncaster), 377

Helwys, Sir Gervase, 278 ff.

Heneage, Sir Thomas, 28

Henri IV, 165 ff., 188, 229, 343

Henry VII, 1, 34, 258, 268

—— VIII, 3, 16, 34, 149, 258

—— Prince of Wales, 141, 240 ff., 250, 252, 257, 260, 266, 280 ff., 329

Hepburn, Francis. See Bothwell, Earl of

Herbert, William. See Pembroke, Earl of

History of the World, The, 8 ff., 61, 74, 129, 132, 134, 138, 243, 252 ff., 298

Holland. See Low Countries

Hooker, John, 57

Howard, Charles, Earl of Nottingham, 40, 58 ff., 96, 120 ff., 143, 152, 159, 175, 183, 197, 232

—— Frances. See Essex, Lady

—— Katharine, Countess of Kildare (Lady Cobham), 175, 192

—— Lord Henry (Earl of Northampton), 165, 172, 175 ff., 198, 208, 218, 244, 275, 278 ff., 286, 388

—— Lord Thomas (Earl of Suffolk), 68, 84 ff., 120 ff., 134 ff., 151, 161, 197, 203

Howell, James, 331

Huguenots, 8 ff., 52, 292

Hume, David, 103, 254, 354

—— Martin, 9, 36, 61, 87, 331, 341 ff.

Humor, 10

Incas, 102 ff., 110 ff.

Inchiquin Ralegh, castle of, 169

India, 19

Indians of America, 15, 49 ff., 104, 106 ff., 235, 265 ff., 294, 301, 307, 311 ff.

Inns of Court, 9

Inquisition, 4 ff., 85, 385

Ireland and the Irish, 5, 14 ff., 32, 40, 58, 60, 62, 66 ff., 95, 101, 104, 121, 142, 148 ff., 169, 302, 343

Ironside, Rev. Ralph, 77

Isham, John, 370

Islands Voyage, 132 ff., 162, 232, 256

Islington, 9

Italians, 21

James I, 19, 51, 53, 56, 81, 108, 142, 155, 158 ff., 170, 175 ff., 186 ff., 192 ff., 213, 220, 226 ff., 231, 233, 239 ff., 241, 244, 246 ff., 257 ff., 263 ff., 272 ff., 285 ff., 289, 292 ff., 299, 304, 309 ff., 313 ff., 334 ff., 350 ff., 354 ff., 372, 378 ff., 384 ff.

—— V of Scotland, 157
Jamestown, 56
Jarnac, battle of, 8
Jeffreys, Judge, 204
Jersey, 167 ff., 189, 202, 392
Jesus, Society of, 39, 83, 195
Jesus, 38
Jezebel, 255
Johnson, Dr., 252
John the Baptist, 38
Jones, Rev. Samuel, 334
Jonson, Ben, 9, 32, 35, 251 ff., 296
Journal, Ralegh's, 302 ff.

Keats, John, 77
Kemys, Laurence, 105, 108, 112 ff., 138, 194, 198, 235, 250, 267 ff., 298, 302, 307, 309, 311 ff., 331, 341, 349
Kerr, Robert, 241, 244, 246 ff., 250, 271 ff.
Ket, Francis, 76
Kilcolman, 69
Kildare, Lady. *See* Howard, Katharine
King, Captain, 341, 345 ff.
King's Lynn, 60
Kinsale, 169, 302, 339
Knollys, Sir William, 13, 172, 213

La Chesnée, 350 ff., 360
Lake, Sir Thomas, 186 ff., 303 ff.
Lamb, Charles, 41
Lane, Ralph, 46, 49
Lang, Andrew, 94
Languedoc, 9
Lanzarote, 303
Lawes, Harry, 392
Le Clerc, 350, 360
Le Febre, 238
Leicester, Earl of, 22, 27, 34 ff., 66
Leigh, Charles, 265
—— John, 265
—— Oliph, 265
Lennox, Duke of, 175, 179, 238
Lenthall, William, 274
Lie, The, 72
Limehouse, 12
Limerick, 21
Lingard, Rev. John, 21, 100, 106, 215
Lisbon, 65 ff., 209
Lismore, 67

Lithgow, William, 385
Low Countries and the Dutch, 6, 12, 27, 35, 68, 120 ff., 126 ff., 134 ff., 138, 142, 194, 211, 242 ff., 265, 289, 319 ff.

McCarthy, Florence, 169
Macaulay, T. B., 145
Mackworth, Captain, 20
Madre de Dios, 96 ff., 101
Madrid, 272, 292, 295, 300, 308, 314, 335, 339, 362, 385
Magi, The Three, 253
Main Plot, 196 ff.
Malby, Sir Nicholas, 20
Manoa, 111 ff., 115, 271
Manourie, Dr., 346 ff., 364, 372, 379, 388 ff.
Mar, Lord, 183
Marêts, Des, 289 ff.
Markham, Sir Griffin, 196, 199, 224, 226 ff., 231, 234
Marlowe, Christopher, 5, 76 ff., 225
Martinez, 110
Mary of England, Queen, 4, 93, 282
—— of Scotland, Queen, 35, 39, 55, 59, 186, 195, 208
Mary Rose, 3
Matthew, Tobias, Bishop of Durham, 190
Mayne, Cuthbert, 39
Medina Sidonia, Duke of, 128
Mendoza, 52 ff.
Mermaid Tavern, 5, 173
Merrick, Sir Gilly, 133, 138 ff.
Mexican Plate Fleet, 136, 144, 299, 333
Mexico, 111, 115
Mezerai, Eudes de, 166
Middle Temple. *See* Inns of Court
Middleton, Captain, 84
Milford Haven, 151
Milton, 70 ff., 77, 91, 115, 145, 211, 256, 392
Moluccas, 29
Moncontour, battle of, 8
Monson, Sir William, 123, 143, 218
Montagu, James, Bishop of Winchester, 355
Montezuma, 115
Montgomeri, Gabriel de, 8
Mont Orgueil, 168

Index 413

Mountjoy, Lord, 163
Munster, 15 ff., 32, 169

Naboth's Vineyard, 259
Nash, Thomas, 80
Nassau, Count Louis of, 8
Naunton, Sir Robert, 1, 7, 14, 16, 23, 27, 314, 358, 368, 386
Neale, Professor, 89, 162
Newfoundland, 12, 43 ff., 329, 334
Ninias, 258
Norfolk, Duke of, 39, 154, 156
Norris, Sir John, 65 ff., 348
North, Captain Rogers, 295, 312, 335
Northampton, Lord. See Howard, Lord Henry
Northumberland, Earl of, 39, 81, 154, 181 ff., 236, 244, 253, 385
North-West Passage, 11, 40 ff.
Norumbega River, 38, 47
Nottingham, Earl of. See Howard, Charles
—— Lady, 375

O'Brien, Murrogh, 21
Oldys, William, 10
O'Neill, see Tyrone, Earl of
Orange, Prince of, 6, 37
Oriel College, Oxford, 7, 39
Orinoco River, 105 ff., 265, 287, 308 ff., 313 ff., 335, 364
Osborne, Francis, 37, 144, 195, 215, 246, 257, 284, 369, 384
Osmund, St., 88
Osorius, Bishop, 130
Overbury, Sir Thomas, 176, 261, 278 ff.
Oxenham, John, 47
Oxford, 7, 28, 39, 130, 296, 391, 395
—— Earl of, 29

Palatine, Prince, 241
Paradise Lost, 115
Paris, 37, 52, 297
Parker, Captain, 312, 323
Parliament, 29, 82, 100, 144, 203, 392
Parma, Prince of, 63
Parsons, Robert, 80
Peirson, John, 175
Pelham, Sir William, 18

Pembroke, Countess of, 221
—— Earl of, 92, 221, 231, 295
Pennington, Captain, 300, 333, 365
Perrot, Sir John, 16 ff., 27
—— Sir Thomas, 17, 64
—— Thomas, 15
Persians, 254
Peru, 101 ff., 111
Peyton, Sir John, 200 ff.
Phelippes, Thomas, 81
Philip II, 4, 20, 48, 52 ff., 59 ff., 121, 127 ff., 142, 149
—— III, 301, 303, 330, 335 ff., 362, 384
Pilgrimage, The, 225, 395
Pizarro, 102, 115
Plymouth, 13, 52, 65, 68, 120, 134, 145, 160, 291, 300, 339, 345
Pocahontas, 56, 264, 282
Pope, Alexander, 255
Pope-Hennessy, Sir John, 14, 26
Popham, Sir John, 203, 247
Portland, 58
Porto Rico, 314, 323
Portsmouth, 68, 285
Portugal and Portuguese, 29, 52, 57, 65 ff., 138, 209
Powhatan, 56
Poyntz, Sir Robert, 50
Prest, Agnes, 2 ff.
Prestall, John, 68
Privateering, 4 ff., 11 ff., 29, 37 ff., 47 ff., 51 ff., 144, 147, 232, 263, 295, 299, 332 ff.
Privy Council, 11, 23, 33, 60, 100, 116, 130, 144, 152, 165, 186, 193, 220, 234, 236, 261, 266, 278, 281, 286, 288, 293, 295, 303, 305, 316, 319, 331, 333 ff., 337 ff., 346, 354 ff., 372, 380, 383
Protestantism, 2 ff., 14 ff., 38 ff.
Puncto Gallo, 309, 311
Puritanism and Puritans, 11, 19, 39 ff.
Pym, John, 385
Pyne, Henry, 302, 372

Quadra, Alvarez de, 59

Ralegh, Carew (son of Sir Walter), 190, 235, 248, 250, 331, 334, 354, 367, 372, 391 ff.

—— Sir Carew, 3, 233, 392, 394
—— City of, 54
—— George, 295, 312, 325
—— Katharine, 3
—— Lady, 9, 88 ff., 104 ff., 145 ff., 158, 167, 170, 175, 177, 200, 224, 233 ff., 236 ff., 241, 247 ff., 252, 263, 284, 296, 306, 329, 341, 345 ff., 351, 353, 358 ff., 372, 383, 389 ff.
—— Sir Walter, family of, 1 ff.; education, 7 ff.; in French wars, 7 ff.; follower of Sir Humphrey Gilbert, 11; in Ireland, 18 ff.; becomes known to Queen Elizabeth, 23 ff.; extravagance, 28 ff.; work in the West, 32; pride and unpopularity, 33 ff.; his Virginian enterprise, 46 ff.; captures the elder Sarmiento, 51 ff.; intrigues with King of Spain, 54 ff.; rise of Essex, 64 ff.; friendship with men of letters, 69 ff.; atheism, 73 ff.; religious tolerance, 81 ff.; acquires Sherborne, 88; marriage and disgrace, 88 ff.; release from imprisonment, 97 ff.; voyage to Guiana, 100 ff.; influence of his *Discoverie of Guiana* on later writers, 114 ff.; at sack of Cadiz, 119 ff.; relations with Cecil, 131 ff.; Islands Voyage, 133 ff.; fall of Essex, 148 ff.; growing unpopularity, 164; entertains ambassadors, 165; Governor of Jersey, 167; Cecil's and Howard's plots against, 170 ff.; King James's reception of, 187; arrest, 193; trial, 197 ff.; reprieve, 229; imprisoned in Tower, 230 ff.; his balsam, 236; political writings, 241 ff.; loses Sherborne, 247 ff.; writings in Tower, 251 ff.; offers to go to Virginia, 263; keeps up connection with Guiana, 265; is released, 281; preparations for last voyage, 284 ff.; negotiations with foreign agents, 287 ff.; difficulties in getting personnel, 295 ff.; talks of seizing Plate Fleet, 299; entertained by Boyle in Ireland, 302; last voyage, 302 ff.; sickness of, 306 ff.; gets news of San Thomé fight, 311 ff.; letters of, from Guiana, 312 ff.; interview with Kemys, 326; question of his truthfulness, 300 ff., 331 ff.; returns from Guiana, 331 ff.; James's *Proclamation* against, 336; arrest, 345; malingers, 347; examination of, 348 ff.; sentenced to die, 362 ff.; last night, 369 ff.; execution of, 369 ff.; effect of his death, 376 ff.; summary of character of, 393; spelling of his name, 394; his supposed illegitimate daughter, 395 ff.
—— Rev. Walter, 392
—— Walter (father of Sir Walter), 1 ff.
—— Walter (son of Sir Walter), 9, 168, 251, 295 ff., 306, 312, 322 ff., 392
—— Wimund, 1
Reeks, Captain, 305
Revenge, 85 ff., 141
Richard II, 133
Richard III, 258
Richelieu, Cardinal, 290
Richmond, 261
Rizzio, David, 188
Roanoke, 49, 56
Rochelle, 379
Rochester, Lord. *See* Kerr, Robert
Roe, Sir Thomas, 263, 270, 283, 284, 295, 317, 328
Rolfe, John, 282. *See also* Pocahontas
Rossetti, D. G., 41, 246

St. John, Sir William, 281, 298, 352
St. Leger, Sir Warham (the elder), 18, 312
—— Sir William, 291, 295, 309, 365
Salisbury, 88, 347, 380
—— Earl of. *See* Cecil, Robert
—— Marquis of, 349
Sancroft, Archbishop, 262, 378
Sanderson, Sir William, 207, 238
San Joseph, 106
Santa Cruz, Marquis of, 60, 62
San Thomé, 113 ff., 268, 293, 311 ff., 331 ff., 371
Santiago, 58
Santo Domingo, 49, 58
Sarmiento (the elder), 51 ff.
Sarmiento (the younger). *See* Gondomar, Count
Sassafras, 146
Savage, Sir Arthur, 179

Savoy, 202, 241, 287
Scarnafissi, Count, 287
Schomburgk, Sir R., 100, 103
Scilly, 61, 68, 302
Scory, Sylvanus, 298, 306
Scotland, 5, 58, 171 ff., 186 ff., 206, 213
Semiramis, 258
Seville, 4, 112, 127, 304
Seymour, Thomas Lord, 87
Shakespeare, William, 1, 5, 10, 92, 103, 114, 133, 150, 173, 263, 282, 374, 387
Sherborne, 88 ff., 93, 132, 175, 225, 232, 235, 237, 247 ff., 261, 267, 284, 303, 346, 391
Shipbuilding, 40, 240, 260
Shirley, Anthony, 301
Shrewsbury, Lady, 170, 363
Sidney, Sir Henry, 16
—— Sir Philip, 5, 16, 25, 39, 64, 87, 220
Smerwick, 20 ff., 69, 169
Smith, Captain John, 282
—— Goldwin, 26
Socinians, 5
Socrates, 222, 226
Somerset, Earl of. See Kerr, Robert
Southampton, Earl of, 90, 141, 147, 161, 189, 192
Spain and Spaniards, 3 ff., 12, 20 ff., 26, 39, 46 ff., 51 ff., 58 ff., 84 ff., 99, 101 ff., 111 ff., 115 ff., 119, 121 ff., 148, 165, 172, 183, 193 ff., 209, 211 ff., 221, 229, 232, 241 ff., 265, 284 ff., 292 ff., 301 ff., 311 ff., 331, 333 ff., 349 ff., 354 ff., 374, 384 ff.
Spence, Rev. Joseph, 255
Spenser, Edmund, 5, 20, 69 ff., 88
Squirrel, 43 ff.
Stafford, Sir E., 90
Standen, Sir Anthony, 120
Stanhope, Sir John, 204
Stannaries, 32, 101, 145
Star Chamber, Court of the, 101, 145, 153, 253
Stationers' Register, 133, 257
Stebbing, W., 19, 152, 154 ff., 193, 215, 222, 311, 333, 378, 393, 394, 396
Strozzi, Peter, 62
Strype, John, 58
Stuart, Lady Arabella, 186, 202, 209, 217

Stukeley, Sir Lewis, 48, 163, 341, 345 ff., 372, 380, 388 ff.
Suffolk, Countess of, 246 ff.
—— Earl of. See Howard, Lord Thomas
Sully, Duke of, 165, 199, 242
Swiftsure, 65
Swinburne, A. C., 41

Tarleton, Richard, 33
Tempest, The, 5, 90, 103, 114, 263
Tennyson, 48, 85, 141
Terceira, 136, 141
Thames, 120, 261, 289 ff., 299
Themistocles, 99
Throckmorton, Arthur, 120, 126, 129, 250
—— Elizabeth. See Ralegh, Lady
—— Sir Nicholas, 93
Thynne, Francis, 369
Tobacco, 51, 239, 300, 319 ff., 336, 372, 381
Topiawari, 108 ff.
Tounson, Rev. Robert, 370 ff., 387
Tower of London, 18, 153, 162, 200, 230, 281 ff., 315, 352, 382
Trenchard, Sir George, 78
Trevelyan, G. M., 384
Trinidad, 105, 112, 271, 309, 311, 313, 320, 330
Turner, Ann, 275, 279
—— Dr., 236
Tyrone, Earl of, 119, 149, 316

Udal, John, 81, 203
United States of America, 349

Van Linschoten, 86
Venezuela, 115, 320, 349
Venice and Venetians, 159, 234, 240, 289
Vere, Sir Francis, 120, 125, 130, 134
Vernon, Elizabeth, Countess of Southampton, 147
Villa Franca, 142
Villiers, George, Duke of Buckingham, 273, 281 ff., 314, 333, 337 ff., 368, 384
—— Sir Edward, 281
Virginia, 46 ff., 68, 80, 93, 111, 146, 232, 263, 270, 282, 334

Waad, Sir William, 197 ff., 203, 235 ff.,
  278
Waldman, Milton, 10, 71, 212, 349, 374
Walsingham, Sir Francis, 22, 24 ff., 40, 53
Warburton, Justice, 204
Warwick, Countess of, 153
Waterford, 14
Watson (Jesuit), 195 ff., 223
—— Sir William, 25
Welldon, Sir Anthony, 185, 238
West Indies, 12, 47, 55, 361
Weston, R., 279
Weymouth, 116, 168
Whiddon, Jacob, 105
White, John, 56
Whitelocke, Captain, 236
Whitney, Captain, 300, 330, 334
Whyte, Rowland, 132, 143, 145
Williams, Charles, 220
—— Sir Roger, 65 ff.
Williamson, J. A., 311
William the Silent, 27
Willoughby, John, 147
Wilson, Sir Thomas, 292, 299, 332 ff.,
  357 ff., 366, 389

Winchester, 203, 223 ff., 226, 363
Wines, farm of, 30, 232
Wingandacoa, 46
Wingina, 46
Winkfield, Sir John, 128
Winwood, Sir Ralph, 271, 279, 288, 297,
  307, 312 ff., 328, 335, 341, 379
Witchcraft, 276
Wokoken, 46, 48
Wollaston (Woolaston), Captain, 330, 334
Wood, Anthony à, 7, 105, 392
Worcester, Earl of, 153, 238
Wotton, Edward, 203
—— Lord, 203
—— Sir Henry, 58, 139, 144, 165, 297,
  392
Wyse, Andrew, 133

Xenophon, 255

Yelverton, Sir Henry, 364
Youghal, 60

Zutphen, 25, 64